Le Corbusier

and the
Concept of Self

Simon Richards

Le Corbusier

and the
Concept of Self

Yale University Press

New Haven and London

For my mother, Aldyth Richards

Designed by Gillian Malpass

Printed in China

Library of Congress Cataloging-in-Publication Data
Richards, Simon, 1973–
Le Corbusier and the concept of self / Simon Richards.
p. cm.
Includes bibliographical references and index.
ISBN 0-300-09565-1
1. Le Corbusier, 1887–1965 – Criticism and interpretation. 2. City planning –
Philosophy – History – 20th century. I. Le Corbusier, 1887–1965. II. Title.
NA1053.J4R53 2003
720'.92--dc21

2003002427

A catalogue record for this book is available from
The British Library

Contents

List of illustrations   vii

Introduction   1
The Argument in Brief   1
Why 'Concepts of Self'?   4
How to Go About It   9
A Two-Part Project   11

I   'The Lawgiver'   19

Preface   21

1   1914–1929: Technocracy   23
The Promise of War   23
'It is "right" and therefore immutable'   28

2   1930–1940: Syndicalism   37
The 'Timid People'   37
'Awakening of Cleanliness'   41

3   1941–1942: Vichy   54
'Through Strange Avatars'   54
'The Lawgiver'   59

II   **The Science of Painting**   67

    Preface   69

4   **Léger and the Purist Object**   73
    A Formal Pursuit?   73
    Léger's 'Knowledge'   80

5   **Conventionalism**   90
    Poincaré: Purist Space   91
    The 'Modulor'   100

6   **Ozenfant's Impasse**   112

III   **'Pascal's *Desideratum*'**   123

    Preface   125

7   **Pascal: Preparing the Machine**   128

8   **'Wisdom Builds Its Own House'**   137
    Alchemy and *Le Poème de l'angle droit*   138
    Jung: A Society of One   158

9   **Bataille and Camus: 'Vers la limite critique'**   171
    'Vers la limite critique'   172
    'The Difference in Blood'   176

    Conclusion   188
    The City as a Source of Interest and Meaning   188
    The Worth of Le Corbusier's Concept of Self   197

    Notes   203

    Bibliography   276

    Acknowledgements   290

    Index   291

Illustrations

1   Le Corbusier. 'Techniques Are the Very Basis of Poetry.' From Le Corbusier, *Prècisions sur un état présent de l'architecture et de l'urbanisme*, 1930.
[© FLC/ADAGP, Paris and DACS, London 2003]   13

2   Le Corbusier. 'February 6th, 1934, in Paris: awakening of cleanliness.' From Le Corbusier, *La Ville radieuse*, 1935.
[© FLC/ADAGP, Paris and DACS, London 2003]   43

3   Le Corbusier. 'Hexagonal France'. From Françoise de Pierrefeu and Le Corbusier, *La Maison des hommes*, 1942.
[© FLC/ADAGP, Paris and DACS, London 2003]   61

4   Le Corbusier. *Nature morte à la pile d'assiettes et au livre*, 1920. The Museum of Modern Art, New York.
[© FLC/ADAGP, Paris and DACS, London 2003; © Photo SCALA]   74

5   Le Corbusier. *Taureau VIII*, 1954.
[© FLC/ADAGP, Paris and DACS, London 2003]   75

6   Fernand Léger. *La Partie de cartes*, 1917. Collection Kröller-Müller Museum, Otterlo.
[© ADAGP, Paris and DACS, London 2003]   83

7   Le Corbusier. *Feuillantines. Etude pour violon et bouteille*, 1926.
[© FLC/ADAGP, Paris and DACS, London 2003]   86

8   Le Corbusier. 'These figures pin down the human body at the decisive points of its occupation of space: they are therefore *anthropocentric*.' From Le Corbusier, *The Modulor 1 and 2*.
[© FLC/ADAGP, Paris and DACS, London 2003]   102

9   Le Corbusier. 'Suddenly light is shed on the problem: three-dimensional city planning.'
[© FLC/ADAGP, Paris and DACS, London 2003]   109

10   Le Corbusier. Scheme of '*iconostase*', from *Le Poème de l'angle droit* (1955), 1989.
[© FLC/ADAGP, Paris and DACS, London 2003]   139

11   Le Corbusier. ' "the individual" / = Man / Each is in his own sack of skin! / (Poem <+).'
[© FLC/ADAGP, Paris and DACS, London 2003]   157

12   Michael Maier. 'Viatorium', 1651. 'The Symbolic City as Centre of the Earth, its Four Protecting Walls Laid Out in a Square: A Typical *Temenos*'.
[© C. G. Jung estate: Küsnacht collection]   164

13   Le Corbusier. Sector 17 city centre (top); Capitol Complex, view of Temple of Shadows, Secretariat and Palace of Assembly (bottom); Chandigarh.
[Author photographs; August 1997]   196

Introduction

The Argument in Brief

Le Corbusier was one of the most influential, controversial, but also inscrutable architects of the twentieth century. I began this research to find out why he made such a drama about separating his public and private lives. To be more specific: why, from the late 1920s onwards, did he hide himself away every morning to paint, and keep those paintings apart from his professional urban and architectural projects for so long? What did it mean that these paintings looked completely different from the ones he painted earlier, as a 'Purist'? Also, how could he masquerade as the quintessential rationalist in public, yet in private create a strange and personal visual mythology?

It did not seem sufficient to say that he used this time to work through certain of the artistic problems from his hectic professional life. Certainly, this was sometimes the case; but it seemed that this private activity was more significant and also different from his public side. The fact that Le Corbusier often drew attention to the split suggests that we should give it more consideration.[1] Obviously, I had to begin by throwing out the mundane answer that everyone needs some privacy. I determined to remain open to the possibility that this was not 'simple' privacy. This approach involved reopening the old debate concerning the matter–spirit dualism that runs through Le Corbusier's work. Every commentator of note has tackled this question, although it has never been satisfactorily resolved.[2]

I sensed that Le Corbusier's public–private split represented two sides of a larger philosophical equation. He appeared to be dramatizing an ideal balance between a self-defining activity that was to be conducted in solitude and was too precious to be contaminated by the other half of the equation: a professional life of bureaucratic frustration, wasted talk and treachery, for which he never had a good word. Perhaps this kind of split between one's public and private life is not so remarkable, and it is difficult not to conclude that Le Corbusier's mornings were simply moments of leisure. But it is clear that these moments were not at all relaxing: they involved artistic struggle and soul-searching. The everyday division of public and private here appeared to represent something more severe – a radical split between 'interior' and 'exterior' realities. Moreover, it emerged in my reading that this split ran throughout Le Corbusier's work, and that he sought to inspire the same thing in every inhabitant of his ideal cities. This split, I thought, was perhaps symptomatic of a particular concept of self that Le Corbusier valued.

So my project came down to the attempt to determine the exact origins, terms, dynamics and consequences of Le Corbusier's concept of self, and this turned out to be a more interesting question than the one I began with. Incidentally, when I use the phrase 'concepts of self', I refer to the vast body of scholarship that seeks to determine the qualities that must be present, or the processes that must be at work, for the individual human being to attain a meaningful and valued sense of self-identity or self-knowledge. I will return to this in a little more depth below.

Le Corbusier's public–private split, at first sight apparently mundane, fanned out into a larger set of metaphysical issues concerning the problem of where knowledge, value and meaning were to be found in the modern world. It became an exploration of such 'exterior' realities as society, science and politics, the 'interior' reality of some vague subjectivity and the question of how these were to be articulated, one against the other, for the formation of a valid sense of self. I also wanted to find out exactly how Le Corbusier's cities were meant to inspire this process.

My answer can be sketched quite simply. Le Corbusier believed there to be two different but complementary ways of engaging with 'reality', which was consequently split into an 'exterior' and an 'interior'. He was plagued by the search for reliable knowledge, but this was not something that he believed could be found external to the self, and certainly not in the upheaval at the beginning of the twentieth century. But beyond the particular circumstances of his time, it was questionable whether anything could be definitively known of exterior reality, which he therefore considered to be of dubious worth. The world, for Le Corbusier, was something to get away from.

So what was Le Corbusier doing with all his monumental attempts to manipulate 'exterior reality' in his urban schemes? In this book, I shall argue that he was trying to settle humankind's relations with the external world. He wanted to put that world into such a shape that it ceased to trouble people, and they would thereby be liberated to pursue more important things. This worked in two ways, 'epistemologically' and 'socio-politically':

Epistemologically   The early twentieth century was a period when certain quarters of the avant-garde were intensely interested in the new innovations in the spatial and mathematical sciences: in particular, with n-dimensional space and non-Euclidean geometry. Le Corbusier set himself against these innovations. Consequently, his projected city schemes sought to reinforce, through the sheer weight of their physical and visual presence, a particular way of 'knowing' the world. This was a stable Euclidean way, although this is not to say Le Corbusier believed Euclid to be 'correct'. Rather, since it was impossible to achieve real certainty regarding external reality, one might as well settle for the least troublesome paradigm.

Socio-politically   Le Corbusier's ideal cities made it very difficult for people to congregate, at least in any other but the most controlled and predetermined manner. Chance encounters were substantially eliminated. The rules of social engagement were always worked out in advance, hence the inordinate provision for sport. Entertainment was best done at home, with Le Corbusier celebrating the gramophone over the germ-ridden concert hall. Also, no provision was made for political participation: once these cities were set up, they were non-negotiable.

But what was this all for? I believe it was intended to 'inspire' people to search for more substantial realities within themselves, through withdrawal into solitude. By the time Le Corbusier had finished with the city, they would have had little choice.

Le Corbusier's project therefore had two stages: it ended with the possibility of each individual attaining some kind of self-knowledge, but before this stage could be reached, all that proved a hindrance had to be eradicated. This included removing all the distractions of the urban domain − its congestion, diseases and luxuries − as well as the belief that one's social life, friendship and love were determining factors of one's identity and meaning. At a more abstract level, it involved attributing some provisional epistemological certainty to the natural universe, so that people did not agonize over whether their rooms had three or four dimensions. Simply put, Le Corbusier sought to check the individual's impetus to depend upon, or be concerned by, things outside the self. This means that his ideal cities, universally considered the objective of all his efforts, were in fact just a means to an end − a preparatory stage.

If my approach is valid, then it is necessary to reject the dominant criticism of Le Corbusier, which maintains that his proposed city schemes would have killed the life of the city. They would do this in at least two ways. First, by eliminating the traditional street − Le Corbusier famously celebrated this as the 'Death of the Street'. Second, by granting only limited space for cafés, community centres, theatres and suchlike, and by dispersing them over great distances. Consequently, it is argued, the social life of the city would unravel. Conclusion: Le Corbusier is guilty of a terrible mistake or oversight.

This criticism has been reiterated verbatim for over seventy years, and Le Corbusier is frequently blamed for the socially alienating high-rise developments of the post-war period.[3] None the less, this criticism is the product of a misunderstanding. Le Corbusier had a clear idea of what people should be doing in his cities. His antisocial urbanism was intentional. It was not a mistake or oversight of which he was unaware.[4]

Why 'Concepts of Self'?

I shall give only a generalized run-down of the reasoning behind this approach, as it will be revisited in greater depth in subsequent publications.[5]

Throughout history, people have attempted to come to an understanding of what it is to be a human being. As mentioned previously, this has involved the attempt to determine the qualities that must be present, or the processes that must be at work, for the individual human being to attain a meaningful and valued sense of self-identity or self-knowledge. The debate has been vigorous and has occupied the attentions of poets, theologians, philosophers, sociologists, psychologists and others.

By 'concepts of self', I refer to the various positions in this immense body of thought. These positions differ radically and so does the terminology. The blanket term 'self', however, has a broader history than certain other terms and is more widely applicable. These other terms tend to be more firmly rooted in the historical and ideological circumstances from which they emerged. For example, there is the transcendental Christian 'soul'; the creative, politicized 'agent' of the Enlightenment; the renegotiable product of cultural discourses and language, the twentieth-century 'subject'; or the term often favoured for ethnic, gender and regional politics, 'identity'.[6]

Two paradigms have proved important to this body of thought, at least in the Western tradition, and perhaps have dominated it.[7] The main ideas can be generalized very crudely as follows:

'The Self-Sufficient Self'   The self is a transcendental entity with a mental or spiritual nature that is capable of being perfected or brought under control. It should not allow itself to be affected by the events that occur around it in the external environment. Consequently, the body and the information gathered through the senses are not constitutive of the self. Individual experience may be unimportant, even undesirable, with all selves tending towards an ideal uniformity. Alternatively, intense soul-searching may result in a violently unique sense of individuality.[8]

'The Self/Other Self'   The self is a fluid process upheld in a complex interchange of social, cultural and linguistic processes. It is embodied and therefore continually affected through the senses by the events that occur 'around' it. In fact, it is not considered possible to conceive the self separately from its external environment and the experiences it has there. Individual experience and social interaction may become fundamental, allowing for the formation of different identities. Alternatively, the environment may have a more controlling, coercive, or destabilizing effect on the self.[9]

The situation is complicated and it is already something of a misrepresentation to categorize it so simply. But the common denominator in all the various positions is that, for good or ill, the self is always influenced by its 'environment'. Obviously, we have to take the term 'environment' in the broadest sense here, referring not only to its physical, built fabric but also to all of the personal, cultural, social and political dynamics that it supports. Most important for us, however, is that this 'equation' is reversible: concepts of the environment are often indebted to concepts of self, and sometimes make assumptions about human beings and their behaviour in accordance with these concepts.

We can get a sense of this by presenting another crude generalization. Theoretical discussions of the city similarly orient themselves between two poles: first, the idea that the city is inherently bad; second, that it is good. This generates two responses as to how the city must be dealt with. First, if one considers the city to be a site of danger, of wasted energies and sinful indulgence, then it must be made subject to stringent order and control. This approach has dominated urban thinking since Plato, through St Augustine and Leon Battista Alberti, and into twentieth-century Modernism. During the Enlightenment, however, it was complemented by another, in which the city came to be considered a valuable sphere of experience in and for itself, providing something that could not be had elsewhere. According to this approach, the city should be nurtured to become richer and less regulated. We can provisionally place figures like David Hume, Georg Simmel and Jane Jacobs in this category, as well as the Surrealists.

Underlying these approaches are assumptions concerning how the individual's life should be lived, which usually are indebted to particular concepts of self. In terms of the first approach, life is considered to become meaningful only under certain precise conditions, in the pursuit of certain morally sanctioned activities, which must be enforced by authority. Here, people are guided or coerced into such things as honest toil, spiritual contemplation and engagement with the high arts. In terms of the second, life is considered to become meaningful only through the individual's immersion in the unregulated mêlée of urban life, and for some writers non-urban living is thought to keep the individual in a state of social and psychological backwardness. Here, people are encouraged to experience the great variety of different things that a large, cosmopolitan city provides, such as involvement in a political community, the exploration of different tastes and entertainments, and the mystique of chance sexual encounters. This latter is currently the dominant way of thinking about the city.[10]

Although these remarks are general, they allow us to see that there is an interesting overlap between concepts of self and approaches to the built environment.

But beyond this, concepts of self are extremely mobile within culture at large. Such concepts are absorbed casually, often unconsciously, and yet they are able to influence our thoughts and actions.[11] Of course, this happens with environmental designers as well. In this case, the concepts are seldom stated explicitly: they are unacknowledged and can be glimpsed only vaguely. However, some architects and urbanists acknowledge openly that a particular concept of self holds a central role in their approach to design, although this is quite rare. In this case the concepts may be elaborated with considerable rigour, but most often they tend to be quite personal, even idiosyncratic.

But exactly how do these concepts manifest themselves in architecture and urbanism? They do so in actual designs and buildings, but only to a certain degree. The arrangements of buildings and towns are indicative of value-laden hierarchies: certain spaces and functions are privileged either through the size of the rooms or buildings in which they are located, or their positioning within the larger scheme. Are they easily accessible and visible, for example, or are they hidden away, suppressed? Tying all this together, there are corridors, paths, roads and meeting places that imply desirable patterns of human movement, interaction and segregation. These elements are often suggestive of social, racial and gender hierarchies, and also of 'life-styles'. But when taken alone, these elements are too broad, and too amenable to transgressive use, to denote any clear concept of self. Therefore it becomes necessary to look at the statements and written theory of architects and urbanists. This has to be our starting-point.

The reason for adopting this approach is to uncover some of the deepest motivations of environmental design, which will serve as a preliminary to discussing its human consequences. The object is not only to gain a better understanding, but also in some cases to initiate a critique.

But there are obvious qualifications that have to be made. For example, it is difficult to claim too much in relation to the legions of modest architectural practitioners and municipal town-planners. These are often straitjacketed by the need to fulfil a client's brief or implement a long-term government strategy, within which they have little room to express their own ideals. It is much more immediately profitable to focus on those designers of international renown and influence who enjoy greater freedom to express their ideals in buildings and writing.[12] This approach is unlikely to yield results in *all* cases, then, but it can be profoundly informative where it does.

To date, only a small amount of academic study has been conducted along these lines. The outstanding example is the volume of essays edited by Dana Cuff and Russell Ellis, *Architects' People* (1989). Cuff and Ellis introduce this book by stating that it 'proceeds on the assumption that it is impossible to design a building without some conception of human activity in and around it'. They assume a polemical position against what they believe to be the neglect of architects on this question:

> Architects are the professional keepers of the knowledge and skills that render the built environment. Theirs is the historic charge to conceive and reconceive design. At the level of imagination and utility they accept this charge and undergo extensive formal training that prepares them to exercise it. *Presumably, they learn somewhere how people do or want to live.*

The point, of course, is that architects learn nothing of the sort. Such things are in fact resented by the architectural community as 'philistine intrusions into pure design'. Even so, there is always an 'implicit actor who lurks in the designer's imagination'. And most often, this 'actor' is not given any real consideration, but instead remains 'a kind of puppet, or *homunculus . . .* an indistinctly motivated lump of somatic stuff'. These 'people' are seldom more than 'passive and unobtrusive' elements in the designer–puppeteer's aesthetic tableau. But by attempting to unearth these 'implicit actors', Cuff and Ellis provided an important step in creating a more 'informed' and 'socially alert' design ethos.[13]

This book is an attempt to find the 'homunculus' hidden in Le Corbusier.

How to Go About It

The concepts of self employed within urban literature tend to be implicit, and Le Corbusier is no exception. Therefore, I shall attempt to draw this out in three sections, each containing three chapters. This requires a rather strange and circuitous course, from politics and economic policy through to poetry and occultism, which, initially, may seem to lead us away from the central question.

Part I, 'The Lawgiver', looks at Le Corbusier's political machinations between the wars, and at the ideal cities he designed to appeal to potential allies. This introduces the suggestion that Le Corbusier was more interested in the spiritual revitalization of the people in his cities than in the cities themselves. Although this offers only a broad sense of Le Corbusier's concept of self, it provides one important insight. It shows how he wanted to cut the ties of interpersonal dependency, provoking people to turn away from their social and political milieu in order to search for something more important and substantial within themselves. These cities, and the political allies he courted in an attempt to get them built, were merely instrumental to this larger purpose.

Part II, 'The Science of Painting', follows up certain leads from the first section, demonstrating that Le Corbusier did not want people to depend upon 'exterior' reality for their life's meaning. But while the first section discusses exterior reality in terms of society and politics, this section approaches it in more abstract terms – as an object of knowledge. Le Corbusier wanted to make the world appear as stable and knowable as possible, so that it ceased to trouble people, who would again be at peace and thus able to think about more important things. He tried to do this, I maintain, through his Purist paintings and the built form of his cities. This epistemological position meant that Le Corbusier had to distance himself from those other members of the avant-garde who were fascinated by new innovations in the theoretical sciences.

Part III, 'Pascal's *Desideratum*', focuses directly on Le Corbusier's philosophy of self. This introduces the idea that Pascal was a major but hitherto unacknowledged influence on Le Corbusier, and served as a rallying point for all these concerns. I believe that Pascal offers the outstanding model and source for Le Corbusier's philosophy. This section also explores how Pascal's metaphysic may have been enriched by Le Corbusier's interest in the occult generally, and alchemy in particular. Finally, I shall demonstrate how two of Le Corbusier's acquaintances 'warned' him that his philosophy of self might be extremely dangerous.

The conclusions drawn in each of these sections give cause for reconsideration of some of the secondary literature on Le Corbusier, and I shall address this in my conclusion. This will apply only to those commentaries that have been especially influential and that continue substantially to dominate opinion. I shall deal with other commentaries along the way. Most importantly, I shall also attempt to assess the lasting worth of Le Corbusier's ideas.

This book represents an attempt to reappraise Le Corbusier's deepest intent. It is not an introduction, and presupposes a rudimentary idea of who he was and what his designs looked like. Illustrations will therefore be kept to a minimum, as there are many well-illustrated books available already.

To begin, it is helpful to sketch out Le Corbusier's philosophy in the broadest terms. 'A Two-Part Project' represents the bare bones that will be fleshed out in the following three sections.

A Two-Part Project

The Acropolis and Parthenon were for Le Corbusier the very pinnacle of human creation. They satisfied both 'reason' and 'passion': 'I can well accept that according to logic, everything here is resolved in accordance with an unsurpassable formula, but why is it that taste – or rather the heart . . . why is it still drawn to the Acropolis?'[1] There appear, then, to be two aspects at work: the former is entirely pragmatic and functional, as revealed by such observations as 'The Parthenon is a product of selection applied to an established standard', while the latter quality ensures that these ruins inspire an artistic response that does not need to be measured or rationalized, a quality that cuts straight into the emotional lives of all individuals: '*There are no symbols attached to these forms; they provoke definite sensations; there is no need of a key in order to understand them.*'[2]

Le Corbusier's philosophy therefore appears to be founded upon a broad dualism of matter and spirit: in the first category are included all those transient, historically bound notions which he considered to be derived from matter, such as reason, mathematics, measurement, government, mechanization, utility and so on; while in the second are to be found only such qualities as derive from spirit, such as emotion, religious faith, divinity and art. The former is bound up with the accumulative knowledge and technical expertise of humankind as it progresses through time: 'reason', we are told, 'is an open account stretching to infinity in which each successive stage is registered; not one tiny grain but adds to it'. But this does not mean that we can only hope to produce transient and therefore valueless things. The spiritual qualities that Le Corbusier discusses seem always to be complete and eternal: for example, 'Human passion, since man was man, has been constant and extends from birth to death; its range being limited by a maximum and a minimum which appears to us constant throughout the ages. This is the gauge by which we can measure the permanence of human creations.'[3]

This important point may be refined through a further example, for which Le Corbusier provided an illustration (fig. 1): 'Ladies and gentlemen, I begin by drawing a line that can separate, in the process of our perceptions . . . the domain of material things, daily events, reasonable tendencies, from that specifically reserved to spiritual ones. Below the line, what exists; above, what one feels.' Those things which belong to the material side of the equation are grouped under three general headings: '*technique . . . sociology . . . economics*', which Le Corbusier considered to be 'commonplace . . . mobile . . . short-lived'. On the spiritual side, however, we 'enter the domain of emotions . . . *poetry . . . these are eternal values* that in all times will relight the flame in the hearts of men'. Providing a foil to the transitoriness of earthly things, then, is a realm where we discover that 'a work of art is immortal and will move us forever'.[4] Thus we 'return to universal law'.[5]

Le Corbusier appears to want a return to constancy and stability in our changeable material world. But two questions need to be raised about his project: how and when did he consider it should happen; and why should it happen? First, it required the intervention of supernaturally gifted individuals at key stages in history: 'an exceptional phenomenon occurring at long intervals . . . perhaps in accordance with the pulsation of a cosmography not yet understood'.[6] Le Corbusier believed the time was ripe for this to happen. He framed a three-part system of the stages of history: first, there is the conflict between humanity and a hostile material environment that cannot be understood or controlled; second, there is greater understanding and control, but still humanity is immured and struggling; finally, there is complete mastery, full knowledge and control:

the great moment is reached at length when every means has been proved, and where a complete equipment assures the perfect carrying

1   Le Corbusier. 'Techniques Are the Very Basis of Poetry.' From Le Corbusier, *Prècisions sur un état présent de l'architecture et de l'urbanisme*, 1930. Croquis de Conférence FLC 30298. © FLC

out of rational schemes. A great calm is created by the power which has been acquired and which can be measured. The mind is able to create in a state of serenity. The period of struggle is over. The period of construction has arrived . . . We can create rational forms, with their basis in geometry . . . *We have in our hands a technical equipment which is the sum of man's acquired knowledge.*[7]

Le Corbusier considered his generation to be at this stage, and believed that he was the man capable of orchestrating the accumulated knowledge of civilization to put humankind on this new footing.[8]

But why should this happen? This process is about finding *rapprochement* with the world, which involves utilizing knowledge so that we are no longer stifled by ignorance or lack of technical expertise. But Le Corbusier went further in characterizing this:

Art is inseparable from being . . . It is intimately linked to the movements of our heart, and it makes the stages of our difficult path through the thickets of this age and all ages, towards a state of awareness. It guides us through time, from the moment when we are crushed by an immense and dominating nature, to that moment of serenity when we have learnt to understand her and to work in harmony with her law . . . the history of civilization, as also the history of the individual.[9]

Here we have something else: as well as knowledge of the world, this process also seems to point towards knowledge of ourselves as individuals. Le Corbusier's historical schema clearly suggests that only at a certain stage is it possible for humanity to lift itself out of the material world that hitherto submerged it. As he says, the 'mission' of art is '*to lift us above disorder*'.[10] The possibility of setting the material world to order at this time, then, perhaps makes possible a self-awareness that was not possible before. Le Corbusier characterizes the culmination of this process as follows:

It is a question of soul, of something which we have at heart; something which is no longer international nor multiple, but individual and cannot be added to by others; something which is *in a man* and the power of which dies within him. It is a question of *Art*.[11]

I shall elaborate on this in the second and third sections, but I should mention also the important influence of the Viennese designer and theorist Adolf Loos, who helped shape Le Corbusier's ideas on self-awareness. Le Corbusier remarked that Loos's 1908 essay 'Ornament and Crime' 'crystallized, in solid form, vague impressions, feelings that are nascent or already well developed but which are hardly ever acknowledged at this time when the fury of "decorative art", the folly of the *Beautiful*, overwhelms and stupefies the simple, instinctive, necessary, and only true sentiment of the *Good*'.[12] He also reprinted the French translation of Loos's essay in the first issue of *L'Esprit nouveau*. But Loos's ideas on design appealed to Le Corbusier because, exactly like him, Loos was never simply or even primarily concerned with design. He was concerned to pave the way for a new modern consciousness – one of complete individuality.

Loos thought that the persistence of ornament, in architecture, clothing and the decorative arts, was a sign of 'degeneracy'. Originally this was a tribal practice through which one's identity, tied to social rank, was indicated to others. This was perfectly permissible for Papuans, but not for modern people. Even so, it was still maintained by those in power – and faked by the bourgeois aspiring to power and prestige – as an outward display of rank which served to underwrite existing social hierarchies and inequalities: 'The state, whose duty it is to impede people in their cultural development, took over the question of development and re-adoption of ornament and made it its own.'[13] The falsification of history in museums was one of the main ways in which this worked: 'Only those objects, covered with decoration, which were little suited to a particular use and were not worn out were kept.'[14]

There is nothing new in this analysis. Far more important, and what has not to my knowledge been pointed out, is Loos's belief that the individual's continued use of ornament was symptomatic of a refusal to evolve and forge an identity that did not depend on society. Famously, he said that '*The evolution of culture is synonymous with the removal of ornament from objects of daily use*.'[15] But the mania for ornament as a manifestation of rank, be it real or pretended, made people dependent on social meanings that were now defunct. These people were forcibly retarded by those who 'want to withhold a recently acquired right, *their self-determination*'.[16] What did Loos mean by '*recently* acquired'? Simply, that this was a new, modern phenomenon:

Primitive men had to differentiate themselves by various colours, modern man needs his clothes as a mask. His individuality is so strong that it can no longer be expressed in terms of items of clothing . . . His own inventions are concentrated on other things.[17]

Loos's attempt to eradicate decoration, then, is not only about eradicating the social distinctions that decoration traditionally upholds. Ultimately it concerns the individual's new-found independence from social categories of identity. The individual is encouraged to forge his own identity, which becomes so unique and 'rich' that it cannot easily be communicated to others. But while on the street, one should present oneself '*in such a way that one stands out the least* . . . In good society, to be conspicuous is bad manners . . . one must not stand out at *the center of culture*.'[18]

The inner spaces of the home and of the soul must be liberated for this crucial development to happen. The architect must be demoted in his responsibilities, providing the 'structure' only, and allowing the individual to fill out the 'interior' for himself: the architect merely sets the scene.[19] He creates an environment as economical, efficient, clean, practical and productive – as standardized – as possible.[20] But he does not invest it with 'meaning', for this is no longer social, but individual. Through this, Loos promises 'culture': 'By culture I mean that *balance of man's inner and outer being* which alone guarantees rational thought and action.'[21]

Le Corbusier wanted the same thing. He, too, condemned the use of ornament as a representation of social rank, which was 'very precisely, the mentality of kings'.[22] Display was for kings and savages, not modern 'citizens':

> in the twentieth century our powers of judgement have developed greatly and we have raised our level of consciousness. Our spiritual needs are different, and higher worlds than those of decoration offer us commensurate experience. It seems justified to affirm: *the more cultivated a person becomes, the more decoration disappears.* (Surely it was Loos who put it so neatly.)[23]

Likewise, he demands the standardization of buildings, objects and clothing to accord with the more or less standard human form and physiology. This again frees us from the wasted time, energy and expense needed to create fancy things, but also frees us from something much more important: as ornament was the means through which social ranks were maintained and

articulated, its eradication is simultaneously the eradication of those ranks
– or more exactly, of the individual's susceptibility to think that this is
where identity is constituted. As Le Corbusier remarks, 'The classes too
have their classification', but the 'special display' of fancy goods allows
them falsely to pitch themselves up this scale of values. Again, the bourgeoisie are especially susceptible to this, and the museum, being biased
towards the ornamental, is the source for the entire sickly mind-set.[24]

But once decoration is gone, so too is this social scale, and the individual
is forced to become his own measure: then 'you will be *master of yourself*
. . . Then comes *inner* cleanness.' The individual can at last confront
himself, and stand out in distinction from those things that formerly
smothered him.[25] The 'naked man' 'seeks to free himself from the dominance of external circumstances', with all richness and individuality now
discovered inside.[26] Once again, this inner richness is so intense that it can
scarce be communicated in the street: socially '*neutralized*' behind his
anonymous English suit, the only thing that betrays the identity of the
modern man is an intriguing glimmer 'in the eyes. That's enough'.[27]

But Le Corbusier goes further than Loos in his discussion of the kind
of individuality that is now available. He was interested in the fable of
Diogenes, the legendary ascetic of antiquity. Diogenes could 'identify the
superfluous and throw it away', which is confirmed both in the discarding
of his cup after seeing a child drink from its hands, and in his insistence
that Alexander the Great, who had offered to grant him any favour, could
do nothing more generous than remove himself from the path of the sun-
light: 'Get out of my light!' If we pursue the metaphor, the utilitarian
stocktaking of what is necessary or superfluous is surely meant to end in
spiritual meditation. But because people are so habituated to relying on
things 'outside' themselves, they are afraid of this: 'If I were to come face
to face with my soul (fearful thought)? What would I say to it?'[28]

Like Loos, Le Corbusier believed that this shift of values must happen
at this precise moment of history, and appears also to have been indebted
to G. W. F. Hegel's philosophy of history.[29] The driving force in Hegel's
philosophy of history is a transcendental spiritual quality, or 'Idea', which
struggles to realize itself in the material world in increasingly perfect forms.
This Idea is revealed on earth by certain 'great individuals of history', who
are 'the most far-sighted among their contemporaries; they know best what
issues are involved, and whatever they do is right'. It is the duty of these

individuals to upgrade the world in stages to a more spiritual plane.[30] The First World War provided Le Corbusier with an insight into how France might evolve in this way, leaving her past behind to forge a powerful technological Utopia. This moment must be seized.

There was an urgency here that remained with Le Corbusier throughout his life: 'A day comes when an idea is ripe . . . Happiness or unhappiness comes from that hour that is gripped in passing, or allowed to flee.'[31] Le Corbusier was therefore primed to initiate this leap into a new phase of history, and the Messianism that informs this statement would justify his attempts to sweep away those powerful reactionary groups of politicians and academicians who had a vested interest in the *status quo*. For Le Corbusier, they were simply destined to step aside.[32]

In sum, we can cautiously generalize that Le Corbusier believed the intelligent deployment of material resources would allow the world and the individual to attain a new pinnacle of self-consciousness. In particular, the individual could forge an identity that did not depend upon society. Also, Le Corbusier believed that the moment was ripe, and that he was ordained to carry through this process.

Part 1

'The Lawgiver'

Preface

In the following three chapters, I shall examine how the ideas discussed above were manifested in 'real' terms. This entails an investigation of Le Corbusier's political dealings between the wars, and the ideal cities he designed to correspond with them: from a technocratic first phase, through a syndicalist second phase and into the outright despotism of his Vichy period. Le Corbusier rarely revealed his political affiliations directly. In fact, he often made statements to the effect that 'I am an architect; no one is going to make a politician of me.'[1] It is therefore necessary to look for broad points of contact, and speculate upon his various isolated and veiled references to political movements and events.

He can be seen pandering to various political figures and movements, so desperate to have his urban ideals implemented as to be oblivious to the ideological inconsistency of these shifts. Thus a number of conflicts develop. Economically, there are his promises that urban redevelopment could provide massive profits for anyone visionary enough to become involved, existing side by side with his hatred of speculative finance and an ultimate belief in a non-profit-making, protectionist economics. Politically, he courted the parliamentary commitment to peaceful, legal channels of reform, combined with a violent and illiberal anti-parliamentarianism. In terms of his outlook as a naturalized Frenchman, his often belligerent nationalism tended to combine with an internationalist outlook.[2]

The social, political and economic situation of inter-war France was complex enough to accommodate all of these viewpoints. Might not Le Corbusier simply be considered an opportunist, then, adopting and abandoning various positions as circumstances dictated? I think something more interesting was happening. I shall endeavour to show that whatever inconsistencies might have been manifest on the political surface of his life, in his mind at least they were all rendered excusable by a coherent philosophy beneath. This is different from mere opportunism, however much one might condemn some of his temporary affiliations.[3]

I believe the ideas presented in the introduction reveal a recurring pattern and set of priorities in Le Corbusier's political machinations. Two things become evident. First, for all the technological idealism of his allies and the cities he designed for them, he was always more concerned with this as the foundation for a spiritual revival. This was most often collective and nationalistic, although it was often individual as well. Second, he always chose those politics that were essentially *anti*-political: Le Corbusier sought to harness political power to build cities in which politics – traditionally understood – had no part. As I have indicated, this was because he was more interested in engendering a spiritual revival, and therefore wanted to draw people's attention away from inconsequential things. So although he considered politics, society and the city to be necessary in a functional sense, they were not an end in themselves. Given that no professional politician has any intention of erasing his own means of existence, however, it is unsurprising that Le Corbusier was consistently disappointed with his allies.

Chapter 1

1914–1929: Technocracy

The Promise of War

The first opportunity for the realization of Charles-Edouard Jeanneret's ideal was the First World War.[1] For Jeanneret (as Le Corbusier was still known before 1920) and others, this lengthy and demanding campaign served the purpose of purging the French of the worst of their pre-war excesses, their greed, luxury and aestheticism, forging them into a co-ordinated modern state. At the outbreak of war, Jeanneret rejoiced:

> We are at a turn of the history of architecture. The engineers have done it all (the only respectable people so far) but the impetus has begun in 1914 and modern Paris will blossom and be born anew. This is where I yearn to be: a mason in the team. I already have my materials to hand and my whole devotion is to the thought of France. And to the hundreds who will be heroes of this new dawn.[2]

As the French High Commission observed in Washington in 1919:

> As the war progressed . . . there developed the need of virtues not commonly regarded as French: patience, perseverance, work, unity. What was

the opinion of France commonly held in 1914? That the race was wearied; the industries behind the times.[3]

But the new collective demands for the mobilization of troops, the general securing of the basic resources of food, clothes, shelter, the manufacture of munitions, and ongoing reconstruction, changed all this. The invasion and widespread destruction of the highly industrialized north-east, for example, cost France half her capacity to produce coal, and some two-thirds of that to manufacture iron, steel and textiles. It became necessary for the government to intervene in private industry and co-ordinate the distribution of raw materials and the manufacture of essentials.[4]

Earlier in the century, French workers generally, together with most small- and medium-scale bourgeois manufacturers, had been hostile to attempts by progressive industrialists to reorganize their factories on Frederick Winslow Taylor's principles of 'scientific management'. In the 1880s, Taylor, an American engineer, had remedied the poor productivity of the American steel industry by scrutinizing the movements of each worker and then devising techniques to purge these movements of all superfluity and make them optimally productive. He also introduced wage incentive systems to reward the workers for adopting such regimentation. Although his scheme was largely limited to factory floor and managerial reorganization, Taylor became for the French the symbol of a much more comprehensive movement towards ever greater efficiency and productivity, now known as 'technocracy': 'Industrial concentration, the assembly line, product standardization, mass marketing, "scientific management," producers' ententes, organizational reform, a "technical state," and a managerial approach to labour relations were only some of the items that it encompassed.'[5] Come the crisis, the French government intervened directly, orchestrating the wholesale imposition of such measures, and the productivity of many war-related industries flourished as a result.

The particular appeal of technocracy for the government was that, based upon the objective standards of science, it served to defuse the factory-floor conflicts of worker and manager at a time when they would have been most disastrous. It masqueraded as an apolitical and classless system of pure productivity from which everyone was likely to benefit. Presided over by the objectivity of the engineer, it was devoid of party-political and class conflict.[6] Furthermore, the system really began to appeal to the

French when it was observed that Henri de Saint-Simon, an early nineteenth-century Utopian socialist, had to some degree anticipated it in his proposals for a hierarchical but frictionless society based on the standards of the engineer. The French could convince themselves that technocracy owed its origins to a Frenchman.[7] Thus arose a new respect for pragmatic design, mass-production and the scientific management of time and labour; in short, a respect for values usually considered to be Anglo-Saxon, but which were now reinstated as traditionally French.[8]

At the outbreak of war, Jeanneret caught the first whiff of his Utopia: 'I see that the propitious moment is at hand.'[9] With the war fully under way, he again exulted: 'Paris will become the rally-point for years not only for the triple, but for the multiple *entente* of nations . . . It will be enough to reach a seventh heaven and sink Bosche progress!'[10] In all likelihood, Jeanneret encountered Taylorism during the war years while researching his Dom-ino housing project in the Bibliothèque Nationale.[11] His move to Paris from Switzerland in the summer of 1917 found him as consultant architect to the Société d'Application du Béton Armé, a collection of engineers and industrialists concerned with solving industrial problems for the war effort. He also established the Société d'Entreprises Industrielles et Etudes and a concrete block factory.

It was towards the end of 1917, in this aura of patriotism and construction, that Jeanneret was introduced to Amédée Ozenfant through a society of artists and intellectuals called Art et Liberté. This nationalistic group had been formed in 1916 to protect French artists from accusations of disseminating German influences. The occasion of their introduction was Jeanneret's search for a publisher for a projected book, *France ou Allemagne*, which pledged to reinvigorate French pride in these native arts.[12] Ozenfant had been engaged on a similar enterprise, a journal entitled *L'Elan*, which in its short run from 1915 to 1916 had been committed to providing 'propaganda for French Art, French independence, in sum, the true French spirit'.[13]

Although Jeanneret's book was never any more than a sketch, a more fruitful collaboration emerged. Four days after the Armistice in November 1918, Jeanneret and Ozenfant published *Après le Cubisme*: 'Art before the Great Test was not "living" enough to invigorate the idle, nor to interest the vigorous; society then was restless, because the directive of life was uncertain, because there was no great collective current to work those

who had to work, nor to tempt to work those who did not have to . . .
Gone are those times.'[14] Their emphasis lay with collective effort over the
economic and artistic individualism that characterized the times before the
war, hence they condemned the fragmentation of the artistic scene into a
plethora of short-lived movements.[15] This gave rise to the 'Purist' movement and its journal, *L'Esprit nouveau*, which first appeared in 1920. The
title of this journal held distinctly patriotic and, more important, spiritual
overtones. Guillaume Apollinaire, for example, used the phrase to denote
the French spirit in its privileged relation to some larger universal spirit:
'Even *L'esprit nouveau*, which has the ambition to note the universal spirit
and does not know how to limit its activities to this or that activity, is none
the less a personal and lyrical expression of the French nation, and claims
to respect it.'[16] The invigorating rhetoric of militarism was also central:

> The War was an insatiable 'client'; never satisfied, always demanding
> better. The orders were to succeed at all costs and death followed a
> mistake remorselessly. We may then affirm that the airplane mobilized
> invention, intelligence and daring: *imagination* and *cold reason*. It is the
> same spirit that built the Parthenon.[17]

Speaking of the necessity for formulating comprehensive plans – both the
plan of a building or a city and the long-term development plan of the
nation – Le Corbusier stated:

> It is a plan of battle. The battle follows and that is the great moment. The
> battle is composed of the impact of masses in space and the *morale* of the
> army is the cluster of predetermined ideas and the driving purpose.[18]

The chief objective of this movement was to perpetuate in peacetime
the momentum of sober co-operation, modernization and national pride,
which had been born of necessity during the war. This new resilience, it
was reasoned, must continue to strengthen the nation for its impending
economic struggles, especially in terms of reconstruction. They stated, 'We
have sought to push aside all forms of futility or disaggregation; we have
sought to bring together the constructive means.'[19] Their proposed use of
Taylorism went beyond industrial efficiency. They reproduced the idealist
interpretation discussed earlier which saw Taylorism as a mechanism for
replacing problematic socio-political hierarchies with a meritocratic élite
of apolitical experts. Politics, as a form of participatory activity, would be

eliminated. Predictably, the Purists were scornful of the way trade unions deferred to the abilities and intelligence of the masses.[20] But from the atmosphere of the original meeting of Ozenfant and Jeanneret, the Purists' rationalization of all spheres of life was intended to result in the spiritual rebirth of the nation. They glimpsed the dawn of a new type of national consciousness which did away with small-scale commerce and party-political infighting.

Although not directly involved in politics during this episode, Jeanneret was surely aware of the career – and failure – of the one politician who might conceivably have brought about his ideal. The Purists had not simply plucked such notions out of the air. These were precisely the notions that flavoured the contemporary political debate as to whether or not a post-war France, with the necessity of survival removed, should return to pre-war economic liberalism and small-scale enterprise. The foremost official proponent of the position identifiable with Jeanneret's was Etienne Clémentel, Minister of Commerce from 1915 to 1919. It was Clémentel's belief that those measures set up for the purposes of war must be maintained after the war and perhaps indefinitely. His rhetoric has a 'Corbusian' ring:

> I have been convinced that a new era is emerging, one in which our old and excessive love of individualism must bow before the necessity of organization and union . . . The war forced us to collaborate. We have lived side by side; we have lived together; we have learned to appreciate the reciprocal efforts that we can make for everyone's benefit. We must certainly continue this union sacrée born from the war; we must multiply our efforts, which will lead, I am convinced, to success and the economic victory of France.[21]

With little political power and a meagre following, Clémentel was able to manoeuvre his ideas into a position of some prominence only by virtue of the fact that others, especially Prime Minister Georges Clemenceau and his Minister of Armaments Louis Loucheur, were too busy waging war to be directly concerned with economic policy until after the Armistice.[22]

Clémentel was somewhat removed from the centre of political action and his scheme was almost purely theoretical, more in tune with his imaginative temperament than with the practical issues of the moment. He also failed to notice the fact that there was little commitment or willingness within the business community, the professional classes or within parliament to preserve the imposed 'étatiste-corporatist realignment of liberal capitalism' for a moment longer than was necessary – quite regardless of its efficacy for waging war.[23] Clémentel's initiatives foundered on a mixture of domestic and international interests, all of which demanded the immediate and full return to free trade and private enterprise.[24]

An example of the consequences of the return to such an uncoordinated system was to be found in post-war reconstruction. After the Armistice, Loucheur was made Minister of Industrial Reconstruction.[25] As well as the need to rebuild some 1,000 destroyed factories, 1,500 schools, 352,000 homes, 62,000 and 5,000 kilometres of roads and railways respectively, there was the necessity of developing the recently annexed region of Alsace-Lorraine, and the recultivation of 3,000,000 acres of land. Coal production was down 74 per cent, pig-iron 81 per cent and steel 63 per cent on pre-war averages.[26] Rather than the formulation of a comprehensive development plan, however, Loucheur handed out indemnities to those home-owners, farmers and private industrialists affected by the war, with which they were free to rebuild in whatever manner took their fancy. The only restriction placed upon them was that they were forbidden *not* to rebuild.[27] Understandably, 'The owners of the heaps of rubble and water-logged foundations often insisted on building on exactly the same site and in the same style.'[28] This was anathema to the ideals of Clémentel and Jeanneret. One possible means for the realization of Jeanneret's ideals had therefore been removed. This occurred within, and as a result of, bourgeois liberal parliamentarianism.

But the most important point to bear in mind is that, for Jeanneret, national planning was not an end in itself. It was meant to provide for a breakthrough in national consciousness.

'It is "right" and therefore immutable'

Le Corbusier was undaunted by the unsatisfactory drift of national politics, and set about the design of his Ville Contemporaine. This scheme is the manifestation of the technocratic approach to the post-war dilemma: utilizing the latest technology in accord with a clear plan, it counters the 'policy of drift and idleness which brings death . . . It sets up *principles* as against the medley of silly little reforms with which we are constantly deceiving ourselves.'[29] The original parameters of this urban project, which Le Corbusier was invited to compose for the 1922 Salon d'Automne, were intended to stop with street furniture.[30] Le Corbusier, however, disregarded the brief and created 'a contemporary city of three million inhabitants'.[31] His plan was saturated with terminology and aspirations aimed at the disciples of Taylorism. Le Corbusier intended to have his plan realized through the agency of such people. The Ville Contemporaine provided an efficient infrastructure of speedy communications, maintained a rigidly hierarchical vision of class relationships with the irrevocable constitution of an objective ruling élite, yet simultaneously offered substantial humanitarian benefits to the lower classes.[32]

All the great cities of the world were brutally competing in 'the mad urge for supremacy', Le Corbusier observed.[33] The commitment to global economic harmony which was dear to many of the technocrats was countered by Le Corbusier's observation that, despite the efforts of organizations like the League of Nations, 'there will not be, there cannot ever be only one single power, for, the day after its advent, a new force will surge forth . . . a vital phenomenon exists, persists, and will never disappear: that of *competition*'.[34] In the Ville Contemporaine, Le Corbusier framed a potent image of a new and aggressive French state, professionally managed, rather than ruled, by the 'brains of the whole nation'.[35] Le Corbusier crystallized the key technocratic ideal, 'the heralded utopian change from power over men to the administration of things'. This system maintains a rigid class hierarchy while sidelining potential insurgency by rationalizing the production and distribution of goods and services.

To reintroduce a topic touched upon earlier, there were two alternatives for dealing with working-class demands: 'redistributive' transfers of property and wealth, in which one class must always prosper at the expense of the other, thereby perpetuating class conflict; and the 'nonredistributive' method, whereby a commitment to optimalization increased the amount of everything so that there was enough for all. Theoretically, this placated the masses, while preventing redistribution of wealth and preserving hierarchical power relations.[36] Technocracy represented the second of these options. Most important, it was anti-political: to run such a system, you needed managers, engineers and logistical experts, not politicians. Le Corbusier championed this in the Ville Contemporaine:

increase production and you will settle the masses. Sanitary rehousing, according to him, was the only way of avoiding revolution. Furthermore, it was the only way of making shift work and the division of labour bearable, although 'If the workman is intelligent he will understand the final end of his labour, and this will fill him with a legitimate pride.'[37] So the new city, being based on the objective lessons of science and 'managed' by an élite of objective professionals, is nominally apolitical, and therefore protected from party-political conflict. It is impervious to change: 'It is the city's business to make itself permanent.'[38] This was shrewdly recognized by Cornelius Gurlitt, a contemporary observer: no provision was made, he noted, 'for public buildings such as churches, schools, theatres, movie houses, stores, post offices, court houses and the like'. In other words, there are no arenas of public participation, and thus little possibility for the formation of a politicized mass consciousness or to exert pressure for change: 'Those who come after Le Corbusier must simply cease wanting to be modern. They must forego any future inno-vations.' Once the system is up and running, any future constitutional change becomes an impossibility. As Gurlitt sarcastically concluded, 'It is "right" and therefore immutable.'[39]

To demonstrate that his proposals were viable, Le Corbusier applied them to a specific site north of the Seine. The resulting Plan Voisin, so-called because of its sponsorship by the Voisin automobile company, was exhibited at the 1925 Exposition des Arts Décoratifs et Industriels Modernes. One of the chief points in its favour was that it 'makes a frontal attack on the most diseased quarters of the city', thus ameliorating poten-tial class unrest.[40] Another means devised by Le Corbusier to entice the capitalist technocrats to support the Plan Voisin was to guarantee massive profits: 'Do we want to see how a state that *wishes* to can earn billions?'[41] 'In my scheme,' he says, 'sky-scrapers accommodating 40,000 employees take 5 per cent. of the available site. Thus actually only 5 per cent. of the population would be dislodged in the rebuilding.'[42] The increased vertical density of the skyscrapers would ensure that the land immediately acquired a worth twenty times its original value, out of which could be taken compensation for the relocated populace.[43] The remaining 95 per cent of unrequisitioned land would consequently become deserted as the businesses housed there migrated into the shining new skyscrapers: free for demolition, this land would then be redeveloped into avenues and parkland, and so the scheme would snowball.[44] The immensely powerful financial trusts must therefore be brought into play.[45]

Such notions would have been simmering among technocrats ever since their first brush with Taylorism during the war. The Taylorist factory thus became 'the nucleic building block of a post-bourgeois world, or at least a secure managerial one'.[46] The most influential figurehead to put such an ideology into practise was Ernest Mercier, who founded the Redressement Français for precisely this purpose in 1925.[47] The Redressement was a response to the failure of Edouard Herriott's Radical–Socialist coalition, the Cartel des Gauches. Initially, the Cartel had been a promising technocratic enterprise, and *L'Esprit nouveau* pinned their hopes upon it by offering support just prior to the Cartel's election victory in May 1924. But inner tensions in the coalition, coupled with its electoral base of small-scale business interests, broke it apart and derailed its technocratic programme in less than a year.[48] Here, then, another politician advocating the kind of ideal Le Corbusier favoured was defeated. The episode highlighted, in ever clearer terms, the constitutional stagnancy of Third Republic parliamentarianism, and its impenetrability behind the interests of bourgeois capital – the 'mur d'argent'.

So, in 1925, Mercier founded the Redressement, which found an immediate ally in Le Corbusier.[49] The reasons that technocracy only caught hold now, rather than during Clémentel's wartime endeavours, was that it had taken several years for the incompetence and deadlock of the Third Republic to become fully apparent. The Redressement provided a rallying point for a professional, 'apolitical' élite of industrialists, engineers and intellectuals, who proposed to reorganize the government and economy along technocratic lines. Their slogan, which captures their frustration with parliamentarianism, was 'Enough politics. We want results.'[50] Emblazoned on the front of their *Bulletin*, where this slogan appeared, was a redoubtable Gaul, ignoring his wounds to rejoin the battle. One of their chief concerns, echoing Le Corbusier, was that of defusing the increasing likelihood of insurgency among the masses. Their chief spokesman, Lucien Romier, warned that unhygienic living conditions made the masses susceptible to Communist propaganda. A strict professional hierarchy was to be maintained, the élite were to be given absolute executive power and would attempt to evade criticism by citing the objectivity of their actions, and the masses were to be placated with better wages, housing, leisure time and welfare programmes. An example of the 'non-redistributive' ideal, this was 'Ford over Marx', material optimalization over material equality. The masses should not hope to lead or influence government, but rather accept their position in the meritocracy: 'What one expects from the workers appears at first glance most simple,' said Mercier: 'It is a question merely of their understanding and accepting the necessities.'[51]

Exactly how these programmes were to be pushed through is less clear. On the one hand, the Redressement was sceptical of parliamentarianism; on the other, they believed that their programme could be put into effect within the existing constitution of the Third Republic. The triumph of the Redressement-backed Union Nationale in 1928, and the support of Loucheur, maintained their faith in the system. Commenting on the failure of Clémentel's initiatives, Romier had earlier suggested that any such measures must be allowed to develop from within the administration, rather than being forcibly imposed upon it from without.[52] Le Corbusier inclined to the anti-parliamentarian approach. He expressed absolute distrust in legal channels, and lamented the absence of a great authoritarian leader who would seize control, as Louis XIV, Colbert, Napoleon I and Haussmann had done in the past. Referring to the Sun-King, he remarked:

> Homage to a great town planner. This despot conceived immense projects and realized them. Over all the country his noble works still fill us with admiration. He was capable of saying, 'We wish it,' or 'Such is our pleasure.'[53]

But in the Redressement, generally speaking, Le Corbusier appeared to have found the allies he needed. He was drafted into their urban study committee, and contributed pamphlets to the *Bulletin* in 1928 in which he outlined the autocratic urban legislature necessary to implement his plan.[54]

When Premier Raymond Poincaré's Union Nationale government was granted exceptional powers to rescue the economy in 1928, however, the channels of parliament were deliberately opened. His initiatives enjoyed clear passage, and a period of steady economic growth began which stripped the Redressement of all basis for complaint. The organization lost its Utopian edge and revealed its true colours by defending its newly prosperous capitalist interests.[55] The modernization drive of the Redressement was never such that they intended fundamentally to alter the Republic, let alone overthrow it. They simply wanted to iron out the worst of its incompetence, consolidate the bourgeois monopoly on private property and strengthen their own interests. They were all too glad to be absorbed back into the parliamentary fold when their grievances had been redressed.[56] Indeed, interest in American models of production only truly took hold in France towards the end of the 1920s, when conservative industrialists and politicians saw in them a means of consolidating their new prosperity, rather than of forging a radical new type of society. Wary of its ideological potential for upsetting the *status quo* – such as the concession of absolute power to the technocrat – the French manifestations of Taylorism were stripped of such overtones and applied in purely pragmatic terms. Fordism, having no problematic Utopian connotations, increasingly came to the fore as the system that provided the safest bulwark for capitalism.[57]

Inevitably, with the rejection of the co-operative social plan, the new productive methods were harnessed to the divisive individualism of industrialists. An example of the extent to which technocracy had left its Utopianism behind is Loucheur's housing legislation of 1928, which made provision for the release of 8,200 million francs between 1929 and 1935 for the construction of some 260,000 'habitations à loyer moderé'.[58] The joy with which Le Corbusier responded to this makes one think his Utopia had dawned:

> This certainly had to happen one day? The Loucheur law . . . places the country for the first time in the face of a gigantic, magnificent, and sensitive problem, if the spirit would seize it, enlighten it, and stir it to give France a historic renown, in the way that the works achieved by the Middle Ages, by Louis XIV, by Napoleon, by Haussmann have become historic.[59]

But this was not the breakthrough Le Corbusier thought. Loucheur's plans represented a bribe for securing middle-class votes in preservation of a 'weak and tottering Republic'.[60] At Loucheur's request, Le Corbusier had provided a house-type which satisfied the parameters of the new law, but he was too jaded to think anything would come of it: 'There is no point of contact between the two sides involved: my plan (which is a way of life) and those for whom the law is made (the potential clients who have not been educated).' As well as the stagnation of government, Le

Corbusier was also convinced of the backwardness of the working classes: 'Workingmen, whose clear-sighted spirit I often love, will loathe our houses; they'll call them "boxes" . . . Here is a dwelling of modern times still awaiting those for whom it is designed.'[61]

The last chance for Le Corbusier's technocratic ideal emerged with the new government of André Tardieu in 1929. A modernizer and rationalist, with a commitment to strong executive authority in the form of a US-style president who could override parliamentary obstruction, Tardieu represented everything Le Corbusier required. He wanted coherent long-term planning, and an end to the *ad hoc* pendulum swing of French politics from 'routine' to 'crisis' ministries. But he too ran aground on the worst excesses of parliamentarianism and party politics.[62] Finally, the reputation of all American models received a blow from the crash on Wall Street in 1929:

> It was mere paper, mere 'bubble' money. And the bubble burst. Suddenly, brutally, this house-of-cards economy collapsed, and the U. S. was filled with hunger marchers.[63]

What conclusions can be drawn from this? First, that Le Corbusier's modernizing initiatives were the foundation for an awakening of national spirit. The Ville Contemporaine was not a hymn to technology, as is commonly thought, but an armature for sustaining this new surge of consciousness. Second, Le Corbusier allied himself with a political movement that was apparently anti-political. There were no politics in the Ville Contemporaine, only objective management. This was not because, as Gurlitt intimates, Le Corbusier was power-hungry. For as well as eliminating the possibility of ordinary people getting involved in political activity, his city also eliminates *social* activity. Night-clubs, cafés, restaurants, concert halls and theatres are good only for wasting time, swapping germs and fraying nerves. It is interesting that when Le Corbusier could not avoid portraying a café or restaurant in one of his cityscapes, he tended to push them to the periphery. And when they were of central focus, he ensured that nobody was ever seen to be using them.[64] Le Corbusier also promises to ameliorate the 'nerve-wracking' visual clutter of the city: 'The eye is overwhelmed, tired and hurt', the 'mind bewildered and worn out and indisposed for its task'.[65] The street, that prime focus of chance encounters, is also eliminated. The only communal activity left is sport, favoured by Le Corbusier primarily because the rules of engagement are laid out in advance and are non-negotiable. The working day is cut, and all the catering and domestic chores of the home are taken over by a co-operative.[66] Le Corbusier is therefore committed to reorienting the daily priorities of ordinary people. He takes many activities, interests and concerns out of their hands until there is not much left for them. In general, he attempts to loosen the ties that make them dependent upon the outside world, especially upon social and political matters. Under his influence, these would have become strictly regulated.

Much of Le Corbusier's rhetoric in this period celebrates the great collective achievements of past epochs, in which the masses were united by a single purpose and found their 'civic pride'. It is this kind of collective movement that he believes will build his new cities.[67] But this is not intended as meaningful social activity, for Le Corbusier has a very peculiar idea of this new collective:

> In terms of town planning, the flat may be considered as a cell. Cells, as a consequence of our social order, are subject to various forms of grouping, to co-operations or to antagonisms which are an essential part of the urban phenomenon. In general, we feel free in our own cell (and our dream is to live in a detached house somewhere in order to feel absolutely free), and reality teaches us that the grouping of cells attacks our freedom and so we dream of a detached house. Our crowded communal life is imposed on us by the very fact of there being towns, a fact which cannot be avoided; and this interference with our liberty affects our happiness, we dream (though fruitlessly) of breaking through this collective phenomenon of which we are the slaves.[68]

It is clear, for Le Corbusier, that the natural human impulse is to pull away from the collective, but the city-based collective is necessary for the workings of society and the economy. The Ville Contemporaine is a mechanism for managing this problem: it is a special type of city that allows the individual to forget the fact of his having to exist in a collective. There will, of course, Le Corbusier maintains, be collective enthusiasm to build the Ville Contemporaine, but this is fuelled by the promise of ultimately 'breaking through' this collective. What remains is 'a *sort* of community', but not community as such.[69]

Le Corbusier's political 'allies' were not prepared to go to this extreme. They only flirted with eradicating the parliamentary structure and party politics during periods of crisis. Once the crisis passed and their interests were met, they slipped back into the fold. Le Corbusier had underestimated the conservatism of these apparent visionaries. He lived the truth of the 'stalemate society'.[70] The following, however, is a clear statement of his intentions:

> The present social system preserves the status quo, opposes any action, eliminates or rejects proposals both pressing and necessary in the public interest. But it is *life* that guided us when we made our plans. Let's go along with *life*. The plan sets out its aims and calls for action. *Let's change the system.*[71]

The next chapter shows the intensification of the above trends and demonstrates that this is predicated upon an underlying concept of self, which Le Corbusier pursues with a ruthless logic.

Chapter 2

1930–1940:
Syndicalism

The 'Timid People'

Central to the ideology of technocracy were two somewhat contradictory positions. First, the expert was to be employed in fine-tuning and eliminating the frictions within an already superior liberal-democratic machine. Second, the expert threatened to demolish this machine, as he believed the commitment to optimize production was incompatible with *laissez-faire* capitalism. The first ideal found greater favour in the relatively stable 1920s. Come the desperate circumstances of the Depression, it was the more drastic formulation that came to the fore. Only now did technocracy develop a real potential for overturning the *status quo*. And this vision became all the more powerful and disturbing when the cult of the objective expert was combined with racialist and nationalist ideals.[1]

Although Le Corbusier's rhetoric conformed to this trend and became increasingly vicious, the underlying ideals remained constant and simple. We can see this by looking at *When the Cathedrals were White: A Journey to the Country of Timid People*. This was published in 1937, as a sermonizing allegory inspired by his visit to the United States two year earlier.[2]

Following a condescending commentary on the state of America, Le
Corbusier maintains that the spiritual superiority of the French over
all nations qualifies them for world leadership. Fundamental to this is Le
Corbusier's diagnosis of a deep psychological malaise within the American psyche, the symptoms of which are recognizable through their obsession with Caravaggio and Surrealism. 'Why Caravaggio?' he asks them:
'Because of the psychological turmoil in that equivocal personality.'[3] And
why Surrealism? For Le Corbusier, this movement represented a com-
memoration of the death of a certain stage of civilization:

> Surrealism is a noble, elegant, artistic, funereal institution . . . What
> liturgy is this? What refined, moving, spectral ceremony? What appeal
> to the past? Is it an entombment? They are burying what was, what has
> ceased to be. They are weeping over the dead. It is an excellent thing.

Beyond this, Surrealism had no positive or constructive qualities to speak
of. But for Le Corbusier, the times must turn towards construction: 'The
new world is waiting for workers!' Rather than help with this task, the
Americans reveal through their artistic preferences that they fear the future,
and are seeking solace in the past. Evoking the image of a perpetually
ascending stairway of progress, Le Corbusier comments: 'Those are singularly disturbed spirits who wish to climb it again, descend it once more,
and consequently to renounce what is before us! Spirits upset by fear,
apprehension, anxiety, anguish – frustration.' Le Corbusier, now on a psychoanalytic high, also traces these symptoms to 'the anxieties of sexual life
. . . an unsatisfied heart'.[4]

Immediately it is clear that Le Corbusier's concern is with psychological
well-being: he believes the time is right to progress towards a healthy spiritual life. But people will not be able to remedy their troubled psyches
until the material world is put into some intelligent order, such that it
ceases to overwhelm them. The Americans, although in material terms the
most dynamic and productive nation, are forced to dedicate all their time
and energy simply to controlling this industrial beast. There is nothing left
over for themselves, which is why they are crazy: 'we do not have a minute
in our lives in which we can make *appraisals*, that is, to try to get to the
bottom of things . . . We are in a whirlwind, we are the whirlwind, we do
not have good judgment about anything that is outside the whirlwind.'[5]

For Le Corbusier, France is the only nation with enough wisdom to
sort out this problem, and he is its self-appointed ambassador to the world.[6]

He no longer justifies his pre-eminence on objective, technocratic grounds, but on the grounds of a genius he has absorbed from his native soil. Fired up with this new sense of right, Le Corbusier pledges to turn his attention back to France for a purge of speculative capitalists, architectural academies and governments committed to the *status quo*.[7] Party politicians come in for particularly harsh attack. Rather than working in accord with humanitarian necessity, like the planner, party politicians are caught in a web of nepotism and publicity. Fear of losing their office far outweighs any commitment to genuine reform: 'they allowed themselves to sink and choke in the most treacherous and execrable quicksands. Disaster, treason, a slap in the face of the sympathetic élite of the world.' Le Corbusier now consciously puts himself above politics:

> But, my dear sir, admit that now you are talking politics. Your argument is political. I am talking about the *plan*, the central idea, the trajectory, the direction. You are the artilleryman who fires the gun at the proper moment, but the plan is the objective at which you are shooting. First you have to know what you are shooting at. Then fire.[8]

Le Corbusier's 'plan' includes primarily the reduction of urban areas to small, super-dense units. This would eliminate the infrastructural maintenance costs of urban sprawl and suburbs, and free ordinary people from having to work unnecessarily long hours to pay for them. It would also eliminate the necessity of commuting, a further constraint on people's freedom.[9]

But alongside this is a plan for a whole new type of authority and society. This would completely do away with the Third Republic, and therefore could hardly count upon it for its implementation. To overcome the self-interest of liberal capitalism and party politics, the 'pontificating coteries', Le Corbusier suggests the return of society to a kind of medieval guild arrangement. Here, he maintains, people existed in raw and frank openness with one another and with the world, free to respond to whatever problems life may present them; truly alive, and not held in thrall by the past. The times were optimistic, pious, clean, progressive, violent, militaristic, and 'Yes, the cathedrals were white, completely white, dazzling and young – and not black, dirty, old. The whole period was fresh and young.'[10]

Already, Le Corbusier maintains, the political institutions of the Republic are proving themselves incapable of containing this new popular sentiment, which is manifest in ever more frequent strike action:

it is fortunate that such 'incidents' occur. Our cities, our 'radiant cities' cannot be built on the basis of our present legislation. The sap of the new times must circulate in worn-out, cruel, inhuman organizations. The new times are near! We shall be able to estimate them through the revolutions which still must take place.

Le Corbusier is careful to stipulate that the nation's productive forces must ultimately be arrayed under the guidance of impartial guild-masters, who are effectively 'medieval' technocrats. He also promises 'the participation of everyone', but 'in an orderly way, and not topsy-turvily; hierarchically, and not de-natured by artificial doctrines'. The people must learn to accept their position within a strict hierarchy, and should not hope for popular sovereignty or the right to vote. None the less, he relishes the thought that 'The French masses are . . . ready for self-examination.' After the frustrations of the 1920s, he is now committed to the rhetoric and, as we shall presently see, even to the practice of violence:

> A new age has begun. A new Middle Age. Through the blood and the sufferings of battles, we must observe the flawless unfolding of the creative work. The interior, the fabric, the nave of the cathedrals was purity itself, but the outside was organised like an army in battle, as hirsute as an army.
>
> Let's break the constraint on our hearts; let's drive away the agony of the unknown . . . let's reconstruct everything . . .
>
> *Above all, let us build for ourselves a new consciousness. That effort does not have a collective basis or character. It finds its support in the depths of each person, in the silence of individual self-examination.*[11]

The pattern is consistent. Le Corbusier is interested in the possibility of the spiritual rebirth of the nation, but this first requires an intelligent deployment of material resources, including the rationalization of the social and political milieu. Without this, the spirit will be drained through unnecessary activities, such as the excessive travelling needed to commute. But here Le Corbusier's concern for the psychological well-being of the individual psyche becomes more apparent. The collective building effort is clearly tied to the building of a new individual consciousness.[12]

'Awakening of Cleanliness'

Le Corbusier's commitment to reorganizing society by violent means, backed up by the ideal of native French values, came directly from the ultra-right political milieu of the 1930s. For Le Corbusier this was not a wholesale change of ideology, merely an intensification of attitudes he had developed earlier.[13]

But one point must be cleared up before proceeding. Le Corbusier concluded *The City of Tomorrow* with a call for a modern Louis XIV to seize control and guide the nation. In the original French version, he adds, 'This is not a declaration of the "Action Française".'[14] The Action Française was the royalist, pro-military movement of Charles Maurras, formed in response to the Dreyfus affair. Maurras insisted that only the monarchy could purge the nation of the decadence imported by the 'four confederate states': Jews, Protestants, Freemasons and foreigners. There was a necessity for wholesale moral cleansing, particularly of self-interested bourgeois capitalism and parliamentary corruption. Before the First World War, Maurras was committed to overthrowing the government by any means necessary, although he especially relished violence. The terrorist wing of the Action Française, the Camelots du Roi, conducted a campaign of physical attacks against their opponents. By 1924, however, when Le Corbusier's statement was published, the Action Française had altered substantially. During the war it had developed some respect for the Republic and became increasingly absorbed into the ideals of traditional conservative parliamentarianism. By the mid-1920s it was committed to seeking a constitutional route to power.[15] Le Corbusier was therefore distancing himself from yet another parliamentary grouping, as incapable as any of effecting change from within the system.

The shift in the Action Française did not go unchallenged. The economist of the movement, Georges Valois, remained committed to the ideal of a revolutionary seizure of power.[16] In the early 1920s he had been attracted to the dynamism of Italian Fascism, against which the Action Française now looked staid and respectable. Maurras remained at heart 'primarily a *littérateur* and political *grondeur*', who Valois believed lacked the necessary 'fascist temperament'. As a movement, they were simply too long established, with an increasingly respectable reputation to uphold.[17] Following heavy electoral defeat for the Action Française in 1924, and the consolidation of leftist power in the Cartel, the parliamentary approach was wholly discredited for Valois. This moment marked a flashpoint for the extreme right, causing an upsurge in the formation and membership of a number of violently reactionary right-wing leagues. Among these was Valois's own breakaway group, the Faisceau des Combattants et des Producteurs, complete with their paramilitary wing, the Légions, and self-publicizing newspaper, *Le Nouveau siècle*. This was the first 'official' Fascist league in France. Valois cast himself in the role of a French Mussolini, and it is probable that Mussolini himself gave financial support to the Faisceau. Through the mediation of a mutual friend, Pierre Winter, Le Corbusier found his name, drawings and ideas featured quite regularly in Valois's *Le Nouveau siècle*. On one occasion Le Corbusier made the front cover as one of the 'animateurs' of the movement, and he also gave a slide demonstration of his urbanism at a Fascist rally. Clearly, he welcomed the association and sought to profit by it.[18]

Le Corbusier's reasons for dissociating himself from the Action Française, then, were not that he found it too extreme and too violent, but because he found it too tame. A curious set of deceptively innocuous comments and photographs in Le Corbusier's *La Ville radieuse* of 1935 provides disturbing evidence of his affiliations. One photograph shows a number of men apparently tearing up the cast-iron street fixtures of Paris (fig. 2). Viewed superficially, this might be interpreted as no more than a reiteration of Le Corbusier's demand for the replacement of wasteful decorative objects with those of proven utility. The caption underneath, however, reveals a more sinister connotation: 'February 6th, 1934, in Paris: awakening of cleanliness'.[19] The date reveals that these are representatives of the combined forces of the extreme right, including the Action Française and newer groupings like the Jeunesses Patriotes and Croix de Feu, who on that day marched on the Chambre des Députés with the intention not only of bringing down the Radical government of Edouard Daladier, but of shattering the entire liberal parliamentary system. They were successful in the former, and almost so in the latter. The rioting involved thousands of protesters and some eight hundred police, and resulted in the hospitalization of at least three hundred, with fifteen deaths.[20]

The occasion of this uprising was the rapid succession of incompetent Radical ministries, some collapsing within weeks, and each one seemingly

2   Le Corbusier. 'February 6th, 1934, in Paris: awakening of cleanliness.' From Le Corbusier, *La Ville radieuse*, 1935. © FLC

less able than the last to push through any financial reform to combat the Depression. What set the match to this touchpaper, however, was the uncovering in autumn 1933 of what became known as the 'Stavisky Scandal'. Serge Alexandre Stavisky was a Jewish financier, a naturalized Ukrainian, whose ill-conceived scam of floating millions of francs' worth of phoney bonds proved over-ambitious. The ensuing investigations revealed that Stavisky's schemes had enjoyed protection from the government and Sûreté at the highest levels. This inflamed the anti-Semitic, xenophobic and anti-parliamentarian sentiments of the extreme right. Stavisky was found, shot dead, in January 1934, and a little later the police official charged with heading the investigation was found tied up and poisoned on a railway track. The extreme right believed this was an attempt by a conspiracy of Radical Jewish freemasons in government to derail the investigations and thereby limit the extent of their complicity in Stavisky's affairs. These events resulted in the riots of 6 February.

All of this combines to make sense of the sinister marginalia of *La Ville radieuse*, in which Le Corbusier condemns the depravity to which the modern conscience has been brought by money: 'the disease has spread', he says, 'moral corruption, embezzlement, betrayal of trust. Percentages, middlemen, a shameful piling up of shady practises.' Shortly afterwards, in a tiny parenthetical remark, the name of Stavisky is mentioned, and nearby is an image of 'The chariot of death / In life after death,' we are told, 'justice will come.'[21] The meaning is inescapable and disturbing: Le Corbusier considered the entire business to be a 'cleansing'. Pointedly contradicting his government-wooing phrases, then, Le Corbusier states that 'Earthly paradise cannot be created by governmental decree.'[22]

The broad political ideology that lay behind all of this was 'syndicalism', which was developed and carried forward from the late nineteenth century by the trade-union federation, the Confédération Générale du Travail (CGT).[23] Generally speaking, syndicalism sought to replace the abuses of speculative finance with a system of co-operative workshops and impartial syndicates. These were to be small committees assembled out of particular segments of the nation's labour forces, which would meet on an equal footing to exchange information and co-ordinate national economic policy. They were deeply anti-republican and anti-parliamentarian, their goal being to dissolve the monolithic centralized state apparatus and disperse political responsibility throughout the country. Power would then be upheld by an elaborate meritocratic hierarchy. For a number of reasons, however, much of the CGT's activism had vanished by the First World War, and it moved gradually on to constitutional parliamentarian ground.[24] It was this 'crise syndicaliste' that caused the fragmentation of 'orthodox' syndicalism, some moving to the extreme left; and others, especially those who believed that the decadent parliamentary state was now in the grip of Dreyfusards, to the extreme right.[25] Here were to be found the likes of Valois, who upheld the ideal of violence and realigned the general syndicalist ideology so as to give absolute authority to the masters of the syndicates. By the 1930s, syndicalism was the prime exponent of the ideal of economic planning, '*planisme*', which promised stringent state-control to remedy the interminable boom–bust cycles of capitalism.[26]

Le Corbusier was exposed to this cluster of ideas.[27] In 1930, he collaborated with Philippe Lamour, another follower of Valois, to edit a syndicalist journal. *Plans* first appeared in early 1931, and Le Corbusier followed it up a year later with editorial work on another journal, *Prélude*, which was the mouthpiece of the Central Committee for Regional and Syndicalist Action. He also contributed to other syndicalist reviews, such as *Grande route* and *L'Homme réel*. With organized labour a minority in France, these journals devised a strategy of blurring class distinctions so as to give syndicalism a wider appeal. They fostered the vision of an organic world order which, in its simple correspondence to universal law and the satisfaction of those inalienable requirements that are natural to everyone, was offered as morally sound and in possession of absolute right. This was a literal transcription of the theories of the early nineteenth-century social philosopher Charles Fourier, with whose work Le Corbusier was acquainted. Fourier had argued that world order and the reconciliation of man with the universe could only occur through the satisfaction of the naturally occurring passions and needs common to all mankind, which were primarily antisocial in nature.[28] Once again, such measures as would be necessary to inaugurate Le Corbusier's system, and such social hierarchies as would be necessary to manage its affairs, were explained as the expression of universal law.[29]

The Ville Radieuse, exhibited at the Brussels conference of the Congrès Internationaux d'Architecture Moderne (CIAM) in 1930, was framed in terms of the same urgency as the Ville Contemporaine had been several years earlier.[30] The accompanying book, which came out in 1935, was substantially comprised of the most important of Le Corbusier's writings for the syndicalist journals. In accordance with the general syndicalist–planiste fraternity, Le Corbusier attempted here to reassert the importance of socio-economic planning in the life of the nation. Taking a natural metaphor, he states that 'the primary form of life consisted of cells that could reproduce by themselves, dividing themselves up, multiplying, and forming an amorphous, quivering, but purposeless mass'. This is offered as an analogy of the aimless growth of a nation or city without a coherent plan, and thus of the meandering economic measures of the Republic. Evolving out of this weak protoplasmic mass, however, the higher forms of life learn to organize their various parts, assigning them different functions, and thereby becoming a thing of formidable efficiency: 'an intention appears, an axis began to form in the centre of this motionless agglomeration. A current, a direction became apparent. An organism was born.'[31] Ostensibly, then, the Ville Radieuse is founded on natural law, with socio-economic planning considered as the societal corollary of the living axes of higher organisms.[32]

The system of government required to orchestrate this effort is also justified in organic terms: 'THE PYRAMID OF NATURAL HIERARCHIES'. The feet of this pyramid of syndicates, or guilds, are found in the nation's working classes, from which arise the representatives of each trade, who in turn meet the representatives of all the other trades at an 'inter-union confer-ence where the main problems of economic interdependence are ham-mered out and a state of balance achieved'. Presiding over all, freed from the drudgery of regulating the economy, the élite are 'at liberty to con-centrate on the country's higher purpose. For it is in works of this supreme authority that the whole philosophy of a civilization will be expressed.'[33] Taking a swipe at Communism, Le Corbusier implies that to reverse this natural order and attempt to install the masses in the place of prominence is as foolhardy as attempting to balance a pyramid on its point.[34] As for public participation and debate, all we hear is that 'A considerable margin should be reserved from the very beginning.'[35] But the Ville Radieuse remains absolutely stable: a natural hierarchy of objective experts, and the satisfaction of the organic needs common to all people, make constitu-tional change undesirable, unnecessary, not to say impossible.[36]

With the ousting of central government in the Ville Radieuse, parties and politics cease to exist. The leaders are unassailable. Essentially they are another group of technocrats, but now they are justified as 'naturally' and 'organically', as opposed to 'rationally', inevitable. The lower classes are considered to be qualified only to comment upon their particular trades, which excludes them from influencing the larger affairs of the nation. This opinion lay at the heart of Le Corbusier's suspicion of the right to uni-versal suffrage.[37] In fact, one of the influences for the 'political' ideals of the Ville Radieuse came from a tobacco factory that Le Corbusier visited in Rotterdam, which was so efficiently run that the workers allegedly became depoliticized – '*there is no proletariat here*'.[38] Good organization – the good city – does away with the need for politics and political con-sciousness. Le Corbusier claimed to have provided 'a doctrine that is neither contemporary, republican, socialist, nor communist, but just *human*'.[39] We are therefore to conclude that 'humans' are not political animals; but neither are they social. As with the Ville Contemporaine, sport is the foremost 'social' activity in the Ville Radieuse. Hence Le Corbusier's famous attack upon the street: there are to be no streets because casual socializing is proscribed. Society is substantially formalized. It is allowed to exist within strict parameters, which are always of an instrumental nature. It is a matter either of bodily health, or thrashing out the logis-tics of production and distribution. But it is not desirable as an end in itself. So when Le Corbusier discusses social 'participation', it is in terms of 'the perpetual *necessity for maintenance*'.[40]

This sets the stage for an upsurge of consciousness, and there are intriguing glimpses of how this might relate to the individual: 'We need a definition of modern consciousness. Without it we cannot keep any clear image of the man for whom we are building the modern home.' This is the most important point of the Ville Radieuse:

The philosophical postulate? Yes, there is one – the keystone of the whole structure.

The present neglect, apparent in all spheres of life, seems to me to lead to the simple question: *Who am I?*

Revision.

Affirmation of the individual.

Recasting of the social structure.[41]

It is also significant for my argument that Le Corbusier should quote favourably the seventeenth-century philosopher and scientist Blaise Pascal, regarding 'The despair that, always, results for men from the inability to remain long enough in their own rooms.' 'Alas,' says Le Corbusier, 'we have reached the point of dreading like some terrible misfortune the possibility of ceasing to be distracted hour by hour, moment by moment, *by events exterior to ourselves.*'[42] As we shall see later, Pascal was committed to splitting the human being in two, between an exterior that ministered to inconsequential things like society, politics and science, and an interior that ministered to its own soul and salvation. Le Corbusier also appears systematically to be shutting down exterior reality as a source of interest, value and meaning.

Le Corbusier envisaged that his plans would overcome all resistance:

There is no authority in existence sufficient to undertake the necessary tasks of our age . . . *The necessary authority must be created* . . . this is the moment when we must dare to cry: *Out of the way there!* . . . I shall tell you who the despot is you are waiting for. The despot is not a man. The despot is the *Plan* . . . a tyrant . . . it will plead its cause, reply to objections, overcome the opposition of private interest, thrust aside outworn customs, rescind outmoded regulations, and create its own authority.[43]

But again, this faltered in the political climate. Syndicalism lost ground as a political force. Léon Blum, leader of the Front Populaire, which came to power in 1936, undermined their strategy of formulating plans. Early in 1934, he dismissed the planistes as wanting merely to stabilize the private sector and therefore prolong the capitalist order: 'the survival of a substantial private sector', he noted, 'is conceived not as a passage, or transition, or advance, but as a relatively stable and durable condition'.[44] By the mid-1930s, the whole ideology of planisme had been devalued, and its proponents were left floundering without any firm political bedrock.[45] CIAM had strong Socialist and Communist elements within it, and although Le Corbusier was most often in conflict with them, he was prepared to publicize such qualities to the Front. Presumably the idea was to win support from the Front, which, being duped by this smokescreen, would not realize that behind it Le Corbusier remained a committedly anti-parliamentarian syndicalist.[46] He was unsuccessful in this. Eventually, however, the Front itself floundered: its inability to remedy the lingering repercussions of the Depression by supporting the modernizing, large-scale sectors of industry left the door open for the return of the Radicals under Daladier. These effected the scaling down of economic planning and state intervention, and reintroduced free trade and the profit motive, to the benefit of small-scale commercial interests. The planiste philosophy was finally discredited when the economy promptly began to recover under these measures.[47]

No doubt sensing the tide of government against him, Le Corbusier was primed to embrace full-blown Fascism. In 1934, Mussolini began to support modern architecture and Le Corbusier was invited to lecture in Rome. He was well received, and declared that 'The present spectacle of Italy, the state of her spiritual powers, announces the imminent dawn of the modern spirit. Her shining purity and force illumine the paths which had been obscured by the cowardly and the profiteers.'[48] On his return, despite failing to woo Mussolini into commissioning the Ville Radieuse, he threw himself into a new phase of militant syndicalist activity.[49] But returning to Le Corbusier's interest in insurgent methods, we should note that the first explicitly violent group he associated with, the Faisceau, had quickly mellowed. Again, this was through having their financial grievances met by Poincaré's stabilization of the economy. It was soon evident that Valois was an aspiring parliamentarian who held pretensions to being called to office 'legitimately' – as had his hero Mussolini. He now remained aloof from calls for violence from discontents within the Faisceau, and refused to respond to violence levelled against the Faisceau. This would have jeopardized his chances of securing broad electoral support from the moderate middle classes.[50]

By the time of the 1934 riots, however, Le Corbusier had developed an interest in some of the newer right-wing anti-parliamentarian leagues, particularly the Croix de Feu veterans' organization of Colonel de la Rocque. Le Corbusier was quoted in the publications of this party, and was flattered by it.[51] La Rocque championed the spiritual purity and inviolability of France: 'Greco-Latin civilisation is incompatible with domination by barbarians, and cannot withstand the invasion of parasites and mercenaries without degenerating', he said, and went on to outline the route to national rebirth that would become central to Vichy: 'Travail, Famille, Patrie'.[52] Buoyed by the impact of these riots, certain quarters had called upon La Rocque to formulate a concerted anti-republican campaign, but he declined. Despite the thrust of his rhetoric, his movement appeared increasingly committed to the Republic. The increasing popularity of the leagues after 1934 led them gradually to reinvent themselves as legitimate parties, even before the Front Populaire government outlawed all paramilitary leagues and demanded such a shift. The Croix, by then the Parti Social Francais (PSF), became a proper working parliamentary party with a centre-reformist programme. And with their economic grievances redressed by Daladier, they came back yet more snugly within the parliamentary fold. Unlike Germany in the 1920s, the fundamentally *petit-bourgeois* commercial interests of these French groups had not suffered such massive inflationary pressures, nor did they suffer nearly so greatly under the 1930s Depression, and so they were always easily persuaded to return to support of the Republic.[53]

As a result of the ongoing difficulties in defining French Fascism, however, several scholars have changed their view. There is a suggestion now that the Croix and PSF were fundamentally anti-parliamentarian, remaining throughout a vigorous militia group determined to use violence to overthrow the Republic. Whatever concessions may have been made to liberal democracy were merely surface froth calculated to disguise the hidden content, and its deeply illiberal, anti-Semitic, even pro-Nazi sympathies. This moderation, of course, was intended to offset the ever-present threat of being legally dissolved by the government, which was not only necessary for the trials of various league chieftains immediately after the 1934 riots, but remained a danger throughout the later 1930s.[54] If this is so, then the groups with which Le Corbusier associated perhaps remained at heart militaristic and revolutionary. And it was not until the capitulation of the Third Republic in June 1940 and the establishment of the Vichy regime that La Rocque was at liberty to show his true authoritarianism and racial intolerance.[55]

Le Corbusier no longer needed to overthrow the Republic. All that had hitherto constrained him, the 'stalemate society', was swept away. Despite the obvious trauma of such a defeat, which came to infuse his writings in this period, it was with genuine enthusiasm and optimism that he took up a post with Vichy. It offered the final and most promising access to the kind of power he craved.

What does this episode show? Although the rhetoric has a disturbing new edge, it is consistent with what I maintain to be Le Corbusier's deeper philosophy. He wants the material world to be brought to order merely as the preparation for a new consciousness, a highly nationalistic consciousness in this case, but also an individual one. He shows concern for the psychic malaise of the Americans, and suggests this could be remedied only by rationalizing the material circumstances of the nation. Intriguingly, he refers to Pascal in terms of the project of self-exploration in solitude, which could be achieved, it seems, only by cutting off one's dependency upon the 'exterior' world. The development of this individual consciousness was also said to be the 'keystone' of the Ville Radieuse.

The possibility of getting involved in activities external to the self was therefore minimized. The 'politics' of the Ville Radieuse, just like those of the Ville Contemporaine, are reduced almost to nothing, and social activity likewise. 'Participation' in this city is reduced to simple 'maintenance': one participates in sport to maintain the body, and participates in 'civic institutions' to maintain the regular production and flow of goods and services. Eric Mumford has commented that although increases in automobile traffic made city streets 'a source of widespread and justifiable concern, CIAM's universal revulsion for the city of streets and interwoven activities seems based on something deeper. Yet that "something" is never disclosed in the denunciations of Le Corbusier, and the need to abolish the street is assumed to be self-evident.'[56] I think that the explanation for this bias, which Le Corbusier fought to make official policy for CIAM, is the belief that the exterior world holds no value or meaning in itself. Consequently, that major attraction for drawing one outside – the bustling street – is abolished. Le Corbusier's cities, it seems, are mechanisms for regulating how much energy and interest the individual should sacrifice to the collective, and the more substantial reserve that must be kept for oneself:

> When the collective functions of the urban community have been organized, then there will be individual liberty for all. Each man will live in an ordered relation to the whole . . . not in slavish subjection to it as he is now. Each man will be his own man, free and happy, because we shall have released in him those interior forces that have no need of sterile personal acquisitions.[57]

It is clear from Mumford's history of CIAM in this period that the tension of individual versus collective was a persistent sticking-point in the attempt to formulate a coherent policy. Generally speaking, most of the internal ideological problems of this organization stemmed from Le Corbusier's dogged attempts to foist his individualist philosophy upon Communist members who were committed to collectivist urban strategies. This caused a pendulum swing within the organization. On those occasions when commitments elsewhere meant Le Corbusier could not attend meetings or conferences, the Communists would have unobstructed passage for their collectivist ideals; and vice versa, Le Corbusier would nudge the organization back to an individualist footing when the Communists were away in Russia.[58]

In fact, the Ville Radieuse originated from precisely this conflict. In 1930, Le Corbusier was asked by the Soviets to complete a questionnaire in response to the competition proposals for a 'Green City' north of Moscow. The competition had been sponsored earlier that year by Soviet labour unions, the brief being to provide a dedicated rest-and-recreation city for the workers. Le Corbusier, in his 'Response to Moscow', heavily criticized the collectivist bias of these proposals, insisting instead that the city should be the home of the 'great spirits'. He drew up plans for a city that might remedy all this collectivism, its apartments being 'independent, closed-off, private, sacred . . . away from all collective pressures'.[59] Shortly afterwards, he rechristened this the 'Ville Radieuse'. From the outset, then, Le Corbusier's canonical city of the 1930s was a polemic against excessively socialized ways of living:

The cornerstone of all modern urbanization is absolute respect for the freedom of the individual . . . I thought that in the U. S. S. R., just as in Paris, a basic human need had to be fulfilled, that of personal solitude. When the door is shut, I can freely enter my own world . . . That's the way I am. At certain times I need solitude.[60]

Le Corbusier illustrated his point with a photograph of himself studying in solitude – 'The Free Man'. The CIAM Communists criticized Le Corbusier's individualism as being symptomatic of what they alleged were his bourgeois liberal-capitalist ideals, a criticism which was echoed by the Soviets upon receipt of the 'Response'.[61] I maintain, however, that this was symptomatic of a deeper philosophical standpoint.

Despite the resistance, sentiments of this kind permeated CIAM. José Luis Sert, for example, who enjoyed a strong mutual respect with Le Corbusier, published *Can Our Cities Survive?* in 1942.[62] A good indication of what was at stake here is that, when Sert approached the American urban critic and historian Lewis Mumford to write the introduction to his book, Mumford refused on the following grounds:

[There is] a serious flaw in the general outline which CIAM prepared . . . The four functions of the city do not seem to me to adequately cover the ground of city planning: dwelling, work, recreation, and transportation are all important. But what of the political, educational, and cultural functions of the city . . . The leisure given by the machine . . . frees [modern man] for a fuller participation in political and cultural activities . . . The organs of political and cultural association are, from my standpoint, the *distinguishing* marks of the city . . . I regard their omission as the chief defect of routine city planning; and their absence from the program of CIAM I find almost inexplicable.[63]

Mumford reiterated the absence of this 'fifth function' in his review of the book in the *New Republic* in 1943, and also complained to an associate: 'Did I tell you that Sert . . . had in accordance with CIAM instructions written his whole book . . . without a single reference to the functions of government, group association or culture?'[64] It was indeed very strange for Sert to invite Mumford to write his introduction, for Mumford was committed to a regionalist idyll of small garden cities.[65] But more fundamentally, Mumford was committed to the polar-opposite urban paradigm, according to which human beings had to participate in the affairs of the city if they were to live meaningful lives. His own ideal cities upheld an organic collectivist vision of 'the primacy of life', based upon 'autonomous but perpetually inter-related organisms as vehicles of life . . . to maintain its life-shape the organism must constantly alter it and renew itself by entering into active relationships with the rest of the environment'.[66] In this case, the 'autonomous' individual finds 'real life' in the interrelationships fomented by the city, and is continually 'altered' and 'renewed' through these relationships. But for Sert and Le Corbusier and, as Mumford realized, probably for CIAM as a whole, this civic ideal was not necessarily valued. Mumford's 'fifth function' was not absent through oversight, as he implies, but through intention: life became meaningful elsewhere than 'in' the city. It seems that individuals must be made to cut their dependencies with the exterior – collective – milieu.[67]

As was demonstrated, even Le Corbusier's political interests in this period are consistent with these priorities. He associated only with those who seemed to promise an end to parliamentary politics, and designed his city accordingly. But again he was disappointed, for generally these 'leagues' were only prepared to challenge the republican structure when their economic interests were not being met. The Faisceau were satisfied by Poincaré, the Croix were satisfied by Daladier, after which both appeared to respect the Republic. Le Corbusier, however, wanted to go the full distance. He genuinely wanted an end to this way of running the world, as it provided too great a 'distraction' from those things that should be taking place inside the individual. This is how he differed from these professional politicians, and it is the only way to understand his statement that 'no one is going to make a politician of me', for in his ideal city politics had no place.[68] It was probably something like this that underlay Le Corbusier's promise that CIAM could 'unite' 'Catalan trade unionists, Muscovite collectivists, Italian fascists'.[69] But rather than 'unite', a Corbusian city would bring politics to an end.

The unprecedented overhaul that was Vichy offered Le Corbusier his last hope. It is this that will concern us in the next chapter, where we will find these patterns confirmed one final time.

Chapter 3

1941–1942: Vichy

'Through Strange Avatars'

The capitulation of France in June 1940, and the establishment of the collaborative Vichy regime under Marshal Philippe Pétain, provided Le Corbusier with what seemed at the time a chance to get his ideal city realized. Perhaps through military *coup d'état*, Pétain created exactly the kind of authority that Le Corbusier admired.[1] Given authority by parliament to frame a new constitution in July, he declared himself head of state and concentrated all legislative and executive powers in his person. He used parliament to undercut parliament. This was backed up by an intense propaganda campaign:

> Propaganda gave Marshal Pétain all the attributes of an *ancien régime* monarch; he was at one and the same time feudal lord, receiving the oath of loyalty from diplomats, magistrates, athletes and pork-butchers; an imperial ruler, sometimes referred to as Philippe 1er; a Christ-like figure who sacrificed himself for the sake of his country; and, like Henri IV, the father of his people, travelling amongst them, sending messages to them, relieving poverty and suffering.[2]

For Le Corbusier, the internecine parliamentarianism and party-political strife of the Third Republic had been swept away: 'The season of political ravings has gone by. Our people heard the war cries of the parties: rivalry, sarcasm, hatred. But since 1934, signs have been written on the skies of France; we have had enough of rottenness.' The triumph of the Nazis was the inevitable result of the cancer of vested interests that had infected the Republic, and which had given rise to such flashpoints as the 1934 riots. Moreover, a prodigious new power, single, ruthless and charismatic, appeared to have been established at last. 'Where can we look for the clenched fist of our national will power?' This question answered itself. Now the nation could broach the 'fundamental question, *What is the purpose of Life?*'[3]

In order to make headway in the new power structure, Le Corbusier first attempted to downplay the national humiliation and trauma. The two books written during the Vichy period, *The Four Routes* and *The Home of Man*, which have been neglected by scholars, provide a fascinating insight into this. The collapse of France is presented as a logical stepping-stone on the road to Utopia.[4] The Second World War is reduced to inconsequential proportions. It is merely the postscript of a global cataclysm, the Industrial Revolution:

> Reconstruction after the ravages of war, rebuilding of devastated areas, is little more than an event of historic periodicity . . . Our present war is only part of the hundred years' war which started with the first locomotive. Our war might well turn out to be the end of that one . . . The hundred years' war is not merely European, it is a universal phenomenon . . . A hundred years during which everything was destroyed, slowly, with determination; everything, a whole civilization . . . But during these hundred years we have also invented, prepared, outlined, initiated the principles and practice of a new civilization.[5]

The actual wars of the previous century are reduced to sideshows. The cause of this 'hundred years' war' is the harnessing of machine technology to the ideals of the free market and consumerism, which has resulted in an unstable world economy. This must now be remedied, the machine humanized to supply only the essential needs of humankind, and increase its leisure time. The end of this more important war signifies the end of what Le Corbusier considers to be the first era of machine civilization.

This will now give way to the second: 'One feels that it might have been the [Second World] war's only *raison d'être* to open up the second era of the machine age.'[6] Formerly, 'The machines were the "individuals", the "souls" of that period, men were . . . an impersonal collective mass.'[7] The second machine age will reverse this equation. It will allow human beings to differentiate themselves from the collective and rediscover their individuality, their 'souls'.

This is consistent with the ideas encountered throughout this section. But in order to have them realized, Le Corbusier's rhetoric assumes an intensity and orientation tailor-made for Vichy. While in the 1920s the spiritual revival was to be led by rational technocrats, who had by the 1930s been transformed into organic syndicalists, now it looked for strength to the rural peasantry. As Le Corbusier said: 'The new machine age (second period) can only be built upon a living countryside . . . sound roots are still there, all that the country needs is to return to what it has been throughout the centuries.'[8] Furthermore, he presents the peasantry not merely as the upholders of ancient values, but also as the repository of practical good sense, and always open to progress. In contrast to the peasantry, the metropolitan intelligentsia are smug, carping reactionaries.[9] This neatly echoed the anti-metropolitan, anti-intellectual and pro-peasant ideology of Vichy.

He also mounts an attack on the backwardness of other nations with his '*International balance sheet*'. He concludes that the French continue to lead the way in national spirit and ancient wisdom, and that the rest of the world are desperate for France to show them the way forward.[10] Although he briefly alludes to a more internationalist sensibility, and suggests that all nations must modernize in harmony with their own national traditions, it is soon revealed that Le Corbusier has a very specific idea of what this means.[11] The students who come from all over the world to learn the Corbusian creed in his Parisian studio will eventually constitute 'an army barbed with optimism arising, an army which will create *to-morrow* and install a world-wide harmony of procedure'. These militaristic allusions blend into French crusading ones when Le Corbusier compares his students to the medieval *compagnons*. Writing his book in Vézelay, a town rich in the history of the crusades, Le Corbusier is inspired by the ghostly forms of horsemen in the morning mist. His own crusaders will similarly go forth and build under a 'universal' French creed.[12] Le Corbusier had earlier considered the medieval crusaders as dissemina-

tors of a universal ideal, which he believed was embraced without a trace
of conflict or resistance:

> When the cathedrals were white, above nationalities concerned with
> themselves, there was a common idea: Christendom was above every-
> thing else. Already, before constructing everywhere the naves of a new
> civilization, a common enthusiasm of spirit had brought together the
> peoples of modern times and had led them, through strange avatars,
> toward Jerusalem, where there was a seat of a universal thought: love.

'An international language reigned wherever the white race was', and the
dissemination of this only 'falsely seems to us like a massacre in which
blood never stopped flowing'.[13] So the French *race* would provide the
ideal, while the right to self-determination of other nations would be
reduced to making only slight, mainly topographical, variations on this
ideal.[14] It was a standard trope among the Catholic community that the
national revolution promised by Vichy was the modern equivalent of the
crusades.[15]

Le Corbusier's next rhetorical step was to champion the French Empire
and colonialism. With the greater part of France under occupation, the
Empire had been hastily resurrected as an enduring symbol of greatness.
Pétain described it as 'this finest jewel in the French crown'.[16] Thus Le
Corbusier's 'four routes' pledge to revitalize 'that magnificent territory so
long abandoned to mortal boredom'.[17] He praises the progressive and
humanitarian planning techniques currently prevailing in the colonies, all
owing to the exemplary 'pioneering' spirit of the colonial officials.[18] And
in those cases where the native colonial administration resists the pat-
ronage of France, its presence must be exerted forcibly. For example, Le
Corbusier states that his scheme for Nemours, which provided for the
industrial regeneration and repopulation of the area with wholesome
family men, was allowed to founder through destructive speculation. The
result will be the ruin of the town through the influx of dissolute,
work-shy untouchables: 'the Maltese, the fugitives from the Kasbah, the
ne'er-do-well from Castille or Aragon, the publican from Marseilles, etc.,
etc., all this riff-raff will slip in'. As it stands, gambling and alcoholism are
rife, and the brothel provides the only stable growth industry. Le Corbusier
is exasperated: 'And they will curse Colonial life!' He demands that France
must be allowed to resume absolute control to ensure for the future the

full implementation of its schemes, in which 'the mother-country would [be] honourably reflected in her smiling colony'.[19]

Although this was the general direction Le Corbusier's rhetoric had been taking throughout the 1930s, it was, I believe, intensified for the benefit of Vichy.[20] He indulged in all the clichés: peasant values, the crusades, Empire and colonialism, racial purity and racial degeneracy. But beneath this lay exactly the same priorities as before. By putting the material world in order, a new consciousness will emerge: it is again time for humanity to be lifted out of the mêlée that formerly smothered it. But now Le Corbusier has formally christened it as the passage from the 'first' to the 'second era of the machine age'.

This new consciousness was framed in nationalist and racialist terms far more pointed than previously encountered. But once again it also has an intriguing personal content. Le Corbusier wanted everyone to confront and reform their own consciousness, and thereby redeem their individualities from the mass of external things that contaminate them. Society provided too many distractions, such as 'cabaret' and 'cinema', and a dependency upon unnecessary goods and luxuries. This was maintained by the 'poisonous', 'lust'-inducing advertising of the mass media, which also subjected people to 'the perfidy of propaganda' of the political parties. This resulted in 'Futile political squabbles in cafés instead of spontaneous happiness, instead of intellectual and moral exercise . . . *Whence loss of individualism*.'[21] De Pierrefeu expresses this very powerfully:

> By the repetition of their attacks they split the person before reducing it to dust and casting it into limbo . . . *artificial dreams* corroding the alert mind and its ability to be alert . . . whose function releases those supreme poisons that man alone is able to exude for man: the *dream of others*. Newspaper, radio, cinema pour out this poison. Numberless images, barrages of slogans with a punch, rhythms repeating lascivious or stupid tunes, crowd and jostle at the door of our senses, the better to lodge within brains made defenceless by the sweeping away of its filter, our memory. Then the subconscious gives way; and, as with a blocked drain, a flood of scoriae, vanities, filth, spreads over the conscience and covers it with a thick film, slow to vanish.[22]

The person is split open by the media, and brainwashed to dream the '*dream of others*' rather than his own. Individuality is lost by continually pinning one's expectations outside oneself. As a response, Le Corbusier seeks to create the home as 'spiritual centre', a sanctuary from all this interference.[23] If left unreformed, the home too is instrumental in deforming the minds of its inhabitants.[24] And again, we have references to Pascal:

> And since leisure will require a man to spend more time in his room (Pascal's *desideratum*) a new concept of home will arise . . . Again and always, I repeat, we must be vigilant, for the whole of our lives and every minute we must be ready to seize the miracle which lies latent in all things. It seems that Pascal, also, said this to Christians, which only goes to prove how right he always was.[25]

The main priority here was the reform of the individual. Le Corbusier sought to prompt the individual to pursue some more meaningful activity by disentangling himself from his external milieu, or by striking the correct balance: 'bringing us again to the alternate equilibrium: individualism, collectivity'.[26] Le Corbusier chose this moment to explain again what lay behind his most famous statement:

> A long time ago, I jumped in where angels feared to tread. I threw into the confused discussion of styles, fashions, snobberies, this argument which was a knock-out: '*The house is a machine for living.*' A thousand utterances have been produced to beat me for having dared that utterance. But when I say 'living' I am not talking of mere material requirements only. I admit certain important extensions which must crown the edifice of man's daily needs. To be able to *think*, or meditate, after the day's work is essential. But in order to become a centre of creative thought, the home must take on an absolutely new character.[27]

The precise nature, terms and dynamics of this mode of selfhood will be explored later. This section concludes by returning to political realities in order to examine exactly what Vichy represented that appealed to Le Corbusier and also what he sought to achieve there.

'The Lawgiver'

In January 1941, Le Corbusier found himself on the temporary Comité d'Études du Bâtiment of Vichy, which was commissioned to formulate plans for reconstruction, and immediately began conspiring with a number of former associates, both syndicalist and technocrat, to accumulate more power.[28] The committee's working life and powers were consequently extended: the new Comité d'Études de l'Habitation et de la Construction Immobilière was charged with permanently framing housing policy on a national scale. It also proposed that seven showpiece urban redevelopments be undertaken, and Le Corbusier contrived to place his plans for Algiers foremost among these.

The syndicalist basis of Vichy was revealed by its formation of a 'Corporation of Architects', which was a tentative step towards the organization of all professions into self-regulating syndicates. Within this Corporation, Le Corbusier schemed to create an élite of master builders, who were to be given absolute power in all national building efforts, free to steamroll existing bye-laws and create factories for the mass pro-duction of building materials. Through the force of its expertise, it would progressively disassociate itself from the State, and acquire substantial autonomy to take whatever measures it considered necessary: 'the Corpo-ration is *one*. The nearer it shall get to this unity, the more forcibly shall the State have to acknowledge the Corporation's mastery over its own destiny.'[29] At the head of this élite was the 'Regulator', or 'Lawgiver', a man of such power that the material fabric of France was effectively his playground. His was the duty of zoning the entire Empire, organizing the distribution and type of agriculture, industry, urban and rural areas, and therefore also of population. Even the President had to secure his approval if he wanted to pass legislation concerning the environment. Financial backing for these initiatives was to be underwritten by the State, with the culture of free trade and speculation almost completely eradicated. Once again, Le Corbusier set the objective planner above the politician. The politician was constrained and sidetracked by concerns of party, finance and public opinion. His profession was one of endless discussion and equivo-cation, while the Lawgiver 'serenely, lucidly puts the world in order'.[30]

The scale of Le Corbusier's vision is best represented through a couple of his sketches (fig. 3). He provides a before-and-after view of 'Hexagonal France', done in coloured crayon, which casually details his completed vision for the national territory. This is handled so cursorily that it barely catches one's attention at first glance, but the proposed trans-formation is immense. The equivalent of thousands of square miles of city, industry, agriculture and infrastructure are 'cut away' and 're-grafted', and

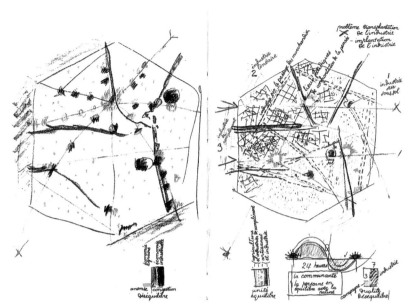

3   Le Corbusier. 'Hexagonal France'. From Françoise de Pierrefeu and Le Corbusier, *La Maison des hommes*, 1942. © FLC

this includes the re-routing of the major waterways. France is reduced to a hexagon, and like all geometric problems the solution is a matter of lines and dots.[31]

But Vichy was no more receptive to Le Corbusier's ideas than the Third Republic. The factionalism and infighting made the former regime seem quite efficient. The closed circle of Pétain and his cronies were moderate pro-republican conservatives. They had little interest in the more dynamic ultra-right groupings.[32] Also, their primary goal was to survive the immediate post-defeat period without conceding yet more power to Germany. All initiatives were therefore geared towards retrenchment and stability. This was not the place for great visionary schemes.[33]

However, there *were* powerful progressive tendencies within the regime. A close-knit group of young technocrats was reluctantly granted substantial powers in the fields of industry and economics.[34] They were committed to comprehensive state intervention and planning, and to modern production and management techniques. The whole initiative was to be orchestrated in a comprehensive ten-year plan. Moreover, all were staffed by allegedly objective planners and logistics experts, untainted by politics. The technocrats appeared to have wrestled free a very powerful hand.

Their efforts failed for three reasons. First, the bureaucracy they created generated a level of confusion and deadlock as hopeless as anything that had gone before. Second, their initiatives were consistently derailed by powerful moderate elements close to Pétain. The most extreme example of this was the propagation of a conspiracy theory, the 'Vichy Synarchy', which condemned the technocrats as being part of a sinister group of Jewish financiers and freemasons.[35] Third, the technocrats were not as progressive and unified as they seemed. They were entrepreneurs afforded an unprecedented opportunity of consolidating themselves in power and accumulating a fortune. Whatever progress they achieved was predominantly the accidental side-effect of their private business interests.[36]

Against this backdrop, Le Corbusier's passage through Vichy assumes the aspect of dark pantomime. It was doomed from the outset.[37] It is ironic that one of Le Corbusier's most powerful supporters, Henri du Moulin de Labarthète, was responsible for conducting the Synarchy witch-hunt, while the technocrats themselves quickly grew impatient with Le Corbusier's attempts to win influence. By July 1941, François Lehideux, who was in charge of Vichy's new planning ministry, the Délégation Générale à l'Equipement National, had sent the message, 'The Minister does not envisage co-operating with Le Corbusier in any way.'[38] In Le Corbusier's words: 'a débâcle cut everything short. The director in charge of *equipment general* said: "neither close – nor far – nor under any circumstances, will I work with Le Corbusier and Pierrefeu".'[39] An indication of just how little Le Corbusier's ideas influenced these technocrats is that Lehideux's ten-year plan made provision for satellite cities, the antithesis of Le Corbusier's urban theory.[40] Undaunted, he attempted to curry favour with Pétain directly, repeatedly requesting a private interview and sending him a copy of his new book, *The Four Routes*. Pétain, however, remained untouchable, deigning only to send a note via his personal secretary that the book contained 'many suggestions for the regeneration of urban life, often happy ones'.[41]

Anticipating official support at any moment, Le Corbusier continued to prepare urban schemes for Algiers.[42] He had first visited the city in 1931, invited to lecture on the city's urban future as part of the ongoing centennial celebrations of the French colonization, and the next year he submitted his first set of plans.[43] At the time, his plans were decisively rejected: Charles Brunel, the Mayor of Algiers, commented that in order to implement the scheme's proposals for uprooting 300,000 inhabitants, 'it would be necessary to have an absolute dictator with the property and even the lives of his subjects at his disposal'.[44]

Through Vichy, however, Le Corbusier believed he had a better chance, and he prepared a final set of plans: the definitive Plan Directeur. Gone was even the pretence of internationalism and natural equality as were found in the early plans, and instead he produced a plan which pointedly re-articulated the dominance of French interests. The Cité d'Affaires, formerly placed symbolically on the border of European and Muslim territories, was now sited unequivocally in the European-owned Agah quarter; while the Europeans themselves were to be housed on the cliffs dominating the ancient cultural heart of the native population, the Casbah. The city, Le Corbusier stated, far from being a site of international cooperation, would become a symbol of 'the mother country reborn from her ashes'.[45] In the summer of 1941, he visited Algiers with a view to imposing this vision, calling upon du Moulin to 'delegate to Le Corbusier the mandate to give orders'.[46] He further courted General Maxime Weygand, Vichy's Governor-General to North Africa, calling for power to steamroll those local bodies determined to impede his efforts:

> In the present administrative state, only the highest authorities of the country can permit the necessary innovations, create the useful precedents, authorize the ignoring of old regulations, permit the Plan to enter into life . . . By an order from above the local plan must be interrupted and its continuance forbidden. This gesture of authority will have a decisive effect on Algerian opinion, showing that the government of Marshal Pétain has taken into consideration the most pressing problems of urbanism and that from now on it intends to impose a new orientation.[47]

Nothing came of this courtship. Darlan, the technocrat, removed Weygand's power in November of that year.[48]

The concluding irony is that when Le Corbusier attempted to advance his plan during a further visit in 1942, and brandished it as though it enjoyed the full support of Vichy, it was rejected on the grounds of being part of a Jewish–Bolshevist conspiracy. In early June, the journal *Travaux Nord Africains* reiterated an attack on Le Corbusier as 'The Trojan Horse of Bolshevism'. The Mayor of Algiers, Rozis, who was even less enamoured of Le Corbusier than his predecessor Brunel, hounded him out of the city on pain of arrest. Utterly disheartened at last, Le Corbusier returned to Vichy, where he received the official verdict of the Algiers City Council: 'In as much as the project is essentially communal . . . we have decided to reject purely and simply the project presented by Le Corbusier.'[49] Less than a month after the first accusations, he had returned to Paris with the words '*Adieux, merdeux Vichy*'.[50] Le Corbusier's political dealings essentially came to an end after this. Yet all along he had maintained, 'I have never played an active part in politics.'[51]

Le Corbusier's pursuit of public allies cannot be considered an end in itself. The numerous shifts that he made, together with his contempt of politics and politicians, suggest that he considered it all to be purely instrumental. As Manfredo Tafuri has observed, 'Too often . . . Le Corbusier's urbanism has been viewed as the ultimate goal of his research.'[52] I believe that Le Corbusier also considered his ideal cities to be instrumental. But instrumental to what end?

This account of Le Corbusier's political history proves that there was a consistent underlying pattern. Despite the opportunistic shifts and the pliability of the rhetoric, it is clear that this was not mere opportunism, for Le Corbusier consistently went for a particular kind of politics. He favoured a politics which promised to eradicate politics: that is, to replace it with non-negotiable structures run by objective experts who would co-ordinate the nation's resources. Instead of politics one had management and logistics. Among the most important motives of this system were the standard physiological requirements of the human being. There was a certain minimum of space, light, leisure and food, below which it would begin to die. Le Corbusier considered it absurd that anyone could find room for discussion or disputation – any room for politics – in this.[53]

The actual groups with which he associated, however, were never the objective experts they pretended to be. They were professional politicians, and their anti-parliamentarian and anti-party-political ideals swiftly evaporated when the Republic redressed their grievances, which were primarily of an economic nature. This pattern recurred in each of the three phases we have examined. Le Corbusier was perhaps naïve in thinking that these people could behave in any other way.

This leads to a more interesting question: why would Le Corbusier favour this kind of politics? He favoured it, I believe, because he seemed to have a particular idea of what made life meaningful for modern people. He was concerned with effecting a spiritual rebirth, which happened on both a national and an individual level. This appeared to work by putting the material world into such a clear and efficient order that it stopped bothering people. It involved the attempt to eradicate politics as an unpredictable and ideologically charged phenomenon which demanded the interest and participation of ordinary people and led to 'Futile political squabbles in cafés'. But as well as 'politics', this also involved the eradication of 'society', at least in terms of its providing an open milieu rich in activities and contacts. The mass media, with its invasive techniques and spurious content, is also likely to have been outlawed. The Ville Contemporaine and the Ville Radieuse only permitted certain limited, non-participatory forms of politics and society. For as long as we continued to be interested in or dependent upon 'events exterior to ourselves', we suffered from 'loss of individualism', of 'soul'.[54]

This first section has shown how a coherent order can be attributed to Le Corbusier's political machinations, and to the social workings of his city, based on the broad outlines of a particular concept of self. Sections two and three will try to determine more exactly what this concept involved.

Part II

The Science of Painting

Preface

This second section, 'The Science of Painting', continues the investigation of Le Corbusier's approach to external reality. The first section showed him seeking to achieve order in the city in social and political terms, so that they could no longer figure as an important part in people's lives. The second concentrates on how Le Corbusier tried to attribute order to the city in terms of knowledge. In other words, I shall investigate his concerns with the natural universe and the question of how it could be truly and reliably *known*. This was an especially acute concern at the time, given the popular interest in those 'new' mathematical and physical sciences which substantially undermined the old ways of understanding the world. What I shall be suggesting here is that Le Corbusier, unlike the majority of the avant-garde, held to old-fashioned ways of viewing the natural universe, and that he attempted to reinforce this through his Purist paintings and the built form of his cities. The reason for this was again his belief that external reality should not concern people unduly. Instead, every effort should be made to make it appear as orderly and non-distracting as possible, so that people could be free to discover true 'knowledge' in themselves.

This attempt to interpret Le Corbusier's scientific outlook commences by looking at Purist aesthetic theory and painting. It might seem strange to try to infer an epistemological theory from an aesthetic theory, but the

Purists were holistic in outlook. They promoted the adoption of a particular attitude to the world, and this included the question of knowledge. Compared with the very substantial interest in Le Corbusier's architectural and urban work, however, relatively little has been generated by his pictorial work. Le Corbusier's painting has been considered 'small beer for the spirit', 'only a pastime'.[1] Yet in 1948 he made the following statement:

> Truly the key to my artistic creation is my pictorial work begun in 1918 and pursued regularly each day. The foundation of my research and intellectual production has its secret in the uninterrupted practice of my painting. It is there that one must find the source of my spiritual freedom, my disinterestedness, my independence, and the faithfulness and integrity of my work.[2]

Furthermore, most of the scholarship that has been undertaken on Le Corbusier's painting, and his Purist painting especially, seems to rest upon two related assumptions. These assumptions persist, but they are not necessarily correct. The first maintains that all of Le Corbusier's art was committed to the discovery of a set of formal laws which he thought would provoke standard emotional responses in the viewer. The second assumption presents the trinity of Le Corbusier, Amédée Ozenfant and Fernand Léger as a coherent and unified group.

I disagree with these assumptions: first, because they contribute to the misunderstanding of the lessons of Corbusian modernism, particularly in terms of its notion of self; second, because they trivialize the richness of the relationships and differences between these three men, with Ozenfant's remarkable writings having suffered most unfairly from this neglect. In examining the truth of these assumptions, I hope to recover Le Corbusier's central project: the search for knowledge of the world and, in opposition to this, of the self. It is here that the full metaphysical significance of his handling of 'public' and 'private' space can be found. The central concern in this second section, then, will be to investigate the epistemology that underlies Le Corbusier's art theory, as well as that of Léger and Ozenfant. I must stress that, for the purposes of this argument, I am more concerned with the theory than with interpreting specific artworks.

The fourth chapter, 'Léger and the Purist Object', will suggest that the Purists wanted to return the viewer of their paintings to objective knowledge of the world. This questions the orthodoxy of interpreting Le

Corbusier's art as purely formal, and preoccupied with inducing some emotional effect in the viewer. It is this formalist interpretation which has lent weight to the tendency to align Le Corbusier with Léger. But I think it is possible to differentiate them in terms of the theories of knowledge and selfhood that are implicit in their writings. Léger seems to uphold the classic modernist paradigm whereby 'subject' and 'object' – or self and world – are considered to be understandable in the same terms and always to interpenetrate each other. The individual human being has no boundaries behind which he could define himself as a distinct entity. Rather, his sense of self is caught up and continually renegotiated in the ebb and flow of everything outside himself. On the other hand, Le Corbusier believed subject and object to be completely distinct entities, corresponding to qualitatively distinct modes of knowledge. This led him to a different understanding and use of artistic form.

Next, in 'Conventionalism', I shall attempt to relate Le Corbusier's approach to knowledge to that of the popular mathematician and physicist Henri Poincaré, with whose works he was directly acquainted. I believe Le Corbusier was indebted to Poincaré's theory that the world could not be definitively known and was therefore a matter of 'conventional' knowledge only. In this case, 'conventional' means a certain approach and set of assumptions which, in the absence of real certainty, are consensually agreed upon as a matter of convenience. I shall be offering a cautious reconsideration of 'functionalism' as the term applies to Le Corbusier, being more about the attainment of some functional understanding of the world than about practical utility or efficiency. Also central to this chapter will be a demonstration of how Le Corbusier's epistemology differs from that upheld by the majority of the avant-garde. Finally, this approach to knowledge will be shown to be fundamental to the 'Modulor' proportional system that Le Corbusier began developing during the Second World War, and which he intended to be used to determine the form of everything in the built environment. His epistemology, then, was literally to be cast in concrete.

The sixth chapter, 'Ozenfant's Impasse', provides an account of the epistemological dilemma in Ozenfant's writings. This is provided for two reasons: first, to contextualize the ferment of ideas in which Le Corbusier participated; second, because Ozenfant discusses Pascal in a very interesting way, and allows us to speculate further upon his importance to Le

Corbusier. Here we find Ozenfant, although similarly indebted to Poincaré's conventionalism, struggling with the desire to find more secure bases of knowledge, and in particular of self-knowledge. The dualist epistemological system of Pascal is introduced by Ozenfant as a tempting option: according to this, real knowledge is to be discovered not by trying to take an objective account of the world, which can only be provisional, but rather through one's withdrawal into solitude and meditation upon God and self. Ultimately, this is rejected by Ozenfant: honest ignorance is for him preferable to a self-knowledge that comes through the sacred, or through the attempt to forge a fully autonomous sense of self. In the twentieth century, he maintains, both these things are delusional and childish. But Le Corbusier, as we shall see, took up the option provided by Pascal.

At this point, having discussed Le Corbusier's notion of an external reality that can only be 'conventionally' understood, it is possible to engage fully with his concept of selfhood as some kind of withdrawal from it. This will occupy us in the final section, 'Pascal's *Desideratum*'.

Chapter 4

Léger and the Purist Object

A Formal Pursuit?

There is an unusual factor in Le Corbusier's career as a visual artist that has made it difficult to understand. By 1923, after three major Purist exhibitions, he made the decision to withdraw his paintings from public view, instead working in complete privacy until 1938, when he began reintroducing his work into the public domain. This private activity grew in importance for him, from something pursued only on weekends to something that was to monopolize his time from 8 a.m. to 1 p.m. every day for the rest of his life.[1] During this period of voluntary exile, both his painting and his architecture underwent a substantial change: from the clean and rational articulation of simple object elements to the exploration of obscure yet allusive figurative symbolism. Le Corbusier increasingly introduced natural elements rather than the machine forms and industrial objects of his earlier years. He also appeared to engage with mythological, religious and occultist themes. The shift from *Nature morte à la pile d'assiettes et au livre* of 1920, to *Taureau VIII* of 1954, gives a compelling sense of how Le Corbusier's painting changed during these years (figs 4, 5).

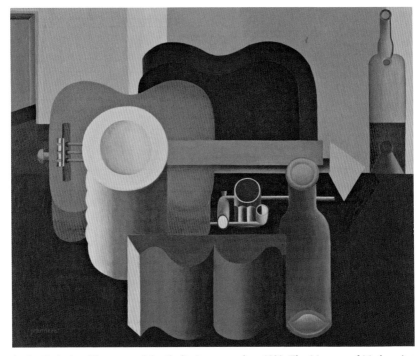

4   Le Corbusier. *Nature morte à la pile d'assiettes et au livre*, 1920. The Museum of Modern Art, New York. Peinture FLC 305. © FLC

Admittedly, this public–private divide was simply another of Le Corbusier's self-aggrandizing myths. As Stanislaus von Moos has observed, this 'daily ritual' was 'a rather publicized privacy'. But as mentioned in the introduction, the persistence with which Le Corbusier elaborated these myths, and this one in particular, encourages a view of them as actual fact. Effectively, such myths constituted Le Corbusier's reality. The almost ritualistic aura of private seclusion which he created around his new studio at 24 rue Nungesser-et-Coli in the early 1930s makes this myth tangible.[2]

One of the ways scholars have dealt with this deliberately provocative split is by smoothing it over. It is maintained that all of Le Corbusier's art – painting and architecture – was committed to the discovery of a set of formal laws which could provoke standard emotional responses in the

5 Le Corbusier.
Taureau VIII, 1954.
Peinture FLC 162.
© FLC

viewer. When he began to lock himself away to paint in the late 1920s, this was only because he craved temporary respite from the political and commercial headaches of his public life, 'the implacable hardships of this *métier* of architect'.[3] These mornings therefore constituted a laboratory in which he might experiment freely and innovate new forms, which would later be transcribed into his architectural projects. The strange new forms with which he began to experiment were not really different from the earlier Purist ones, but were simply attempts to extend his formal vocabulary and maximize its expressive power. This interpretation has become the dominant one. Although I want to propose an alternative to this 'formalist' approach, there is much to recommend it.[4]

In the Purists' most representative and mature theoretical statement, the essay 'Purism' of 1920, the demand is explicitly made for a universally transmissible formal language. A distinction is made between 'primary' and 'secondary' forms and colours: the 'primary' being those which correspond to the fundamental psycho-physiological perceptive mechanism of humankind at large, and which affect everyone identically; while the 'secondary', corresponding to hereditary and cultural variations, are more specific to the individual's experience and therefore variable in their action and limited in their effect. An illuminating example is provided in the response of the Frenchman, African and Laplander when presented with a cube: all will react to this primary form in a consistent manner; but when it is covered with a particular arrangement of dots, probably only the dissolute Frenchman will make the specific secondary association of gambling. The most compelling form, for the Purists, would be that which strikes a balance between the universalized abstraction of the primary and the culture-specific resonances of the secondary. In specific pictorial terms, this is found in the common objects of everyday life, the bottle, carafe, pipe, glass, plate, guitar and so on. Such a language would ensure the artist's ability 'to place the spectator in the state he wishes'. This ideal is set against the obscurantism of much contemporary art, 'an art of symbols', with its highly allusive symbolism. This symbolism requires 'a literature whose goal is to explain, to give the key, to reveal the secret language, to permit comprehension'. The Purist vocabulary would work directly, without mediation. The goal, it seems, was to inscribe the underlying laws of the universe into the forms of the painting. And perception of these would throw the spectator into a state of cosmic bliss, of 'mathematical lyricism'.[5]

All of this was reiterated in Le Corbusier's canonical architectural text several years later, where the pictorial language is rendered into 'Mass', 'Surface' and 'Plan': '*There are no symbols attached to these forms: they provoke definite sensations; there is no need of a key in order to understand them.*' 'THE SIGHT OF THEM AFFECTS US IMMEDIATELY', whether we be 'the child, the savage [or] the metaphysician'. Again, we have 'A thought which reveals itself without word or sound, but solely by means of shapes which stand in a certain relationship to one another'.[6] Much later, when commenting on the early Purist preoccupation with still life, Le Corbusier appeared to put the seal on this formalist approach:

> With such bareness and poverty of subject matter you have to scrape your brains rather thoroughly to create a plastic symphony capable of renewal. Spheres, cones and cylinders.[7]

In fact, he appeared to disregard the importance of these objects *as* objects: 'Until 1928, *not objects*, glasses, and bottles but supports for geometry, instigators of proportion.'[8]

When Le Corbusier and Ozenfant began experimenting with a more organic formal vocabulary towards the end of the 1920s, and when Le Corbusier began to conduct this work in private seclusion, it could easily be glossed over as the continuation of the search for formal affect. Le Corbusier himself explained that the 'objets à réaction poétique' of 'rocks and flints, shells and splinters of wood, butcher's bones and roots of trees . . . were intended to renew and enrich' the established Purist vocabulary.[9] Besides, Purist theory had proposed a hierarchy of subject matter in which the human figure assumed the apex. It is therefore possible that the early Purist paintings, with their emphasis on domestic objects, were only a partial application of this theory. And it is likewise possible that this later 'organic' development was not a change of tack, but was instead symptomatic of a more thorough application.[10] Also, the hard-line formalist Léger was closely involved with the Purists at this time, and the compelling visual affinity of this late-1920s material with some of his figurative neoclassicism invariably colours our interpretation and leads us back to the seemingly closed world of Purist formalism. Says Green, 'Ultimately it was [Léger's] attitude to the object as essentially and overridingly a "plastic fact", a *formal* incident in painting, that Le Corbusier shared – the formalism of Purism was not altogether superseded.'[11]

The formalist interpretation is much too strong to be overturned. But the seamless way in which it reconciles Le Corbusier's public–private split, and his Purist and post-Purist work, does not in my opinion do full justice to their differences. I consider it necessary to offer a cautious alternative. First, to say that Le Corbusier was using this private time to develop some formal vocabulary later to be applied in his public works does not give a sense of how unique and precious this time clearly was to him. Here, written in 1953, is his own dramatic characterization of what painting had come to mean for him:

> I behaved like a combatant among men. And painting, ripped from the hands of the clock, made the private gardens of my freedom bloom. What an extraordinary thing! Because it is of enormous benefit to confront one's self freely and in solitude, to open the flood-gates to internal forces – for once personal, individual, unrestricted, intimate and free from all pretension. I worked for myself, with myself alone as judge, and not a complaisant one either[12] . . . [these paintings are] intimate and entirely indiscrete manifestations of the *self* . . . welling up from the depths of the unconscious.[13]

Recalling his earlier references to painting as providing 'spiritual freedom' and 'independence', I would argue that something *different* was going on in these late figurative works. There is more here than some 'form' workshop: there is a sense of an emerging self, somehow torn away and articulated in opposition to something outside it, something that might compromise it. This is all the more remarkable when we consider Le Corbusier's condemnation of 'individualistic' art in the essay 'Purism': 'anything of universal value is worth more than anything of merely individual value'.[14] How can individualism be upheld as of crucial importance in one form of artistic activity, but rejected as worthless in another? Similarly, the recurrence of certain symbolic elements in the post-1920s work points to a personal meaning, a content beyond mere formalism.

This leads me to believe that there are two different purposes implicit in these two types of painting, and that neither of them is necessarily 'formal'. I suggest they are both concerned with knowledge: the late work seems committed to self-knowledge, which I will return to in the third section. But to what knowledge is Purist painting committed? The answer comes directly from the Purists themselves. Beyond the attempt to move the viewer through its form, what is the effect of a Purist painting? 'Our concept of the object comes from the *total knowledge* of it, a knowledge acquired by the experience of our senses, tactile knowledge, knowledge of its materials, its volume, its profile, of all of its properties.' Classic single-point perspective is criticized for taking a particular viewpoint and thus giving 'an incomplete angle'. None the less, even 'the usual perpective view only acts as *the shutter-release for the memory of these experiences*'.[15] The multiple viewpoints of a Purist painting, then, offer a more comprehensive opportunity to recall the experienced reality of these objects: more angles facilitate better recollection and, presumably, better *knowledge*. Colour, despite its generally 'disaggregating' effects on the defining form, is none the less also of some use in this project:

> Given the play of memory, acquired in looking at nature, logical and organic habits are created in us which confer on each object a qualifying, and hence constructive colour; thus blue cannot be used to create a volume that should 'come forward,' because our eye, accustomed to seeing blue in depths (sky, sea), in backgrounds and in distant objects (horizons), does not permit with impunity the reversing of these conditions. Hence a plane that comes forward can never be blue; it could be green (grass), brown (earth).

Again, one is brought back to one's memories and experience of the world: it is the duty of art not to conflict with what one already knows and has experienced to be true. A more irresponsible or arbitrary deployment of form and colour would only engender confusion in the spectator. Against the universalizing tendencies of the 'primary', as discussed above, we have here an emphasis on the 'secondary', on those phenomena deriving from our specific culture and heredity: 'The secondary standard of memory, recall of visual experience and of our harmonization of the world'. These paintings deliver us back to our world of immediate experience, which represents our 'objective' reality: 'a painting is an artificial formation which, by appropriate means, should lead to the objectification of an entire "world"'.[16] This is how Le Corbusier characterized the importance of the 'object' some years later:

> The concentration of intention on the proper object. The attention concentrated on the object. The object must be deliberately created,

completely created, conceived for some purpose, made perfectly. The perfect object is a living organism; it is animated by the spirit of truth. We have in us a direct command which is the spirit of truth and which recognizes the true object within the limelight.[17]

Beyond being merely 'formalist', then, Purist painting sought to objectify the world. This objectification, it would seem, involved presenting objects in such a form – and with such colours – that they remind the spectator of the world he already knows and is comfortable with. But considered more technically, what epistemological paradigm informed this strange position? If this knowledge is 'total' and objective, why should it need to be 'artificially' reinforced in this way, and to what end?

Léger's 'Knowledge'

I shall return to the origins of this approach to knowledge in the next chapter. But first, I want to look at Léger's approach to the objects in his paintings, which betrays a fundamentally different notion of the world and of the knowledge that could be had of it. I shall examine Léger's aesthetic theory with a view to understanding his notion of the relationship between the human being and its exterior milieu, between subject and object, in the modern world. It is here that the essential point of his difference from Le Corbusier is found: Léger's approach implies a subject–object continuity that is inimical to Le Corbusier's dualism.

There are four observations to be made. The first is to point out Léger's love of the chaotic and violent spectacle of modern life, which is closely aligned with his fascination for war. There is something morbidly self-destructive in his accounts of the capacity of the machine and mass media to interpenetrate, to compromise the integrity of the human subject. Modern man, he says, 'drinks in the whole of this vital instantaneity, which cuts through him in every direction. He is a sponge: sensation of being a sponge, transparency, acuteness, new realism.'[18] But as well as relying on his own wartime experiences, and a loose affinity with Futurism, he also probably borrowed from the 'Intuitionist' philosopher Henri Bergson, whose ideas were very much in vogue in the years surrounding the war. According to Bergson, the essence of reality was in experience: it could not be known through science, which attempts to compartmentalize all phenomena into digestible units, but rather only through the action of an individual consciousness which fabricates around itself a world of interminable flux, of 'duration' or *lived* time. Thus, space and time are convulsed, distances, bodies and objects lose their integrity and flow into one another, past and present intermingle. As Green comments, Léger's 'emphasis . . . was on the quality of modern *experience* . . . rather than on the *structure*'. For Léger, the art appropriate to the age must be forged by imaginatively improvising upon these phenomena; phenomena in which the individual subject is not only inextricably implicated in the world, but indeed must lose himself in it to *know* it.[19]

Second, how are objects and people conceived by Léger? Everything that is caught up in this modern state seems to be levelled by it: there are no longer any qualitative differences between phenomena, be they buildings, machines or even the human body. Nor are there different ways of gaining knowledge of them. Everything is collapsed into the same formal-epistemological field, becoming 'objects' of formal worth only: 'everything is of equal interest . . . the human face or the human body is of no weightier plastic interest than a tree, a plant, a piece of rock, or a pile of rope'. Again, 'For me the human body is no more important than keys or velocipedes . . . For me, these are plastically valuable objects to make use of as I choose.'[20] What is left of the individual human being, then? Not much. Of key interest here is Léger's criticism of the clean and confined Corbusian living space. Léger had supplied several paintings for Le Corbusier's Pavillon de L'Esprit Nouveau of 1925, and marks this as the date when the cube and white wall came to architectural prominence. Here one saw

> the white wall appear with all the consequences it involved: a new, habitable rectangle or a false start. What was going to happen on this white wall?
>
> This habitable rectangle, though freed from decorative values, was a rectangle all the same, with its precise boundaries; the rectangular prison cell has always existed. Light had taken possession of it. *The object, the individual, exhibited in this new atmosphere, became visible, took on its total value, height and volume. One became aware of its true dimension within the four walls.*

But Léger found this situation intolerable, and demanded it be altered through colour:

> The white wall accepted its partial destruction through applications of color; naturally the choice of colors had to be established. This was done, and the permanent, habitable rectangle of four white walls became an elastic rectangle. I say elastic because each color applied, even when shaded, has a mobile effect. *Visual distances become relative. The rectangle disappears, its boundaries and its depths eroded. The modern individual now finds himself in a vital arrangement that has been entirely renewed* . . . It is a kind of law: colors advance or recede from the sensory point of view. Naturally, if you destroy the habitable surface, what I call 'the habitable rectangle,' *you make it into another rectangle that has no physical limitations and cannot be measured* . . . the visual relationship between you and the wall disappears.[21]

Space and objects are set shifting, rendered equivocal, and the fully defined individual that stood out in the initial Corbusian cube is lost in the flux.

This can be traced quite clearly in some of Léger's paintings.[22] In *Les Disques dans la ville* of 1920–21, for example, Léger incorporates what appear to be four vaguely human figures in the swirling forms of the city. These figures are never presented whole and distinct, however. Two of them appear flattened out, and may be little more than images on advertising billboards. The other two, more rounded and robotic, give a sense that they are emerging from some automated production line. More intimate, domestic pieces such as *Femme et nature morte* and *Le Grand Déjeuner* of 1921, again seem to be committed to merging their human figures into their surroundings. In *Femme et nature morte* the figure is almost completely lost, while in *Le Grand Déjeuner* it is only a handful of motifs, such as fingers, toes, and a uniform set of faces, that prevent the figures from sinking back into the anonymity of pure form. And except for the table in *Le Grand Déjeuner*, these environments obey no conventional laws of space. One of Léger's most striking works in this vein is *La Partie des cartes* of 1917 (fig. 6). Here is a group of three card players who are barely distinguishable among the forms that cut them open at almost every point. It is meaningless to talk about background or foreground in this painting as everything is treated equally, the billows of pipe-smoke being no less substantial than the fragments of arm and torso. Again, slight motifs

6   Fernand Léger. *La Partie de cartes*, 1917. Collection Kröller-Müller Museum, Otterlo.

such as their different military insignia and medals are barely adequate to identify the card players as individual human beings. In none of these paintings is it possible to know what is advancing or receding, or where objects and people stand in relation to one another – either spatially or idealistically.

The third observation I want to make concerns how this aesthetic was made manifest in Léger's politics. In terms of the masses and their potential for individual identity, this belief in the formal equivalence of all phenomena leads to predictable consequences: the ideal collectivization of society. Thus, the 'prejudice of the individual-as-king is gone . . . the individual-as-king [must be] really willing to become a means like the rest'.[23] Accordingly, Léger goes into raptures at the *Spartakiades*, an immense public spectacle where the collective social order of the Czechoslovak Republic was dramatized by a mass parade of people in geometric and rhythmic harmony.[24] I believe that this is what Léger meant by the 'New Realism'.[25] The definitive work on this kind of phenomenon, Siegfried

Kracauer's 'The Mass Ornament' of 1927, deals with it in a very similar way. He considers the grid forms of these mass gymnastic displays to be symbolic of Enlightenment rationality. This has purged mankind of its pre-modern sense of 'individuality' and 'soul', which are the age-old products of religious and mythological thinking, and promises to usher in a more socialized or even mass consciousness.[26] People become particles in a formal pattern, all identical.[27] Léger demands that art likewise be purely formal, purged of its 'subject', of all anecdotal or symbolic content. I think we must take this as parallel to his eradication, here, of the individual human 'subject', with its now anachronistic content of an individual soul.[28]

My final observation is as follows. Art, says Léger, must be taken out of the museums and made readily available everywhere, and our snobbishness overcome to allow us to recognize it in a wide variety of popular sources: in the shop display, in the machine, in cheap reproductions, and so on.[29] The reason for all this is that art, and colour especially, is said to answer a fundamental physiological need. It serves to distract and comfort the masses, offering them some respite in the midst of the disorienting modern flux, allowing them briefly to forget their miserable living and working conditions. 'It is necessary', he says, 'to distract man from his enormous and often disagreeable labors.' Colour can make the cold seem warm, the sooty and grimy seem clean; moreover, it can subliminally coerce the worker to be cleaner, smarter, more affable.[30] The psychological boon of this formal art, then, is linked to the attempt to provide a distraction from harsh reality.

To summarize these four points: first, Léger's individual is interpenetrated by all the phenomena of modernity, especially the mass media. Indeed, he or she is now indivisible from that which formerly might have been considered to lie 'outside' the self. Second, the human subject is collapsed into the object world to such a degree that there is no longer any qualitative distinction between the two, both being known and of interest only as form. Third, this has 'collectivist' political connotations, which also involves the eradication of the individual. Fourth, this 'new reality' is so disruptive and traumatic that people need to be distracted from it. More generally, the elimination of a 'subject' or content from art, which is now purely formal, seems to run hand in hand with the elimination of the human subject.

These four points are symptomatic of a fundamentally different conception of art, its relationship to the world and to the individual, than that which we have seen emerging with Purism. For Léger, subject and object are considered to be understandable in the same formal terms. The individual is effectively continuous with everything outside himself. Purism, however, seems to have been committed to returning the viewer to a stable, albeit somehow artificial, knowledge of the object world. Also, discussing his later, 'private' art, Le Corbusier clearly indicated that he was plumbing the depths of his own unique subjectivity. Far from being eradicated, it was undoubtedly a strong source of knowledge, value and meaning for him. The two things – subject and object – were held apart. They were not considered to be of merely formal interest, as they seem to have been for Léger.

To return to the example of the Corbusian cube, what did Léger find so objectionable about the way it worked? He objected to its perfect clarity, its impeccably defined boundaries and sense of stability. These were qualities against which the individual stood out distinctly, his own sense of dimension and volume – his 'total value' – easily legible. In response, Léger demanded that colour be introduced to 'elasticize' the walls. Now the walls appeared to advance and recede, and all sense of distance was relativized. Nothing in this hypothetical room was allowed to stand out, and the results were demonstrated in some of his paintings. I believe that Léger's proposed modification of the Corbusian cube is attributable to a different concept of knowing and being – a different metaphysics. For Léger, the individual exists anonymously *as* form, and is immersed in a larger continuity. But the Corbusian cube indicates something different: a commitment to objectify the world, against which the individual may begin to stand out on his or her own terms. The key, here, is the attempt to define the world and self in a discontinuous field of experience. And one might also remember that Le Corbusier wanted to keep the mass media out of his 'cube', for this interpenetrated and compromised the inhabitant's individuality. But it was precisely this dissolution of self that Léger celebrated, the mass media providing that 'vital instantaneity, which cuts through him in every direction'.[31]

The theory suggests this, but I think it is also borne out by Le Corbusier's Purist painting. The objects in these paintings are presented

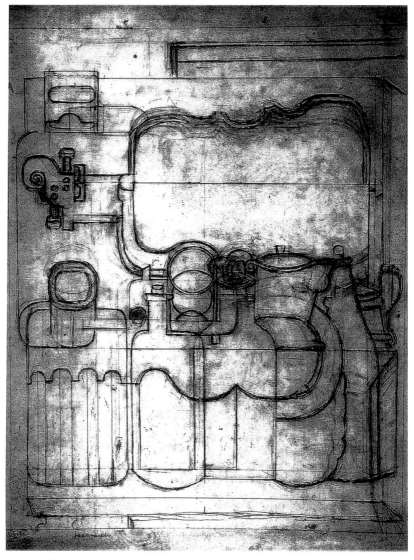

7   Le Corbusier. *Feuillantines. Etude pour violon et bouteille*, 1926. Dessin FLC 2365. © FLC

more as relating to concrete objects in the world than as being spring-boards for the exploration of form. I believe these paintings aspire to a quasi-scientific presentation of objects. In fact, they are barely paintings at all: they consciously press as close as possible to being simple engineering blueprints. Perhaps the best sense of this comes from the meticulous precision of Le Corbusier's preparatory sketches (fig. 7). The addition of colour in the finished pieces lessens this impact somewhat, but I think the overall sense of engineered precision remains. In this sense, Le Corbusier's Purist paintings are the small-scale domestic equivalent of his city blueprints. They, too, seek to settle humankind's relations with a world that has become too intrusive and disruptive, by attributing some order to this world. Typically, each object in a Purist painting is represented from several of its most definitive viewpoints: often simultaneously in plan, elevation and profile. And occasionally, this may also be combined with a 45° downward view. The whole ensemble is always comfortably centred and seldom transgresses the frame. Although the objects are always meticulously arranged and frequently overlap, I feel there is little real sense of flow or continuity between them. The aura is one of perfect repose, and each object, unproblematically contained within its contours, is fully identifiable in itself.

Purist paintings seem to have different priorities than those of a Léger still life, such as *Nature morte à la chope* of 1921–2. They demonstrate very simply where things are and what they look like. They refuse to present the viewer with anything he does not already know about his milieu. They are self-consciously unremarkable and obvious. As Curtis remarks, Purism held the 'ambition of finding a static order behind contemporary existence'.[32] That is, the Purists were not interested in indulging the potential chaos and flux of contemporary existence, as was Léger.[33] And against the orderly milieu that the Purists provide, the individual might presumably turn his attentions towards those 'intimate and entirely indiscrete manifestations of the *self* . . . welling up from the depths of the unconscious'.[34] That is, with the object world properly re-established within its boundaries, the subject might begin to perceive itself as distinct.

Green's interpretation of this material occupies a position midway between the orthodox formalist one and my own, and it is helpful to look at it briefly. Complementing the opinion that Le Corbusier shared Léger's 'attitude to the object as essentially and overridingly a "plastic fact", a *formal* incident in painting', Green observes that 'No form which takes part in the pictorial composition is unconnected with its palpable existence *outside* the painting.'[35] He identifies an epistemological tension in Le Corbusier's early nature studies between the imposition of some ideal formal lawfulness upon external nature and the more submissive observation and acceptance of the object as it already exists: 'His control over what he chose to look at was always clear; but so too was its autonomous presence in its own space.' Art was therefore an epistemological 'testing-ground' upon which Le Corbusier could negotiate his relationship with the external milieu: 'It marks out the interval', says Le Corbusier, 'between the moment when a vast and dominant nature overwhelms, and that when man, having acquired serenity, has a conception of that same nature and works in harmony with its law.' And as Green intriguingly goes on to suggest, this was just 'one side of another opposition: between the individual and the social'. This tension continued throughout early Purism: it was a tension between the attempt to hold back from the external milieu, to define and distance its objects as somehow other; and the attempt to uncover the formal truths underlying and therefore unifying all phenomena, including humankind and its milieu. But ultimately, Green maintains, this was resolved. The clearly defined lines of the Purists' painted objects began to loosen, the mechanical formal vocabulary was enriched with organic forms, and everything began flowing into everything else. This revealed that 'fundamentally the formal exigencies and the geometric order of [Le Corbusier's] art *were* his priorities'; and by the late-1920s, 'the shift was to be once and for all concluded [with] the new, more homogenous view of man and nature [and society]'.[36] Thus we are brought back to something very much like Léger's formalism.

I believe Green makes an important point by noting that this material seems to explore the epistemological boundary between the individual and the natural and social realities that surround him, even though he concludes that this schism was overcome. I would like to keep open this aspect of Green's reading by suggesting that Le Corbusier was determined to hold the individual and external reality completely and indefinitely apart, and that an important factor in this was the attempt to attribute some kind of 'objective' order to this reality. Le Corbusier's differences with Léger, then, rest upon a fundamental divergence of views as to where truly valid selfhood is found: either through immersion in the world, to such an extent that individuality is dissolved into the collective; or through the withholding of oneself from the world.

In order to understand how Le Corbusier's individual was meant to hold himself back, one must first try to understand his thoughts on scientific method. Only then can one turn directly to his philosophy of self.

Chapter 5

Conventionalism

I have taken this route specifically to open up the larger metaphysical issues that underlie this cluster of art theories. By suggesting that Le Corbusier's painting was not 'formalist' in the same manner as Léger's painting, I began also to suggest that it did not have the same kind of outlook on the world and on the self. It appeared to involve a different approach to the way knowledge of these things could be attained. Ultimately, this would entail a particular concept of selfhood; but prior to this, it was necessary to establish a particular concept of the world.

This chapter explores the latter in terms of the kind of science 'favoured' by the Purists, which can be attributed to their reading of the popular scientist Henri Poincaré, and also notes how this differed from the science favoured by the majority of the avant-garde. The next stage is to investigate how this manifested itself in Le Corbusier's later proportional system, the 'Modulor'. As with Le Corbusier's theory of Purist painting, I shall argue that the Modulor was not primarily about achieving good proportion, but about achieving satisfactory knowledge. And this kind of knowledge, steeped in the lessons of Poincaré, could never be certain: at best it could be 'conventional' or provisional, a matter of *functional* convenience.

Poincaré: Purist Space

I should like to suggest a new model for Le Corbusier's understanding of the mechanisms through which knowledge of the world might be gained. If we recall what was said above in relation to Purist painting, it would seem that Le Corbusier's notion of what constituted knowledge of the world had little to do with absolute truth: rather, it had something to do with the convenience and comfort of recollection, knowledge simply being that to which we have grown accustomed. The rather offhand connotations of this are crucial, and should be kept in mind.

Consequently the Purists were unimpressed, to the point of hostility, by the most recent theoretical innovations in mathematical science. In his essay of 1916, 'Notes sur la Cubisme', Ozenfant criticized certain of the 'minor' Cubists – 'neither artists nor scholars, but veritable ignoramuses' – for what he believed was a naïve acceptance of recent four-dimensional space theories. Not only did such theories go against mankind's three-dimensional mode of visual perception, but the attempt to inscribe some hypothetical fourth dimension on to a two-dimensional canvas was obviously ludicrous. The whole enterprise remained purely speculative:

> Crisis, because contrary to all reason certain ignoramuses have banished the third dimension as outmoded, to the benefit of a new dimension called the fourth. But as the fourth dimension is purely hypothetical (the plastic sense of man remains conditioned by his senses, which are three dimensional) why do this? . . . they forget that it is preposterous to claim to materialize the fourth dimension using a medium of two dimensions . . . in a plastic work three dimensions provide the necessary perspective, and one must affirm that there is no work of art without perspective . . . in the interests of Cubism, and of Art, it would be desirable that artists – architects of matter having as their materials the properties of matter in space – learn as much as possible about organic laws, in order to prevent too much gossiping and the transgression of these same laws.[1]

Art, then, must attempt to reinforce the conventional lawfulness of matter. Purism did this by presenting the objective world from a number of the most logical angles. This was taken up unchanged in 1918 in

Ozenfant and Le Corbusier's *Après le Cubisme*, with the addition that non-Euclidean geometry was now mentioned as well, and so too was its endorsement by the most prominent Cubist 'ignoramuses': Albert Gleizes and Jean Metzinger. The 'marvellous game' of these new spatial theories might be conceivable in an abstract sense, but they were 'without any contact with the real world'.[2]

But what did these things entail? Gleizes and Metzinger's essay of 1912, 'Du Cubisme', gives an indication of what the Purists were reacting against:

> This [painterly] space we have negligently confused with pure visual space or with Euclidean space.
>
> If we wished to tie the painter's space to a particular geometry, we should have to refer it to the non-Euclidean scientists . . .
>
> As for visual space, we know that it results from the harmony of the sensations of convergence and accommodation of the eye.
>
> For the picture, a flat surface, the accommodation is negative. Therefore the convergence which perspective teaches us to simulate cannot evoke the idea of depth.[3]

The initial argument, it seems, is for the absolute separation of the space of the painting from the concretely observable space of 'reality', the two being irreconcilable: 'There are no direct means', they say, 'of evaluating the processes thanks to which the relations between the world and the thought of a man are rendered perceptible to us.' And to those who insist, as the Purists would do, that art should reproduce the phenomena of the objective world, 'Let us remind them that we visit an exhibition to contemplate painting and to enjoy it, not to enlarge our knowledge of geography, anatomy, etc.'[4] But Gleizes and Metzinger go further than this, insisting not only that the world is non-representable, but that it is in a state of continual flux:

> objective or conventional reality, this world intermediate between another's consciousness and our own never ceases to fluctuate according to the will of race, religion, scientific theory, etc., although humanity has laboured from time immemorial *to hold it fast* . . . Henceforth objective knowledge at last regarded as chimerical, and all the crowd understands by natural form proven to be *convention*.[5]

So what is the painter meant to do, according to this theory? Reality, according to Gleizes and Metzinger, cannot be truly or finally known, and it is nonsensical to attempt to present it as such. Indeed, reality changes with everyone's perceptions: 'An object has not one absolute form, it has several . . . As many images of the object as eyes to contemplate it, as many images of essence as minds to understand it . . . to the eyes of most people the external world is amorphous.' Rather than '*present distinct objects*', then, the painter must provide 'a veritable fusion of objects'. The object is 'transubstantiated', so that it might '[reserve] an infinity of replies to an infinity of questions'. But this is not to end in some chaos of unknowing. Rather, there is a commitment to establish a flexible, consensual understanding of the universe, through a 'reciprocity of concessions': 'we cannot enjoy ourselves in isolation; we wish to dazzle others with that which we daily snatch from the sensate world, and in return we wish others to show us their trophies'. This is reconciled through painting, that 'plane of higher reality'.[6] Despite their disclaimer that Cubist painting had nothing to do with knowledge, then, it seems to be a mechanism for the endless renegotiation of spatial knowledge. Unable to come to any settled understanding of the object world, human beings continually compare experiences in pursuit of what they ideally hold in common.[7]

Much of this position can be attributed to the general fascination for the new mathematical sciences at this time. Linda Dalrymple Henderson has charted the development and popular dissemination of theories concerning non-Euclidean and multi-dimensional space, revealing that they had at least as many variations as practitioners.[8] But generally speaking, non-Euclidean geometry made a case for the curvature of space, which challenged the age-old paradigm of its being orthogonal and the mathematical laws that hitherto had explained it.[9] Many in the artistic avantgarde believed this to have invalidated the system of linear perspective, while 'traditional means of rendering objects could hardly be adequate if no absolute, unchanging form for an object could be posited'. Theories of four- or *n*-dimensional space generally argued for the presence of higher spatial dimensions that complemented the usual three, and that united them into increasingly complex continuous structures *at* this higher level.[10] These theories were exciting and broad enough to be popularized in a variety of ways. This happened through the publications of the 'hyperspace philosophers', who transformed dry mathematics into more accessible terms; through the science-fiction of H. G. Wells and Edwin A. Abbott, for example; and also, perhaps most influentially, through its association with the burgeoning occult revival, which tended to conceptualize the fourth dimension as a higher, transcendental mode of being. The combined effect was that the fourth dimension was almost a household word by the early twentieth century. Of course, the formal and spatial opportunities on offer also fired the imagination of much of the artistic avant-garde. But as Henderson cautioned, 'the fourth dimension could be all things to all people'.[11]

Although by no means responsible for the initial Cubist innovations of Pablo Picasso and Georges Braque, these ideas were sufficiently widespread and evocative to be grafted on to these manifestations after the event by Apollinaire, Juan Gris, and Gleizes and Metzinger. Picasso and Braque remained aloof, but the younger Puteaux-Courbevoie group of Cubists, and Metzinger especially, appear to have taken an active interest in these issues.[12] Even Léger, who remained on the periphery of this group, was indirectly implicated by Apollinaire, who praised his efforts 'to get rid of perspective, of that miserable tricky perspective, of that fourth dimension in reverse'.[13] Apollinaire maintained that Cubism was not interested in achieving any 'real resemblance' to the objects of the world as they are perceived or experienced, but rather in the larger 'conceptual' truth. This art was 'more cerebral than sensual', it rejected everyday 'human' proportions and sought 'metaphysical forms'. He also said that:

> It is the social function of great poets and artists to continually renew the appearance nature has for the eyes of men. Without poets, without artists, men would soon weary of nature's monotony.[14]

This was represented in painting in various ways. Most obviously, it entailed the rejection of traditional three-dimensional perspective, which was considered a superficial way of viewing the world. This was done through the recombination of multiple, successively perceived viewpoints of the object into a single image, which was intended to represent its enmeshment in a higher spatio-temporal continuity. Objects were often transparent, distances were ambiguous, and inter-flowing forms and grid-like armatures could be used to imply the underlying continuity of all phenomena.

It is unlikely that the Cubists had any first-hand knowledge of the new spatial theories, however, and their detailed understanding was nonexistent. They picked it up more through occultist channels than through scientific ones, and even then, this seldom involved any committed research but was more likely to have come from their participation in what amounted to a new salon culture of fashionable occultism.[15] Even so, they had an intuitive understanding of the single irreducible point common to the whole discourse: overlooking the diversities of the various positions, we can cautiously generalize that any interest here was symptomatic of a desire to immerse and lose oneself in the higher reality of a multi-dimensional universe. Undoubtedly there were spiritual connotations of redemption at work here, which ran parallel with the political desire to overturn the value-laden conventions of nineteenth-century scientific positivism and the Beaux-Arts tradition, and thus of the bourgeoisie that upheld them.[16]

I consider this to be especially important. The ideal of spatio-temporal continuity which the new mathematics and new occultism provided inter-locked at an intuitive level with the collectivist bedrock of left-wing politics: 'immersion' could thus be regarded as redemption from an old order of discontinuous being. The rhetoric here proved extremely flexible. The value-laden discontinuities of space, art, politics and society were all to be collapsed into and resolved at a transcendental level of reality, with the flow of all into all. Most important, the autonomous individual was liquidated. As Tom Gibbons observes, the fusion of objects and their sur-roundings in Cubist paintings 'may be seen as a method of depicting the most fundamental belief of the occult-idealist tradition: that the separate-ness of individual existences, whether of objects or of living creatures, is merely apparent, and that all are, in transcendental reality, part of one interpenetrating and indivisible unity'.[17] Henderson confirms that the fourth dimension, especially in its occultist manifestations, was tied to the tradition of philosophical 'monism'. That is, it sought the oneness of self and universe, the dissolution of 'subject' into 'object', and consequently the end of autonomous 'self-consciousness'.[18]

The Purists' rejection of these new sciences would appear to make them conservatives at several levels. Indeed, their thesis, with its championing of perspective, proportion, good drawing and the like, is essentially Beaux-Arts.[19] But what exactly was meant by the Purists' criticism of the way the avant-garde subscribed to these new sciences? The answer is that they believed that reality should be fixed in knowledge, or 'held fast' in 'conventions', if we adopt the scornful tone of Gleizes and Metzinger. But why would they want to do this? We remember from the first section that at this time the Purists were engaged in a constructive programme to put France in order. They feared that the disruption brought about by the war would never end. Le Corbusier was especially sensitive to the interminable social and political upheaval, and we have seen that he intended to remedy this by putting an end to society and politics through the order of his cities. It is customary to regard this creation of order as the end point of Le Corbusier's activity, but we should remember that this order was intended as a precursor to the forging of a new national and individual consciousness. I suggest that these social and political initiatives were accompanied by an epistemological one, and for the same reasons: to end unnecessary disruption and focus attention upon more important things. Ultimately, it was Pascal who informed the Purists in this kind of epistemology, and his theories will be discussed in due course. But first, we must take account of the contemporary influence of Poincaré.

Ozenfant considered the philosopher–mathematician Henri Poincaré, one of the foremost scholars and popularizers of the new sciences in France in the years surrounding the turn of the century, to be his mentor. After settling in Paris in 1906, Ozenfant attended Poincaré's lectures at the Collège de France, and was later to recall that his works 'were the essential creators of my thought'.[20] He also gave a copy of Poincaré's *Science et methode* to Le Corbusier in late 1920.[21] Gibbons maintains that the Cubists were unlikely to have read such texts, although they liked to name-drop.[22] But the Purists prided themselves on what they believed to be a more responsible, serious-minded engagement.

Poincaré's epistemology was as follows. He argued that 'geometric' space, unlike 'perceptual' space, was not necessarily three-dimensional. This means that what we perceive with the senses and what we conceive with the mind do not necessarily correspond. Perceptual space was governed by certain three-dimensional geometric conventions. But this was because our physiology, our body, psyche, senses and sense of balance, were so configured that we automatically experienced space as three-dimensional and Euclidean. By responding to the concrete objects of the world, the human organism created and maintained a three-dimensional grid around itself. This automatic response was bolstered by our ongoing personal experience of the world, and was also passed down to us through our ancestors

– the three-dimensional paradigm was somehow genetically inscribed. If we did not experience space in this way, says Poincaré, we would be unable to negotiate our world. It was therefore necessary for simple survival. But contrary to what our body told us, it was possible to conceive of multi-dimensional, non-Euclidean mathematics which exhibited all the internal logic and coherence of our 'ordinary' mathematics. It was also possible to conceive of hypothetical beings and worlds that lived in accordance with these new spatial paradigms. But these were merely hypothetical, and Poincaré never believed that our world and our spatial experiences could be anything other than three-dimensional.

But in such a scheme, could anything be considered 'knowledge' or 'truth'? Poincaré famously leap-frogged the debate as to whether space was in fact 'Euclidean'. This debate was held between the conservatives and radicals in the field: those who wanted to keep the old spatial paradigms, and those who wanted to innovate new ones. The conservatives maintained that space was Euclidean and corresponded to an *a priori* Euclidean 'grid' in the mind, while the radicals tried to prove through empirical observation that space was in fact non-Euclidean. Poincaré attacked these positions with the thesis that *a priori* judgements and empirical observations were both beside the point. The various hypotheses by which we attempted to understand the nature of space, he said, were in abstract terms all equally plausible. The notion of proof was inapplicable, because they could *all* be proved. Ultimately, whichever way we chose to think about these things was simply a matter of convenience, of 'convention':

> One may ask what these hypotheses are. Are they experimental facts, analytic judgment or synthetic *a priori* judgments? We must respond negatively to these three questions. If these hypotheses were experimental facts, geometry would be subject to unceasing revision and would not be an exact science; if they were synthetic *a priori* judgments or, even more, analytic judgments, it would be impossible to remove one and establish a system on its negation . . .
>
> Thus, the fundamental hypotheses of geometry are not experimental facts; it is however, the observation of certain physical phenomena which accounts for the choice of certain hypotheses among all possible ones.

On the other hand, the group chosen is only more convenient than the others and [one] cannot say that Euclidean geometry is true . . . Euclidean Geometry is, and will remain, the most convenient.[23]

But this was not mere convenience. Poincaré differentiates himself from the 'nominalist' approach, which said that our choice of epistemological conventions was random and arbitrary. Instead, he believed our 'choice' to be unavoidable – a necessary product of our physiological make-up. Questions of absolute 'truth' and 'knowledge' were sidelined. All we had were our bodies, and whether it was true or not, these bodies would always give us the sense of a three-dimensional universe that all human beings held in common. And as well as being unavoidable, the Euclidean paradigm was also the most useful for taking practical, 'industrious' action in the world. Conventional 'knowledge' was favoured because it was the most functional. Rather than fighting against this natural reflex, then, Poincaré recommended we submit to it. It is revealing that he also criticized Bergson's belief that space could be reconfigured through experience.[24]

The Purists, I think, concentrated upon this 'conventionalist' approach to knowledge. As the new sciences gained in popularity, particularly through the personality of Albert Einstein, *L'Esprit nouveau* did indeed give more space to their discussion. But this remained at a speculative level, and was never taken seriously enough to warrant consideration as a genuinely viable way of understanding the world. The Purist affinity for Platonic solids, then, did not betoken an interest in ideal form. Rather, it suggested a desire to make objects concretely manifest in three-dimensional Euclidean space.[25] I think it may have been this that led Le Corbusier to reminisce that the years '1922–23' were characterized by the 'constipation of Henri *Poincaré*'.[26] This characterization shows Le Corbusier understood Poincaré quite well.

Keeping in mind Poincaré's 'personal experience and heredity', I think Purist painting seeks to recall the viewer to his prior knowledge of three-dimensional space and the objects it defines and contains. The viewer has come to know this through 'logical and organic habits'.[27] The tight boundaries of the painted object, its unequivocal surfaces and edges, recall those of the object itself, which in turn serves to inscribe that object *and* the viewer into Euclidean space.[28] It is interesting that Poincaré said that our knowledge of the world was generated by our experience of objects from

different angles, and that 'solid bodies' were fundamental to our understanding of three-dimensional space: 'in order to visualize a figure in space,
do we not all visualize successively the various possible perspectives of this
figure?'[29] Accordingly, Purist objects are presented from various viewpoints. It was a serious misunderstanding by Gleizes and Metzinger to
think that Poincaré encouraged them to present successive viewpoints as
a means of breaking the three-dimensional paradigm, for in fact he considered it the best way to reify this paradigm.[30]

This paradigm was applicable to Purist architecture and urbanism as
well, except that, unlike the painting, it did not function at a remove
and was thus more effective. That is to say, the imaginary stroller in a
Corbusian building or city from the 1920s would be directly presented
with vista after vista against which to test his conventional understanding
of objects and space, which is repeatedly and unfailingly confirmed.
Through regularity of forms, the crispness of edges, planes and sight-lines,
and most compellingly through sheer mass, I believe that Le Corbusier's
cities cast this paradigm back into concrete. Distances and shapes remain
stable and predictable, they answer all prior expectations. Unlike Apollinaire's Cubism, they deliberately presented a 'monotonous' picture of
the world. They are conventionally determined, and therefore reliable
enough.[31]

Euclidean space is reified here as a reliable and functional epistemological paradigm, although not necessarily as 'truth'. Did the Purists truly consider the classical Euclidean model to be the only basis for knowing the
world, something true in actual fact? I do not think so. They were as aware
of contemporary scientific challenges and innovations as any of their contemporaries, if not more so. But their championing of Euclidean space was
a conscious decision, more one of convenience than real belief. It
was also rooted in the physiology and experience of human beings as the
necessary way of negotiating the world. Ultimately, however, truth
about external reality did not seem to matter.

But why did they do this? In maintaining this particular notion of
the 'object', they also held open a particular notion of the 'subject': one
that did not entail the dissolution of the one into the other. Given their
indebtedness to Poincaré, who said that it was impossible to gain any real
knowledge of external reality, it was cursorily glossed over. Attention
could now be turned to interior reality.

The 'Modulor'

To reduce Le Corbusier's 'understanding' of the world solely to Euclid would be a misrepresentation. I have singled out this example from his early professional history primarily as a convenient way to make a point. Le Corbusier was not so consistent or confident that he could place his trust in any single such system: rather, he crowded together a fairly comprehensive variety of epistemological paradigms. It seems this was always with a view to establishing order in the world, which thereby did not threaten to compromise the boundaries of the autonomous self. But what is important is that his general mode of engagement with external reality remained the same throughout his life. It was a matter of functional *rapprochement*, rather than real knowledge or truth.

The 'Modulor', Le Corbusier's project to formulate a comprehensive proportioning system, provides a compelling picture of this, and I would like to show how it was intended to work. Again, I believe this is primarily an epistemological mechanism, and only incidentally a formal one. It is also worth looking into as it gives a clearer intimation of how the individual must effectively be lifted out of the objective world in order to come to know himself. The way in which these ideals were manifested in Le Corbusier's buildings and city designs will become clear. My reappraisal of the Modulor will centre around three questions: what kind of knowledge does the Modulor provide, was this knowledge reliable, and what was its final purpose?

THE MODULOR AS 'KNOWLEDGE'

Le Corbusier began to formulate the Modulor in occupied Paris in 1942, after his retreat from Vichy. This was done both in clandestine meetings with fellow members of the newly formed *Association des Constructeurs pour une Rénovation Architecturale* (ASCORAL) and in correspondence with various amateur and professional mathematicians.[32] The purpose was to unite the foot-and-inch and metric systems of measurement, and consequently those parts of the globe that use these different systems.[33] For the future, he envisaged a new convention of measurement to replace the old:

> The next generation will know nothing of the conflict between the metre and the foot-and-inch; the generation after it will know only the

universal measures. The conventional signs of today will have been abandoned, forgotten. What I once rashly called 'abstract' will be *the conventional number of the day*.[34]

But beyond these practical considerations, why did Le Corbusier reject
these measuring systems? The foot-and-inch, while praised for being heir
to the historical tradition of grounding measurements in the proportions
of the human body, and therefore true to our bodily experience of the
world, is rejected because of its cumbersome nature. The metric is considered convenient yet inhuman, having no relation to the human body
at all. It is pure abstraction: 'I am seriously angry with the metre (forty-
millionth part of the meridian of the earth) for having *desubstantiated* itself
as it has done, and for having placed itself so perfectly, so dangerously, so
unhappily outside the human scale.' The metric leads to the alienation of
mankind from those objective bodily measurements of which it is
reminded every day. To continue construction with this system serves only
to make man insecure and unsure of himself in an alien environment, one
that literally does not fit and that he does not know.[35]

Predictably central to the Modulor, then, is a criticism of the speculative abstractions of the new mathematics, which Le Corbusier satirizes
appropriately as tending towards esotericism and mysticism. He dramatizes
this by cryptically reproducing a key passage from François Rabelais's
Gargantua and Pantagruel, in which the protagonists travel via 'the port of
Mataeotechny — the Home of Useless Knowledge' to consult the Oracle
in the 'Kingdom of the Quintessence'.[36] After being flummoxed by various
mystical sciences, rites and number symbolism, the protagonists are granted
the Priestess Bacbuc's final warning — a warning against all knowledge
seekers: 'all men's knowledge . . . is hardly an infinitesimal fraction of all
that exists'. The moral is clear: try to get on with whatever knowledge
you already have, and do not rely upon ever knowing much more.[37] In
Le Corbusier's own words: 'I interpret: act, and you shall see the miracle.
Do not seek a gloss! Do not try to escape!'[38] He is scrupulous, then, about
presenting the Modulor as the paradigm of down-to-earth empiricism. To
bring the 'boundless', 'unlimited' and 'intangible' phenomena of the new
sciences, lampooned as a quasi-magical practice, directly into the everyday
built environment would be simply irresponsible: 'Being a builder and not
an art pundit,' he says, 'I think that *today* . . . any door that offers an escape

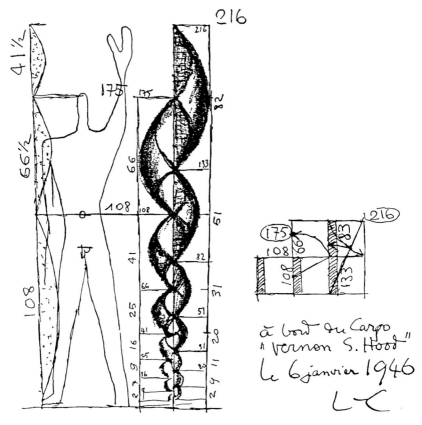

8   Le Corbusier. 'These figures pin down the human body at the decisive points of its occupation of space: they are therefore *anthropocentric*.' From Le Corbusier, *The Modulor 1 and 2*. FLC 32287. © FLC

is dangerous. By so saying, by so doing, I am relegating myself to the inferior rank of a simple labourer. All the better! Thanks!'[39]

The proportions of the Modulor seem to be committed to reinforcing a particular kind of knowledge of space, but how is this knowledge put together? First, out of the concrete dimensions of the human body: 'These figures pin down the human body at the decisive points of its occupation of space: they are therefore *anthropocentric*' (fig. 8). Measures are again to 'be *made flesh*, the living expression of our universe, *ours*, the universe of men, the only one conceivable to our intelligence'.[40] The sense that theoretically a more fundamental understanding of the universe may be possible, but that this is beyond us, recalls Poincaré quite neatly. Second, the proportions of the Modulor are intended to recall our ordinary perceptual knowledge and experience of the world: 'I have stayed within the realm of concrete things, within the field of human psycho-physiology. I have concerned myself only with objects falling under the jurisdiction of the eye.'[41] Le Corbusier believes that the perceptual apparatus of the human body, and sight in particular, limit the amount and the kind of knowledge it can have of the world: 'The cone of vision is in front, concentrated upon a concrete field which is, in reality, a limited one, and limited still more by the spirit, which, hidden behind the physical apparatus, can interpret, appreciate and measure only that which it has time to grasp.' Le Corbusier illustrates this with a sketch, which is intended to show that our knowledge of space is not conceptual and homogenous like a grid, but instead is rooted in our individual physiologies and experience.[42] By no means, then, can we have any fuller knowledge. The world we experience must forever exclude the forms 'issuing' from the new sciences, 'the philosopher's polyhedrons'.[43] Again, this recalls Poincaré very closely.

Everything in the Modulor is intended to recall us to what we already know. It is essentially a collection of epistemological conventions bundled together for convenience. The volume *Modulor 2* is substantially made up of comments on the system from a wide variety of interested parties, which Le Corbusier either attacks or commends. Le Corbusier enjoys the suggestion by the mathematician Andreas Speiser that the Modulor, in 'appealing simultaneously to geometry and numbers', fuses the 'two means [we have] of understanding the outside world':

1. Numbers. By their effect, we 'posit' the other person – sympathy, order, harmony, beauty, etc.; in short, everything that is of the mind.

2. Space. This gives us objects without interest, without life, without beauty, but 'having extension' (lying outstretched, standing, present, etc.).[44]

These epistemological conventions recall the dual Pythagorean–Platonic tradition which lies at the basis of most proportional systems throughout

Western history. 'This tradition has a double aspect: it consists of numerical relationships (harmonious intervals of the Greek musical scale: 1st, 2nd, 3rd, 4th) and of perfect geometrical figures: equilateral triangle, rectangle, isosceles triangle, square, pentagon (elements of the five regular solid bodies).'[45] Le Corbusier presents the Modulor as the culmination of this heritage, and also as a fusion of all the proportional conventions which emerged in history from one or the other of these broad trends.[46]

The Modulor was an intricate attempt to synthesize a variety of proportional systems, which were apprehended primarily in terms of the epistemological paradigms that underlay them. It was also an attempt to return people to the world they had come to know through their everyday perceptual experience, much like Purist painting appeared to be. It was, in this sense, more concerned with knowledge than form or proportion. And indeed, there were even some tentative suggestions that the Modulor was broad enough to absorb the new non-Euclidean and 'space–time' paradigms, although these were not made by Le Corbusier himself.[47]

'FUNCTIONAL' KNOWLEDGE

But just how objective or truthful is the knowledge that the Modulor represents? Predictably, given Le Corbusier's indebtedness to conventionalism, it is not absolutely reliable. This is revealed throughout by the undercurrent of confusion as to whether the Modulor stems from empirical observation and method, or from Le Corbusier's own conceit. He begins the first book by warning the reader that the Modulor is the product of the tumultuous fortunes and interests of his personal life-experience, which is, '*The very opposite of an encyclopaedic bookshelf, where volumes of wisdom are tidily ranged*'. The 'facts and ideas' here were never dispassionately 'known' or objectively 'classified'.[48] He further distances himself from any pretensions towards objectivity with the observation that this system has not emerged from any official body of experts, but rather from an 'ordinary man' who is 'the product of a certain *milieu*', and moreover one that 'has, on occasion, created an environment to fit himself'.[49] It is therefore not surprising to find Le Corbusier agonizing that the Modulor may be completely arbitrary, just one alternative among many:

assuming that the 'Modulor' is the key to the 'door of the miracle of numbers', if only in a very limited sphere, is that door merely one of a hundred or a thousand miraculous doors which may or do exist in that sphere, or have we, by sheer hazard, opened the one and only door that was waiting to be discovered? . . . that question is always at the fore-front of my mind.[50]

But, for all his 'trembling with anxiety to know and make sure', he never appears to arrive at certainty: 'one day', he observes, 'a solution appeared along the way. Is it *the* solution? We have nothing to prove it.' One receives an ever clearer impression that this system is no more than a stop-gap, but also that a stopgap is all one can ever hope to have in such an enterprise – in the search for knowledge. The Modulor is committed to 'rounding-off', to seeking a 'compromise'. Eventually, Le Corbusier con-cludes: 'I have gained one certainty . . . I have made a good model of an efficient working tool.'[51]

Given that Le Corbusier was preoccupied with attaining certainty in knowledge throughout this entire project of the Modulor, what are we to make of his apparent failure to achieve it? To put it another way: if it could be admitted that the epistemology of the Modulor was merely 'con-ventional' and therefore possibly wrong, then of what *use* was it? The answer is that it was intended to settle our relations with the world. And given that real knowledge was unattainable, it was necessary to select the most convenient knowledge. Hence the question of whether the 'knowl-edge' it represented was true or not is incidental: the knowledge was *instru-mental*, it needed merely to provide a 'good enough' account of exterior reality such that it ceased to trouble or enthral us. It is possible here to offer a cautious redefinition of 'functionalism' as the term related to Le Corbusier. His functionalism was as much about gaining a functional understanding of the world as it was about the more obvious practical utility or convenience of his buildings.

THE MODULOR AT WORK

The Modulor was a fusion of various epistemological conventions, but the fact that it was flawed at a theoretical level is quite unimportant.[52] Rather, the significance lies in the intention. We remember that, with Purism, the

Euclidean was consciously settled upon as a convenient but not necessarily correct way of understanding the world. This was intended to hold off the uncertainties engendered by the new sciences and embraced by the more typical modernists.[53] The Modulor is just a more comprehensive, if more cumbersome, version of this. If the Euclideanism of Purism was a tightrope that stopped one falling into uncertainty, the Modulor is a densely woven safety net: 'a flawless fabric formed of stitches of every dimension'.[54] And this approach to the 'object' world again ended with a particular notion of the 'subject'.

The fundamental purpose of the Modulor, as Le Corbusier envisaged it, was to fracture the underlying continuity of all phenomena. That is, in order not to feel absorbed and overwhelmed by the universe, humankind must break it down into manageable chunks. This provides evidence both of the power of human agency, and simultaneously of the ability of the individual to stand out as distinct from nature. This is something that Le Corbusier applies to all spheres of understanding and activity, be they natural or social, temporal or spatial, and these frequently overlap in his terminology. For example, he admires how Pythagoras articulated the continuity of sound into a handful of 'conventional' intervals, which became the basis of Western music.[55] And on a more comprehensive scale:

> It takes only twenty-six letters to write tens of thousands of words in fifty languages. The Universe, at our present state of awareness, is composed of ninety-two elements. All arithmetic is written with ten figures, and music with seven notes. The year has four seasons, twelve months, and days composed of twenty-four hours.

To remain immersed in a universe of phenomena that have not been articulated into measures adequate to our limited understanding will give us only 'hell on earth, omnipresent and virulent everywhere'.[56] And note how Le Corbusier does not question whether these ways of understanding are correct or not: they correspond merely to 'our present state of awareness' and are good enough. The Modulor is intended to do exactly the same: like the musical scale, its divisions are similarly considered 'rungs'.[57] As an 'example' of this, Le Corbusier provided an account of how he dealt with the Musée National d'Art Moderne in Paris on the occasion of an exhibition of his paintings there in 1953–4. Appalled by the dimensions of the hall that he was allocated in this 'inhuman palace', he employed the proportions of the Modulor to partition it into a series of intimate spaces 'designed to the human scale'.[58] The bodies and objects within could now stand out clearly, no longer threatened by dissolution into an over-large, even formless space.

But ultimately, what does this represent? It represents a 'battle' between humankind and the universe, which Le Corbusier dramatizes as 'this duet, this duel, this alliance, this struggle, this difference and this sameness of the destinies of the one (man) and the other (the universe)'.[59] And his various 'technics', such as the Modulor, give evidence of his 'subtlety and astuteness [in] refusing to accept defeat'.[60] But what, with the universe reduced to these conventional measures, does humanity gain? This is absolutely the crux of the matter, the point where Le Corbusier's 'object'-world opens out into that of the 'subject'. Le Corbusier recollects a lecture by Hans Kayser in the 1951 'Divine Proportion' conference in Milan, in which he discussed the worth of these epistemological conventions:

> Present-day society is faced with the inexorable fatality of a collectivism which threatens more and more to submerge it. Total absorption of the individual by his profession, by his duties towards the collective, by the ever-growing difficulties which undermine any attempt to think calmly. In this deafening noise of our era it is time to use powerful counterweights if one wants to prevent mankind being reduced to the existence of termites by the scourge of anti-personalism. Quiet work, away from interference and without aspiration towards the outward world, could make such a counterweight . . .
>
> In the pervading chaos, Kayser offers a sanctuary to man. In this direction, on this ground, we are once again – happily – far from the conference table; once again, we are men.[61]

Of crucial importance is the way this passage has moved us from a discussion of breaking up the continuity of the natural universe, to that of breaking up the continuity of some social collective. External reality, be it social or natural, is something that must be reduced to a conventional order so that it may be escaped. When represented in this way, we understand that the Modulor is also intended to settle matters with our most abstract milieu: space and the universe. The Modulor exhibits the same priorities as we saw with Le Corbusier's social and political commitments:

it ends with the redemption of the individual from his environment, from
that which would liquidize him.[62] It is the 'counterweight' to save us from
'anti-personalism'.

A building or a city built in accordance with the Modulor would automatically cast these epistemological paradigms in concrete.[63] This would
provide an environment that is intended to be grasped easily as an object
of knowledge. In a world convulsed by the new sciences, Le Corbusier
would provide a city that reproduces edges, surfaces and volumes in accordance with long-established ways of understanding space. The regularity
here would allow of no uncertainty, but should one doubt it, confirmation was easily obtained. Le Corbusier makes provision for little hillocks
throughout his cities from which 'unexpected perspectives' can be viewed.
And perfectly straight, cross-city highways would without fail return the
doubter to his prior knowledge of perspectivally exact space. The caption
to one of Le Corbusier's meticulous Ville Contemporaine persepectives
reads as follows: 'Suddenly light is shed on the problem: three-dimensional
city planning'[64] (fig. 9). This effect was also provided by the arrangement
of windows in the interior of Ozenfant's studio in Paris, which Le Corbusier designed and built in 1923–4.[65]

Moreover, Le Corbusier's cities would be encased in glass. But what
exactly would an observer standing in front of one of these windows see?
The answer is nothing. Imagine yourself in a top-floor apartment of one
of the 'set-back' housing blocks. The walls are soundproofed, the neighbours cannot be heard, and conditioned air means that the windows are
sealed shut. The immense window taking up an entire side of the apartment promises a magnificent view, but the view directly down reveals only
the tops of trees, and one knows little of the activities that might be going
on below; while the view directly across reveals only a solid wall of apartment blocks at up to four hundred metres distance.

The only image that this city would signify to its inhabitants is that of
a world that had been set to order. But this did not represent a love of
order in and for itself. This city is a mechanism dedicated to demonstrating beyond all doubt the lack of all interest and meaning in exterior
phenomena. Even if one went outside for a stroll, one would find this
confirmed. Le Corbusier provides a revealing vignette of this scenario:
'Readers, try to walk in that new city and try to benefit.'[66] This 'reader'
would be disappointed: while standing in the middle of it, he would barely

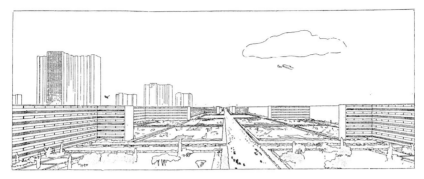

9   Le Corbusier. 'Suddenly light is shed on the problem: three-dimensional city planning.'
From Le Corbuier, *Cité contemporaine pour 3 millions d'habitants*, 1922. Plan FLC 30827. © FLC

be able to find Le Corbusier's city. This city would dematerialize. At the
most obvious level, to look up, one would notice that the buildings are
hidden behind a screen of trees. But also, more subtly, the main adminis-
trative and commercial skyscrapers are completely clad in glass, and the
apartment blocks very substantially so. The only function Le Corbusier
attributes to his glass is that of 'reflecting': it does not afford the glance
free passage through to the interior, but rather reflects the surrounding sky
and foliage. If one could glimpse a building through the trees, one would
only see more trees in reflection. The city therefore vanishes into the elements. One cannot even find the city by holding one's gaze at eye level:
the buildings have been lifted up on *pilotis*, and one sees only unobstructed
lawn and parkland, spreading from one horizon to the other. Again, as in
the apartment, nothing can seen or heard: 'Healthy air, almost noiseless.
You can no longer see any buildings! . . . There is absolute quiet. Where
would noise come from?' And if by some fluke one is successful in
glimpsing the city, one would have to conclude that everything is '*the same
. . . the same*'.[67] Le Corbusier provided a series of sketches of city views,
in which almost nothing of the city is visible.[68]

These cities are visually unengaging, and neither do they engage any of
our other senses.[69] But this is not some fault of which Le Corbusier was
unaware. In my opinion, these cities are intended as a self-fulfilling
prophecy of the fact that the environment should be considered meaningless and of little interest. External reality should not be our foremost
concern. Once the stroller had recognized this, he could return to his her-

metic cell where he is 'completely shut off'.[70] The promise is of 'total
silence and total solitude . . . The house is sealed fast!'[71] Once back inside,
one might pursue:

> An elevated activity: to manage, by means of those stimulants which for
> us are the achievements of life – that is, music, books, the creations of
> the spirit – to lead a life that is truly one's own, truly oneself. That
> means a life that is *individual*; and thus *the individual is placed on the highest
> level, the only level*, but detached from the secondary level of his tools.
> These activities of the spirit, this introspection, which can delve only a
> little way, or very deeply, is life itself, that is, one's internal life, one's
> true life. So in no sense has life been killed, thank God! And neither
> has the individual.[72]

To conclude this chapter: Le Corbusier wanted to present external reality
in terms of some kind of 'conventional' knowledge, in such a way that it
could be provisionally understood, given the absence of real certainty. His
approach to form and proportion, first in his Purist period and later in
the Modulor, allowed this 'knowledge' to be made manifest in the physical structure and visual impact of his architectural and urban designs especially. This knowledge, and the city buildings that represented it, were
somehow instrumental. They were not an end in themselves, but merely
prepared the ground for something more important to happen. As such,
they were as discreet and self-effacing as possible. The only visual or symbolic interest they projected was that of a world reduced to conventional
order. This notion of an unobtrusive, almost invisible city goes against the
popular tendency to consider Le Corbusier's cityscapes as among the most
monolithic and imposing in urban history.

But where did all this end? Let's return to a point raised in the
Modulor: 'Nothing exists except what is deep within us, and the
"Modulor" only does the housework, no more.'[73] External reality as a
whole must be ordered. This relates not only to efficiency and productivity, as we saw in the first section, but also to making external reality
understandable. Both of these 'allowed' the individual to begin searching
for more substantial realities within. It is crucial in this light that Le Corbusier considered 'architecture' and 'metaphysics' to be 'Two consecutive
phenomena: the one overtakes the other, and passes it.'[74] Architecture first;

metaphysics second. Consequently, Le Corbusier limits his own professional responsibility: 'I do not and never shall deny that there is a metaphysical science linked to a thousand and one meanings. But I am a man concerned with building.'[75] It seems that Le Corbusier provides only one half of the whole scenario. He does not presume to provide a meaningful environment for his imaginary populace; rather, he provides an environment that does not distract them from the search for their own, inner meaning. This all appeared to rest upon a distinctly pre-modernist notion of 'subject' and 'object', one which persisted in considering them radically separate and susceptible to different kinds of understanding, and which valued them differently.[76]

This approach to gaining knowledge of the external world remained unchanged throughout Le Corbusier's life. In his sketchbook of 1961, he pondered the nature of the museum as the container and symbol of the current state of knowledge. When presented in the traditional structure of 'dome', 'pediment', 'colonnade' and 'façade', there is a tendency for knowledge and museum to be '<u>cherished respected adored</u>'. But Le Corbusier resolves that knowledge is only about '<u>knowing the present contingency</u>'. It can never be definitive, merely having a *functional* role in society: 'The <u>Museum</u> is <u>part</u> of <u>the contemporary tool-kit</u>.' Consequently, he proposes making new electronic museum–laboratories dedicated to '<u>scientific decision-making</u>'. As knowledge was unstable and ever-developing, these museums would be capable of 'unlimited growth'.[77] I believe this general approach is attributable to the early influence of Poincaré.

Chapter 6

Ozenfant's Impasse

I want to end this section with a discussion of Ozenfant's opinions on these issues. There are three reasons for this: first, because it underscores how issues of knowledge and selfhood were considered important by this section of the avant-garde; second, because it helps us begin to understand the intellectual differences between Ozenfant and Le Corbusier, which have not to my knowledge been treated in the secondary literature; and third, because looking at Ozenfant's 'rejection' of Pascal provides a richer sense of what was at stake when Le Corbusier 'adopted' him. By speculating upon Le Corbusier's adoption of this and related ways of thought, it is possible to access the central features of his system.

What is meant by Ozenfant's 'rejection' of Pascal? Ozenfant's *Foundations of Modern Art*, published in 1928, is an attempt to gain certainty in knowledge by scrutinizing the merits and disadvantages of various approaches.[1] It is a rich and complicated book, which could be considered a book about 'art' only if approached superficially. Different ways of gaining knowledge are all tangled up together by Ozenfant, successively endorsed, rejected and resurrected. Finally, however, he is forced into a submission of defeat: he concedes mankind's ineradicable ignorance.[2] But along the way, Ozenfant tortures himself about what it would mean to take Pascal's advice: is it any longer valid to find certainty in the sacred, and in the self? Different answers to this question invoke different concepts of what it is to be human in the modern world. A brief outline of Ozenfant's dilemma will clarify his relationship with Le Corbusier.

Initially, he demands that the 'distractions' of contemporary life and art be replaced by 'the fundamental "constants" of humanity'.[3] Ozenfant characterizes 'distractions' as all those pointless needs and activities that prevented humanity from thinking about its wretchedness, ignorance and fear of death. 'Constants', in turn, are discussed in terms of the biological 'tropisms' that draw organisms towards certain stimuli necessary for their survival, such as that which draws plants to the light.[4] Later, Ozenfant refines this into the '*Theory of Preforms*', according to which we are all filled with certain needs or 'preforms' which demand that the corresponding 'form' be provided:

> Are not our needs and the fulfilling facts comparable to a moulding and its symmetrical mould? Similarly: the relationship between lovers, and between the first member of an equation and the second member which satisfies it, etc. Are not our known and unconscious needs a set of negative *structures*?
>
> When the positive structure is unveiled, the pre-existence in us of the coinciding negative structure is *revealed*.

The forms provided by 'ART', which is understood as including the more obvious visual arts as well as philosophy, science, religion and so on, must provide the interlocking positive structures. It is a type of revelation of knowledge that is already 'known' within us, albeit in negative form.[5] 'It reveals our gods', Ozenfant says, 'physical, metaphysical'.[6]

Knowledge is therefore a matter of form, and the more abstract this form is, the more effectively it satisfies our preforms. Architecture and music are consequently the foremost means of attaining such knowledge, but in painting Purism leads the field. In dealing with the objective aspects of things, it circumvents the limitations of culturally specific meaning systems. 'Every form', we are told, 'has its specific mode of expression (the language of plastic) independent of its purely ideological significance (the language of the sign).' The one is a 'cryptogram', whose 'key' must be learned and meaning deciphered or 'projected'. While the other is 'categorical' and 'compelling': it 'imposes its imperious edict upon us'.[7]

This is the ideal: direct access to knowledge through form. And this knowledge fulfils a need within each human being, interlocking with and effectively completing the individual. Also important is that it frees the individual from meaningless 'distractions'. But something in this appears to trouble Ozenfant, and by worrying over it he undermines himself almost entirely. Recalling Poincaré, he says that these constants come to us through the mediation of various epistemological conventions or 'modalities'. Although only approximations, these are as close as we can get to an understanding of the world:

> What is important is to be able, even remotely, to intuit or feel certain constants. It matters little whether they be arithmetical, geometrical, logarithmical, or appertain to some other system: the important thing is that they should be present. If they are, even though too uncertain to constitute a precise technic, yet they will be certain enough to fecundate a trend, a spirit, an ethic, an aesthetic.[8]

Initially, this appears not to be a problem for Ozenfant: humankind has never done anything other than propose and substitute one more or less inadequate convention for another, be it scientific, artistic or religious:

> Causality and determinism are mere words. Words often deceive us. They lead us to suppose they must stand for reality, when they often merely adorn lay figures. As peremptory as a fiat from the Vatican, they go back to a time when Man believed he knew something, and that, some day, he would know all: they are the moulds in which faith is stored . . . God, in such an event, would be a creation of mankind, a dressing for a perpetual wound, a stop-gap for a hole in our souls.[9]

Ozenfant seems to consider this process of introducing conventions to be inevitable, and given his debt to Poincaré this is not surprising:

> Man is unable to perceive the universe except through the geometric filter of his sensations. Nothing can move us but what is adapted to the perceiving of our brains. When we become aware of phenomena which are not directly perceptible, it is because some intermediary apparatus has adapted them to our organs. Establishing a fact is equivalent to adapting its structure to our own.[10]

In this way, the 'apparent chaos' of the universe is provisionally reduced to humankind's measure. No longer overwhelmed by their ignorance or fear, people can get on with the business of civilization well enough.[11] Again, it is 'art' – be it philosophy, religion, science or art proper – that communicates these conventions.

But closer attention reveals Ozenfant's unease. He is not unequivocally committed to the conventionalist philosophy, and is troubled that it can apparently never end in certainty: 'truth in its essence must necessarily escape us', and we must become 'resigned to our basic ignorance'.[12] Speaking of science, he says that it does not proceed by degrees to an increasingly complete body of knowledge and 'ultimate' or 'definitive' truth. On the contrary, 'Science is a palliative to our need to know. The Bread the scientist offers us is not the pure flour of truth, but still it is eatable and tastes good.' Earlier scientific conventions can therefore never be superseded or bettered in any real terms. We merely substitute new 'themes' and 'modalities', almost like fashions, so it does not really matter which ones we choose to indulge. All such conventions are now understood not to offer any real knowledge, but merely to be tricks for temporarily offsetting our ignorance. Ancient conventions might serve equally well in soothing us as our modern ones: 'many so-called antiquated theories, even when contradictory, are poems which assuage'. Accordingly, science 'set out to say the final word, and has instead become one of the arts of illusion. Its creations are but eloquent similitudes.'[13]

We remember that, initially, Ozenfant criticized modern life for its distractions, and sought to replace them with 'constants' which fulfilled an inner longing. These constants were the knowledge-forms which interlocked with the 'preforms' within each human being. But after consideration, this 'knowledge' was revealed to be, at best, a matter of flimsy and changeable conventions, and these conventions merely served to distract humanity from its 'basic ignorance' in a manner that was indistinguishable from those initial distractions from which Ozenfant wanted to escape. But can certainty be found anywhere? Ozenfant refused to give up the hunt. He believed that in modern times this question becomes especially acute, for the increase in leisure time provided by technology would soon force people to think about the more important metaphysical issues. There would simply not be enough distractions to keep them occupied all the time. At this point, Ozenfant effectively opened the door for Le Corbusier, while refusing to go through it himself.

Conceive the frightful emotional and intellectual situation of future humanity, with nothing to do and brains more questioning than ever before. The masses will find themselves in the frightful waste that Nero knew, despite the succour of science, which no longer attempts to explain: and with no help from faith. Possibly there will be attempts to believe. But can the wish suffice? *Will they stultify themselves to believe?* It becomes difficult to do so when one has had time to think. Did Pascal succeed? He died, rather mad, of terror and despair.

The remark about Pascal's fate is not true, but Ozenfant is making a polemical point: any search for certainty in the sacred is insane.[14] Speaking of the heroic attempts to understand the universe through scientific reason, he further remarks that 'the nineteenth century experienced very little of the torment of the physicist Pascal, who forced himself to have faith, realising the terrible snares that lay in wait for man in that sterile solitude where science awaited him'.[15] Reason, having failed as 'conventionalism', seems to point towards an alternative approach that must now succeed. But, crucially, religion is no longer capable of providing us with certainty either:

> as nothing in the universe can help us truly to prove anything whatever, and consequently to demonstrate the falsity of a religious belief, silence is best. Believe who can, that is all that can be said. Faith is impervious to criticism. To believe is to feel there is an absolute, and he who believes knows. It is a question of Grace. The Jansenists were right. That is why on Sundays I often turn my 5 h.p. in the direction of Port-Royal-des-Champs (the high plateau of which serves as an aerodrome for the Farman Company), in the vague hope of somehow finding faith or, failing which, its illusion, among the wings that float about the sky, miraculously almost.

Pascal was affiliated with the Jansenists of Port-Royal, as we shall see. But Ozenfant now suggests that any belief in 'such a transcendental reality' can arise only if one is prepared to 'Stultify oneself (Pascal's way out)'.[16] When the modern man looks up to find God, however, and if he has strength to be honest with himself, he sees only aeroplanes.

Ozenfant 'resolves' the dilemma of our fruitless search for certainty in an unexpected way: he demands that we liquidate our sense of individuality. This is his reasoning: our lingering belief that we are autonomous beings encourages us to think too highly of ourselves, and it is only this individual hubris that leads us to believe we have any right to certainty regarding the big metaphysical questions. If we do not want to continue suffering in this way, it is therefore better that we forgo those claims to individuality which lie at the root of our suffering. Individuality is effectively a disease, the cause of our symptoms. But to cut it away should not be too painful an operation, because autonomous selfhood, Ozenfant maintains, is a delusion in any case.

This is a dramatic conclusion, and clearly deserves attention. With art, science and religion failing to give us certainty, where is it to be found? Ozenfant suggests that we can achieve certainty only through thoughtless immersion in the present moment.

> the only absolute reality is the sensating of the present. I FEEL THERE-FORE I AM . . . The might of the present! That is certitude itself . . . Truth is the particular sentiment of trueness each of us may have . . . And since our ideas as to the relative values of all things are now clear, is not that a certitude gained and a stable basis found at last? . . . We were seeking certitude: now at last we find it in the conviction that neither logically nor scientifically can we ever acquire it. That itself is a certitude. Let us make it our foundation.[17]

But this moment in which we concede to our ignorance is like a 'mosquito sting', so painful that it must be avoided. Therefore those 'arts' which initially were meant to uncover our constants are, through their failure, recommissioned into distracting us from this one unendurable certainty:

> Art is actual, it is a reality intercepting that other reality, pain. A narcotic, but a salubrious one. Beneficent euphoria! . . . I have always defined the object of art as the easing the pain of reality, the helping us to EVADE reality.[18]

We recognize our puniness in the face of the universe, which ends in complete self-effacement: 'our blind egocentricity corrects itself, because we see where we stand in the ensemble of things . . . and then our gaze must turn within, upon our own abyss, in search of that ineffable axis which is the abscissa of the vast Whole'.[19] 'Art' must return us to this state: 'The great forces of art dominate and silence in us the chatter of our passing individuality and recall us to the sense of our pettiness: thus for a time they deliver us from the burden of ourselves . . . they make us forget ourselves.'[20] It would seem that the only way to deal with our ignorance and insignificance, which are irremediable, is by fully effacing our sense of self and with it our questioning nature.

This is a convoluted and troubled set of reflections, but we can sum them up as follows. Ozenfant began with the desire to replace the 'Vacillating and the Fashionable' with the 'Universal and the Permanent': 'This book is in favour of "constants" and against the conventions dictated by circumstance.'[21] These constants would replace our various distractions. But Ozenfant was unable to find certainty, not even in the tempting alternative held open by Pascal. So the problem was resolved by positing a new, monolithic distraction: we are to be distracted from that sense of individual selfhood that believes itself worthy of satisfaction in these matters. We are to be 'lost' in some infinitely greater and more important whole, where our self-awareness and the pain it generates are shown to be utterly inconsequential. The 'individual' is recalled to his 'pettiness'. Hopefully, the current 'egotism' and 'anarchy of the Self' through which we fashion ourselves into 'innumerable tiny Phoenixes, all busily preoccupied with their own individualities', might be remedied.[22]

Ozenfant explores the same themes in a more freewheeling form in his diary from 1931–4, *Journey Through Life*.[23] Again, he attacks Pascal and everything that he represents. For example, he states that all attempts at comprehension are inherently 'rationalizing', thus to seek the 'mysterious' is merely to indulge in 'naive rationalism': 'We take our attempts at comprehension for mystic flights. See Pascal.'[24] Rather than admit their ignorance, feeble-minded people like Pascal contrive some mysterious second tier of knowledge. And knowledge of the self as some discrete unit is again abandoned by Ozenfant:

> It is curious to think of oneself . . . as pierced, constantly, by cosmic rays and wireless rays, and to reflect that nothing in ourselves and nothing in anything actually adheres to any other thing. Talk of the abhorred void! That is what we are — empty forces and an empty universe, my dear old Pascal.[25]

More generally, this is an attack on a 'dualist' approach to the world: the division of matter and spirit is just a conceit to cover our inability to comprehend certain phenomena.[26] With his theory of a 'hypermaterial' universe, Ozenfant reduces all phenomena to a 'play of waves' at different frequencies. Thus he is able to conclude this book more optimistically than the last. For the moment, we appear able to comprehend only those waves that vibrate at a frequency amenable to our senses and intellectual apparatus, but given the fact that the universe is 'singular', it is only a matter of refining these in order to comprehend the whole system:

> The quality of a product can be measured. From steel to thought, everything in the world is a play of waves. Once we are satisfied that our entire physical and moral being is a play of waves and that our sensations, ideas and feelings are effects of the same unifying phenomenon, I see no reason for declaring, a priori, that we shall never be able to measure them . . . And so by a curious 'looping' we have arrived at a generalised materialism which is really an *immaterialism* . . . Can floundering humanity be dragged out of the debilitating marshes of dogmatic religiosity by the great tractor of materialism? Certainly it can, if Matter is understood in the sense I have given it. It is the starting-point of an *all-wave philosophy* – we might call it *Hypermaterialism* – which will form the basis of the mystic Gospel of immaterialism: an immaterialist materialism.

The attempts to read the wave-forms that are produced by human beings by assessing 'the reactions of works of art on the sentient subject', might have failed so far; but 'no doubt it is only a matter of discovering a suitable apparatus'.[27] Ozenfant therefore concludes with 'a very pleasing form of Monism'.[28] Everything and everyone is made up of interpenetrating waves that one day might be understood fully.

This is linked to a demand for the artist to develop a coherent socio-political consciousness and commitment, and Ozenfant discusses the steps of his own socialist awakening from the mid-1920s onwards, strongly condemning those artists who refuse to engage. I think this can be taken as an attack on Le Corbusier:

> The artist, as a man, must inevitably share the common fate. Yet some, disgusted by the social impotence and ugliness of present-day conditions, shut themselves up. They think they can serve their art by isolating themselves. We see them suffocating, morally speaking, in the

horrible glass bell of the airpump. Their work is obviously useless, out of touch with everything.[29]

Ozenfant accordingly gives up the 'private laboratory work' of early Purism.[30] Similarly, he abandons the 'theatrical divinities' and 'antiquated symbols' of the first, 'mythological' stage of his painting, *Life*.[31]

From the mêlée of these two books, Ozenfant appears to come to two different conclusions: *Foundations of Modern Art* ends in a despair of unknowing, the individual rendered inconsequential and helpless; *Journey Through Life* reopens the possibility of gaining knowledge, with the individual now understood as being of the same order of phenomena as the 'waves' which interpenetrate it. But most important, and what both books hold in common beyond their explorations of epistemology, is the eradication of the individual as an autonomous entity. Individuality is abolished as the worst kind of delusion and conceit. This feeds into a 'collectivist' politics in an obvious way. The affinities with Léger are also obvious, and it is worth noting that he and Ozenfant opened their joint art school in 1925, the year when Ozenfant and Le Corbusier split acrimoniously.

Ozenfant differed from Le Corbusier here on every point. Le Corbusier was not worried that his knowledge of 'external' reality was merely conventional. We have seen this in the case of the Modulor. The world was at best to be provisionally understood and ordered so that it stopped being a matter of concern. It was certainly not to be agonized over, and certainly not to the extent that, in order to avoid this agony, one had to liquidate the sense of individual selfhood that sustained it. Nor was the individual to be 'understood' in the same terms as all other phenomena, such as in the 'play of waves'. The Modulor seemed to 'end' with the individual's pursuit of some more substantial knowledge of himself in solitude. And Le Corbusier's post-Purist painting, pursued in the 'horrible glass bell' and displaying those 'antiquated symbols' criticized by Ozenfant, points to the same thing.

Given that so much of Ozenfant's position was symbolized by his rejection and ridicule of Pascal, we have to begin to think seriously about what Le Corbusier meant by the following statements:

And since leisure will require a man to spend more time in his room (Pascal's *desideratum*) a new concept of home will arise . . . Again and always, I repeat, we must be vigilant, for the whole of our lives and every minute we must be ready to seize the miracle which lies latent in all things. It seems that Pascal, also, said this to Christians, which only goes to prove how right he always was.[32]

Again, what did he mean by favourably citing Pascal on 'The despair that, always, results for men from the inability to remain long enough in their own rooms'?[33] These statements give an intriguing indication that Le Corbusier subscribed to a fundamentally different philosophy of selfhood than Ozenfant.

In the first section, we saw how Le Corbusier sought to use his cities to put order into society and politics, so that people no longer had the opportunity of participating in them. In this second section, we have seen him doing something different yet related. Again, he appears to be attempting to put the world in order, but in more abstract terms as an object of knowledge. He prefers to attribute a 'conventional' epistemological order to the world, rather than risk the uncertainties of the rest of the avant-garde, who were fascinated by the new sciences. The point of this, it seems, was that as the world could never be definitively known, one should settle for the most convenient paradigm. By doing so, the individual was freed to search for more substantial knowledge within himself. We also tried to read evidence of this epistemological standpoint into Le Corbusier's Purist paintings, Modulor proportional system and ideal cities.

This enabled us to appreciate how Le Corbusier differed from those ordinarily considered to be his closest intellectual peers. Both Ozenfant and Léger explored the idea of the intimate enmeshment of the individual and his milieu, although they did it in different ways. Ozenfant allowed himself to be torn in all directions by the hypothetical search for certainty, and concluded not only that it was impossible to have knowledge of the world and of the self, but also that we should liquidate our individualities to prevent us from asking such futile questions. He later said that the individual should content himself with anonymity in some cosmic continuum. More simply, Léger was excited by the experience of urban modernity, with its dissonant clash of energy and signs. He considered the individual to be an integral part of this flux of experience. In fact, the exterior milieu interpenetrated the individual so completely that he could no longer distinguish himself from it. Léger aspired to 'be a sensibility completely subject to the new state of things', creatively adjusting himself to all these 'external manifestations'.[34] But despite their different approaches, both Léger and Ozenfant welcomed the end of the 'individual-as-king' – the extinguishing of 'tiny Phoenixes'. Beyond the more abstract and existential reasons that can be adduced, this standpoint was also tied to the collectivist nature of their politics.

Everything we have seen with Le Corbusier suggests that he wanted the exact opposite.[35] He sought to preserve individuality as something sacred, which was to be achieved by making the individual less dependent upon his exterior milieu. In the final section, 'Pascal's *Desideratum*', we shall enter fully into the spiritual and selfhood side of the equation.

Part III
'Pascal's *Desideratum*'

Preface

It is now possible to explore in more detail the origins, terms, dynamics and consequences of Le Corbusier's concept of self.

Mysticism and occultism have been acknowledged as central to much of modernist art and literature. In fact, the general picture that emerges is that it would be unusual for an artist not to have some connection with them.[1] But when the subject is broached in relation to Le Corbusier's 'private' iconographic paintings, which seem to have some kind of esoteric content, one of two things tends to happen. Either this esotericism is accepted enthusiastically and uncritically, which leads to gross over-interpretation. Or else it is smoothed over as something of an embarrassment to Le Corbusier – a regrettable idiosyncrasy in an otherwise logical mind.

In the former camp, it is maintained that Le Corbusier's private work was a departure from Purism, representing an attempt to forge 'an extremely personal iconographic system'. I think this is generally correct, but the results have been frustrating. In order to understand Le Corbusier's iconography, attempts are made to establish links with the astrological, occult, mythological and religious iconographies of mankind throughout history. Predictably, this generates such complex and allusive explanations that little can be concluded with certainty, although *certainty* in these cases seems almost taboo. Moon goddesses, solar bulls, mercurial waters, hermaphrodites, cosmic eggs and perceptive nipples all feature much more heavily than is warranted.[2] Commentators exult in the advantages of this approach, while in fact pointing out its chief drawback: 'The possibilities for this type of interpretation are endless . . . the analogical speculation begins to run away with itself.'[3]

This justifiably leads to scepticism and a refusal to become entangled in iconography. Green, for example, maintains that there is no mysterious content in these later images, and attempts to incorporate them within his formalist thesis. The 'subject-matter' of these symbols may be 'unexpected' and 'unknown', but they 'were never to be taken as the obscure traces of hidden systems of meaning'. Instead, says Green, Le Corbusier was simply trying to extend his vocabulary of forms. These impenetrable images therefore *meant* nothing, they had no content: they were 'forms released from the usual function of sign and symbol, and *by their release* made available to architecture'.[4] Tim Benton is simply damning: he gives little credence to these mystical pretensions. After a study of mystical, alchemical and Jungian texts during the Second World War, Le Corbusier 'embarked on a number of overtly "poetic" statements . . . in which he tried to formulate his very personal set of beliefs'. Even so, Benton warns, we should not be duped into taking this too seriously: 'There was clearly a danger here not only of a failure to communicate, but of the growth of an introspective and closed system of belief whose lack of comprehensibility would itself become the proof of his own prophetic destiny.' Much of this material is 'often intentionally mystifying and obstructive . . . Le Corbusier was as capable as anyone of dropping into empty words'.[5] Le Corbusier does rather invite this attack:

> [painting] is a bitter struggle, terrifying, pitiless, unseen; a duel between the artist and himself, the struggle goes on inside, hidden on the surface. If the artist tells, he is betraying himself!'[6]

The approach I want to take for this final section, however, lies between the two. I believe that Le Corbusier's private work did have a genuine mystical or occult content. It was not mere obscurantism or play with forms. But I also believe that this iconography should not be overly indulged: it is full of gaps and blind alleys, and does not form a coherent system. Therefore, I shall not be providing another archaeological analysis and reconstruction of Le Corbusier's iconography, or of the paintings in which it is manifest, but instead will take a much simpler approach. I shall approach this symbolism, or rather its *presence*, as broadly representative of the particular concept of self that Le Corbusier valued, and that he sought to inspire in the honeycombs of his cities.

Pascal has surfaced in various ways throughout this study, so in the seventh chapter, 'Preparing the Machine', I speculate upon the influence of his philosophy, which provides a compelling framework for all the relevant issues. It provides the classic paradigm of the dualism that has been surfacing with increasing clarity throughout our study of Le Corbusier, including the balance of knowledge of external reality with a sacred 'knowledge' of self, their corresponding somehow to public and private space, and their basis in two qualitatively distinct 'languages'. The antisocial underpinning of this system will also become apparent.

Chapter eight, 'Wisdom Builds Its Own House', will consider how Pascal's metaphysic may have been echoed in Le Corbusier's interest in the occult generally, and alchemy in particular. *Le Poème de l'angle droit*, the most important document detailing these concerns, will be of special interest here, as will the popular occultism of Kurt Seligmann and the alchemical psychology of Carl Gustav Jung, which will help redefine our understanding of Le Corbusier's philosophy of selfhood. But apart from clarifying the psychological terms of this, Jung also voices concerns about its dangers.

The final chapter, 'Bataille and Camus: "Vers la limite critique"' will explore these dangers more fully. I shall be relying on Georges Bataille's *The Accursed Share* (1949) and Albert Camus's *The Rebel* (1951), inscribed copies of which were sent to Le Corbusier when he was working on his *Poème*. A close reading of these books reveals that they were arguing broadly in favour of the kind of self upheld by Le Corbusier, but also that they were deeply troubled by its potential dangers. These books were perhaps intended as a warning to Le Corbusier, and the notes he made in his copies suggest that he was not deaf to this.

I consider the association with Camus and Bataille to be especially important. In pointing to the dangers of a self-identity forged in antisocial solitude, they open up the field for what I consider to be an appropriate critique of Le Corbusier and his legacy. I shall suggest briefly how this might be pursued in my conclusion.

Chapter 7

Pascal:
Preparing the Machine

In my opinion, Le Corbusier's philosophy owes a much greater debt to Blaise Pascal than to René Descartes, although it is the latter who seems to figure in the secondary literature as the most significant influence from the Enlightenment era.[1] To my knowledge, no scholar or writer has discussed the influence of Pascal on Le Corbusier. But as has been shown, Le Corbusier employed the escape clause that Ozenfant rejected. So what exactly was 'Pascal's *Desideratum*', and why was Pascal 'always right'?

I shall treat this in three brief sections: the first introduces Pascal's distinction between knowledge of exterior and interior realities, how they must be approached and valued differently, and how they are articulated in different 'languages'. Second, I want to demonstrate that Pascal thought reason was of use only for putting the external world in some provisional order, such that it might cease to distract one from meditation. I also note how this manifested itself in Pascal's opinions about the worth of social contact. Third, I address his demands for solitude and self-knowledge, and show how these issues were manifest in Le Corbusier.

REASON VERSUS PARADOX

Born in 1623, Pascal received his passion for mathematics from his father, who conducted his education personally. This isolation from the contacts of normal schooling intensified an already prodigious intelligence, and by seventeen Pascal began a distinguished career as a mathematician by publishing his first treatise, on conic sections. He also went on to make important contributions to physics, invented a calculating machine and organized the first public-transport system in Paris. But his practical side was complemented by a spiritual one. Unlike many of his peers in the scientific community, Pascal was worried that intellectual advances were causing a spiritual vacuum in humanity. Pascal was deeply devout, the most important event of his life being a personal 'visitation' by Christ in 1654. He also defended the Jansenist movement from papal charges of heterodoxy, which resulted in the *Provincial Letters* of 1656–7.[2]

He began to formulate his spiritual outlook systematically in the *Pensées*, a hotchpotch of notes and essays left in various stages of completion upon his death in 1662. These were intended as a defence of his peculiar and personal religious views against the encroachments of modern science.[3] His main adversary was Descartes, who in his *Discourse on Method* of 1637 maintained that all phenomena could be fully understood by reason. This included the human psyche, which was centred on a '*rational* soul': its tendency to make mistakes and uphold faulty knowledge could be put right simply by recalibrating it according to the 'method'. God's existence was also a matter of rational proof, as verifiable 'as any geometric demonstration can be'.[4]

In response, Pascal made a demonstration of reason's inadequacy, which clearly informed some of the ideas we found Ozenfant toying with. As human beings, said Pascal, we are suspended in a material universe which extends to infinity all around us, beyond the reach of our perception and understanding:

> what is man in nature? A nothing compared to the infinite, a whole compared to the nothing, a middle point between all and nothing, infinitely remote from an understanding of the extremes; the end of things and their principles are unattainably hidden from him in impenetrable secrecy.

Equally incapable of seeing the nothingness from which he emerges and the infinity in which he is engulfed.[5]

But unlike Ozenfant, according to whom knowledge of the whole can be predicted from our knowledge of the 'middle point', Pascal says that not even this middle point is knowable. We have no stable ground upon which to build such knowledge. Howsoever we may strive to find something firm and irreducible, 'to know the principles of things and go on from there to know everything', these remain 'infinitely divisible' and 'never allow of any finality':

> We are floating in a medium of vast extent, always drifting uncertainly, blown to and fro; whenever we think we have reached a fixed point to which we can cling and make fast, it shifts and leaves us behind; if we follow it, it eludes our grasp, slips away, and flees eternally before us. Nothing stands still for us. This is our natural state and yet the state most contrary to our inclinations. We burn with desire to find a firm footing, an ultimate, lasting base on which to build a tower rising up to infinity, but our whole foundation cracks and the earth opens up into the depths of the abyss.[6]

What we know of our universe, then, is merely provisional, and there is consequently no real reason for choosing one explanation over another. Pascal's system dabbles in a kind of conventionalism: 'In the perspective of these infinites, all finites are equal and I see no reason to settle our imagination on one rather than another . . . *Nothing more is ours (what we call ours is by convention).*'[7] In real terms, we remain ignorant.[8] And reason ultimately must concede that it can provide knowledge of almost nothing:

> Reason's last step is the recognition that there are an infinite number of things which are beyond it. It is merely fallible if it does not go as far as to realize that. If natural things are beyond it, what are we to say about supernatural things?[9]

Of course Pascal believed real knowledge *could* be attained, but only of certain things and through certain channels, and these did not include knowledge of the universe through reason and the mind, but only knowledge of God and self through paradox and the heart. It was only this latter 'knowledge' that truly deserved the name.[10] Appropriately, the contents of the mind and the heart were to be articulated through different 'languages', the former being rational and discursive, the latter non-rational, indulging paradox through images and symbols.

For Pascal, this was found in the miraculous and prophetic imagery of Scripture, and one might best prepare oneself for the possibility of grace by pondering upon such imagery. Their obscurity and contradictoriness were intended to work as a deterrent to the wicked and to encourage the dedicated to persevere. Indeed, it was often the actual impossibility of what they said that was considered to provide their surest proof. To be able to believe in these paradoxes was a sign of the individual's spiritual strength. 'Everything that is incomprehensible', says Pascal, 'does not cease to exist.' Such proofs cannot be reasonably disputed, precisely because they are outside the purview of reason.[11]

THE USE OF REASON

This did not mean that reason was useless. It had an important, albeit preliminary, part to play in a larger scheme: 'it is not through the proud activity of our reason but through its simple submission that we can *really know ourselves*'.[12] Although reason could not provide humanity with knowledge directly, it could hold open the possibility of receiving it from elsewhere – from God. The individual could merely prepare himself and wait passively for this, a moment of grace that might or might not occur.[13]

This preparation involved cutting ties with those activities and expectations which distracted one from the 'wretchedness' of one's soul. Whatever satisfaction one did derive from interacting with the external environment, be it through socializing, gambling, whoring, through one's prestige, intelligence or beauty, was only the momentary satisfaction of forgetting one's true condition: 'They have a secret instinct driving them to seek external diversion and occupation, and this is the result of the constant sense of wretchedness.'[14] But there was no real solace in this, 'because it comes from somewhere else, from outside'.[15] None the less, we are driven on an unending treadmill of such pursuits, for even the slightest moment of stop, leaving us alone with our wretchedness, is terrifying. Our dislike of stillness and boredom is at root revealed to be this full-blown metaphysical terror: 'take away their diversion and you will see them bored to extinction. Then they will feel their nullity without recognizing it, for nothing could be more wretched than to be intolerably depressed as soon as one is reduced to introspection with no means of diversion.'[16]

'*Preparing the machine*' is the foremost task of reason.[17] The 'machine' is the human being, and reason 'prepared' it through reasoned arguments about the impossibility of ever finding any satisfaction or stable knowledge outside oneself. But further than this, Pascal demanded that reason be used for the organization – the routinization – of all the remaining, ordinary aspects of life and activity.

A good example of this is the famous 'Wager', in which Pascal attempts to convince his audience that, as it is impossible to establish reasonable proof of God's existence, it is none the less reasonable to place a bet in favour of His existence: 'if you win you win everything, if you lose you lose nothing . . . there is an infinity of infinitely happy life to be won . . . and what you are staking is finite'.[18] Although his audience would hopefully be won over by this certainty, true salvation would only come to a predetermined few. Even so, he encourages them all to adopt the routine of faith, to follow the example of those who

> behaved just as if they did believe, taking holy water, having masses said, and so on. That will make you believe quite naturally, and will make you more docile . . . Now what harm will come to you from choosing this course? You will be faithful, honest, humble, grateful, full of good works, a sincere, true friend.[19]

Although few will enjoy the genuine religious experience, Pascal demands that we be remade as seemingly devout 'automatons'. We must allow our actions to be prescribed by religious 'habit' which 'inclines the automaton'.[20] That is, the automaton is inclined away from all the diversions and distractions of society. With his priorities realigned into waiting for God, the individual becomes machine-like and super-efficient in his social life.

But 'social life' would not persist in any other than the most functional form. Pascal considered all human relations to be pointless, and any kind of interpersonal knowledge and love an impossibility. As we encounter and can judge one another only in terms of external qualities that are constantly shifting, he said, we must remain forever incomprehensible to one another. Asking the question 'What is the self?', he concludes that it is something that cannot be fathomed by or communicated to others.[21] Consequently, he urges us not to become attached to other 'transitory creatures'.[22]

One's social interactions were of no direct consequence or meaning in themselves. When allowed to run wild they were a terrible distraction. But when properly organized by reason they could form the foundations of religious faith.

'PASCAL'S *DESIDERATUM*'

With the individual finally weaned from society, he had ample time to confront the soul's wretchedness in solitude. This is Pascal's *desideratum*: 'I have often said that the sole cause of man's unhappiness is that he does not know how to stay quietly in his room.' Of course, we prefer the forgetfulness of our diversions: 'That is why men are so fond of hustle and bustle; that is why prison is such a fearful punishment; that is why the pleasures of solitude are so incomprehensible.'[23] But we must be made to endure it as a profitable trial-by-fire. We are to imitate the solitude of Christ.[24]

There is an ambiguous quality to the self in Pascal's *Pensées* that he appears to find keenly troubling. Clearly he has a hatred of the notion of the self as some seat of frivolous social pleasure, but the individual's act of turning away from the exterior environment is itself a fresh retreat into and exaltation of the self. The self here acquires a hint of the sacred which Pascal simultaneously relishes and believes to be an affront to God: 'Men, it is in vain that you seek within yourselves the cure for your miseries. All your intelligence can only bring you to realize that it is not within yourselves that you will find either truth or good.'[25] Paradoxically, Pascal advocates a turning towards the self which is simultaneously its 'annihilation':

> as we cannot love what is outside us, we must love a being who is within us but is not our own self . . . and is both ourselves and not ourselves . . . True conversion consists of self-annihilation before the universal being.[26]

On the one hand, then, 'the bias towards self is the beginning of all disorder'; while, on the other, it is the only access to salvation.[27]

Interestingly, those Jansenists that set up their community in Port-Royal-des-Champs just outside Paris became known as the 'solitaries'.[28] This paradox can only be understood if we consider it in terms of the withdrawal of self from immersion in a realm of social and sensual indulgence, and its re-immersion within a sacred one. Even so, it remains an unresolved problem for Pascal that although it is necessary for us to seek this sacred sense of self, it represents a challenge to God and to organized religion, and is profoundly antisocial.[29]

To sum up: for Pascal, reason does not give us access to knowledge, and society does not allow us to live meaningful lives. Reason should be used to give us a provisional understanding of natural phenomena, to put order into our societies, and to help us realize that we can only find real meaning in antisocial solitude. Our life's meaning was somehow accessed through sacred images and paradox, although it rendered us completely incomprehensible to our erstwhile fellow citizens. But even if nothing came of this, the individual would at least be a more effective and considerate automaton. A system geared to the pursuit of sacredness in solitude is underwritten by a 'social life' of the utmost mechanical orderliness.[30]

Pascal only provides one half of the ideal whole: he sets the parameters within which meaning and knowledge may come to the individual. He prepares the machine. Ultimately, the individual must fill out the other half for himself. And the greater his success in this, the further he is taken away from what remains of society. From Descartes's aggressiveness and outright control, then, which dissected the human heart and presumed to recalibrate the individual soul as a matter of method, Pascal's inquiries stopped at the boundaries of the individual. He sought merely to make the individual's heart receptive to its own ineffable meaning.

To recall Le Corbusier's words:

> leisure will require a man to spend more time in his room (Pascal's *desideratum*) . . . we must be vigilant, for the whole of our lives and every minute we must be ready to seize the miracle which lies latent in all things. It seems that Pascal, also, said this to Christians, which only goes to prove how right he always was.[31]

Given our earlier discussion of Le Corbusier's 'scientific' outlook, which is clearly indebted to Pascal as well as to Poincaré, we begin to understand just how much is revealed by these lines. Probably referring to Descartes's treatment of the human heart, Le Corbusier mentions 'Those who dissect but do not see: knowledge through reason'. Against this, he sets 'Illumination'.[32] Pascal's system, which demonstrates how these two halves are meant to work together, provides the key for unlocking Le Corbusier's dualism. It shows that his cities, so widely considered to be the ultimate objectives of his ideals, were merely a preparatory ground. Once completed, they would compel the individual to turn his attentions within, simultaneously within the private cell and within his soul. In the end, 'a basic human need had to be fulfilled, that of personal solitude. When the door is shut, I can freely enter my own world.'[33] On the subject of distractions, Le Corbusier raved:

> Then *background noise* to fill in the holes, the emptiness. Musical noise, coloured noise, embroidered noise or batiked noise. A low volume of noise, a high volume of noise, reading the newspaper (description of the actions of others), cinemas, dance-halls, Pigalle's . . . in order to get away from oneself, never be alone. 'If I were to come face to face with my soul (fearful thought)? What would I say to it? Watch out!'
>
>   Thus they keep their distractions on the go to avoid having to face themselves.[34]

Exactly like Pascal, Le Corbusier's individual must not be allowed to evade the wretched condition of his soul with distractions.[35]

To discuss these issues any further, however, one has to come to grips with the paradox that A. J. Krailsheimer has identified in Pascal: 'Pascal is thus in the paradoxical position of appealing to reason in order to communicate truths which, on his own showing, are outside its province.'[36] Le Corbusier likewise cannot speak directly about this other side, though it is possible to locate a few more clues that seem to point in this direction.

But in my opinion, the crucially important point is how Pascal's model, although ending in a concept of selfhood that was fundamentally antisocial, was built upon a social order of the utmost mechanical orderliness. People were to become machine-like, their interactions strictly regulated and predictable, so as to prepare them for spirituality. This, I think, provided the germ for the mechanical orderliness of Le Corbusier's cities. It also led him to qualify his controversial statement that the house was 'a machine for living in' by saying that 'living' itself was not machine-like:

But when I say 'living' I am not talking of mere material requirements only. I admit certain important extensions which must crown the edifice of man's daily needs. To be able to *think*, or meditate, after the day's work is essential. But in order to become a centre of creative thought, the home must take on an absolutely new character . . . *the reason for living* . . . [is] the most beautiful of subjects.[37]

For the remainder of this section, I am going to investigate more precisely how the general concept of self and the sacred that was found in Pascal was made manifest in Le Corbusier's work. Although it was twisted in several ways, the underlying paradigm remains that of Pascal.

Chapter 8

'Wisdom Builds
Its Own House'

In this chapter, I shall first analyse Le Corbusier's *Le Poème de l'angle droit*, particularly in terms of its alchemical symbolism, and also note Le Corbusier's interest in the occult generally, which I attribute to the considerable influence of Kurt Seligmann during this period. I shall then introduce Carl Gustav Jung's work on alchemical psychology, another body of work that was highly topical at this time. Jung provides the link between occultism and an elaborate psychological model of selfhood, and it is useful to look at this in order to understand what may have been the psychological dynamics of Le Corbusier's model.

Every point from now on is predicated upon Le Corbusier's belief that one's identity could only be forged in opposition to the dominant conventions of society, which I have demonstrated in the previous chapters. The alchemical material offers a fresh, albeit increasingly extreme, variation on Pascal's metaphysic. These are the qualities that would have made it attractive to Le Corbusier.

Alchemy and *Le Poème de l'angle droit*

THREE ALCHEMICAL THEMES

Le Poème de l'angle droit, which contains visual images as well as verse, is of special interest because it comprises the most complete compendium of Le Corbusier's personal iconography, which appears only in fragmented form elsewhere. The closest anything comes to the comprehensiveness of the *Poème* is the mural Le Corbusier painted in the refectory of his Pavillon Suisse in 1948, and this contains a mere four of the nineteen separate scenes that make up the *Poème* – neither does it contain any text.[1] I shall therefore limit my analysis of Le Corbusier's iconography to the *Poème*.[2] It is, however, a complex and allusive document, and can be manipulated to support almost any reading. Le Corbusier enjoyed this obscurity, and probably cultivated it deliberately.[3] With this in mind, we need to proceed cautiously.

The *Poème* was allegedly composed over seven years, from 1947 to 1953, and this is intended to be significant; for the poem itself is arranged into seven 'levels', 'A' through 'G'.[4] This is no conventional poem. It is subdivided into levels, each of which represents a particular colour-coded 'theme'; and each level is further subdivided into free-form mini-poems of varying number and length that explore their relative themes. These mini-poems seem both to stand independently, and also to contribute enriching facets to the particular level in which they are situated. The themes are as follows: 'milieu' (environment), 'esprit' (spirit), 'chair' (flesh), 'fusion', 'caractères' (characters), 'offre – la main ouverte' (offering – the open hand) and 'outil' (tool). To complicate matters further, each mini-poem is handwritten, with the few lines of each page weaving around a multitude of cryptic images which at times reflect the text and at others seem completely arbitrary. More important, in terms of the poem's visual impact, each mini-poem is headed by an emblematic lithograph.

Le Corbusier presents this schema in terms of an '*iconostase*', in which can be seen the seven thematic levels and the individual lithographs relating to each mini-poem. The iconostasis functions as an unhelpful table of contents, but also as a literal iconostasis: these lithographs were meant to be detached from the text of the *Poème* and assembled upright into a structure approximately seven feet high and five feet wide[5] (fig. 10). Le

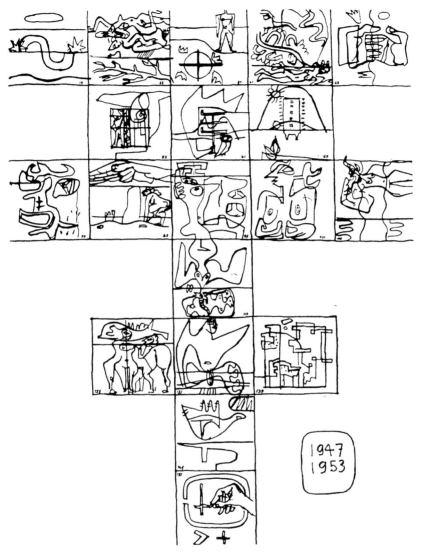

10   Le Corbusier. Scheme of '*iconostase*', from *Le Poème de l'angle droit* (1955), 1989. Iconostase.
© FLC

Corbusier had been fascinated with the mystique and power of the icons and icon-screens encountered during his voyage through the Near East. The following is his description of the church of the Monastery of Filotheou:

> There are ex-votos or acts of faith, all probably in intentional or symbolic order, with each scene occupying its hierarchical place, and what's more, each subject and each figure painted to a predetermined size and scale in accordance with some strong, subtle meaning . . . Add to this an iconostasis sparkling with its gold between the marble paving and the triumphal arch, hiding behind the wall all the legends of the Passion and isolating the secret of the apse. But being too tired (or not methodical enough), we visitors too hurried and too distracted, did not examine these invaluable museums of Byzantine painting. Rather we often railed against the horrible restorations, turning our backs to the painted book open before our eyes, whose every page merited understanding and love.

These youthful sentiments were ratified by being published so late in Le Corbusier's life. I think they were intended as a warning that we should take Le Corbusier's iconostasis seriously, to approach it as the boundary of his own personal sacrament. It was in the presence of an iconostasis that the young Jeanneret first enjoyed the 'the poignant sensation of feeling *absolutely* alone'.[6]

The preparatory notes for the *Poème* offer intriguing glimpses of a fascination with all kinds of symbolism, including the number symbolism of the *iconostase*:

> 4 is the number of solid matter
> 3 [is the number] of divine power
> 4 + 3 = 7 = fulfilment
> . . . = fulfilment of god in matter.[7]

But perhaps no less strange is that Le Corbusier also had a couple of Shakespearean sonnets on his mind when beginning to compose his *Poème*, a bundle of notes dating from 1947 showing what appears to be a keen interest in personally interpreting sonnets 56 and 64.[8] Thematically, the first asks 'Sweet love, renew thy force'; while the second laments 'That Time will come and take my love away'.[9] And at the foot of one of his translations, Le Corbusier wrote:

L'Espace indicible
Space beyond Words.[10]

The notion of 'L'Espace indicible' – 'ineffable space'   is central to the *Poème*. Perhaps, then, it is intended as some strange love poem. But what kind of love can be associated simultaneously with the sacred, and with 'Space beyond Words'? These are the key questions which can help us understand the *Poème* and Le Corbusier's philosophy of selfhood.

We can take our lead from the poem and lithograph located at the dead centre of the iconostasis, 'D.3 fusion', where Le Corbusier introduces alchemy. I believe this to be the keystone of all these poems, and it is useful to quote it at length:

Sitting on too many mediating causes
seated at the side of our lives
and the others there
and everywhere is the: 'No!'
And always more against
than for
Do not then condemn he
who wants to take his part of the
risks of life. Let
the metals fuse
tolerate the alchemists who
besides leave you outside
the cause
It is through the doors of the
open eyes that glances
exchanged have been able to lead to
the violent act of communion . . .
Then we will not be
at rest sitting at the side of our lives.[11]

The first half of this poem seems to demand that we should not let our lives pass by. We must engage in some kind of activity: the individual must 'take his part', even though this involves 'risk'. It also seems to suggest that 'others' may resist or resent those who take such action, but encourages them to refrain from 'condemnation'. After this, there is a clue as to what this activity may be. It involves alchemical fusion, and the plea that it be 'tolerated' is reiterated. But despite the resentment, the goal of this seems to be a new 'communion' of people, even though it is tainted somehow with 'violence'. The poem ends as it began, implying that we must not idle our lives away.

This can be reduced to three central themes: alchemical fusion; the alchemist's assumption of some kind of responsibility for himself; and a plea that this activity be tolerated. I believe these themes are central to the *Poème* and make all the others cohere. More than this, these are probably the three determining concerns in Le Corbusier's entire career: they point to the specific concept of selfhood that he wanted explored by each individual in the cells of his cities. To obtain this crucial meaning, it is necessary to turn these concerns into questions: what is the nature and meaning of the alchemical fusion? What is the nature of the alchemist's responsibility and why is it necessary that he should assume it? And why should any plea for its toleration need to be made – why do people feel resentful of it? After provisionally answering these questions, I shall return to investigate the *Poème* more closely.

SELIGMANN: 'WISDOM BUILDS ITS OWN HOUSE'

A sense of what may have been meant by the above themes can be obtained by examining two contemporary sources relating to alchemy, those of Seligmann and Jung – the first definitely known to Le Corbusier and the second almost inevitably so. We have to do this as Le Corbusier leaves the question open. Here, I shall concentrate on Seligmann's more straightforward account and consult Jung later to understand the psychological connotations.

Alchemy was a popular topic throughout the first half of the twentieth century. It was represented by a good deal of serious historical research, provided the themes and imagery for popular novels, and also began to be re-evaluated along interesting new psychological lines. Predictably, it held great fascination for the avant-garde.[12] Seligmann was the foremost popular authority on occultism for the French avant-garde from the late 1920s onwards, and a quasi-official occultist 'adviser' to the Surrealists especially. He was a fairly important ethnographer and painter, and a collector of original occultist treatises and artefacts. He was well connected within avant-garde circles and orchestrated the relocation of many artists to the United States at the time of the Second World War. He knew and exhibited with Ozenfant and Léger, and it is almost inconceivable that Le Corbusier was unaware of his ideas. Seligmann's *The Mirror of Magic: A History of Magic in the Western World* was published in 1948 and translated into French for 1956. Le Corbusier possessed a copy of this translation, and although this came after his *Poème*, I think we can consider it symptomatic of a set of interests that had existed in him for some time.[13] Besides, Seligmann had been publishing articles for many years before this point, and his book was substantially compiled from these pieces.[14] I do not want to insist that Seligmann had any direct influence upon Le Corbusier, but I think Seligmann's ideas on alchemy are likely to have substantially determined the general atmosphere from which Le Corbusier drew his own.[15] It is worth mentioning that Le Corbusier's brother had introduced him to alchemy early in life.[16]

The largest chapter in Seligmann's book deals specifically with alchemy, and seems to give direct answers to the three questions above. It is revealing that these were of fundamental concern to Seligmann as well as Le Corbusier. According to Seligmann, the alchemist understood all matter to be imperfect. It was composed of the four elements or 'essences' – earth, air, fire and water – but held the potential to evolve slowly towards a state of perfection. This impetus was maintained by the fifth element, or 'quintessence', which, mixed in with the other four, possessed the same generative power as God used to animate the universe. The alchemist sought to assume control and accelerate this process. He began by extracting this quintessence or 'lapis philosophorum' from base matter – the 'prima materia' – and then cleansed this matter of its impurities. This cleansing allowed for the next step, when the quintessense would be fused again with the prima materia, thus effecting its transformation to a higher stage of material perfection. This fusion or 'chymical wedding' took place in a vessel known as the 'vas Hermetis', and the process would be repeated until the seven stages of the work – the 'opus circulare' – were completed: from lead, through various intermediary metals, to gold. Every aspect of this process, the materials, instruments, transformations and so on, were written about symbolically, with the male–female dualism of the 'wedding' being especially important. This practice flowered into an iconographic system of absurd complexity.[17]

This only becomes relevant when it is realized that it represents alchemy in a literal and practical sense. It should be read at another level: although replete with internal metaphor, the entire discipline was itself a symbol for something else. The transformations that the alchemist wrought upon matter were merely the outward symbols of a transformation in the alchemist's spiritual life. The secret vessel in which the fusion was made, although nominally a glass retort, earthenware jug, oven or furnace, 'was nothing more than the alchemist himself'.[18] The marriage of elements with their male–female personifications was symbolic of the achievement of spiritual balance within the alchemist, who became known as 'hermaphrodite' or 'androgyne'.[19] 'Thus the transmutation of base metals into gold', concludes Seligmann, 'was accompanied by another transmutation, that of man, and the seven steps, or stages, of the alchemical process were the symbols decking the path to blessedness.'[20]

Now I can try to answer the questions I posed above. First, what is the nature and meaning of the alchemical fusion? It is the achievement of a particular kind of inner psychic harmony. This feeds directly into the second and third questions: what is the nature of the alchemist's responsibility and why is it necessary that he should assume it? And why should any plea for its toleration need to be made? Alchemical fusion leads to blessedness, but what is crucial about the alchemist's responsibility is that he pursues this salvation as a personal project: the responsibility lies entirely with himself. Consequently, the alchemist is a recluse, minimizing his contacts not only with his external social milieu and its values, but also more drastically turning away from a public religion that he considers unequal to the task of his salvation:

> In all the ramifications of society, alchemy had taken root, yet it did not participate in its life. The alchemists lived in seclusion, *as if protesting tacitly against their environment*. The soul of the alchemist could find no peace in the teachings of the established dogma . . . Wisdom builds its own house, they used to say . . . These 'specialists' were mystics without being orthodox Christians, scientists without following the learning of their time, artisans unable to teach others what they knew. They were sectarians, problem-children of society.[21]

Alchemists were fundamentally antisocial, and sought to carve out value and meaning for themselves, entirely in private and on their own terms.

As this was a spiritual endeavour, the alchemist was considered heterodox and often prosecuted as such. Beyond the reflex of shutting out society, however, the iconography of alchemy was explicitly heterodox and frequently satanic, a debt it owed to Gnosticism.[22] Alchemists were always subject to resentment and persecution, then, but the essential fact of their heterodoxy remained: the desire for self-salvation. Their antisocial stance also remained.[23]

I think this allows a better understanding of what may have been meant by those three themes identified in Le Corbusier's poem 'D.3', and also of the concept of selfhood that was central to his design philosophy. This poem implied that we should seek alchemical fusion as a personal responsibility, and asked that it be tolerated by others. Why? If we follow Seligmann, the alchemical fusion was symbolic of the achievement of perfect spiritual balance. This was a responsibility that the alchemist was obliged to take upon himself as he believed that organized religion could not provide it for him. Meaning was found for oneself in solitude. The demand for toleration of this kind of activity was necessary because the alchemist put himself in a dangerous position with regard to society: his withdrawal involved an implicit criticism of its structures and beliefs – a 'tacit protest'. Add to this the explicit heterodoxy of his iconography, and it is clear that the alchemist opened himself to the possibility of violent reprisal. It was perhaps this that made the venture, as the poem suggests, a 'risk'.

'WHO IS BEELZEBUB?'

With this in mind, I would like to return to Le Corbusier's *Poème* and offer an interpretation. I hope to show that it can be read in terms of a complex metaphor of his entire philosophy, passing from the initial demand for a functional understanding of the world to the ultimate retreat into solitude. Although this highly allusive and obscure material invites over-interpretation, I shall try to avoid it.[24]

In the first level, 'milieu', we see the scientific-conventionalist line played out again. Here, we seem to find humanity attempting to come to some arrangement with the natural universe. Initially, in poem 'A.1', humanity seems overwhelmed by the immensity and power of its milieu. 'The sun' is the 'master of our lives / far off indifferent / He is the visitor – a lord – / he enters our house'.[25] But this visitor seems not to be a

kindly one. 'He' comes only to dictate to us the conditions of our existence, particularly our enslavement under the twenty-four-hour rhythm of
our solar system. This is a 'Punctual machine turning / since time
immemorial'.

> But brutally
> he breaks it twice –
> morning and evening. Continuity
> belongs to him while he
> imposes on us the alternative –
> night and day – the two rhythms
> which rule our destiny:
>> A sun rises
>> A sun sets
>> A sun rises anew.[26]

The sun 'rules our destiny', he 'imposes' his will upon us 'brutally'. The
lithograph of this poem shows the changeless pattern of the sun's movement. So we get a sense of the puniness of humanity, which Le Corbusier
also dramatizes quite comically. The sun, it seems, is rather absent-minded
– or simply 'indifferent' – and has to remind himself every night that what
appear to be 'mould', 'puddles' and 'wrinkles' from his viewpoint are
forests, oceans and mountains from ours:

> In setting goodnight he says
> to this mould (oh trees)
> to these puddles everywhere
> (oh seas) and to our haughty
> wrinkles (Alps, Andes and
> Himalayas). And the lamps
> are lit.[27]

What he takes for 'lamps', we take for stars. Poem 'A.2' confirms the influence of the sun. It is dedicated to showing how the sun heats the oceans
to make possible the condensation of clouds and their movements around
the globe. But the imagery is clearly militaristic, which again was perhaps
intended to demonstrate the hostility of our milieu.[28]

After this, in poem 'A.3', I believe humanity's attempt to seek some
form of *rapprochement* with its milieu is seen. The celestial rhythms betray

the existence of certain natural laws to which man must submit, and use to his advantage. But initially, in the face of such immensity, and unable to understand the nature of space, it seems that there is a tendency to concede defeat:

> The face turned toward the sky
> Considers the space inconceivable
> until now beyond grasp.
> To rest supine to sleep
> – to die
> The back to the soil . . .[29]

Le Corbusier, however, refuses to lie down. The lithograph shows a man standing up in what is probably intended to be defiance of his milieu:

> But I put myself upright!
> Because you are upright
> you are fit for action.
> Upright on the terrestrial plateau
> of things knowable you
> contract with nature an
> act of solidarity: it is the right angle
> Upright in front of the sea vertical
> There you are on your legs.[30]

The man seems to find in nature a way of understanding space, symbolized by the right angle, and this knowledge is necessary as the basis of 'action'. This brings to mind those comments made earlier about conventionalism, and like conventionalism, this knowledge appears to be little more than a provisional arrangement. It can make no claim to absolute truth.

This can be seen by jumping to poem 'G.3 outil', which is dedicated to the right angle. The lithograph shows a hand tracing out this 'sign':

> It is the answer and the guide
> the fact
> an answer
> a choice
> It is simple and naked

> but knowable
> The savants discuss
> the relativity of its precision
> But conscience
> has made it a sign
> It is the answer and the guide
> the fact
> my answer
> my choice.[31]

Note how Le Corbusier does not dispute the 'relativity of the precision' of the right angle. Rather, he makes subtle play with its being '*the*' definitive answer, '*an*' answer, or only '*mine*'. It is 'conscience' that makes it a 'sign', nothing more. It is useful to remember Le Corbusier's uncertainties over the Modulor: to the question 'Is it *the* solution?', he can conclude only that it is 'an efficient working tool'. The right angle, likewise, is only a functional tool.[32] The 'milieu' level ends, in poem 'A.5', with what appears to be an uneasy stand-off between two forces. The lines flow into one another to give a sense of reconciliation passing into resentment and back again:

> Between poles reigns the tension
> of fluids working on the
> liquidation of contradictory
> accounts proposes an
> end to the hatred of
> irreconcilables ripens the union
> fruit of confrontation.

Given what has dominated the other poems, it is likely that this stand-off represents the way humanity comes to terms with its milieu. This is symbolized in the lithograph by a pair of interlocking hands. This 'necessary reconciliation', Le Corbusier concludes, is the 'Sole possibility of survival / offered to life'.[33] Again, this seems to recall Poincaré's thesis that a functional understanding of our milieu is the necessary starting-point for our survival as a species.

Le Corbusier seems to indicate that there are two reasons for having such a provisional science. The first, already introduced, is about bare survival: only by attempting to understand his environment can man protect himself from its hostility, and we saw in poem 'A.3' that when he refuses to do this, he effectively concedes 'to die'. This theme perhaps informs the poem immediately afterwards, which multiplies the imagery of death and decay and implies that this is to be found everywhere in our world, which appears to be treacherous underfoot.[34] The second reason for having such science emerges logically from the first, and forms the thematic core of the second tier of poems. Here we seem to see how this science should be used in the construction of our built environment. The Modulor is introduced as the proper 'tool' for this job in poem 'B.2':

> To place at the tips of one's fingers
> above all in one's head an
> agile tool capable of swelling
> the harvest of invention
> clearing the route of thorns
> and doing the housework will give
> liberty to your liberty . . .
> Here is proportion!
> the proportion which puts
> order in our
> relations with our
> surroundings.[35]

So the Modulor allows us to 'order our relations with our surroundings'. But it also 'clears the route of thorns', somehow 'giving liberty to our liberty', which indicates that this 'housework' perhaps makes something else possible. A clue as to what this may be lies in Le Corbusier's remark that 'Nothing exists except what is deep within us, and the "Modulor" only does the housework, no more.'[36] It seems that, by creating an orderly environment which no longer threatens or distracts us, we can be liberated into our inner lives. The next two lithographs and poems, 'B.3' and 'B.4', are concerned with the two main building types through which Le Corbusier sought to achieve this: the individual house lifted on *pilotis*, and the communal 'Unité'.[37]

To summarize so far: the first and second tiers of the *Poème* seem to explore how humanity must achieve some kind of functional *rapprochement* with its milieu, and how this involves a provisional 'knowledge' of it. This knowledge is fundamental to the conceptual tools that we use to order our built environment, such as the right angle and Modulor. There are two reasons for this: first, bare survival; second, perhaps, to make possible the exploration of an inner life. If this *is* what the first and second tiers are about, then the third and fourth tiers seem to follow quite logically. I believe that they are concerned with the inner life. In particular, tier C can be read as introducing what I consider to be the alchemist's sense of selfhood, which we remember is not broached explicitly until poem 'D.3'. The imagery becomes much more complex and allusive from now on, and we have to be even more cautious in trying to interpret it.

This concept of self is broached in several ways. Poem 'C.1' is concerned, I think, with the theme of rebellion. Le Corbusier recalls the creation of an icon that was very important to his later work, and which is displayed in the corresponding lithograph. It is an image of a 'bull' that he discovered by chance in a sketch he had made of a pebble and piece of wood, or rather through his obsessive reworking of this sketch during his voluntary exile in Ozon in the early months of the Second World War.[38]

> The elements of a vision
> collect together. The key is a
> stump of dead wood and a pebble
> gathered in a sunken Pyrenean lane. Some
> oxen of burden pass
> every day in front of my window.
> Because of being designed and redesigned
> the ox – pebble and root –
> becomes bull.[39]

Le Corbusier seems to interpret this bull in two ways. One of them is rather comical, and it is difficult to take it seriously. Le Corbusier says this image reminds him of his pet dog:

> Here he is awakened dog.
> Thus after eight years
> fixes the memory of 'Pinceau'
> so-named, my dog.

> He became evil
> without knowing it and I had to
> kill him.[40]

But he also equates the bull image with an altogether more troublesome
beast and rebellion:

> Armed with animated apparati
> by dispositions in order to disclose
> to seize to stave-in to taste all
> senses alert here is the hunt
> armed to the teeth
> muzzle and nostril eye and
> horn hair bristled-up
> goes away in war
>   Beelzebub
> Who is after all
>   Beelzebub?[41]

To my mind, one can make sense of this strange poem by considering Le Corbusier's interpretations of the bull image as pointing to the
'awakening' of a certain kind of self-awareness. This self-awareness
appears to be violently aggressive towards authority and is considered
'evil'. 'Pinceau' rebels against the authority of Le Corbusier as master;
while 'Beelzebub' is gathering arms for what can only be his rebellion
against God. The most dramatic point of this poem is Le Corbusier's
question: 'Who is Beelzebub?' Le Corbusier declines to answer. But
perhaps we can speculate by allowing Seligmann to respond: '*Satan is an
individualist*. He upsets the commandments of heaven which enforce a
definite moral conduct.'[42]

Poems 'C.2' and 'C.4' belong together as pendants to this tier's central
poem. Both of them ostensibly seem to be concerned with 'love' and
'woman', and the fact that this tier is presented under the theme of 'chair'
– or 'flesh' – leads one to suspect that they represent sexual love. But again
I think they are more concerned with the theme of selfhood as the balance
or union of psychological opposites. This is how Le Corbusier characterizes love in 'C.2':

One could be two and of two
and yet not combine the things
that it would be essential to
put each in presence of the other
alas quite blind not seeing
that which he holds of the ineffable
at arm's length.[43]

And in 'C.4':

The men tell
of women in their poems
and their music
They bear on their sides an
eternal laceration from top
to bottom. They are but
half, not feeding
life but by halves
And the second part comes
to them and fuses.[44]

I do not believe this represents any conventional notion of sexual love. It seems instead to point to something less obvious. There is a demand that 'men' fix the 'eternal laceration' that renders them incomplete. 'They are but half' and need to 'fuse' with the 'second part'. Poem 'C.2' seems to suggest that this second half is already present in the individual, and just needs to be 'combined' properly: 'one could be two and of two / and yet not combine'. A further sense that these poems do not represent sexual love is that the lover arrives – 'the woman passes' – in the 'profound home . . . / in the great cavern of / sleep'.[45] I believe that these poems can be seen as referring to the alchemist's discovery of self through the alignment of the conflicting parts of the psyche. It is perhaps this that explains the undercurrent of psychic androgyny, which was shown to be an important theme in alchemy.

In poem 'C.3', these ideas are explored again, and I would like to present it at some length before analyzing it. The most immediately striking thing is how Le Corbusier stretches out the verses. The result is that one is almost forced to read them at a tortuously slow speed, which I suspect was intended to make one think that something important is being conveyed:

> In these things here understood
> an absolute sublime accomplishment
> intervenes it is the harmony
> of time the penetration of
> forms the proportion – the ineffable
> finally subtracted
> from control
> of
> reason
> carried beyond
> all
> daily
> realities
> admitted
> to the heart
> of an
> illumination
> God
> incarnate
> in
> the illusion
> the perception
> of truth
> . . .
>
> Yet one
> must
> be on
> the earth and
> present
> to
> attend
> one's own
> wedding
> to be

in one's home
in the sack of one's skin
to do one's affairs for oneself
and give thanks to the Creator.[46]

The poem begins by presenting the 'love' that thematically unites this tier as an extremely important event, a 'sublime accomplishment'. It then goes on to suggest that this 'ineffable' thing can be achieved only by 'subtracting' it from the 'control of reason', and also by 'carrying it beyond all daily realities'. Beyond reason and the everyday, it seems that the 'heart' receives some 'illumination', perhaps from God, and it is here that one might approach 'truth'. The second half of the poem again seems to focus upon how this might be achieved. The dominant refrain is revealing, as it continually comes back to 'oneself': one must attend one's own wedding, in one's own home, in the sack of one's skin, doing one's affairs for oneself. This is a strange notion of love. I believe that these images recall the central ideas of Pascal's philosophy: first, reason cannot give access to truth or meaning, nor can our daily social lives; second, this can be granted only by God, as a revelation which visits the heart; third, utter solitude is the prerequisite of this revelation.[47] Also, I think the reference to 'one's own wedding' can be seen as referring to the 'chymical wedding' of alchemy, in which the conflicting sides of the psyche are fused to allow one to discover a personal, unorthodox sense of the sacred.

The next tier, 'fusion', contains the single poem 'D.3', and we have already speculated upon what this involved: the achievement of personal salvation as a responsibility owed to oneself, and the plea that this antisocial activity be tolerated. Although this is slippery material, then, I think it is plausible to say that the *Poème* revisits many of the dominant philosophical themes from Le Corbusier's career. Levels A, B and G appeared to explore how humanity must achieve a working balance with its milieu, or external reality, by means of conventional knowledge and techniques. Levels C and D appeared to explore how the individual was then freed to cultivate self-awareness and search for the sacred within himself. I do not wish to trace these ideas through the three poems of level E, which with their references to 'fish', 'horses' and 'amazons' almost defy interpretation. But as this level is dedicated to the theme of 'caractères', one might speculate that these poems explore the different types of 'character' that emerge out of the self-scrutiny of the previous poems. Certainly, there are further references to self-discovery, and to its being tied to the home:

> I mirrored myself in this character
> and found myself there
> found at home
> found.[48]

A final suggestion that thematically this revolves around the project of self-definition is provided by 'F.3', the 'Open Hand' lithograph and poem.[49] The 'Open Hand' can most obviously be taken as symbolic of an ideal equanimity and generosity, a preparedness to make exchanges for mutual advantage:

> It is open since
> all is present available
> seizable
> Open to receive
> Open also that each
> may come to take
> . . .
> Full hand I received
> Full hand I give.[50]

But it is interesting that Le Corbusier conceived of the hand in another way:

> The hand which contains so many interior lines and so many meanings in its outline, in its texture. It contains the personality of the individual; one would like to say that the most hidden, the most secret, the most personal, the most unseizable things could be well revealed by an exact feature, a line of the hand, by the muscles of the hand, by the silhouette of the hand.[51]

It is also worth noting that a small cache of press-cuttings in Le Corbusier's archives is comprised of illustrations and photographs of all manner of hands.[52] Included in this, and the only thing that begins to explain the obsession, are a couple of articles by the contemporary astrologist Marie-Louise Sondaz, 'Destiny and the Stars: the Four Elements' and 'The Hands that Speak'. Both these articles point to the limitations of rational-scientific approaches to knowledge, and argue that occult approaches should be used as an alternative. Sondaz seems to think they are especially relevant for understanding the self, and this dominates in the discussion of palmistry:

> The form of the hand, its balance, its proportion, the quality and the colour of its skin, the value of its mounts, reveal the temperament and the character of the individual as reliably as the deeper examinations of psychology . . . [this remains] mysterious, because still nothing is able to explain how all the important points of our life find themselves marked in advance in the hand.[53]

Perhaps the Open Hand, the culmination of the *Poème*, represents self-hood.[54] And the monumental Open Hand that Le Corbusier fought to have installed over his work in Chandigarh is perhaps the largest tangible example of an artist's signature.[55]

This is as much of Le Corbusier's iconography as I believe can be interpreted with any reasonable certainty. But we have gleaned enough to be able to summarize the *Poème* as follows: the individual must achieve a conventionalized *rapprochement* with his natural environment such that it no longer threatens or distracts him. Once this is achieved, he is free to seek out more important things in solitude. This also seems to involve the rejection of human contact in society: 'In the final account', Le Corbusier says, 'the dialogue is reduced to a man alone, face to face with himself, the struggle of Jacob with the angel, within man himself!'[56]

Of course, Le Corbusier did not intend us all to become alchemists or mystics as such. But I think he *did* seek to inspire the general psychic dynamic through which the individual turned away from his external milieu in order to make his life meaningful. He continued to explore these ideas up until the end of his life:

> There are some things which you don't have the right to violate: the secret which is in every being, a great limitless void where you either can or cannot place your own notion of the sacred – individual, completely individual. This is also called conscience and it is the tool of measurement of responsibility or of feelings, reaching out to the graspable and the ineffable. We are granted a little space, some time. Everyone is inside his own skin, in the sack of his skin.[57]

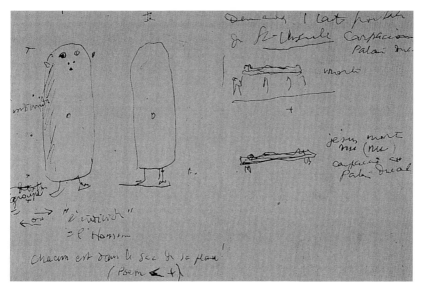

11   Le Corbusier. ' "the individual" / = Man / Each is in his own sack of skin! / (Poem <+).'
Carnet T70 04/08/1963 – 30/08/1964 p. 7. © FLC

Ozenfant may have complained, 'Every belief has been bled white or abolished, and we are left stewing in our own skins.'[58] But Ozenfant hated the concept of the individual, and it is clear that Le Corbusier sought to keep us stewing. Le Corbusier always carried a sketchbook with him wherever he went, jotting down sketches and ideas on all manner of topics, and it is clear from his sketchbook of 1963–4 that the verses of his *Poème* continued to play on his mind. He begins one page with the words 'the individual / the group', as if weighing up the two: did the individual '=' the group, or should it be a case of the individual 'or' the group? Then he seems to make up his mind anew: '"the individual" / = Man / Each is in his own sack of skin! / (Poem <+)'. Le Corbusier sketched his resolve with a front and back view of a man literally bound up in a sack of skin, and looking distinctly nonplussed about it (fig. 11).[59]

* * *

Jung: A Society of One

The previous section tried to elucidate the sense of self Le Corbusier sought to inspire, but did not explain its psychological terms and dynamics, nor the potential dangers. Jung's alchemical psychology can be consulted provisionally to remedy this.

The first attempt to link psychology with alchemy was made by the Viennese psychologist Herbert Silberer in 1914, with his *Probleme der Mystik und Ihrer Symbolik*. Silberer had interpreted an alchemical legend in terms of Jung's theory of 'introversion', but Jung himself was not convinced. He thought the link was 'off the beaten track and rather silly'. It was not until 1928, and his introduction to an ancient text of Chinese alchemy, that Jung changed his mind.[60] He committed much of the remainder of his life to a comprehensive mapping of the psychological content of alchemy. Everything he produced from this point onwards was 'alchemical', and everything he had done hitherto was reoriented so as to bring it into line with alchemy. Further, he actually lived the alchemical model of selfhood.

Given that Jung's work was so popular during these years, it is questionable whether anyone could refer to alchemy and conceivably not be referring to him. There is general agreement that Le Corbusier must have been doing so. Given the absence of direct evidence, it is chiefly Le Corbusier's late artistic and poetic imagery that leads to this opinion.[61] The connection becomes slightly more compelling if we note that Seligmann cited Jung as being responsible for the fullest exploration of the psychological connotations of alchemy.[62] But although it is not feasible to establish a direct line of influence, I think it is also unnecessary. These ideas were in the air. Le Corbusier's philosophy of selfhood seems to hold much in common with that of Jung, and we can use him cautiously to flesh out those issues that remain implicit to Le Corbusier, though this must remain speculative.[63]

The following summary will explore four issues in Jung's work. First, how humanity had reached a stage in history at which its participation with the world must be severed. Second and third, the alchemist's heterodox self-salvation and how this had to happen in a special 'place'. Finally, the potential dangers of this mode of selfhood, and also how these dangers were considered worth the risk.[64]

PARTICIPATION AND WITHDRAWAL

Alchemy for Jung was a confusion of two different kinds of knowledge: of self, and of the world. This confusion happened because both the alchemist and his historical milieu were relatively 'immature'. First, the alchemist was ignorant of the real laws and constitution of matter, so he tried to clarify it with magical, mythical and religious meanings. These meanings were products of his own psyche, and therefore appeared less mysterious to him than the material world itself.[65] But, in a contradictory way, he also needed to get rid of these psychic contents because he was too immature to deal with them properly – that is, internally. His unconscious was pursuing a self-perfecting process of 'individuation': 'Individuation means becoming a single, homogenous being, and, in so far as "in-dividuality" embraces our innermost, last and incomparable uniqueness, it also implies becoming one's own self. We could therefore translate individuation as "come to selfhood" or "self-realisation".'[66] But this process was so difficult and dangerous that it had to be externalized. These psychic transformations could be managed more easily when projected into alchemical transformations in the laboratory.

To summarize: first, the alchemist could not understand the material world on its own terms, so he projected his psyche into it; second, he was fearful of confronting his psyche on *its* own terms, so he projected it into the world. The same thing happened for different reasons, but the end result was still a muddle. This was known as *'participation mystique'*: a primitive state which found the individual enmeshed in the world.[67]

But humankind apparently outgrew this state. During the Enlightenment, the development of more effective scientific methods allowed the world to be understood in its proper terms. Alchemy became the material science of chemistry, and unconscious projections were increasingly withdrawn back into the psyche:

Our forefathers, being even more naïvely constituted than ourselves, projected their unconscious contents directly into matter. Matter, however, could easily take up such projections, because at that time it was a practically unknown and incomprehensible entity. And whenever man encounters something mysterious he projects his own assumptions into it without the slightest self-criticism. But since chemical matter nowadays is something we know fairly well, we can no longer project as freely as our ancestors did . . . Consciousness develops in civilized man by the acquisition of knowledge and by the withdrawal of projections. These are recognized as psychic contents and are reintegrated with the psyche.[68]

Participation mystique was at an end. The individual could finally be extricated from his milieu, and by reintegrating his psychic contents he began his individuation properly. Self-knowledge therefore followed knowledge of the external world. It was the second part of a two-part project.[69]

I believe this recalls the general drift of Le Corbusier's philosophy. But it finds another echo when Le Corbusier notes that during earlier ages, 'the moment when we are crushed by an immense and dominating nature . . . the fear of the unexplained', the cosmos had been rendered provisionally knowable through artistic and symbolic means. That is, through an 'integration' or 'intervention' of human beings and their milieu indistinguishable from Jung's *participation mystique*. Le Corbusier characterized this as the 'folk' mentality. But in the present,

> We have learnt about such things from science books and have a much more extensive and precise knowledge of them. We are brought face to face with the phenomenon of the cosmos through treatises, documentary pictures, and graphs . . . We now approach the mystery of nature scientifically . . . [and enjoy] the serenity of knowledge.

Science is merely a 'tool', however, and 'we have in no way added to our satisfaction unless our spirit is nourished and our heart enriched'. Exactly as with Jung, we no longer participate so directly in this objective world. We do not need to project our inner life into external phenomena in order to make them comprehensible, as they are now comprehensible on their own terms. Only now are we free to withdraw ourselves. This split 'will leave a void around us – a void whose silence will favour inner work. The work of art will find there its atmosphere.'[70]

THE ALCHEMIST'S HETERODOXY

Although his knowledge of himself and the world was muddled, the alchemist represented something very important for Jung: the stage in history at which the individual could begin to discover his own meaning in defiance of those provided by society.[71] This worked both in a religious and in a secular way.

To begin with the religious, individuation consisted of a personal confrontation of the rational ego with the unconscious, which for Jung contained the original religious experience, or '*numinosum*'. This manifested itself through various 'archetypal' symbols. But this confrontation was so disruptive that hitherto it had been projected into the rituals and imagery of organized religion, which deflected the confrontation. Therefore, until the birth of alchemy, people experienced only a watered-down version of the pure *numinosum* – 'codified and dogmatized'. Dogma helped deflect the full force of the sacred unconscious.[72] But the alchemist sought a more direct and personal confrontation. He was no longer prepared to rely on external observances prepared for some collective, which could scarcely touch the internal life of the individual. The alchemist took the responsibility for his salvation upon himself, creating his own religious myth from the symbolic material erupting from his unconscious. Thus alchemy represented a particular historical situation in which the 'collective dominants' of religious life had become 'obsolete'.[73] It was fundamentally blasphemous:

> the Christian *opus* is an *operari* in honour of God the redeemer undertaken by man who stands in need of redemption, while the alchemical *opus* is the labour of Man the Redeemer in the cause of the divine world-soul slumbering and awaiting redemption in matter. The Christian earns the fruits of grace *ex opere operato* ['by the performed work'], but the alchemist creates for himself – *ex opere operantis* ['by the work of the operator'] in the most literal sense – a 'panacea for life' which he regards either as a substitute for the Church's means of grace or as the complement and parallel of the divine work of redemption that is continued in man . . . all these myth-pictures represent a drama of the human psyche on the further side of consciousness, showing *man as both the one to be redeemed and the redeemer*.[74]

The alchemist 'mirrors' himself in Christ.[75] Inevitably, they are 'decided solitaries; each has his say in his own way'.[76]

But as well as rejecting religion, the alchemist rejected all sources of value and meaning external to himself: specifically, those of science and society. He rejected science because of its pretence that it could lead to definitive truth. This was a fallacy coined during the Enlightenment. Although science was useful for technological progress, to rely too heavily upon it was symptomatic of a psyche that was dangerously off-kilter: 'One-sidedness, though it lends momentum, is a mark of barbarism.' Such knowledge was useful and functional, but not meaningful.[77] The alchemist also rejected society, which 'levelled' everyone down to a 'conceptual average': 'As a social unit he has lost his individuality and become a mere abstract number in the bureau of statistics. He can only play the role of an interchangeable unit of infinitesimal importance.'[78] Rather than develop his individuality, this 'unit' was encouraged to waste his time and energy with distractions outside himself:

> Indeed, it seems as if all the personal entanglements and dramatic changes of fortune that make up the intensity of life were nothing but hesitations, timid shrinkings, almost like petty complications and meticulous excuses for not facing the finality of this strange and uncanny process of crystallization . . . Western man is held in thrall by the 'ten thousand things'; he sees only particulars, he is ego-bound and thing-bound.[79]

But the proper route leads us into solitude: 'Fundamentally it is a question of polar opposites: the collective or the individual, society or personality.'[80]

The individual who pursues this course would not be welcomed by his society. In cultivating his individuality to this degree, he renders himself 'incomparable' and 'unknowable' – 'an irrational datum'.[81] In a statement that fully reveals the challenge that this represents to all dominant social conventions and religious orthodoxies, Jung states that the individual must align himself with all 'those tendencies that represent the *antisocial* elements in man's psychic structure – what I call the "statistical criminal" in every-body'.[82] The individual becomes so alien to everything 'outside' that he can only be considered criminal.

Even the 'language' in which he articulated his individuality would be an affront to normal social standards. It would be an incomprehensible collage of all the available mythic and religious iconographies, utterly resistant to rational-discursive analysis.[83] This represented, for Jung, a distinct genre of 'visionary' art, which 'bursts asunder our human standards of value and of aesthetic form . . . the primordial experiences rend from top to bottom the curtain upon which is painted the picture of an ordered world'.[84]

TEMENOS

This process was meant to happen in a special 'place' that protected one's individuality from outside contamination: the 'temenos'.

Jung believes this eruption of symbols to be a disorienting event for the individual. The fact that these new meanings and values are so different from all those he had formerly taken from society is a cause of confusion, fear and shame. He feels immediately 'isolated' and 'alienated' from society. But this does not matter, because out of these symbols the individual constructs a private 'phantasmagoric' society 'as a substitute for loss of contact with other people'.[85] But as his individuality grows, he becomes more comfortable with this situation and constructs a psychic home in which he might fraternize with his new society:

> The fact that the dreamer stands rooted to the centre is a compensation of his almost insuperable desire to run away from the unconscious. He experienced an agreeable feeling of relief after this vision – and rightly, since he has succeeded in establishing a temenos, a taboo area where he will be able to meet the unconscious. His isolation, so uncanny before, is now endowed with meaning and purpose, and thus robbed of its terrors.[86]

The temenos is figured in many different ways: as a city square, garden, room and prison cell, a sacred precinct set apart for the gods, among other things (fig. 12). But they all represent that safe place in which the individual can create a new society for himself and discover his own meaning free from external influences: 'the idea is to protect what is within from the intrusion and admixture of what is without, as well as to prevent it from escaping'.[87]

But the temenos could also be real. Jung's own temenos was his 'Tower' at Bollingen, which he began building in the early 1920s and periodically extended to commemorate the milestones of his psychological maturation. In 1950, he inscribed a stone monument with alchemical maxims to 'express' and 'explain' the Tower, but this was a strange kind of communication: 'It is a manifestation of the occupant,' he says, 'but one which

12   Michael Maier. 'Viatorium',
1651. 'The Symbolic City as Centre
of the Earth, its Four Protecting
Walls Laid Out in a Square: A
Typical *Temenos.*'

remains incomprehensible to others.'[88] So the temenos is the site for the
individual's creation of a personal society which renders him antisocial and
incomprehensible – a 'sacred egoism'.[89]

The *temenos* is also interesting in terms of Jung's characterization of
space. He believed actual space and the space of the psyche to be completely different. The psyche was impossible to 'localize' in space, it was
'something that has taken root in the midst of our measurable, ponder-
able, three-dimensional reality, that differs bafflingly from this in every
respect and in all its parts, and yet reflects it . . . it occupies no space'.[90]
After a heart attack in 1944, he returned reluctantly from his near-death
ecstasy to the material world:

> Disappointed, I thought, 'Now I must return to the "box system" again.'
> For it seemed to me as if behind the horizon of the cosmos a three-
> dimensional world had been artificially built up, in which each person
> sat by himself in a little box . . . Although my belief in the world

returned to me, I have never since entirely freed myself of the impression that this life is a segment of existence which is enacted in a three-dimensional boxlike universe especially set up for it.[91]

The 'real' space of bodily existence is therefore an artificial, three-dimensional box system. But this is a necessary site for the cultivation of a psychic space that reaches beyond all boundaries.[92] As Jung said of his own love of building, which extended to building toy towns, 'the building game was only a beginning. It released a stream of fantasies . . . I was on the way to building my own myth.'[93]

I think this comes close to Le Corbusier's notion of space and building. We saw how he sought to establish a regular three-dimensional city, which was also 'artificial' – or *conventional* – in that it did not necessarily correspond to the 'truth' about space. These contained boxes that were utterly self-contained, indeed hermetically sealed. There was no contamination from outside, be it from sound, sight or society. This external world was made deliberately unenthralling. Once secure in his box, the individual could do little else than explore the boundless inner space of 'l'espace indicible'. It is also interesting to observe that in a book that builds up to a comprehensive discussion of 'Mass-Production Houses', Le Corbusier traces the origins of the home to the act of squaring off a sanctuary for the gods.[94]

DANGERS AND REDEMPTION

Jung adduces several reasons why individuation must be attempted.[95] But although eradicating some dangers, it creates another: this is the danger of every individual becoming the centre of their own little universe. This would result in the inflation of one's sense of self-worth and an unwillingness to be circumscribed by social conventions and laws – that is, if one could be persuaded to interact with society at all. Emerging from this is the predictable social backlash against such extremes of individuality, which is taken as implicit criticism of what society has to offer. 'Naturally,' says Jung, 'society has an indisputable right to protect itself against arrant subjectivisms.'[96] But the individual is unlikely to submit to this persecution willingly. Given that he now considers himself his own judge and jury, he is fully at liberty to perpetrate his own violences back upon society.[97]

So there are a number of dangerous and unattractive alternatives on offer. Perhaps the individual will continue to comply with society. This means he will remain a slave to everyday distractions and the watered-down spirituality of the church, and never fully realize himself as an individual. But if he does try to realize himself, one of two things will probably happen: either he will be hunted down as deviant and heterodox, or he himself will become the hunter. Striking the correct balance between conscious and unconscious sources – between society and solitude – seems impossibly difficult. It is disruptive at the least, and more usually explosive. None the less, for Jung, individuation *must* be attempted.[98] There is one major boon, it seems, which outweighs all the dangers of creating a world of sociopaths.

Although this whole enterprise seemed to be deeply antisocial, it was meant to provide for a new kind of society. This society would be a vibrant spiritual one, comprising individuals who have all developed a personal relationship with some inner 'God'. This would replace the current society which hangs together merely because of its mass-mindedness, a condition which makes it too weak to seek anything better. Jung seeks an ideal balance: 'Just as man, as a social being, cannot in the long run exist without a tie to the community, so the individual will never find the real justification for his existence, and his own spiritual and moral autonomy, anywhere except in an extramundane principle capable of relativizing the overpowering influence of external factors.'[99] And beyond this, the process of individuation would also make all individuals aware of their unity on the deepest level of the 'collective unconscious'. The initial trials of solitude, and the inevitable dangers, are therefore only temporary. The individual would finally be rewarded with a sense of interpersonal connection and 'oceanic' immersion far greater than that possible within any overtly social gathering. From an extreme of solitude that flirts with the psychopathic, the self would open out into a new, blissful community.[100]

It is significant that for all Le Corbusier's allusions to self-confrontation in solitude and the rejection of society, his reformation of individual consciousness itself appeared to be only a necessary precursor to the revitalization of collective life:

It is through the individual reformation of consciousness that the reformation of collective consciousness will be accomplished. When consciousness shall have passed beyond the agonies of its present incertitudes, collective allegiances will develop and a new world will replace a fallen one. That takes time – years are needed, years of sincere self-examination, inner reflection, interior awareness. A collectivity is valuable only through the equilibrium of its material needs. A civilization exists only through the whole immeasurable utterance of an entire society. When individual consciousness has been changed, and only then, the collective mechanism, set right again, will function on a *true axis* . . . Above all, let us build for ourselves a new consciousness. That effort does not have a collective basis or character. It finds its support in the depths of each person, in the silence of individual self-examination; great sacrifices may be required in order that this new consciousness, aroused everywhere, may be the great universal consciousness, the lever of fruitful deeds.[101]

Through the reform of individual consciousness, we access some kind of universal, super-social consciousness. Elsewhere, the dynamic seems again to proceed from the individual back to a 'revised' and 'recast' society:

The philosophical postulate? Yes, there is one – the keystone of the whole structure.

The present neglect, apparent in all spheres of life, seems to me to lead inevitably to the simple question: *Who am I?*

Revision.

Affirmation of the individual.

Recasting of the social structure.[102]

This sense of a new 'communion' is also present in the *Poème*. After the incremental build-up to the exploration of self in solitude, Le Corbusier says:

> It is through the doors of the
> open eyes that glances
> exchanged have been able to lead to
> the violent act of communion.[103]

It is interesting that this communion somehow holds the potential of 'violence'. This new society would be based on difference, not similarity. It would be a society of individuals who have made themselves incomprehensible to each other through what Le Corbusier calls 'immeasurable utterances'. Jung hints that this would result in a society of eccentrics, held together by the fascination their eccentricities exerted on all the other eccentrics.

But it is difficult to understand, and Jung neglects to explain, how the initial impasse could be superseded. The individual rejects the collective as useless and meaningless, the collective responds with the demonization of the individual, and the claims of each intensify in a self-perpetuating process of increasing polarization and violence. This problem is abandoned at deadlock.

These are the terms, dynamics and dangers of alchemy, and Jungian alchemical psychology, as they relate to a specifically heterodox sense of self. This sense of self revolved around the three alchemical themes that were introduced as central to Le Corbusier's *Poème*. The fact that these themes could be identified as central to Jung and Seligmann seems to suggest that Le Corbusier shared these interests, although it is difficult to point towards any definitive lines of influence. But Le Corbusier evidently participated in the general fascination for occultism and mysticism that flourished among the avant-garde during these years.

The three themes can be summarized as follows. First, an attempt must be made to come to terms with one's own psyche by 'fusing' its conflicting parts. Second, this represented a kind of spiritual salvation, which the individual had to conduct as a responsibility towards himself, his social and religious milieu being inadequate. This also involved abandoning rationalism as a means of understanding the self. Consequently, the individual expressed or confronted himself in terms of incomprehensible symbols. Third, the resulting resentment and disruption between individual and collective demanded caution from both sides.

Consulting Jung permitted speculation as to how the elements in such a philosophy of self may have related to one another in a 'psychological' sense, and this gave rise to another cluster of ideas. Jung maintained that this mode of self had only become possible at this particular stage in history: self-knowledge must follow knowledge of the world. He showed how this had to happen in a special 'place' – the *temenos*. And he maintained that the individual would ideally proceed out of solitude into a new spiritual community. These ideas also seemed to find compelling echoes in Le Corbusier.

To conclude this chapter, I want to suggest that Le Corbusier was more directly fascinated with heresy as a source of his self-identity. This was not simply a theoretical position, but was felt personally. There were some Albigensian Cathar connections in Le Corbusier's home region of the Swiss Jura. The Albigensians of southern France were descended from the Gnostics, and represented the greatest heterodox threat to orthodox Catholicism in the Middle Ages. Pope Innocent III authorized the deployment of Catholic-backed armies from the north to crush them in the early 1300s. And indeed, it was substantially as a result of this experience that the Dominicans, the first order committed solely to policing heterodoxy, were founded.[104] Probably some Albigensians fled persecution into the Swiss mountains. In a brief vignette sketching his ancestry and 'homeland', Le Corbusier spoke of his descent from this outstanding heterodox stock: 'La Chaux-de-Fonds,' he said, 'three thousand feet high in the Jura, was a place of refuge sustained by the victims of successive religious and political persecutions from the early middle ages until, and including, Russian pre-Revolutionary days.' Speaking of medieval Provence and Languedoc, the twin foci of the Catholic church's so-called 'Albigensian Crusade', Le Corbusier 'reminisces' about how 'the glow of fires rose over the villages, and it was pitiable to see such beautiful country reduced to this miserable condition'.[105] It is interesting in this connection to note that Le Corbusier's archives contain a French edition of *The Bible Standard* from late 1964. This edition is chiefly made up of a sustained and inflammatory attack on papal abuse and corruption through the ages, with special attention being given to the murderous suppression of heretics.[106] And in 1941, Le Corbusier recalled an aeroplane flight over the cities of the M'zab in central Algeria:

M'zab is the country of thirst and death. The Mozabites, banished, execrated by Islam, heretics marked out for slaughter, arrived here one day – the whole people – and it was so far away, and the land so appallingly barren, that they were left in peace; hunger and thirst, it was thought, would soon make an end of them. That was a thousand years ago!

They built the seven cities of the M'zab and laid out the seven oases.

These cities, with their lush plantations and shade, and 'blind street walls' behind which each house enjoyed its own interior garden, clearly recall Le Corbusier's own cities.[107]

But what is the meaning of all this heterodoxy? I believe it is precisely that alchemical one noted above: Le Corbusier loved the idea of a self-identity that could be forged in opposition to the dominant mores of society. It is essential in this connection to note that in amongst discussing his family's alleged Albigensian roots, Le Corbusier also mentions their interest in the great literature of former ages, especially Rabelais. The card announcing his mother's death also displayed the family motto: 'THAT WHICH YOU DO, DO IT', from '"The Kingdom of the Quintessence", 5th book by Rabelais'.[108] This refers to the chapter in *Gargantua and Pantagruel* in which the heroes arrive in a strange country steeped in alchemical and occultist lore and are immediately told how to address the queen:

> Entelechy is her real name, and anyone who calls her by any other – can go and shit himself! . . . Entelechy, which means perfection.[109]

As a term, 'entelechy' referred to the soul generally, but it was used more specifically in alchemy to mean the *perfection* of soul and attainment of individuality – as such, it was used by Jung.[110] In drawing our attention to these things, Le Corbusier appears to want to identify himself and his family with heterodoxy and alchemy in the same breath. When combined with the M'zab reference, it is possible to conclude that Le Corbusier was building cities for 'heretics' just like himself, in which one might take upon oneself the hardships of isolated self-exploration and all its consequences.[111] The term 'Purism' also perhaps takes on a richer aura when we note that the word 'Cathar' is derived from the Greek *katharos*, meaning 'pure'.[112]

It is easy to understand how the alchemical model of self might appeal instinctively to someone already interested in Pascal, the underlying dynamic being very similar. I do not, however, think it viable to press for any more links between these particular protagonists. But is it possible to make the idea that Le Corbusier was committed to this concept of self slightly more compelling? The dilemma of its being 'dangerous' points the way. This will be my main concern for the final chapter.

Chapter 9

Bataille and Camus: 'Vers la limite critique'

It is obvious that to become the centre of one's own universe might lead to an inflation of self-worth, and that this could become pathological. But was Le Corbusier aware of this? There is good evidence that he was, and I want to use it as final confirmation that he was designing his cities with precisely these ideas in mind.

I shall introduce two sources familiar to Le Corbusier: Georges Bataille's *The Accursed Share* and Albert Camus's *The Rebel*, which their authors sent to him on publication in 1949 and 1951 respectively.[1] It might seem odd to 'ally' Le Corbusier with a maverick surrealist and an existentialist novelist, but none the less there is some justification. I discovered these texts in Le Corbusier's personal library while trying to ascertain what he might have been reading, and what ideas he might have had in mind, while composing his *Poème*. His reception of these books falls within its period of composition, and it is clear that the ideas contained in them influenced, or at least mirrored, its progress. This was definitely the case with Camus. During the period when Le Corbusier was preoccupied with a concept of self based on solitude, both Camus and Bataille sent him books which dealt extensively with the dangers of such an outlook. I think this represents an implicit acknowledgment that they were concerned with the same cluster of problems. It is particularly interesting that Camus, one of the great intellectual leaders of the Resistance, should be associated with Le Corbusier, the Vichy collaborator. It seems that this particular issue of selfhood was considered important enough to override ordinary resentments and differences. I intend to give an account of Le Corbusier's reading of these books, and to try to infer the influence they might have had on him. As with my account of Seligmann and Jung, however, it is probably more plausible to think of Camus, Bataille and Le Corbusier as pursuing parallel and mutually illuminating lines of enquiry than to insist upon influences.

Both Bataille and Camus pondered the problem of withdrawing from social interaction and external sources of value, and both said that two contradictory factors had to be taken into account. On the one hand, this withdrawal was thought to be essential in order to experience aspects of human existence without which life is meaningless. On the other hand, it might lead one to the most violent kinds of antisocial sentiment and activities. This posed a paradox which Camus and Bataille found difficult to resolve, although they did manage to suggest how the risk might be minimized or avoided.

First, I shall introduce those passages that Le Corbusier singled out for comment, or simply highlighted, in his personal copies of these works. With our attention provisionally focused, I shall then consult Bataille and Camus for clarification.

'Vers la limite critique'

What do these books hold in common, the one contributing to a larger 'Essay on General Economy' and the other an attempt to understand the nature of rebellion? And what is their relevance to Le Corbusier?

The central thesis of Bataille's *The Accursed Share* is that the meaning of life was found not in the world of objects and utility, but through their violent negation:

> Once the resources are dissipated, there remains the prestige *acquired* by the one who wastes. The waste is an ostentatious squandering to this

end, with a view to superiority over others that he attributes to himself by this means. But he misuses the negation he makes of the utility of the resources he wastes, bringing into contradiction not only himself but man's entire existence. The latter thus enters into an ambiguity where it remains: It places the values, the prestige and the truth of life in the negation of the servile use of possessions, but at the same time it makes a servile use of this negation.[2]

Le Corbusier highlighted this passage with the words, '= le mot juste!' This is an interesting point to have chosen for agreement. Le Corbusier has isolated Bataille's discussion of the ambiguity of the Mexican and North American tribal custom of 'potlatch', which involved the giving of gifts seemingly without profit. Bataille took such squander as symbolic of the fracturing of man's enslavement to the utilitarian values of the object world and society. This negation initiated his return to the sacred, and was also the first step in discovering one's selfhood. As can be seen from this passage, however, Bataille believed the potlatch ceremony was spoiled, because the gift-giving was put to another social, utilitarian end: symbolically, it put the recipient under an obligation of gratitude to the giver. For Bataille, then, the negation of society, which allowed one to glimpse one's individuality, should not be allowed to reify society by taking on another social use. Selfhood must be found away from society, and it is perhaps this that Le Corbusier approves with his comment. This seems to run parallel with my observation that utility and functionalism were not important to Le Corbusier; or rather, that they were only the first stage of a much larger project that ended with the discovery of self.[3]

It is also important that Le Corbusier should have highlighted the section in which Bataille outlined his 'economy' as a two-part project. 'Doubtless it is paradoxical', says Bataille with regard to his study of the material economy, 'to tie a truth so intimate as that of *self-consciousness* (the return of being to full and irreducible sovereignty) to these completely external determinations.' 'But,' he continues, 'it is the starting point and the basis, not the completion, of *self-consciousness*.' Completion is found in the 'pure intimacy' of 'mystical contemplation', in the 'truth that silence alone does not betray'.[4] As well as annotating the main body of text, Le Corbusier also provided a summary of special points of interest on the flyleaf, such as in the following, which is related to the above passages:

In this perspective of man liberated through action, having effected a perfect adequation of himself to *things*, man would have them behind him, as it were; they would no longer enslave him. A new chapter would begin, where man would finally be free to return to his own intimate truth, to freely dispose of the being that he *will be*, that he is not now because he is servile.[5]

The individual seeks a 'perfect adequation' with the object world, then, but only in order to break its stranglehold and escape from it into an exploration of self. This seems to confirm trends we have already seen in Le Corbusier. It is also essential that he should draw special attention to Bataille's discussion of how, in the attempt of man to rediscover the sacred and with it his individuality, 'the mistake of all religion is to always give man a contradictory answer: *an external form of intimacy*'.[6] Organized religion cannot give adequate access to the sacred.

Finally, there is a passage in *The Accursed Share* which summarizes the paradoxical dynamic explored in various forms throughout the entire book:

> And if I thus consume immoderately, I reveal to my fellow beings that which I am *intimately*: Consumption is the way in which *separate* beings communicate. Everything shows through, everything is open and infinite between those who consume intensely. But nothing counts then; violence is released and it breaks forth without limits, as the heat increases.[7]

Through the 'destruction' or 'consumption' of the objects of the material world, the individual is able not only to fathom his own depths, but also to reveal to others his true nature. This allows for a deeper kind of community, but a community linked to violence. In his personal copy, Le Corbusier isolated this centrally important passage, annotating it with the following:

poème de <+
'fusion'[8]

It is in the 'fusion' section of his *Poème* that he talks about the shift from a self forged in solitude to 'the violent act of communion'.[9]

What caught Le Corbusier's attention in Bataille's text? I suggest that he was interested in those passages that refer to a concept of self that is found through the negation of the object world of society and its values – in particular, through the negation of organized religion. This seems to relate to Le Corbusier's own two-part project: one settled one's relations with exterior reality only in order to turn one's attention inwards. And from this withdrawal, the individual seems to open out again into a new relationship with others, although this is potentially violent. These themes in Bataille seem to mirror quite closely those we found in Le Corbusier.

Somewhat similar ground is covered in Camus's *The Rebel*. Here is one of the most crucial passages:

> Moderation, born of rebellion, can only live by rebellion. It is a perpetual conflict, continually created and mastered by the intelligence. It does not triumph either in the impossible or in the abyss. It finds its equilibrium through them. Whatever we may do, excess will always keep its place in the heart of man, in the place where solitude is found. We all carry within us our places of exile, our crimes, and our ravages. But our task is not to unleash them on the world.[10]

In his personal copy, Le Corbusier surrounded this with the words: 'vers la limite critique . . . le dilemme tragique': 'towards the critical limit . . . the tragic dilemma'. The 'critical limit' that concerns Camus is precisely that at which the individual's right to forge his own meaning in contempt of society spills over into the desire to attack and transform that which he has left behind. And yet, says Camus, without this rebellion we are not truly alive. Le Corbusier seems to have identified himself with this concern by scratching his symbol for the *Poème* alongside: '<+'.[11]

It is also telling that Camus should mention, and Le Corbusier should single out in his notes, 'the admirable efflorescence of the Albigensian heresy'. Camus equates this 'efflorescence' with the initial life-affirming moment of revolt which so quickly passes either into organized forms of violence or, as in this case, is crushed by organized religion in the form of the Inquisition.[12] As Camus says elsewhere, 'To kill God and to build a Church is the constant and contradictory purpose of rebellion'; thus, 'if the rebel blasphemes it is in the hope of finding a new god'.[13]

Given Camus's exploration of these themes, which again seem to mirror Le Corbusier's own interests, it is little wonder that Le Corbusier appears to have sent a manuscript copy of the *Poème* to him:

My dear Camus,
    Humbly I take the liberty of presenting you with another draft of my 'Poem of the Right Angle' (text) for safe-keeping, and if by chance

you have some advice to give me concerning any obscurities or inaccuracies that you are able to find, and also on syntactical or other faults, I would receive them with pleasure.

Amicably yours

LE CORBUSIER.[14]

This is compelling evidence of a close relationship. But most intriguing, given the reference to 'obscurities' and 'inaccuracies', is the clear suggestion that Le Corbusier sought to represent Camus's position in his *Poème*, which he is anxious not to *mis*-represent. Or perhaps they shared a joint position. The year of this letter, 1952, seems to have been quite rich with projects involving both men. There was also, for example, a projected film or 'drama' on the subject of the Marseilles Unité – the everyday life inside as well as its relations with the city – which Le Corbusier and Camus were to script jointly.[15] I believe this represents an implicit intellectual agreement concerning their vision of the city and how life becomes meaningful within it.[16]

What does Le Corbusier isolate in Camus? First, the necessity of rebellion as a life-affirming action; second, this rebellion being linked to solitude and the discovery of a new god in place of organized religion; and third, the possibility that this may erupt in violence, both by the individual against his society, and by society against the individual. This seems related to those themes he isolated in Bataille.

I believe this is a valuable set of clues for gaining new insights into Le Corbusier's concerns, and I would like to clarify what was at stake by expanding upon the main ideas. Although Camus, Bataille and Le Corbusier no doubt pursued their reflections for the most part independently of each other, I believe they were all involved in working through the consequences of highly problematic concepts of selfhood that have many interesting points in common.

'The Difference in Blood'

THE ACCURSED SHARE

Bataille's *The Accursed Share* is an economic treatise, but not a conventional one. In fact, the obvious notion of economics as the attempt to understand commerce, trade and industry as a rational-utilitarian science is for him only 'particular' economy. More important is his 'general' economy, which maintains that the cosmos has a surplus of energy which must be squandered without use: 'Beyond our immediate ends man's activity in fact pursues the useless and infinite fulfilment of the universe.' Beyond 'particular' economy, with its focus on the world of materialism, comes 'general' economy which must destroy it – both in the *actual* destruction of objects and in some other, perhaps metaphorical, waste of energy.[17]

But this useless wastage does have a use as it provides for the 'sovereignty' or self-awareness of the individual: 'what it aims at is consciousness, what it looks to from the outset is the *self-consciousness* of man'.[18] How did this work? For Bataille, the object world turned the individual into an object as well: rendered transparent, fully 'knowable', he was consequently more amenable to its purposes. The impetus to squander things uselessly was therefore an attack by the individual upon this condition. By these means, he protests that he is not susceptible to the same rational-utilitarian analysis as everything else in this object world, and that he cannot forge any meaningful sense of individuality through his dealings with it. The resulting sense of self is ineffable:

> The world of *intimacy* is as antithetical to the *real* world as immoderation is to moderation, madness to reason, drunkenness to lucidity. There is moderation only in the object, reason only in the identity of the object with itself, lucidity only in the distinct knowledge of objects. The world of the subject is the night: that changeable, infinitely suspect night which, in the sleep of reason, *produces monsters* . . . And if I thus consume immoderately, I reveal to my fellow beings that which I am *intimately*: *Consumption* is the way in which *separate* beings communicate.

Clearly, this new awareness of self serves to reconnect humanity at a deeper level, a level beyond the utilitarian social one. With the objectivity of this real world destroyed, the individual 'receives a sacred communication from it, which restores him in turn to interior freedom'.[19] So 'wastage' is a sacred act, a radical but necessary means for the discovery of self and some deeper social communion.

But when does this happen? According to Bataille, it happens only *after* the material world has reached such a stage of efficiency and order that the necessities of life are adequately provided for all. Then wastage emerges to fritter away the surplus: 'The limit of growth being reached, life, without being in a closed container, at least enters into ebullition: Without exploding, its extreme exuberance pours out into a movement always bordering on ebullition.'[20] But for Bataille, this new situation does not involve the outright rejection of the object world as it is a necessary part of existence, and the individual sacrifices part of himself in service to it. The utilitarian world continues to exist, then, but it reminds the individual by its insistently banal presence that it cannot provide him with meaning – it *disappoints* him in this:

> The multitude has surrendered to the somnolence of production, living the mechanical existence – half-ludicrous, half-revolting – of *things*. But conscious thought reaches the last degree of alertness in the same movement. On the one hand it pursues, in an extension of technical activity, the investigation that leads to an increasingly clear and distinct knowledge of *things*. In itself science limits consciousness to objects; it does not lead to *self-consciousness* (it can know the subject only by taking it for an object, for a *thing*); but it contributes to the wakefulness by accustoming us to the precision and by *disappointing* us: For it acknowledges its limits, it admits its powerlessness to arrive at *self-consciousness*. On the other hand, thought does not at all abandon, in the face of industrial development, man's basic desire to find himself (to have a sovereign existence) beyond a useful action that he cannot avoid. This desire has only become more insistent.

It is only after fully coming to terms with the world that mankind is freed to seek the sacred elsewhere: 'having effected a perfect adequation of himself to *things*', says Bataille, 'man would have them behind him, as it were; they would no longer enslave him. A new chapter would begin, where man would finally be free to return to his own intimate truth.' In fact, the clearer and more objectively the external milieu manifests itself, the greater is the individual's realization of its inadequacy, and the greater his determination to forge something more substantial for himself.[21]

But beyond rejecting economics, this also involves the rejection of rational-scientific method. That is, it is granted that science can come to some understanding of the object world, but it cannot offer any real insights into the interior life of individuals: 'It would serve no purpose to neglect the rules of rigorous investigation, which proceeds slowly and methodically. But how can we solve the enigma, how can we measure up to the universe if we content ourselves with the slumber of *conventional* knowledge?'[22] Such 'conventional' knowledge is merely the functional tool we use to make sense of our milieu and to turn it to commercial account, but the sovereign 'moment remains outside, short of or beyond, all knowledge'. It is attainable 'Only by cancelling, or at least neutralizing, every operation of knowledge within ourselves'. Prior to this moment, the individual's identity is tied to the causality of the world. Everything is judged and identified according to its present and future usefulness, which is a matter of rational calculation and commerce. But after this moment, the individual is purged of this rational workaday structure. He articulates his new sense of self through irrational visions, acts and paradox. He is no longer an accountable 'thing' in the world of objects.[23] Finally, this involves the rejection of 'institutional' religion as well. In the past, says Bataille, humankind was too immature to experience this sacred sense of self internally, so it was projected into external ritual. But now it must be confronted by each individual in solitude.[24]

Individuality is found by disavowing the object world, its laws and institutions, and this necessarily involves some kind of 'violence'. This violence may involve the outright destruction of objects and people, such as in human sacrifice, but nowadays it is more likely to involve simply pouring scorn on the rational-utilitarian basis of the object world. Bataille therefore advocates a tempered kind of rebellion, one that has a proper 'domain' in which violence might reign, but there is always the danger that this will break out of its confines.[25] The most effective and indeed safest way to break away from the world and experience the 'pure intimacy' of sacred self-consciousness, 'comes down in fact, as in the experience of the mystics, to intellectual contemplation, "without shape or form," as against the seductive appearance of "visions," divinities and myths'.[26] In this way, the individual discovers his full individuality. But once again, this initial detachment of oneself ideally ends not in isolation and violence but in the return to a more profound human connection at a deeper, spiritual level: 'The individuals break loose, but a breaking-loose that melts them and blends them indiscriminately with their fellow beings helps to connect them together.'[27]

This closely parallels Le Corbusier's concept of self and the way his ideal cities worked. The world is brought to some stage of functional efficiency and legibility. But only in order that the individual may perceive its spiritual and social bankruptcy. This prompts the individual to turn to solitude and discover his own meaning on antisocial grounds. Hopefully, the violence this entails will open out into a new spiritual society.

BATAILLE'S ALIGNMENT WITH CAMUS

Camus's *The Rebel* represents the next step. The affinity between these writers on this subject is illustrated by Bataille's review and defence of Camus's book. Bataille specifically aligns their two positions, using each to fill out the gaps of the other so as to present a single, fairly consistent thesis.

Camus's *The Rebel* is a study of the impulse to revolt that has riven Western society from the late eighteenth century onwards. But it is more specifically an attempt to work through a dilemma. How is it possible to allow for this revolt against society, which permits the fundamental act of self-discovery, and yet prevent it from spiralling into antisocial violence. This is what Le Corbusier called the 'tragic dilemma' – the 'critical limit'.

Camus's presentation of the dilemma encourages Bataille to rethink his own response. This 'Revolt leaves the rebel faced with a dilemma which depresses him: if it is pure and headstrong he will reject the exercise of all power, will push powerlessness to the point of nourishing himself with the complacency of incontinent language. If he compromises with a quest for power, then his revolt becomes allied with the spirit of subordination.'[28] This can be put more simply. Either the rebel becomes utterly withdrawn from society, which means he is self-aware but sustained entirely by his own little world and 'language' – 'complacent' and 'incontinent'. Or else the rebel refuses to remain withdrawn, pours his revolt back into the world and tries to subordinate it to his own ideals. This pursuit of self-awareness seems indivisible from criminal activity.[29]

Bataille resolves the dilemma in a slightly different way than before. It is perversely pragmatic. He proposes moderation and restraint, but in the form of the individual consenting to be split in two. There is an unimportant part of himself that can be handed over to society, conforming with the utilitarian demands it makes of him. And there is an inalienable part of himself through which he achieves sovereignty, and which must be held in reserve.

This part of him which is never reducible to the law, which derives from the immensity of being within him, which is an end in itself and cannot be treated as a means - he knows he can spare it by working, by allowing another – reducible – part of himself to submit to the law . . . the 'rebel' knows that he can do a certain amount of work, on condition that he does not make his *whole* life a cog in the system subordinated to the requirements of work. And it is also the effect of *restraint* within him no longer to aspire to that power he struggles against.

Effectively, this is a part-time commitment to self-awareness. But Bataille now believes this to be a more 'profound' rejection of the exterior world than outright violence, for by limiting himself in this way the individual 'maintains so much violence within him'. This has another 'benefit': by refusing violence, the individual acknowledges his 'complicity' with other human beings. But this is a disturbing complicity. With everyone conducting their mini-revolts alone, there comes the paradoxical recognition that in this need to reject each other they find the common factor of their humanity. Human beings are united anew through recognition of their shared hatred. This represents the basis of a new society.[30] So this revolt is most beneficial when upheld in 'poetry', rather than in 'the vehemence and strategems of realist politics'.[31]

In conclusion, Bataille maintains that there are two sides to the human personality that are incapable of resolution. At best, they can be brought to a mutually suspicious and often outright destructive stand-off. This psychic stand-off is handled in the way we fit ourselves into our environment: certain portions of the self are auctioned off to the outside, but there is nothing much of interest there. It is therefore necessary to keep the more crucial portions in antisocial reserve.

THE REBEL

Camus's *The Rebel* is less optimistic than Bataille about the ease of the problem's resolution, and therefore more morbidly preoccupied with its dangers. Even so, Camus comes by a different route to essentially the same conclusion. He approaches the problem through an attempt to account for how the great rebellions of the last two centuries have ended with the establishment of revolutionary regimes that rationally endorse and systematically pursue murder. Is there anything of value in rebellion that is worth preserving? And if so, how is this possible?[32]

He begins at once with a discussion of the dangers of solitude. Although it symbolizes the initial moment of rebellion, it must not persist. The rebel's initial ' "no" affirms the existence of a borderline'. It is the individual's most fundamental right to set up this 'limit', at which point 'Knowledge is born and conscience awakened'. Nothing must be allowed to transgress or 'infringe' upon this. True rebellion, however, 'contrary to present opinion and despite the fact that it springs from everything that is most strictly individualistic in man, undermines the very conception of the individual'. It is here that Camus believes the true value of solitude is discovered. It allows the individual to realize that all people hold the desire of breaking away from the moribund values and institutions of society. As yet, this realization is 'still indeterminate', but he is vaguely aware of suffering as a 'collective experience'. This commits him anew to the common good.[33] Rebellion, then,

> plays the same role as does the '*cogito*' in the category of thought: it is the first clue. But this clue lures the individual from his solitude. Rebellion is the common ground on which every man bases his first values. I *rebel* − therefore we *exist*.[34]

Rebellion is the prerequisite of existence, and this existence is collective. But even so, 'At this limit, the "we are" paradoxically defines a new form of individualism.'[35] Although superficially it seems that the rebel assumes a negative and destructive position, in fact he rediscovers all that is positive. It is a 'passionate affirmation'.[36]

But the rebel's withdrawal from society does not end so happily. It always dangerously misfires.[37] This can take two courses. Either this solitude turns outward into 'revolution', which for Camus represents the institutionalization of the original moment of rebellion. Because of the initial rejection of the ethical fetters of organized religion, law and custom, revolution manifests itself as a rationally justifiable project of violence and murder. This is symbolized, for Camus, in the inauguration of the French Revolutionary 'Terror': 'by guillotining God [Louis XVI as beneficiary of the Divine Right of Kings] on 21 January 1793, [the revolutionaries] deprived themselves, forever, of the right to proscribe crime or to censure wicked instincts'. Alternatively, the other 'course' is symbolized by the

Marquis de Sade: unable to subjugate the world to his immediate satisfaction, the rebel turns further inward, and shuts himself away behind the boundaries of an imaginary domain where his personal values and violence hold full sway. Even so, 'Every ethic conceived in solitude implies the exercise of power.'[38]

So there is a choice, but only between different types of 'crime': 'There are crimes of passion and crimes of logic. The line that divides them is not clear.'[39] The initial rebellious moment is an essential component of human being, but there seems to be no way of avoiding murderous destruction in one form or another: either in mind or deed, in solitude or in society. All rebellion makes 'an appeal to the essence of being', but then it slips into murder. 'Is this contradiction inevitable?' Camus asks. 'Does it characterize or betray the value of rebellion?'[40] This violence certainly does betray the value of rebellion, the value being the awareness of solidarity with other human beings. Camus makes the following statement about the outbreak of violence:

> At this exact point, the limit is exceeded, rebellion is first betrayed and then logically assassinated for it has never affirmed – in its purest form – anything but *the existence of a limit and the divided existence that we represent*: it is not, originally, the total negation of all existence. Quite the contrary, it says yes and no simultaneously. *It is the rejection of one part of existence in the name of another part which it exalts.*[41]

This leads to a paradox. Violent action must be taken in the real world, but it must not be allowed to destroy that newly won individuality and solidarity which the initial moment of rebellion reveals.[42] This rebellion is legitimate only if it does not transgress these limits, yet without the transgression it remains in a state of mere potential, and sterile. Somehow, the rebel must not 'flee this tension'. He must find a way to exist on this borderline.[43]

This paradox is worked over in various forms throughout the latter parts of Camus's book. One way it is 'resolved' is by his outlining a provisional ethos for responsible political action.[44] But most importantly, the sense of selfhood 'already made manifest in the act of insurrection . . . can be best described by examining it in its pure state – in artistic creation'.[45] Art most effectively sustains this metaphysical moment for Camus: 'Rebellion can be observed here in its pure state and in its original complexities.'[46] Rather than taking on the 'real' world and scuppering itself through violence, art is a form of rebellion which fabricates a new world and new knowledge for itself:

> In every rebellion is to be found the metaphysical demand for unity, the impossibility of capturing it and the construction of a substitute universe. Rebellion, from this point of view, is a fabricator of substitute universes. This also defines art . . . All rebel thought . . . is either expressed in rhetoric or in a closed universe . . . In these sealed worlds, man can reign and have knowledge at last.[47]

Camus's favourite artists and writers rely on motifs such as 'prisons', 'isolated castles' and 'solitary heights'.

But what kind of art did Camus have in mind? Again, there were two extremes that he thought must be avoided. First, pure abstraction or 'formalism' was the equivalent of de Sade's type of rebellion, forgoing all relations with the real world and creating instead a personal, but sterile and uncommunicative, new world. Second, 'realism' was equivalent to the revolutionary mind-set that seeks too literal a correspondence with and control over the real world. The artist cannot reject the world entirely, then, but rather must work with its elements and imaginatively transform them. This proper rebellious art therefore uses a kind of mutated figuration:

> The realist artist and the formal artist try to find unity where it does not exist, in reality in its crudest state, or in imaginative creation which wants to expel all reality. On the contrary, unity in art appears at the limit of the transformation which the artist imposes on reality . . . Language destroyed by irrational negation becomes lost in verbal delirium; subject to deterministic ideology it is summed up in the word of command. Half-way between the two lies art.[48]

Such art represents the ideal point of controlled rebellion against the real world. It permits the individual to sustain, but not to spoil, the beneficial experience of a violently antisocial sense of self. This art occupies the middle ground between solitude and society.[49] It constitutes a critical stepping back from the ceaseless change of history and material things, but not their outright rejection. Too much solitude remains for Camus not only sterile, but also dangerous.

Whatever we may do, excess will always keep its place in the heart of man where solitude is found. We all carry within us our places of exile, our crimes, and our ravages. But our task is not to unleash them on the world.[50]

This was precisely what Le Corbusier christened the 'critical limit' – the 'tragic dilemma'. We are not alive if we do not seek that which distinguishes us from all other human beings, but we must stop short of 'consecrating the difference in blood'.[51]

It is easy to understand why the ideas introduced in this section might have been of interest to Le Corbusier: they all deal with a philosophy of selfhood that, in general terms, he had been thinking about through much of his adult life. Of all these figures, however, the only influence that it is possible to prove is that of Pascal. But it is clear that Le Corbusier had much in common with the others. I believe he is likely to have been interested in them because of the ways in which they gave fresh consideration to a set of ideas that he had developed independently, rather than because they were of any formative influence.

It is true that they approach their ideas in different ways and with different agendas, and frequently these differences can be accounted for by their degree of morbidity and despair. Even so, they are remarkably consistent. With minor qualifications, the following summary applies to them all. First, they maintained that genuine selfhood could be forged only by rejecting society, which required solitude. Second, in order to discover or express its uniqueness, the individual relied upon artistic or sacred symbolism. Third, this involved the danger that the new sense of self, unfettered by social values, would become violently sociopathic and also provoke the resentment and violence of society itself. But finally, as this renaissance of the individual consciousness was meant to open out into a renaissance of the collective, it was considered worth the risk.

This also represents the closest it is possible to come to a 'definition' of Le Corbusier's concept of self. Being an architect and urbanist, however, he had a particular way of dealing with its potential dangers. Rather than having to make pleas for toleration from the individual as it defined itself against society, and vice versa, Le Corbusier would hold them apart through the physical fabric of the city itself. The city was a complicated mechanism for negotiating what the individual should give to each of these extremes. It was a controlling 'framework': 'Human consciousness is in need of a revelation. We need a framework for the contemporary consciousness.'[52] Le Corbusier could also provoke us into taking stock of ourselves by eliminating all the points of interest that would ordinarily be found in the city. His city, the logistical systems and knowledge associated with it, were purely functional, but only in order to liberate and simultaneously contain the profoundly dangerous and *dysfunctional* atom of each individual.

I believe ideas of this kind may have informed Le Corbusier's late artistic practice and his decision to keep this work separated from the rest of his life for so long. And although he considered this private production to emerge from a valuable process of solitude and merciless self-exploration, he was conscious of the dangers of admitting no outside criteria against which to judge himself. One senses the desire for a mutually regulating flow between the two extremes, with neither outright abstraction nor outright realism being permitted. This exactly reproduces Camus's position on art:

> Without a dealer, and without a fixed market value, I have the good fortune to paint without selling. That carries with it a certain danger. One remains the only judge of oneself, one lives alone (in painting only, for heaven knows that I am in contact with men and their passions in architecture and city planning!). One lives alone in the dilemma peculiar to artists: confidence against doubt.
>
> Another consequence: the taste for a rarefied kind of painting, very remote, nourished by a hundred forces piled up behind a wall of hermetism. For all that, my hands wish to seize physical things and to bring the human into that empty space. There is a tide ceaselessly rising toward the spiritual, and ebbing toward the substantial realities of life. Abstract or representational art? I am not of the generation which nowadays can deliberately choose abstraction alone. In its headlong rhythm my life is too strenuous for that, and I need to keep in contact with living beings.[53]

Earlier, Le Corbusier had offered the choice:

> Architecture or Revolution.
> Revolution can be avoided.[54]

Given what has been discussed, it is appropriate to modify this: while collective *revolution* might be avoided, perhaps individual *rebellion*, 'the revolt of human consciousness', cannot.[55] It serves to maintain that sacred portion of self that must not be handed over to society.

Conclusion

There are two things I want to do in this conclusion, and both involve introducing some new material. First, I shall summarize the conclusions from the above three sections, and show how they invite the reconsideration of certain influential commentaries. Unlike the commentaries encountered so far, these are perhaps more clearly 'motivated' – they approach Le Corbusier from within their own agendas. It is for this reason that they need to be treated separately. This will also provide a foil against which I might further clarify my ideas on Le Corbusier's concept of self. Second, I want to address a question: is Le Corbusier's concept of self of any use or value today? This will involve determining where he sits on the scale of opposing urban paradigms that I mentioned in my introduction. It is also important to be aware of the broad trends concerning how the self has been conceptualized from the beginning of the twentieth century.

The City as a Source of Interest and Meaning

In the first section, 'The Lawgiver', I looked at Le Corbusier's political machinations between the wars, and also at the ideal cities he designed for potential political clients. Despite some extraordinary and often disturbing manœuvring on his part, it transpired that it was not as opportunistic as might first be thought. His theory, rhetoric and city designs all provided evidence that a coherent concept of self underlay them. This concept involved forcibly severing those ties that encouraged the individual to be dependent upon the social and political activities that ordinarily characterize the city. Consequently, in Le Corbusier's ideal cities there were no streets for casual socializing, few venues for formal socializing, and politics had been taken over by apolitical experts. It is also likely that the mass media would be censored, given that it was believed to keep people in a state of hypertension over political issues, and to be psychologically invasive and disruptive. 'Participation' in the affairs of the city was reduced to the non-negotiable 'maintenance' of an already perfect machine, and socializing was reduced to sport. In both cases, the rules of engagement were established in advance. Chance was abolished. Everything was geared towards discouraging people from depending upon things outside themselves, which was intended to inspire them to reclaim their individualities. Le Corbusier's choice of political allies and ideologies was also consistent with these priorities. He always favoured those that promised to eradicate politics as a form of participatory activity.

An important branch of criticism of Le Corbusier seems to overlook this, or at least to overlook the possibility that it was intentional. Several of these have been mentioned already, but we can revisit the issue by looking at Jane Jacobs in *The Death and Life of Great American Cities* and Richard Sennett in *The Uses of Disorder: Personal Identity and City Life*.[1]

Jacobs has a personal love for the richness of inner-city life, which she considers to be a fragile ecosystem that can survive only the subtlest planning interventions. She proposes four 'generators of diversity' that will gently foment an interesting, safe and trusting street culture. Out of this would emerge informal political communities versatile enough to defend their interests not only against ordinary criminals, but also against a demonic 'City Hall' committed to bulldozing their neighbourhoods under the banner of Corbusian planning. Life, for Jacobs, is made meaningful in this collective struggle for survival, and the more intense the struggle, the more *living* the life. Indeed, one gets a sense that it is only through community networks and interpersonal relationships that people can be said to exist at all. Without this, they remain anonymous, their identities evaporate. The organic interrelation of all the parts in Jacobs's city is reminiscent of Lewis Mumford, and so too is the sense that the human being can find its life's meaning only through complete immersion in this urban ecosystem, and through allowing itself to be shaped and transformed by it.[2]

Sennett takes this to a more complicated extreme. For him, the 'Purist' city is for adolescents. 'Adolescence' is understood as the period during which the individual is given increasing responsibility for his actions but has insufficient experience to be able to make informed choices. Consequently, the adolescent closes himself off and finds his identity behind a safe mental barrier that permits only certain sanctioned ideas and activities. Anything that does not fall within these limited parameters is dismissed as worthless, which gives rise to intolerance and violence. The orderly and predictable Corbusian city provides no challenge to this pre-established pattern of expectations. But in order to fracture the adolescent mind-set, says Sennett, the city must allow for the play of difference and discord. Official law and order, and the emergency services, must very substantially withdraw. The resulting anarchy would be less dangerous than the bigotry that flourishes in Purist cities, as people would be compelled to thrash out a tolerant working balance simply in order to avoid utter destruction. This is the 'survival community', and in responding to its challenges the inner potential of the individual would be realized. As with Jacobs, life and self-identity become meaningful only in the struggle of the collective.[3]

Despite their differences, the positions of Jacobs and Sennett are based upon the belief that society is good, and that humans require participation in a rich and diverse community. Their arguments have provided a powerful focus for the so-called 'New Urbanism' and 'Community Architecture' initiatives, under which people are encouraged to become closely involved in the long-term urban development of their neighbourhoods.[4] This involvement ideally results in the politicization of the neighbourhood, and the clarification of their relationships and collective needs. Both Jacobs and Sennett condemn Le Corbusier's ideal city on the grounds that it would destroy the community as an effective political force. But to attack Le Corbusier from this standpoint is to overlook the possibility that the absence of this kind of community and politics in his ideal cities was not an irresponsible oversight, as Jacobs and Sennett present it, but was intentional. Mumford's similar reaction to the antisocial bias of CIAM urbanism and Sert appeared at the end of the second chapter. But when

Le Corbusier celebrated his Unité building-type as 'the *vertical commune* without politics', it was for a good reason.[5] I have tried to demonstrate that his proposals were consistent with a particular ideal of what made human life meaningful, and that this did not involve society or politics. It is probably the strangeness of this ideal that provokes such emotional reactions against his work.[6]

The second section, 'The Science of Painting', showed that Le Corbusier wanted not only to establish order in our relations with society and politics, but also to establish order in our relations with the physical world and universe. He subscribed to Poincaré's 'conventionalism', which maintained that as physical laws could never be definitively known, we should conform to those epistemological paradigms that seemed to work and corresponded to our experience. This 'knowledge' involved achieving a functional balance with external reality, and was the necessary starting-point for human survival. But although external reality could not be definitively known, Le Corbusier believed that when the individual extricated himself from this reality he could achieve definitive knowledge of himself. This involved keeping 'subject' and 'object' apart in a way that distinguished Le Corbusier from those ordinarily thought to be closest to him, Léger and Ozenfant, and also from those others who were interested in immersing the individual in the higher spatial dimensions theoretically provided by the new sciences. Le Corbusier tried to achieve this by designing cities that were as 'objective' as possible. They were deliberately orderly, plain, unenthralling and predictable, and would continually have recalled the inhabitant to his prior knowledge and experience of space. This also seemed to work for the domestic objects of Purist paintings. As with Le Corbusier's socio-political initiatives, this was intended to cut the individual's dependency upon things external to the self.

This reading is overlooked by another important cluster of commentaries. These approach Le Corbusier from 'typological', 'semiological' and 'phenomenological' perspectives, and although these terms sound imposing, they can, for the purpose of my argument, be understood quite simply and as fundamentally similar. They are all concerned with studying and promoting the urban milieu as a rich source of interest and meaning in the lives of human beings. The typological approach is the only one that is specifically architectural, so we should give it special consideration.

The 'type' is the shape you arrive at when you try to obtain the 'average' of a type of building – be it a church, hospital, prison, house or whatever – throughout its history. It is an historically derived 'formal' consensus, found by 'comparing and superimposing'. Despite all the variations throughout history, it will always look essentially the same.[7] This is Giulio Carlo Argan's classic formulation from 1963.[8]

But the most influential typological text is Aldo Rossi's *The Architecture of the City*. Rossi believes that cities and human beings are analogous, created through similar processes. Both are subject to a unique set of events or 'experiences' that happen only to them. These experiences leave traces in the 'memory', which ties all these traces together in order to create an individual 'identity' and 'consciousness'. But how does a city remember? A city remembers through its architecture. The preservation of old architecture in the city is the same thing as the preservation of old memories in the mind. And if a city can remember in this way, if it can hold on to traces of its old architecture and yet still remain open to change in the future, then it will be able to develop an identity that becomes ever more rich and unique over time. But if a city loses too many of its historical buildings, it will effectively suffer memory loss and the loss of its identity. The built environment, then, can demonstrate to people the proper trajectory of their lives. And of course, people are even more intimately linked to their environment by the fact that their experiences always happen in particular places. The architect must reinforce this human–urban symbiosis through the sensitive use of 'types'.[9]

Typology was an attack upon architectural and urban modernism, especially its deliberate attempt to break with history and innovate completely new forms. Respect for the type made possible the rehabilitation of historical meaning in a way that was flexible enough to allow for those meanings to change as and when new circumstances dictated. But in order not to fracture this meaning completely, changes to the inherited stock of types – and consequently to the fabric of the city – must be gradual and respectful.

Attempts are persistently made to trace the typological precedents concealed within Le Corbusier's work. A good deal of Alan Colquhoun's work has been dedicated to this, and von Moos has supported him. Colquhoun maintains that the modernists, and Le Corbusier especially, were deluding themselves by thinking that they could eradicate historical referents from their buildings. They had insisted that form followed function or other programmatic requirements, and that their architecture was consequently self-referential. But this, Colquhoun maintains, only led to a vacuum of meaning that was filled with other kinds of symbolism. Colquhoun therefore concludes that all architecture is imprisoned within a pre-existing vocabulary of historical types. As types are inescapable, the architect should work with them in a respectful way, 'modifying' them according to new circumstances.[10] However, given that Le Corbusier consistently and dramatically tried to subvert historical types, such as by turning columns into *pilotis* to lift buildings off the ground, typologists have to go to considerable lengths to make their case.[11]

It is a truism to say that design cannot disregard its history, but to trace the historical meanings of Le Corbusier's 'types' is again to disregard the fact of his intent. He intended that the forms of his cities should be cut loose from all inherited systems of meaning, because he thought 'meaning' ought to be found not in one's urban milieu but in oneself. Consequently, he made every attempt to purge his ideal city of meaning. Indeed, one of the key ways he did this was to force a radical break with history. As far as possible, his ideal cities demanded a *tabula rasa*. The Ville Voisin for Paris, for example, proposed to save only certain outstanding historical artefacts from demolition, which were to be isolated in the vast parks. But they were dead museum pieces, no longer part of the evolving historical texture that typologists value.[12] Le Corbusier's plans for Moscow, which became the Ville Radieuse, were even more disrespectful of the history bound up in the pre-existing urban milieu. It was, he said, 'impossible to dream of harmonizing the city of the past with the present and future'.[13]

For the same reason, it is necessary to question those attempts to approach Le Corbusier from 'semiological' and 'phenomenological' perspectives. As these are based on non-architectural disciplines, they will not be treated in such depth here.

Phenomenology is a branch of philosophy that attempts to understand the world in a way that prioritizes direct experience, rather than using abstract theoretical systems. The phenomenological approach to architecture is committed to providing environments that heighten the quality of lived experience. It is more popularly referred to as 'place-making' and has amounted in recent years to orthodoxy. Place-making involves such things as providing points of interest for all the five senses; providing clues for the triggering of memory, imagination, daydreams and desire; and otherwise attempting to give the individual a sense of his or her immersion in an inconceivably rich and varied phenomenal reality. This reality ranges from the most mundane domestic object, through the social milieu, towards mystical notions of union with nature, the cosmos and God, and the individual is meant to absorb it all in a non-stop reverie bordering on ecstasy. It is allegedly in this *total* experience – by realizing our preordained place in this scheme – that we achieve our 'identity' and 'being'. Architecture should make us feel 'at home' here and allow us to 'dwell'.[14]

Geoffrey Baker believes a reappraisal along these lines would be necessary to humanize Le Corbusier's cities. These cities did not allow people to 'be', 'in-the-world': 'His city proposals were excruciatingly boring.' They 'failed to give man an existential footing', while properly they should 'enable man to comprehend his world through the medium of buildings'. The philosopher Henri Lefebvre criticizes Le Corbusier's city designs for being more concerned with providing some unattainable '"objective" knowledge of "reality"' than with providing places more responsive to the living experiences of human beings: 'The user's space is *lived* – not represented (or conceived).' And alluding to Le Corbusier's infamous maxim, Karsten Harries criticizes 'our technological culture, which insists not so much on dwellings as on machines for working and living'. This architecture is 'inhuman' because it is founded upon 'a self-displacement which transforms man from an embodied self into a pure thinking subject'.[15] Le Corbusier might have dismissed these critics as ignorant of his deepest intentions.

Semiology is the study of signs and symbols in language, and is concerned especially with the processes through which meaning is sustained, transformed and transmitted. Although it is clear that architecture does not work exactly like language, attempts have been made to understand the mechanisms through which it upholds meaning. Behind this lies the belief that architecture has an important role in communicating the socio-cultural ideals of its day, and that it should be made more effective and responsible in this. Like typology, this approach became popular in the 1960s as an attack upon modernism's attempt to evade meaning: Charles Jencks said that 'Meaning' was 'Inevitable, yet Denied'.[16]

In relation to Le Corbusier, Jencks maintained that 'the architect's creativity is somewhat dependent on his using a pre-existent syntax (or structure and technology) and semantics (or the conventional connotations of doors, windows, stairways, etc.) . . . architecture is more flexible, permissive and changing than language, but at the same time less powerful for manipulating ideas and communicating'. Le Corbusier handled his 'language' so flexibly that he revealed the 'arbitrary nature of the architectural sign'. Even so, this language was 'functionally stable', and 'This coherence of use allows one . . . to read off the semantic meaning.' Jencks consequently proposed the 'systematic deciphering and classification' of Le Corbusier's language, and began by identifying forty consistently recurring 'words'.[17]

Underlying all of these critical approaches, in my opinion, is a refusal to pay attention to Le Corbusier's intentions. They presuppose that the individual must continually be attending to the city, enthralled by everything going on outside itself, be it 'society', 'politics', 'history', 'signs', 'experiences' or other 'phenomena'. This leads them either to condemn Le Corbusier for not conforming to their philosophy, or to attempt to recast him until he does conform. In so doing, they reveal that they conceive the city differently than he did. They believe that people are indivisible from their urban milieu. Le Corbusier believed the opposite. What these commentators might take to be failure or oversight, Le Corbusier might take to be success.

I was in Chandigarh for the Golden Jubilee of Indian Independence on 17 August 1997. This experience gave me a useful insight into how Le Corbusier's cities were meant to work, although I did not expect or welcome this insight at the time. It seemed that every town and city in the country was engaged in some kind of street festival, which intensified as midnight approached. Expecting a similar event in Chandigarh, my friend and I wandered late into the streets and city centre and found them deserted. Our presence served only to arouse the suspicion of the police, so we hurried back to our hotel room and watched the festivals elsewhere on television. Initially I was disappointed, but later I realized that I had no right to be. It is misguided to demand experiences from Le Corbusier's cities that they cannot and were never intended to provide. Given the extraordinary vibrancy of other Indian cities it is difficult to avoid the suspicion, however disturbing it might be, that the situation in Chandigarh is a direct and deliberate product of its architectural forms. These serve to overawe and alienate the individual rather than provide a reassuring place for socializing (fig. 13).[18]

13   Le Corbusier. Sector 17 city centre (top); Capitol Complex, view of Temple of Shadows, Secretariat and Palace of Assembly (bottom); Chandigarh.

Umberto Eco seemed to recognize that Le Corbusier was attempting something along these lines. Le Corbusier's design

> moves outside the accepted typology . . . the architect has preceded architectural design with an examination of certain new social exigencies, certain 'existential' desiderata, certain tendencies in the development of the modern city and life within it, and has traced out . . . a semantic system of certain future exigencies . . . on the basis of which new functions and new architectural forms might come into being.[19]

Le Corbusier fractures the existing social code in accordance with a new ideal of living – new 'existential *desiderata*'. This is precisely why his cities are devoid of those processes and qualities that are thought important to bind society together: there was to be no society. As discussed in my final section, Le Corbusier's new 'existential *desiderata*' came from Pascal. This connection clarified the nature and possible consequences of Le Corbusier's philosophy of self, which involved the individual turning his back on society to search for knowledge, value and meaning within. This act was profoundly antisocial, and also dangerous: there was the danger that society would persecute the individual, and that the individual would persecute society.

I believe that this concept of self was of central importance to Le Corbusier and conditioned a broad range of his thought and activities, from politics to poetry. I also believe that, on the basis of this understanding, it is possible to make an appropriate critique of Le Corbusier and his legacy. To finish, I should like to outline how this critique might be pursued.

The Worth of Le Corbusier's Concept of Self

Is Le Corbusier's concept of self of any use or value today? To answer this, it is necessary to re-establish its precedents and context in the broadest terms.

In the introduction, I suggested that urban literature has been dominated by two broad paradigms, and that these involved broad concepts of self. The first paradigm believed that the city – when considered a rich, diverse and unpredictable milieu – was evil, and sought to reform it in an orderly way. This was intended to ensure that people would make worthwhile use of their lives, which would be lived within strict, pre-ordained parameters. The second paradigm believed that the city was good, and sought to nurture all those factors that made it rich, diverse and unpredictable. Again, this was intended to ensure that people would make worthwhile use of their lives. But now, life would become worthwhile through immersion in the challenges and experiences of the unregulated city. These paradigms underlie urban literature, and are seldom explicitly stated.

It is obvious that Le Corbusier's urban philosophy belongs with the former, but it also represents the most extreme and perhaps final version of this paradigm. We can understand this by considering how Le Corbusier stands against the two other great figures in this tradition, Plato and Alberti.

Plato believed that the internal workings of the psyche and those of the city republic were unbalanced, but they could be realigned simultaneously. The city would be divided into a tripartite structure of 'Rulers', 'Auxiliaries' and 'Third Class', and the faculties inside each mind would be reconfigured to correspond with this hierarchy: 'reason', 'spirit' and 'appetite'. This proper balance of elements represented 'justice'. Plato proposed to achieve this by erasing and rebuilding the city and psyche. Not even memory or history would remain to remind people of their former lives:

> The first thing our artists must do . . . – and it's not easy – is to wipe the slate of human society and human habits clean. For our philosophic artists differ at once from all others in being unwilling to start work on an individual or a city, or draw out laws, until they have given, or have made themselves, a clean canvas.

Human beings were fickle and likely to be tempted into all manner of wasteful activities. But they were also malleable, and with careful management they could be made good.[20]

Although Alberti was also convinced of the viciousness of human nature and of the city, he did not believe either could be reformed. At best, they could be managed. His architectural treatise can be read as an urban survival guide for important men, keeping them one step ahead of the treachery, murder and vice that not only surrounded them on all sides but also flourished in their own homes and families. The physical structure of the city became an elaborate mechanism for managing and surviving human nature. Listening tubes and secret passageways riddled the palace, travel was restricted between 'zones' to prevent the formation of an organized mob, and fortifications warded off outside attacks. Even beautiful decoration had the underlying motive of soothing the enemy. The city was necessary as the seat of commerce and government. But once one's affairs were concluded, it was best to retreat to the suburban villa.[21]

To modern ears, Alberti and Plato seem extreme. But both worked within the intellectual expectations of their time. Neither of them had any idea that there might be another way of thinking about the city. It is interesting in this regard to note the lesson of one of Alberti's elder contemporaries, the humanist teacher Guarino of Verona, on how properly to assign praise or blame:

> Remember when you praise the countryside or denounce the city to take the reasons for the praise or blame from four 'places'. That is, show that utility, pleasure, virtue and excellence belong to the country. Contrariwise, damage, wretchedness, defects and flaws belong to the city.[22]

The ease and immediacy with which Guarino settles upon his examples seems to suggest an unspoken law: the city is always blameworthy. The possibility of an alternative way of thinking only emerged later, during the Enlightenment, when cities became so large and cosmopolitan that new qualities and potentials began to be discerned in them. Increasingly, the unregulated city was viewed as having many positive things to offer people. To be sure, ordinary people had no doubt lived with this fact from time immemorial, but it was only in these more secular times that writers seriously began to justify the city on such grounds.[23]

By the time Le Corbusier came to formulate his ideas, this second paradigm was dominant. Consequently, he was always working against what most people had for a long time considered to be the proper use of the city, particularly in terms of what the city was thought to contribute to the quality and richness of their lives. In the same decade that Le Corbusier presented his Ville Contemporaine, for example, Louis Aragon published *Le Paysan de Paris* and André Breton published *Nadja*.

Aragon documents the activities in a covered arcade of shops, the 'passage de l'opera'. Mysterious places like this seemed to generate new ways of living, 'entirely new types of person . . . hitherto unknown species', and Aragon attacked the planning initiatives which threatened to destroy them. Also, he believed that the individual who immerses himself in such places 'shall once again plumb his own depths'. Breton begins his novel with the question 'Who am I?', but shortly insists that 'categorical self-evaluation' is impossible. Instead, by assessing their responses to a labyrinthine city full of incident and intrigue, Breton and Aragon are able to gain insights into their own unconscious motivations. This allows them continually to reinvent themselves. Breton makes the following comment, which explains the situation perfectly: 'As far as I am concerned, a mind's arrangement with regard to certain objects is even more important than its regard for certain arrangements of objects, these two kinds of arrangement controlling between them all forms of sensibility.' The alternatives are these: do I change the city to suit myself, or do I change myself in response to the city? Le Corbusier does the former, Breton the latter, hoping that his experiences 'will be of a nature to send some men rushing out into the street'.[24] Although these ideas came from the avant-garde of the time and are extreme in their own way, I believe they are broadly representative of what has become the 'normal' way of thinking about the city.

But beyond concerns for the city, it is possible to evaluate Le Corbusier in terms of his concept of self, which seems to have nothing in common with the dominant trends of twentieth-century thought on the subject. I mentioned in the introduction that surveys of the philosophy of self tend to identify two broad paradigms, which I called the 'self-sufficient' and the 'self/other'. These have run side by side throughout history, with one never fully eclipsing the other, but there has been a distinct shift in the balance of power. Precisely when this shift occurred is open to debate: some situate it in the Enlightenment, which is the period I favour, others in the twentieth century.[25] But even so, few nowadays maintain that the self is an ideally discrete entity that needs to be shut off from the distracting influence of its environment. Instead, it is widely agreed that the self is comprehensively mediated, enriched, conditioned and even produced by its environment. I have discussed several of the main trends and theorists already, but it is useful to give a further indication of some of the major contemporary manifestations.[26]

Anthony Giddens, for example, follows in the tradition of sociologists like George Herbert Mead and Erving Goffman, who argue that the self is maintained through social interaction and role-play, although some trace of autonomous control or 'agency' remains to the individual in these accounts. For Giddens, the individual is involved in a mutually influential or 'reflexive' negotiation with global-institutional forces on more or less equal terms, and through which it constructs an ongoing 'narrative of self-identity'.[27] Contemporary 'governmental' theorists like Nikolas Rose are heir to the position developed by Michel Foucault, which takes a less sanguine view of the individual's relationship with power. Rose concurs that the psychological sciences are less concerned with providing knowledge than with producing 'psy'-techniques. These allow governments to infiltrate the psyche by various subtle and indirect means and enforce 'normalized' character structures. The individual consequently becomes self-policing and biddable.[28] Kenneth Gergen has taken over the 'subject-of-language' thesis first discussed by philosophers like Jacques Derrida. The individual is 'saturated' by the different 'languages' of society which results in a traumatic state of 'multiphrenia': it has no stable core of knowledge, value or meaning, it is full of conflicting ideas and potentials, and all its choices are potentially arbitrary. At first the individual will attempt to stabilize the situation by favouring a hard-line ideological viewpoint or identity from which to condemn the others, but ultimately the experience of being forced to incorporate so many 'languages' should lead to a more tolerant 'relational' self and society.[29]

Again, this is only a sketch of a vast body of theory, but despite their differences it is possible to recognize two fundamental beliefs in its more representative works. The first is a belief that, for good or ill, the individual is dependent upon its social milieu for meaning and identity. Scholars occasionally discuss cases when individuality is overemphasized to the detriment of society, but this tends to be condemned as sickness or vanity.[30] The second belief is that the individual is continually changing. Sometimes these changes are orderly and cumulative, sometimes arbitrary or enforced, but selfhood remains an ongoing *process*, not an end. Le Corbusier's philosophy of self, however, emphasized precisely the opposite of these two beliefs: the individual's disconnection from its milieu − social, political and natural − for the definitive realization of self.[31]

It was perhaps a suspicion that his ideas were inconsistent with the general drift of opinion that led Le Corbusier to ponder whether 'my *Poème de l'>+* is perhaps only a song of goodbye to a fleeting epoch'.[32]

By the early 1960s, Team 10, the group of architects that broke away from CIAM, could celebrate the end of Le Corbusier's 'old', 'deterministic', 'Euclidean groove' and the mode of living that it implied.[33] Even one of Le Corbusier's long-term collaborators, Maxwell Fry, came to feel he had lost contact with the lives and expectations of ordinary people: 'I imagine that he peopled his buildings, where indeed they gave the impression of being peopled, by figments of his own creation, unendowed with normal human attributes; and that as he grew older and more withdrawn, these counted for less than the elemental forms reaching forward to ultimate ruination.'[34]

Although Le Corbusier's thesis is probably no more extreme than those of Plato and Alberti, he was more of an extremist by advancing it against the grain of his times and against ordinary expectations of living. In terms of current thinking about the uses of cities and the nature of self, Le Corbusier's philosophy occupies a difficult, if not untenable, position.[35] Affinities with Jung, Camus and Bataille ensure that he was not completely alone in his thoughts. But there must be an ethical difference between exploring these ideas in literature and seeking to build cities in which people would be forced to explore them in their real lives. And there is also the question of how far Le Corbusier lived up to this ideal himself, as he was certainly no monk.

In this 'real' sense, Le Corbusier's concept of self is of questionable worth. But Le Corbusier himself was exemplary. He was aware that his proposals presupposed a particular concept of self. I think he was also aware that such issues are unavoidable in all architecture and urbanism. The central object of this profession has always been the design of human beings. This awareness is no longer common or welcome in architectural and urban circles, but it is always implicit. The necessary precondition for any responsible design ethos is that these issues be drawn out and treated more seriously. I hope the broad-based approach I have adopted for understanding Le Corbusier may offer some clues for unearthing the hidden 'homunculi' of other important architects and urbanists.

Notes

For reasons of space, references to written works will usually be kept to name, date of publication and page numbers, with full details reserved for the bibliography. Occasionally, the original publication date differs from that of the edition consulted, but this will be noted only where chronology has some bearing on the issues under discussion. Because of the frequency with which Le Corbusier's writings are consulted I refer to their titles also, and occasionally do likewise for other important primary sources.

Introduction

1   I agree with Christopher Green's point that although this public–private split *was* something of a self-aggrandizing myth on Le Corbusier's part, and not always carried out in the actual circumstances of his life, the persistence with which he drew attention to it compels us to take it seriously: 'the myth was an essential component in the entire structure of his thinking'. ('The architect as artist', in Michael Raeburn and Victoria Wilson [eds], 1987, pp. 111–12.) Alan Colquhoun has remarked that 'Over the last 60 years the work of Le Corbusier has been the subject of two very different types of commentary. These might be called, respectively, myth-reinforcing or myth-destroying.' ('Books. The Le Corbusier Centenary', in *Journal of the Society of Architectural Historians*, vol. 49, no. 1, March 1990, p. 96.) Charles Jencks's argument that Le Corbusier should be ranked an 'Exemplary Creator' alongside several other 'heroically productive titans' is the most recent act of myth-reinforcement, while the opposite is

provided by Mardges Bacon: 'Experience rarely changed his preconceptions; reality rarely challenged his myths.' (Jencks, 2000, pp. 256–361, quotation from p. 356; Bacon, 2001, p. 158.) A more profitable approach, however, is the one suggested by Green, which indulges Le Corbusier's *intent* but without resorting to flattery.

2   Le Corbusier's dualism is interpreted in countless ways, including function versus form, engineering versus architecture, 'Dionysian' versus 'Apollonian', nautical versus aeronautical, good versus evil, and so on. Commentators will often switch between these interpretations freely. (Reyner Banham, 1960, pp. 226, 259, 262. Kenneth Frampton, 1980, p. 149; 2001, pp. 174, 202–3. William Curtis, 1982, p. 105; 1984, p. 41. Colquhoun, 'Architecture and Engineering: Le Corbusier and the Paradox of Reason', in Colquhoun, 1989, pp. 90, 99, 101, 115. Jencks, 1977, p. 142, 147–8; 1987, pp. 179–81. Stanislaus von Moos, 'Le Corbusier as Painter', trans. Jane O. Newman and John H. Smith, in Frampton [ed.], 1980, pp. 102–4.)

3   The earliest example is Cornelius Gurlitt, 'Le Corbusier and the "Pack-Donkey's Way"' (1929), in Peter Serenyi (ed.), 1975, pp. 122–3. For the latest, see Bacon, 2001, pp. 63–4, 74, 157–8. Other examples include Peter Hall, 1996, pp. 203–40, and Vincent Scully, 'The Architecture of Community', in Katz, 1994, pp. 221–30. To give *all* the instances of where this criticism appears, however, would be to give an almost complete bibliography of Le Corbusier scholarship. We shall encounter several more examples later.

4   More than anyone, Umberto Eco has suspected this: '[Le Corbusier] moves outside the accepted typology . . . [because he] has preceded architectural design with an examination of certain new social exigencies, certain "existential" desiderata, certain tendencies in the development of the modern city and life within it, and has traced out . . . a semantic system of certain future exigencies . . . on the basis of which new functions and new architectural forms might come into being.' ('Function and Sign: The Semiotics of Architecture' [1980], in Neil Leach [ed.], 1997, pp. 182–204, quotation from p. 197.)

5   I am conducting a research project with Professor Jules Lubbock in the Department of Art History and Theory at the University of Essex, investigating 'Concepts of Self in the Theory and Practice of Architecture and Town-Planning since 1945'. The Arts and Humanities Research Board is funding this research, which is scheduled for completion in 2005.

6   'These terminological differences are not always especially significant, primarily because all these terms can be said to denote a concern with the subjectivity of the individual. However, others argue that such terminological differences are worth close attention, if only because these differences reflect deep historical and political transitions.' Even so, the different terms indicate 'conceptualizations of selfhood' that are 'squarely pitched between those that deny the agency of human subjects and argue in favour of the person's determination by social structures

. . . and those that celebrate the authenticity and creativity of the self". (Anthony Elliott, 2001, p. 9; see also pp. 2–4.) This polarity is fundamental to the discourse of the self.

7   My account is taken from a reading of many of the primary sources and several commentaries and anthologies: Elliott, 2001; Roy Porter (ed.), 1997; Shaun Gallagher and Jonathan Shear (eds), 1999; Paul du Gay et al. (eds), 2000.

8   This paradigm has taken countless individual forms that are frequently contradictory. They may be profoundly religious or sacrilegious, rational or emotional, peaceful or violent, social or antisocial. But generally they all privilege some form of autonomous self-discovery or self-creation away from the debilitating effects and constraints of the 'environment'. Here and throughout, we have to take the term 'environment' in the broadest sense, referring not only to its physical, built fabric but also to all of the personal, cultural, social and political dynamics that it supports.

   The concept of self under this paradigm may take a Christian Protestant form, as in the personal cultivation of the soul through study, prayer and hard work, and resistance to the temptations of the flesh. It may be philosophical: René Descartes considered the information that came through the senses to be untrustworthy, and therefore employed pure reason to strip himself of all he had learned and find the final, irreducible point of knowledge. This was the 'thinking' self discovered through rational thought, but also the *source* of rational thought that could open out and understand the world anew. (*Discourse on Method*, 1637; *Meditations on First Philosophy*, 1641.) The shift from a mindset restricted by social and religious conventions towards one of full self-determination and moral accountability may be interpreted as the basis of nascent democracy and civil liberty. (John Stuart Mill, *On Liberty*, 1859.) The same general process, with less emphasis on democracy, might be presented as the genius of a uniquely gifted historical culture. (Jacob Burckhardt, *The Civilization of the Renaissance in Italy*, 1859.) It might even take the form of the angst-ridden self-centredness of the Romantics and Existentialists, which arguably found their spiritual origin in Jean-Jacques Rousseau's *Confessions* (1782).

   Despite their variety, all of these examples seek out a self that is ideally autonomous, whole and authentic. (See n. 7 above for secondary references.)

9   Again, there is a great variety of individual positions within this paradigm, but all maintain that the self is articulated through negotiation with 'environmental' factors. The differences arise around the question of the *degree* to which the environment influences the individual. Is there some core or process of self that continues to exist substantially independent from its environment? Or is the self utterly conditioned, even *produced*, by its environment?

   On one side is John Locke's revolutionary thesis, which was the first to give prominence to such factors as 'experience', 'time' and 'memory'. Locke maintained that the individual articulated his or her experiences in the world into a unique biographical narrative of individual identity. Memory held the pieces of this narrative together, allowing one to become increasingly differentiated as an individual identity through time. (*An Essay Concerning Human Understanding*, 1690.) Georg Simmel considered the proper trajectory of life to be the successive transgression of 'boundaries', social and psychological. The individual moved into ever larger and more differentiated social groupings, within which he or she could come to recognize and express their own uniqueness. ('Group Expansion and the Development of Individuality', 1908; 'Subjective Culture', 1908; 'The Transcendent Character of Life', 1918.)

George Herbert Mead maintained that the self is elaborated through the use of shared language in social interaction. This process – 'symbolic interactionism' – *socializes* the self, but it is not completely 'passive'. On the contrary, it allows the individual to distinguish and maintain a critical distance between the 'I' and the 'Me': the 'I' is the *unsocialized* part of the self, ego-driven and including spontaneous dreams and desires; the 'Me' is its respectable public face. This distinction allows the individual to preserve some autonomy and creative agency, and hence to exert a reciprocal influence on the social structure. (*Mind, Self and Society*, 1934.) The elements of role-play in Mead's model are amplified by Erving Goffman. Goffman maintained that the self was continually refashioned in response to changing social circumstances and expectations, in order to appear 'competent'. But again, as in Mead, the self was not completely passive: the playing-out of roles allowed for it to be concretized in reality, and also acted as a façade for the maintenance of a reflective and creative presence behind the scenes. (*The Presentation of Self in Everyday Life*, 1956.)

Alternatively, many argue that the 'subject' has little or no mastery over its environment. The earliest and still the most radical thesis is that of David Hume, who maintained that there was no evidence to prove we were anything other than an unrelated 'bundle' of perceptions, produced by sensations flooding in from outside. The self was a 'fiction', and it was only our fear that prevented us from conceding the fact. (*A Treatise on Human Nature*, 1739.)

This has been taken up in many different forms, with theorists variously arguing that the 'subject' is not a self-constituted, purposeful agent, but instead a product of language and discourse. Perhaps most memorable in this vein is Michel Foucault, who argued that the self is comprehensively conditioned by the psychological and sexual 'norms' established by ostensibly objective scientific research. These norms are enforced through institutional regimes like asylums, prisons, hospitals and schools, and disseminated less directly through such channels as the popular media. The self becomes inculcated into a strict regime of self-policing, unable to deviate from the norm. (*Discipline and Punish*, 1975; see also Louis Althusser, 'Ideology and Ideological State Apparatuses', 1971.)

Others, such as Jacques Derrida, have emphasized different consequences of the 'subject-of-language' idea. Derrida has argued that the self is rendered unstable due to the unstable nature of the language through which it attempts to articulate itself. 'Meaning' is sustained through the exclusion of some 'other' element which is opposing and inadmissible: 'black' and 'white', for example. But this *other* remains as a reminder of incompleteness and exclusion to 'divide and haunt'. Therefore meaning, and with it the identity of the individual, can never stabilize: they are subject to endless 'slippage' and 'deferral'. (Derrida, '*Différance*', 1972; see also Emile Benveniste, 'Subjectivity in Language', 1958.)

Despite their variety, the self under this paradigm is always changing, malleable and unstable. (See n. 7 above for secondary references.)

10   These ideas have taken many different forms in the theoretical work of architects and urbanists, as well as in other kinds of scholarly and imaginative literature that deal with the phenomenon of the city. I shall give some examples in my conclusion.

11   Elliott, 2001, pp. 6–8, 11–12.

12   It is a part of our current project, however, to consider how these issues affect more 'ordinary' practice. (See n. 5 above.)

13   Dana Cuff and Russell Ellis (eds), 1989, pp. 3–11; quotations from pp. 3 (emphasis added), 5, 7, 8. Several of the contributors went beyond this remit, and started to advocate certain concepts of the 'person' that they personally favoured. Therefore the volume occasionally became prey to the very abuses it sought to remedy. Certain essays, however, offered model examples of how to pursue such research: see Paul Groth, 'Nonpeople: A Case Study of Public Architects and Impaired Social Vision', pp. 213–38. This volume also drew attention to some important earlier work: Sidney N. Brower et al., 1966, pp. 228–33; Lambert van der Laan and Andries Piersma, 1982, pp. 411–26. Another crucial study is by K. Michael Hays, who investigated how twentieth-century challenges to Humanist ideals of individual autonomy and stability were reflected in the work of Hannes Meyer and Ludwig Hilberseimer. Increasingly, the 'subject' was considered to be a renegotiable product of cultural forces, and this shift found compelling echoes in their approach to design. Hays also makes the useful general point that 'precise potentials of meaningful action are produced and made available . . . in the architectural objects and their subject-productive force'. (1992, *passim*; quotation from p. 7.) Also relevant is Jean Hertel La Marche, 1995. La Marche attempts to map the notion of the 'subject' in several of the most important twentieth-century architects, and one chapter is dedicated to Le Corbusier. He alleges that Le Corbusier wanted to fix the psyches of 'his' people, which were split between concerns for past and present. This is wrong, as will become clear as we proceed. But the most problematic thing about La Marche's thesis is that he is less interested in the concepts of the 'subject' upheld by his chosen architects than in demonstrating how 'naïve' they are when put up against Jacques Lacan. La

Marche's research, then, is tied to the questionable agenda of formulating 'a Lacanian architecture'. I do, however, agree with his general point that 'The aggressive role that architects played toward the subject in the early part of the century narrowly focussed the subject's experience.' (See esp. pp. 1–40, 86–101; quotations from pp. 87, 91.)

A Two-Part Project

1   Le Corbusier, *Journey to the East* (1966), 1987, p. 216. Because of the frequency with which I have to refer to Le Corbusier's writings, I shall provide only a shortened version of their titles after the initial reference.

2   Le Corbusier, *Towards a New Architecture* (1923), 1989, pp. 133, 211. The 'establishment of a standard' is said to 'involve exhausting every practical and reasonable possibility and extracting from them a recognized type comfortable to its functions, with a maximum output and a minimum use of means'. (p. 137).

3   Le Corbusier, *The City of Tomorrow* (1924), 1987, pp. 45–6.

4   Le Corbusier, *Precisions on the Present State of Architecture and City Planning* (1930), 1991, pp. 35–6.

5   *Towards*, p. 212; see also pp. 208–9, on the 'axis' or 'criterion of harmony' inside us all which 'leads us to assume a unity of conduct in the universe and to admit a single will behind it'; and p. 203: manifestations of the spiritual side 'arouse, deep within us and beyond our sense, a resonance, a sort of sounding board which begins to vibrate. An indefinable trace of the Absolute which lies in the depths of our being.' See also *City*, p. 48, for a list of the kinds of artefact which Le Corbusier believes give evidence of this. Upon visiting Athens for the first time in 1911, he appears to have bought a copy of Ernest Renan's essay 'Prière sur l'Acropole', where the Parthenon is described as 'the one perfect manifestation on earth (aside from the advent of Christ) of the universal "Ideal"'. (Paul Venable Turner, 1977, pp. 99–100.)

6   *Towards*, p. 165. See also *Precisions*, pp. 31–2, 218, on this 'visionary', 'poet', and 'prophet'; and Le Corbusier, *The Decorative Art of Today* (1925), 1987, p. 181, on the 'initiate', 'the man of greater strength who will explain'.

7   *City*, pp. 35–6, 150; more generally, see pp. 29–39 on 'Sensibility Comes Into Play'. These historical stages were later formulated as '*Archaism*', '*Naturalism*' and '*Hieratism*'. (*Decorative*, p. 122; see also p. 214 on the cyclical nature of this process.)

8   See *City*, pp. 38 and 141–58 on 'Our Technical Equipment'.

9   *Decorative*, p. 118.

10   *City*, p. 36.

11   Ibid., p. 150.

12   Le Corbusier to Francis Jourdain, 1913, cited in Nancy J. Troy, 1991, p. 80. Le Corbusier was acquainted with the work of Loos no later than 1912–13, when

the journal *Les Cahiers d'aujourd'hui* published several of Loos's essays. He may have been introduced to it earlier, however, in the pioneering design studios of Auguste Perret and Peter Behrens. (Troy, 1991, p. 79; see also Jencks, 1987, p. 22 and Turner, 1977, p. 44.) There is scarce an opinion in Le Corbusier's thesis on the necessity of reforming the decorative arts which cannot be traced to Loos. (See Lubbock, 1995, pp. 301–12.)

13 Loos, 'Ornament and Crime' (1908), trans. Wilfred Wang, in Yehuda Safran (ed.), 1985, p. 100.

14 Loos, 'Architecture' (1910), in ibid., p. 105. On the aspiring bourgeois's love of expensive-looking fakery and the willingness of designers to cater to this taste, see Loos, 1982: 'Interiors: A Prelude' (1898), pp. 19–20; 'Building Materials' (1898), p. 64; 'Furniture' (1898), pp. 77–8.

15 Loos, 'Ornament and Crime', p. 100.

16 Loos, 'Ladies' Fashion' (1898), in Loos, 1982, p. 102 (emphasis added).

17 Loos, 'Ornament and Crime', p. 103. This is the reason for Loos's love of the anonymous modern suit, and the house must be similarly anonymous: 'The house should be discrete on the outside; its entire richness should be disclosed on the inside.' (Loos, 'Vernacular Art' [1914], in Safran [ed.], 1985, p. 113.)

18 Adolf Loos, 'Men's Fashion' (1898), in Loos, 1982, pp. 11–12.

19 See Loos, 'The Story of a Poor Rich Man' (1900), trans. Harold Meek, in Gustav Künstler and Ludwig Münz, 1966, pp. 223–5. This comic fable provides the most memorable account of Loos's belief in the inviolability of the home interior. A 'poor rich man' is terrorized by his 'famous architect', who coordinates all aspects of the interior and then forbids his client to change anything. All domestic identity and intimacy, and the right to self-determination, are thus thrown over for the socially derived standards of design. The Belgian architect Henry van de Velde was probably intended to take the brunt of this satire: in 1895 he not only designed a house for his wife, but also the clothes in which she would best harmonize with its decor. (Frampton, 'Adolf Loos and the Crisis of Culture: 1896–1931', in Safran [ed.], 1985, pp. 8, 11; see also Loos, 'Interiors in the Rotunda' [1898], in Loos, 1982, pp. 22–7.)

20 See Loos, 'Culture' (1908), in Safran (ed.), 1985, p. 97, in which Loos champions the productivity and efficiency of the 'Anglo-Saxon' civilization over the laziness and backwardness of the 'Latin'. He characterizes this in terms of the industrious pig who loves to get dirty and clean himself afresh for more action, versus the lazy cat who recycles her dirt with her tongue. On the symbolism of hygiene-as-progress, see Loos, 'The Plumbers' (1898), in Künstler and Münz, 1966, pp. 219–22. Also, on Loos's concern for economic thrift and standardization, see 'Ornament and Crime', pp. 101–2; 'Vernacular Art', p. 113; Loos, 'Review of the Arts and Crafts' (1898) in Loos, 1982, p. 104; Safran, 'Adolf Loos: the Archimedean point', in Safran (ed.), 1985, p. 33.

21 Loos, 'Architecture', p. 104 (emphasis added).

22 *Precisions*, p. 107.

23 *Decorative*, p. 85; see also pp. 118, 134.

24 Ibid., pp. 86–7. On standardization, museums, love of the past, architectural training and shoddy manufacture, see ibid., pp. 69–79 on 'Type-needs. Type-furniture'; *Precisions*, pp. 105–21 on 'The Undertaking of Furniture'; *Decorative*, pp. 3–37, 54; esp. pp. 15–23 on 'Other icons: the museums'; *Journey*, p. 173; *Towards*, pp. 14, 94–5. For attacks on the bourgeoisie, see *Decorative*, pp. 6, 20, 27–8, 37 and 52. Le Corbusier liked to symbolize their folly through literary characters like Alfred Jarry's Père Ubu and Gustave Flaubert's Monsieur Homais. (See Jarry, 1997; Flaubert, 1992.)

25 *Decorative*, p. 188; see also p. 189 on 'The Law of Ripolin'.

26 Ibid., p. 22. See also p. 42: 'There is no longer such a thing as a private palace; luxury no longer resides in the Aubusson carpet but has moved up to the brain'; and p. 77: 'the human spirit is more at home behind our foreheads than beneath gilt and carved baldacchinos'.

27 *Precisions*, p. 107.

28 *Decorative*, pp. 31, 166, 180.

29 Turner has traced Le Corbusier's introduction to some form of German philosophical idealism through Henry Provensal's *L'art de demain* (1904) and Édouard Schuré's *Les grands initiés* (1889). (Turner, 1977; 1971, pp. 214–24.) See also Colquhoun, 'Architecture and Engineering: Le Corbusier and the Paradox of Reason', pp. 90–92, 103.

30 Such individuals 'have made themselves the instruments of the substantial spirit . . . this substance is the sole aim, the sole power, and the sole end which is willed by such individuals; it seeks satisfaction through them and is accomplished by them'. (G. W. F. Hegel, 1975, pp. 84–5.)

31 *Precisions*, p. 192.

32 For further references to the inexorable right of these 'great men', see Hegel, 1975, pp. 52, 59–60, 84–5. Le Corbusier reproduces these sentiments in *City*, pp. 15–16, 18, 39, 43; *Decorative*, pp. 35, 43; *Precisions*, p. 31. See also Loos: 'No one has tried to put his podgy hand into the spokes of the turning wheel of time without having that hand torn off.' (Loos, 'Cultural Degeneration' [1908], in Safran [ed.], 1985, p. 98.) Lubbock traces Loos's ideas to the social-evolutionary doctrine of Herbert Spencer. (1983, pp. 43–9.)

'The Lawgiver': Preface

1 *City*, p. 301.

2 He assumed French citizenship in 1930. (Raeburn and Wilson [eds.], 1987, p. 348.) Jencks reckons that 'Like a true son of the Enlightenment [Le Corbusier]

would accept only ideals as his guide, ideals based on reason. This allowed him . . . to remain free from partisan involvements in a sort of apolitical opportunism . . . All the clients had to be persuaded by idealist arguments (instead of party sentiments) and had to be enlightened paternalists.' Jencks calls this 'idealist liberalism'. (1987, p. 112.) This is questionable: not only was Le Corbusier openly implicated with various partisan movements, but these were often violently illiberal. 'Reason' and 'objectivity' were just costumes to be donned as appropriate. We also have to question the following statement from Maurice Jardot: 'Radically opposed to the big-business approach common among architects and planners to-day, this truly great man has never sought the favour of influential clients.' ('Introduction', in Le Corbusier, *My Work*, 1960, p. 12.)

3   Von Moos has stated that Le Corbusier was blameworthy for elevating 'socio-economic forces, institutional patterns and ideology . . . to the level of universal and natural laws'. This should be reversed: Le Corbusier started with an abstract ideal, and adopted certain of the most promising political and socio-economic forces as vehicles to realize it. ('From the "City for 3 Million Inhabitants" to the "Plan Voisin"', in Serenyi [ed.], 1975, pp. 125–6.)

1   1914–1929: Technocracy

1   Charles-Edouard Jeanneret first began using the pseudonym 'Le Corbusier' in 1920, when he and Amédée Ozenfant were collaborating on articles for the self-publicizing 'Purist' journal, *L'Esprit nouveau*. It is likely that this was a ruse to convince their readership that the journal had a greater number of contributors. Yet the pseudonym was also employed as a symbol of Jeanneret's self-perceived ideological maturity after 1920.

2   Jeanneret to Max DuBois, 24 June 1914, cited in Joyce Lowman, 1976, p. 230.

3   Information Bureau of the French High Commission, *What France Has Done in the War*, 1919, cited in Kenneth Silver, 1977, p. 60. Maurice Barrés noted, 'We had come to be regarded as jaded triflers, far too affluent and light-hearted, with pleasure as our only concern.' (*The Undying Spirit of France*, New Haven, 1917, cited in ibid., p. 59.)

4   Richard F. Kuisel, 1981, p. 31.

5   Ibid., p. 77. For a full account of 'technocracy' in this period, see pp. 76–92. See also Kuisel, 1973, pp. 53–99; Mary McLeod, 1983, pp. 132–47; Charles S. Maier, 1970, pp. 27–61. By 1914, Henri le Chatelier had translated Taylor's major written works into French.

6   Kuisel, 1981, pp. 76–7; McLeod, 1983, pp. 133–4; Maier, 1970, pp. 29–31; Eric Hobsbawm, 1987, pp. 44–5. Regardless of such sentiments, the trade unions were quick to demand higher wages and social-welfare measures, which were granted by the government out of fear of strike action. By 1920, trade union member-

ship had risen to over 2,000,000, with the workers over-optimistically believing themselves to be as indispensable in peacetime as they had been during the war. (Arthur Marwick, 1974, pp. 73–5, 90; D. W. Brogan, 1940, p. 558.)

7 Maier, 1970, p. 38; McLeod, 1983, pp. 134–5. On the appeal of Saint-Simonianism to the political right and left, see Fishman, 1977 (a), pp. 248–51.

8 The eagerness with which the French masses absorbed rationalization appeared to betray a desire to redress the Prussian defeat of 1870–71, and the popular myth of their national dissolution and frivolousness. (Silver, 1977, pp. 59–60; David Stevenson, 1979, p. 878.)

9 Jeanneret to DuBois, 15 September 1914, cited in Eleanor Gregh, 'The Dom-ino Idea', in Frampton (ed.), 1979, p. 78.

10 Jeanneret to DuBois, 9 March 1915, cited in Lowman, 1976, p. 231. Jeanneret put similar sentiments in his sketchbook of 1915. He maintained that the goods in the Printemps department store were 'the most beautiful that can be demanded of the present age . . . Thus the Krauts are routed . . . it's more than enough to completely offset the Hun.' He also said that these national tensions were 'A necessary piece of rehabilitation'. (*Le Corbusier Sketchbooks. Volume 1, 1914–1948*, 1981, p. 8, entry nos. 97, 99.)

11 In 1917, Le Corbusier called Taylorism 'the horrible and ineluctable life of tomorrow', although he praised it highly in many of his subsequent publications. (Jeanneret to William Ritter, 25 December 1917, in McLeod, 1983, p. 135. See also Brian Brace Taylor, 'Le Corbusier at Pessac', in Serenyi [ed.], 1975, pp. 98–9.) The Dom-ino constituted Le Corbusier's main creative outlet during the war years. Back in his home town of La Chaux-de-Fonds since 1911, he otherwise had to deal with criticisms of his teaching initiatives at the local art school, a building slump lasting from 1912–16, and the recriminations and financial wrangles over the Villa Schwob of 1917. 'This profession drives one to support autocracy,' he complained. (Jeanneret to Ritter, 9 May 1913, cited in ibid., p. 77; see also pp. 75–9 and Lowman, 1976, *passim*.)

12 This introduction was orchestrated by Perret, who became vice-president of Art et Liberté's governing board in December 1916. Earlier, Jeanneret had helped Perret formulate the defence of his Théâtre des Champs-Elysées of 1915. Perret had been attacked that summer in a newspaper article by Léon Daudet, a member of the right-wing group Action Française, who condemned its stripped neo-classical forms as betraying sympathies with 'L'ART BOCHE'. (Troy, 1991, pp. 82–4.)

13 *L'Élan*, no. 1, 1915, cited in ibid., p. 84. The title of this journal was intended to encapsulate a mystical, ancient Gallic sense of gritty determination in the face of overwhelming odds. (Silver, 1977, p. 56.)

14 Jeanneret and Ozenfant, *Après le Cubisme* (1918), 1975, cited in ibid., p. 57.

15 Jeanneret and Ozenfant, 'Purism' (1921), 1964, p. 35.

16 Guillaume Apollinaire, 'L'esprit nouveau et les poètes', in *Mercure de France*, vol. 130, December 1918, cited in Silver, p. 58.

17 *Towards*, p. 109.

18 Ibid., p. 180; see also Silver, 1977, p. 58.

19 'Purism', pp. 72–3; see also Silver, 1977, p. 56.

20 McLeod, 1983, pp. 137–9. The editors of *L'Esprit nouveau* recommended the Saint-Simonian journal, *Le Producteur*, as essential reading. See also Maier, 1970, p. 38.

21 Etienne Clémentel, *L'Expansion Economique*, 1917, and 'Address to the Budget Commission of the Chamber', May 1918, cited in Kuisel, 1981, p. 40.

22 Marc Trachtenberg, 1977, pp. 315–7. Clémentel's vision was roughly as follows: he was committed to a comprehensively state-organized and planned economy, which was to replace the divisiveness of free-market economics. The Ministry of Commerce was to be responsible for coordinating all this activity, ensuring that firms within the same industry co-operate with one another, sharing knowledge and dividing their markets equitably. At the international level, this system would be underwritten by an inter-Allied economic entente, providing a constant pool of raw materials to be allocated between nations on the basis of need, together with a system of preferential trade tariffs between member states. The entire system was to be put into the hands of impartial, apolitical experts from each national administration. (Ibid., pp. 319–26, 329–30; Kuisel, 1981, p. 47; Marwick, 1974, p. 48.)

23 Kuisel, 1981, pp. 42–4, 48; quotation from p. 44. See also Maier, 1970, p. 38; Trachtenberg, 1977, pp. 318, 325–6.

24 Louis Loucheur demanded the immediate re-establishment of free trade, which was unanimously applauded by the business community and received status as official policy after the 1919 election victory of Georges Clemenceau's right-wing Bloc National coalition. Two years later, Clémentel made a further attempt to reintroduce his ideals of industrial co-operation, planning and control, through the formation of a national employers' union, the Confédération Générale de la Production Française. This scheme faltered on the desires of private businessmen to remain free of all governmental controls. (Kuisel, 1981, pp. 50–57; Trachtenberg, 1977, pp. 340–41.) On the influence of Great Britain and the United States in this matter, as well as the issue of reparations, see ibid., pp. 321–2, 332–40; Stevenson, 1979, pp. 877, 883–5, 894; Elizabeth Wiskemann, 1985, pp. 14, 38–9, 44–8, 70-1.

25 Kuisel, 1981, p. 50.

26 For these and other statistics, see Silver, 1977, p. 58; Marwick, 1974, p. 55.

27 Kuisel, 1981, pp. 69–70.

28 Brogan, 1940, p. 600.

29 *City*, pp. 93, 288.

30 Von Moos, 'From the "City for 3 Million Inhabitants" to the "Plan Voisin"', p. 126.

31 *City*, p. 163; see also *My Work*, p. 62.

32 *City, passim*; see esp. pp. 163–78 on 'A Contemporary City'.

33 Ibid., p. 87.

34 *Precisions*, p. 180; see also *City*, p. 12. See McLeod, 1983, p. 146, n. 49, for remarks on the French 'Pan-Europe' movement, which was committed to European economic integration.

35 *City*, p. 187; see pp. 181–93 on 'The Working Day' for an account of the commercial efficiency of the Ville Contemporaine.

36 Maier, 1970, pp. 31–2, 43; quotation from p. 32; Fishman, 1977 (a), pp. 248–51.

37 *Towards*, pp. 274–8; quotation from p. 275. More generally, see pp. 271–89 on 'Architecture or Revolution', and *City*, p. 86.

38 Ibid., p. 53.

39 Gurlitt, 'Le Corbusier and the "Pack-Donkey's Way" ', pp. 122–3. This is not *entirely* true: see *City*, pp. 245–7 on '*Theatres, public halls, etc.*', p. 239 on 'restaurants and cafés', and pp. 171–2, 217. But Gurlitt's general observation that Le Corbusier shifted emphasis away from the social and political activities of the city is correct.

40 *City*, p. 280; see also pp. 256–7, 284, and 277–89 on 'The Centre of Paris'. By 1919, seventeen districts with an unacceptably high death rate had been recognized by the Parisian authorities and the Plan Voisin was committed to the removal of a number of these. (Tim Benton, 'Urbanism', in Raeburn and Wilson [eds], 1987, p. 204.) 'In the 1920s alone, Paris proper lost 16,000 residents due to severe overcrowding and the general deterioration of living conditions.' (Peggy A. Phillips, 1978, pp. 413–4, n. 1; see also McLeod, 1983, pp. 136 and 145, n. 33.)

41 *Precisions*, p. 178.

42 *City*, p. 297; more generally, see pp. 293–301 on 'Finance and Realization'.

43 Ibid., p. 295; see also *Precisions*, pp. 182–4, where a four- to ten-fold increase in land value is estimated.

44 *City*, p. 297. As Anthony Sutcliffe has discussed, Le Corbusier's calculations are riddled with elementary oversights: for example, 'higher densities at a given point mean lower densities and therefore lower values elsewhere'. ('A Vision of Utopia: Optimistic Foundations of Le Corbusier's *Doctrine d'urbanisme*', in Walden [ed.], 1977, p. 235.)

45 *City*, p. 154.

46 Maier, 1970, p. 32.

47 Ibid., p. 57.

48 See McLeod, 1983, pp. 138–9; Tony Judt, 1976, pp. 199–215.

49 The following information on the Redressement Français is taken from Kuisel, 1981, pp. 76, 88–90; Maier, 1970, pp. 37–9, 57–9; McLeod, 1983, pp. 139–43.

50 Cited in ibid., p. 142.

51 Ernest Mercier, *La Production et le travail*, Paris, 1927, cited in Maier, 1970, p. 59.

52 Trachtenberg, 1977, p. 341.

53 *City*, p. 302; see also pp. 253–73 on 'Physic or Surgery'.

54 McLeod, 1983, pp. 142–3.

55 Kuisel, 1981, pp. 74–6, 89–90; Maier, 1970, pp. 58–9.

56 Klaus-Jürgen Müller, 1976, pp. 87–92.

57 Maier, 1970, pp. 37, 54–6.

58 McLeod, 1983, pp. 136, 143; Benton, 'Urbanism', pp. 205 and 207, n. 31; Taylor, 'Le Corbusier at Pessac', pp. 100–01.

59 Le Corbusier, 'Réflexions à propose de la loi Loucheur', in *Revue des vivants*, August 1928, cited in McLeod, 1983, p. 143.

60 Phillips, 1978, pp. 406–7.

61 *My Work*, p. 86; *Precisions*, pp. 93–5. By the late 1920s, Le Corbusier had ample reason for such pessimism: in 1925, for example, the sugar industrialist Henri Frugès commissioned the construction of a housing settlement at Pessac, near Bordeaux, which Le Corbusier was at liberty to use as a testing ground for his most radical theories. First, the authorities blocked plans for the introduction of facilities for running water, and then refused the right to sell these dwellings on the basis of this lack of water. Next, the workers for whom they were built refused to move in. Finally, when the workers eventually settled, they transformed their houses beyond recognition. (Le Corbusier, *The Radiant City* [1935], 1967, pp. 144–5; *When the Cathedrals were White: A Journey to the Country of Timid People* [1937], 1947, p. 15. Steen Eiler Rasmussen, 'Le Corbusier: The Architecture of Tomorrow?', in Serenyi [ed.], 1975, pp. 90–91; Phillipe Boudin, 'Lived-In Architecture', in ibid., pp. 92–4; Taylor, 'Le Corbusier at Pessac', pp. 95–102; Jencks, 1987, pp. 68–75.)

62 See Trachtenberg, 1977, pp. 331–2, 335; Kuisel, 1981, pp. 90–92; Mildred Schlesinger, 1974, pp. 476–501; and esp. Monique Claque, 1973, pp. 105–29.

63 *Radiant*, p. 74.

64 See the drawing in *City*, pp. 245–6.

65 Ibid., p. 71; see also pp. 84, 86.

66 Ibid., pp. 167–70, 197–205, 214–20. Le Corbusier criticizes bohemian café life and the energy wasted in night-clubs and restaurants. (*Decorative*, p. 213; *Towards*, p. 14.)

67 *The City*, pp. 240–44. Further celebrations of the nobility of collective achievement can be found on pp. 52, 130 and 141–58 on 'Our Technical Equipment'.

68 Ibid., pp. 211–12.

69 Ibid., p. 217 (emphasis added).

70 Stanley Hoffman coined the term 'stalemate society'. Stalemate was maintained in the Third Republic through a broad 'republican synthesis' which was deeply resistant to change. It included peasants, private and official white-collar workers, small- and medium-scale shopkeepers and manufacturers, and landed notables. The preservation of the family and economic individualism were paramount. Politically, the republican synthesis involved a precarious balance of authoritarianism and liberal democracy: the former with just enough power to override

any impetus towards substantial reform through parliamentary channels, the latter with just enough power to offset any slide into the worst abuses of out-and-out authoritarianism. ('Paradoxes of the French Political Community', in Hoffmann et al., 1963, pp. 3–60 and *passim*.)

71   *Radiant*, p. 8 (emphasis added); see also McLeod, 1983, p. 143.

2   1930–1940: Syndicalism

1   Maier, 1970, pp. 32–5, traces these positions to their two American champions: Herbert Hoover, the 'ameliorist', versus Thorstein Veblen, the 'revolutionary'. See also pp. 35–54 for an account of xenophobia throughout inter-war Europe.

2   The most comprehensive study of Le Corbusier's relationship with America is Bacon, 2001: see esp. pp. 6–14, 137–41 for her account of how *Cathedrals* built upon a European literary culture of '*américanisme*'.

3   *Cathedrals*, p. 138.

4   Ibid., pp. 145–8; see also Jencks, 1987, p. 107.

5   *Cathedrals*, p. 82; see also p. 35.

6   According to Le Corbusier, America had not achieved its amazing progress through any special acuity of mind or purpose, but only through the self-generating energy of money. France, then, steeped in a long tradition of philosophical thought, must assume the position of wise father-figure over America, which is calling out for guidance. (Ibid., pp. 127–8; see also pp. 39, 92, 96–8, 111–12, 123, 141, 166, 213–14.)

7   For Le Corbusier's ferocious attacks on these institutions, see ibid., pp. 13, 77, 115, 119.

8   Ibid., pp. 178–80.

9   Ibid., pp. 171–8. See also François de Pierrefeu and Le Corbusier, *The Home of Man* (1942), 1948, pp. 59–65.

10   *Cathedrals*, pp. xxi, 3–9, 114–20; quotation from p. xxi.

11   Ibid., pp. 8, 63, n. 1, 119–20, 132, 217 (emphasis added).

12   The Americans did not entirely let Le Corbusier get away with his behaviour and opinions whilst over there in 1935 and afterwards. See Geoffrey Hellman, 1947, who caricatures him as an amusing, absent-minded eccentric.

13   Christopher Green clarified for me the fact that Le Corbusier indulges in two types of nationalist strategy: a rational version, rooted in the civilizing ideals of the Enlightenment; and a visceral version, rooted in race and peasant values. We shall see both of these played out with increasing wiliness from now on. (30 January 2001.)

14   Cited in McLeod, 1983, p. 139.

15   Robert Gildea, 1994, pp. 309–10, 315; Joel Blatt, 1981, pp. 260–77; Richard Griffiths, 1978, pp. 733–6.

16   The following information on Georges Valois is taken from ibid., pp. 736–7; Blatt, 1981, pp. 271–6; Gildea, 1994, pp. 315–17; Kuisel, 1981, pp. 81–2; and esp. Jules Levey, 1973, pp. 279–304.

17   Ibid., p. 287; Blatt, 1981, p. 282.

18   Fishman, 1977 (a), p. 255; Mark Antliff, 'La Cité française: George Valois, Le Corbusier, and Fascist Theories of Urbanism', in Matthew Affron and Antliff (eds), 1997, pp. 135–7. Antliff argues, however, that there was a deep divide between the ideals of Valois and Le Corbusier. Valois was committed to the 'vitalist' ideals of the anarcho-syndicalist theorist Georges Sorel, who sought to revitalize worker and bourgeois class identity by placing them in mutual antagonism. Obviously, this involved the overthrow of democracy, which tried to assuage class rivalries. Antliff observes that Le Corbusier's cities sought the opposite of Valois: to place the classes in a frictionless idyll. This is an extremely useful point, for as we have seen, Le Corbusier found socially derived categories of identity abhorrent. Antliff's suggestion that Le Corbusier was also too liberal and pro-parliamentarian for the Faisceau, however, is questionable (pp. 134–70, *passim*).

19   *Radiant*, p. 23.

20   This and the following information on the riots of 6 February 1934, is taken from Roger Price, 1993, pp. 235–8; Alfred Cobham, 1965, pp. 137–46; Martin Kitchen, 1988, pp. 219–21.

21   *Radiant*, pp. 14–15; see also p. 70.

22   Ibid., p. 73. For a sense of Le Corbusier's anti-Semitism, see *Journey*, p. 138, and esp. p. 258, n. 4, for the passage excised from the published text.

23   The following information on syndicalism is taken from Fishman, 1977 (a), pp. 253–5; Phillips, 1978, pp. 398–401; Kuisel, 1981, pp. 77–81; McLeod, 1980, pp. 56 and 81, n. 8.

24   One of the reasons for the mellowing of the CGT was that it could only secure consistent strike success through the support of high-ranking parliamentary officials. See Gerald C. Friedman, 1997, pp. 174–81.

25   Wayne Thorpe, 1996, pp. 559–63 and *passim*; Gildea, 1994, pp. 311–15; Jack J. Roth, 1977, pp. 231–5 and *passim*.

26   Kuisel, 1981, pp. 93–100.

27   A major influence on the formation of Le Corbusier's ideas here was the proto-syndicalist watchmaking industry of his native town of La Chaux-de-Fonds. (Jencks, 1987, pp. 17–18.)

28   Peter Serenyi, 1967, pp. 277–9 and *passim*.

29   Fishman, 1977 (a), p. 256; Kuisel, 1981, p. 101; McLeod, 1980, pp. 56–7; Frampton, 1980, p. 185. Reproductions of the journal *Prélude* are included as the fifth part of *La Ville radieuse*, pp. 174–94.

30   CIAM was formed in 1928 out of all parties of the European architectural and urban avant-garde. The flashpoint that brought them together was the League of Nations competition 'scandal'. Le Corbusier's proposals, originally voted as

the winning ones, were dismissed on a technicality by one of the jurors: they were mechanical reproductions rather than the original ink drawings. This was pointed out by an influential figure from the Ecole des Beaux-Arts, Charles Lemaresquier. The commission was then given to the neo-classical design of Nénot and Flegenheimer, with the adjudicating committee adding 50 per cent to the specified budget of the competition brief so as to cover this more expensive scheme. Furthermore, the winners were asked to rework their design, and did so to such an extent that Le Corbusier attempted to sue the League of Nations for turning a blind eye to what he believed was the plagiarism of his original proposals. (*Radiant*, p. 18; *My Work*, pp. 49–50, 79; *The Athens Charter* [1943], 1973, p. 4. See also Benton, 'League of Nations competition, Geneva', in Raeburn and Wilson [eds], 1987, pp. 172–3; and esp. Eric Mumford, 2000, pp. 9–16.)

31 *Radiant*, p. 81.
32 The Ville Radieuse offered another socio-economic panacea, this time intended to remedy depression. It involved two things: first, eradication of the manufacture of useless consumer goods, which was perpetuated only to benefit the capitalist order and as a stopgap against unemployment; second, the comprehensive mobilization of land for immediate redevelopment, so as to uproot the nation's unproductive parasites. (Ibid., pp. 10, 72–4, 112, 148–9, 177, 341.)
33 Ibid., pp. 192–3.
34 Ibid., p. 136.
35 Ibid., p. 168.
36 Ibid., pp. 8, 37, 99 and *passim*.
37 Fishman, 1977 (a), p. 257.
38 *Radiant*, pp. 178–9.
39 Ibid., p. 10. See also p. 99: he refuses to 'bend either to the right or to the left'; and again, 'We must *concern ourselves with man*, not with capitalism or communism; with *man's happiness*, not with company dividends; with the *satisfaction of man's deepest instincts*, not with the race of success being run between the managements of two companies or corporations' (p. 69).
40 Ibid., p. 179; see also p. 151, where social participation is talked about in terms of Taylorism. Also, pp. 64–8 on 'Leisure, an Imminent Threat'; and pp. 119–26 on the 'Death of the Street'. Jencks has commented interestingly on how Le Corbusier 'can so easily confuse a unified communal effort like harmonious factory-work with political participation, or the necessary plurality of views in the public realm'. But he misses the point with his argument that Le Corbusier's interest in 'active participation' betrayed some ideal of public life as a valuable and meaningful sphere of experience, and that his efforts were intended to 'result in a much richer and more responsive environment'. Le Corbusier's efforts were committed to making participation in the environment as efficient as possible,

but certainly not a source of enjoyment. (1987, p. 123; see also pp. 120–26 on 'Participation and the Radiant City'.) Obviously, I also disagree with Frampton's argument that the Ville Radieuse provides for 'a *dialectic of socio-political participation*'. (1969, p. 543.)

41 *Radiant*, p. 97. See also p. 177 on individual and collective 'spiritual joy', and p. 94: 'The keystone of the theory behind this city is the *liberty of the individual*. Its aim is to create respect for that liberty, to bring it to an authentic fruition, to destroy our present slavery.'

42 Ibid., pp. 150–51 (emphasis added).

43 Ibid., pp. 113, 153–4. Le Corbusier echoed the complaints of fellow syndicalists who were jealous that France had no Stalin, Mussolini or Hitler of her own. (Fishman, 1977 [a], p. 265.) His commitment to a legal, constitutional route to success had all but vanished, although he continued to flirt with it: see *Radiant*, pp. 94 (in which he claims that his scheme awaited only 'a "yes" from a government with the will and the determination to see it through!') and 97. He also continued to entice potential backers with promises that his city redevelopments would generate massive profits (pp. 71, 102). And a further attempt to secure backing was that of brandishing the threat of an imminent aerial poison-gas attack: the airless corridor streets and courtyards of the traditional masonry city would prevent the gas from dispersing and ensure complete loss of life. '*Not one existing city*', he threatens, '*will be spared: fire, collapse, death by gas. Nothingness!*' By virtue of its immense open spaces, however, the Ville Radieuse would allow the gas to dissipate harmlessly, its high-rise apartment blocks would allow the populace to climb above the danger, and even a direct hit could be survived by virtue of armour-plated roofs. Lieutenant-Colonel Vauthier, Inspector General of Aerial Defence, agreed with Le Corbusier's argument, and delivered a lecture entitled 'Urbanism and Architecture in the Face of Danger from the Air' at the 1937 CIAM congress in Paris (pp. 60–61, 171; see also *Precisions*, p. 192; Mumford, 2000, p. 113).

44 Léon Blum, in *Le Populaire*, 25 January 1934, cited in Kuisel, 1981, p. 114. A Socialist party conference later that year resolved that quickly seizing power was more important than drafting long-term plans. Besides, circumstances change, and once power was gained, any preconceived plans might prove to be inappropriate or unnecessarily restrictive. As Blum concluded, 'the public is faced with such a variety and sample of plans that when you present yours you will find the boutique full and the shopper already a bit discouraged'. (Parti Socialiste, *31ᵉ Congrès national tenu à Toulouse*, May 1934, cited in ibid., p. 115.)

45 Among the most humiliating of all Le Corbusier's attempts to court officialdom was that acted out under the Front, through his involvement with the Paris International Exhibition of 1937. Despite his manipulation of various groups, simultaneously from both left and right, from whom he could scarce withhold

his contempt, he was unable to secure sufficient support or financial backing for any of his more ambitious projects. From his original intention of being appointed sole designer for the entire exhibition, to that of providing various massive skyscrapers, to that of designing a museum, he was finally obliged to erect little more than a tent, and this sited in a singularly inauspicious position. (Danilo Udovicki-Selb, 1997, pp. 42–63, *passim*; *Cathedrals*, pp. 21–4, 113; *My Work*, pp. 51, 128–9; Dawn Ades, 'Paris 1937: Art and the Power of Nations', in Ades et al., 1995, pp. 58–62; Marko Daniel, 'Spain: Culture at War', in ibid., pp. 63–8.)

46   Mumford, 2000, p. 110.

47   Kuisel, 1981, pp. 116–27; Pierre Martin, 1991, pp. 45–75, *passim*.

48   Le Corbusier, in *Stile futuristica*, vol. 1, no. 2, August 1934, cited in Fishman, 1977 (a), pp. 267–8; see also Jencks, 1987, pp. 129–31.

49   Fishman, 1977 (a), p. 268.

50   Levey, 1973, pp. 279, 294 ff.; Kuisel, 1981, pp. 81–2; Allen Douglas, 1984, pp. 689-712, *passim*.

51   Udovicki-Selb, 1997, pp. 47–8, and 61, n. 31.

52   Lieutenant-Colonel de La Rocque, *Service Public*, Paris, 1934, cited in Gildea, 1994, p. 321.

53   Ibid., pp. 320–22; Müller, 1976, pp. 94–9; William D. Irvine, 1974, pp. 534–62, *passim*; Robert J. Soucy, 1966, pp. 27–55, *passim*.

54   Irvine, 1991, pp. 271–95, *passim*; Soucy, 1991, pp. 159–88, *passim*.

55   Ibid., pp. 165, 167–8, 173–4, 178–81; Irvine, 1991, p. 274.

56   Mumford, 2000, p. 56.

57   *Radiant*, p. 152; see also p. 182: 'Our problem is man . . . placed by the laws of nature in that rich, perilous and total equation: INDIVIDUAL-COLLECTIVITY.' Le Corbusier's opinion on this remained unchanged throughout his life: 'Whatever the individual can do by himself, do not try to have it done collectively. / The collective intervenes at the point where the individual fails.' (*Le Corbusier Sketchbooks. Volume 2, 1950–1954*, 1981, p. 20, entry no. 221. This is from a sketchbook dated 1950.)

58   Mumford, 2000, pp. 16–44, 49–50. A good example of this conflict is the saga over the publication of the resolutions from the 1933 CIAM congress on the 'Functional City'. Little consensus emerged, but different groups quickly published their own versions of what was 'resolved' there. In his address, Le Corbusier immediately demanded that urbanism must manage those 'two contradictory and hostile fates', individualism versus collectivity. (CIAM 4, proceedings of 30 July 1930, cited in ibid., p. 79.) And in a report heavily influenced by Le Corbusier, published that year as 'Resolutions', the first point was as follows: '1° The city should provide liberty for the individual and the benefits of collective action on both the material and the spiritual plane.' (*Radiant*, p. 188.) The report by another group, published almost simultaneously as

'Constatations', made no mention of this. Discussions over the form and content of the official book-length publication of these proceedings continued for several years. Finally, Le Corbusier published the 'official' view independently as *La Charte d'Athènes*, and again inserted a clause demanding 'the effulgence of the individual within the framework of civic obligation'. (*Athens Charter*, p. 44: 'Life flourishes only to the extent of accord between the two contradictory principles that govern the human personality: the individual and the collective.') For a full account, see Mumford, 2000, pp. 73–91, 94–5, 116–9, 123–4.

59   Le Corbusier, 'Réponse à un questionnaire de Moscou', cited in Jean-Louis Cohen, 1992, p. 146. The 'Réponse' was translated and published as an appendix to the Russian translation of *Urbanisme* in 1933.

60   *Radiant*, p. 9.

61   For details, see Jean-Louis Cohen, 1992, pp. 126–63 on ' "Response to Moscow" and the "Origins of the Ville Radieuse" ', and esp. pp. 150–56 for the Communists' response to the 'morbid fantasy' of bourgeois individualism. More generally, see Mumford, 2000, pp. 44–9 on 'Le Corbusier, the Green City, and His ' "Response to Moscow" ', and *Precisions*, pp. 259–66 on 'The Atmosphere of Moscow'.

62   José Luis Sert, *Can Our Cities Survive? An ABC of Urban Problems, Their Analyses, Their Solutions, Based on the Proposals Formulated by the CIAM*, Cambridge, Mass., 1942. This was Sert's own 'official' account of the 1933 conference. (See n. 58 above.)

63   Lewis Mumford to Sert, 28 December 1940, cited in Mumford, 2000, pp. 133–4.

64   Mumford to F. J. Osborn, 27 November 1942, cited in ibid., p. 132; see also p. 142.

65   See Hall, 1998, pp. 6–7, 782–95 for an account of Mumford's contribution to the attempt to prevent the further urbanization of New York.

66   Mumford, *The Culture of Cities*, New York, 1938, p. 301, cited in ibid., pp. 791–2.

67   Mumford had seen examples of Le Corbusier's architecture and visited his atelier in Paris in 1932, but in a subsequent essay on modern housing he declined to mention this. (Bacon, 2001, p. 24.)

68   *City*, p. 301.

69   *Radiant*, p. 188.

3   1941–1942: Vichy

1   For evidence of Le Corbusier's long-standing respect for Philippe Pétain, see *Radiant*, pp. 154–5.

2   Gildea, 1994, p. 25; see also p. 79.

3   'And, before that seemingly impossible task, crushing, chimerical, it was necessary to open the cracks which eventually would undermine the bastions of lethargy

and routine, opening up sites for reconstruction. The cracks have started, the bastions topple; we must clear the ground . . . And then we can build again.' At last, 'a huge petrification of selfish interests and ties, as it were compounded of baleful prejudices, theories, systems, has crashed to the ground'. (Le Corbusier, *The Four Routes*, [1941], 1947, pp. 201, 204 and 192; *Home*, p. 14.) *Home* is split into two sections, the first comprised of de Pierrefeu's text, the second of Le Corbusier's drawings and diagrams. Although de Pierrefeu insists that 'here are two trains of thought which move independently' (p. 12), the most cursory reading reveals that he has been deeply inculcated into the Corbusian creed and is manœuvring his argument towards a demand that Vichy give Le Corbusier a more powerful role. For this reason, I shall be treating de Pierrefeu's text as a reliable transcript of Le Corbusier's own ideals. Winter is also cited as an important contributor.

4   *Routes*, pp. 15, 19.

5   Ibid., pp. 8, 17–18, 204; see pp. 81–5 for Le Corbusier's arguments that the railways set the trend for all subsequent machine-based outrages against humanity.

6   Ibid., p. 17, also pp. 22, 26, 154. See also *Home*, p. 57, *Cathedrals*, pp. 202–6, and *Sketchbooks. Vol. 1*, p. 28, entry nos. 616 ff. concerning how the First Machine Age has disrupted the sexual equilibrium of modern men and women. This is from a sketchbook dated 1932–3.

7   *Routes*, p. 76.

8   Ibid., pp. 68–71; quotations from pp. 69, 70.

9   Le Corbusier provided a visitors' book for his Temps Nouveaux Pavilion of 1937, in which he observed how the 'considered, serious, well-reasoned and always weighty opinion of the Provinces' sat against the 'invective, challenge, ravings' of the Parisians. Allegedly, the provinces called for the speedy implementation of Le Corbusier's ideals. (Ibid., pp. 202–3.)

10 No nation escapes this censure. The Dutch, for example, are obsessed with 'pure thought', while the Italians are obsessed with 'flesh' and the 'body'. The emphasis throughout is on 'changing' 'the soul of a people'. (Ibid., pp. 119–29, 195; quotations from pp. 122, 125.) On the ancient spiritual wisdom of the French, see pp. 195, 201, and for the belief that other nations are pleading for guidance, see *Home*, p. 14 and *Routes*, p. 127: 'Our nonchalance in this connection is inconceivable, especially in view of the tireless insistence of other nations . . . They are looking to us. They say: will the French never make a move?'

11 Le Corbusier's internationalist bluff is most elegantly put in *Routes*, p. 129: 'We must persevere and discover, each on his own ground, that sap which issues from the compost of ages, sap that gives a crop of *natural* flowers and releases diverse essences. A happy profusion of the spirit's harvest; contrasted gems infinitely varied and resplendent.'

12 Ibid., pp. 130–38, 143–4; quotation from p. 131. See also p. 203: 'I feel that one could well preach a crusade by means of modern town-planning.'

13   *Cathedrals*, pp. 4, 6, 32. Commenting on the multinational melting-pot of America, Le Corbusier maintains that the strongest 'racial echoes' are French, which appear by natural selection always to bubble irresistibly to the surface (p. 128). Further references to race as a biologically determined fact can be found in *Home*, p. 38.

14   The world's diversity will 'be expressed in unity, and not cacophonous'. (*Routes*, pp. 132–3; see also p. 159.)

15   Gildea, 1994, pp. 229–30. This kind of national arrogance was endemic to Vichy France.

16   Pétain, speech of 3 September 1940, cited in Gildea, 1994, p. 128.

17   *Routes*, p. 139.

18   Ibid., pp. 115–17.

19   Ibid., pp. 88–92; quotations from pp. 91–2. See *Radiant*, pp. 310–18 for an account of the Nemours project of 1934–5. See also *Cathedrals*, p. 36, where Le Corbusier noted how France brought her benefits to Morocco, 'benefits which were somewhat imposed but which must be considered the indispensable signs of civilization'.

20   Similarly, upon defeat, Pétain had immediately set about the resurrection of the myth of native French greatness. The defeat itself was bustled into the wings, and the spotlight allowed to fall on the courage displayed by the French in the face of impossible odds: 'Our flag remains spotless', said Pétain. 'Our army has fought bravely and loyally. But inferior in arms and numbers it was obliged to request an end to hostilities.' (Pétain, speech of 23 June 1940, cited in Gildea, 1994, p. 128.) But even so, 'the renaissance of France will be fruit of this suffering'. (Pétain, speech of 16 June 1940, cited in ibid.) This was echoed almost verbatim by Le Corbusier and de Pierrefeu. The war constituted a welcome wake-up call: 'Hence the hour to build proved not to be that of Victory . . . When foolish beatitude has been a drug, suffering must herald the awakening.' (*Home*, p. 16; see also pp. 13–14 and *Routes*, pp. 11–20 on 'When Peace Takes Over The Roads'.)

21   *Home*, p. 14 (emphasis added); *Routes*, p. 195. On how easily the masses are 'bedazzled' and 'distracted' by the media, and the fact that architectural and urban projects increasingly exploit these techniques, see pp. 125–6, 147–8, 201. See also *Sketchbooks. Vol. 1*, p. 21, entry nos. 444–7. In this sketchbook of 1931, Le Corbusier notes sarcastically that the only thing likely to sway public opinion in favour of his Plan Voisin would be to present it amid great pomp and pageantry. In a sketchbook of 1955–6, Le Corbusier reiterated his attack on the mass media in similarly contemptuous terms, concluding that it 'profoundly hurts the serious consideration of life'. (*Le Corbusier Sketchbooks. Volume 3, 1954–1957*, 1982, p. 52, entry nos. 639–40.)

22   *Home*, p. 19; more generally, see pp. 18–20 and Clive Entwistle's introductory remarks on the 'forfeiture of inner freedom' by 'becoming slaves to an

ever-multiplying brood of otherwise unnecessary obligations, disorders, and diseases' (p. 8).

23   Beatriz Colomina considers the fact that Le Corbusier photographed his architecture as evidence that he was infatuated with the mass media, and sought to introduce its invasive techniques and spurious content into modern ways of living. Obviously, she disregards his powerful statements to the contrary. (1994, *passim.*)

24   'Because one's home, one's working place . . . do not merely act as shells for the life of individuals and society; they go deeper, reach within this life, impregnate, colour it by a thousand various approaches.' (*Home*, p. 14.)

25   *Routes*, pp. 18, 100.

26   Ibid., p. 70; see also *Home*, p. 29, where we hear of how the individual, 'once freed from the shackles of misery, drink or mental drugs', may be inspired to fill his leisure time with all kinds of 'personal creation', which 'means a gain for both the individual and society'. This constitutes a 'pendulum', an 'internal balance', which pulls the individual back from complete and unthinking immersion in society.

27   *Routes*, p. 161; see also *Precisions*, pp. 86–7: 'If the expression has infuriated, it is because it contains the word "machine," representing evidently in all minds the idea of functioning, of efficiency, of work, of production. And the term "for living," representing exactly the concepts of ethics, of social standing, of the organization of existence, on which there is the most complete disagreement.' Le Corbusier explains that his statement was intended to raise the question of '*the reason for living . . .* the most beautiful of subjects'.

28   This came through the influence of a notoriously authoritarian official, Marcel Peyrouton. Peyrouton was Minister of the Interior and Governor General of Algiers when Le Corbusier presented his plans for that city throughout the early 1930s. He was one of those ousted for being overly authoritarian during the Front Populaire purge of colonial administrators in 1936. (William B. Cohen, 1972, pp. 376–7; Fishman, 1977 (a), pp. 271–2. See *Radiant*, p. 248 for a transcript of one of Le Corbusier's letters to Peyrouton.) The following information concerning Le Corbusier's relations with Vichy is taken from Fishman, 1977 (a), pp. 271–9; McLeod, 1980, pp. 71–9; Jencks, 1987, pp. 131–3.

29   *Home*, p. 43.

30   Le Corbusier, *Poésie sur Alger*, Paris, 1950, cited in Fishman, 1977 (a), pp. 273–4; *Home*, pp. 30–38, 44–50, 52, 132; *Routes*, pp. 160–61, 165–7, 201. One can infer what must be the supernatural talents of the Lawgiver by noting that the 'Master Builder', who appears to be one rung lower on this 'professional' hierarchy, already contains the trinity of architect, engineer, and humanist: 'This trinity – could it but be fully realised within one man – would for an instant imprison a ray of that Trinity to which we owe the creation and upholding of our world, and which one was justified in calling the Great Architect of the Universe.' (*Home*, p. 32.)

31　Ibid., pp. 73–5. See also *Routes*, p. 165, where Le Corbusier defends himself by implying that he is *unable* to think in small scale.

32　Gildea, 1994, pp. 326–8. Pétain's circle descended from the era of the Action Française *after* Maurras had substantially turned it into a legitimate parliamentary party.

33　Hoffman, 1963, pp. 34–41; see also pp. 42–52, 58–60 for an account of how the new Vichy institutions, although taken over by the post-war governments and briefly reoriented towards genuine progress and modernization, were quickly allowed to slip back into a state of bureaucratic stagnancy perhaps even worse than that of the Third Republic.

34　This transfer of responsibility was made only because Pétain and the Vice-President of the Council of Ministers, Pierre Laval, had to concede their incompetence in these matters. These technocrats were eventually assembled under Laval's successor, Admiral François Darlan. The following information on the internal organization and factionalism of Vichy is taken from Kuisel, 1970, pp. 365–98; 1981, pp. 128–56. Compare also Steven M. Zdatny, who slightly idealizes the power and motives of the technocratic faction within Vichy, with Adrian Jones, who maintains that they were not pursuing a coherent, socially conscious campaign but rather their individual business interests. (Zdatny, 1986, pp. 155–79; Jones, 1986, pp. 1–31.) A further account of the resistance to economic and industrial modernization within Vichy can be found in Joseph Jones, 1982, pp. 541–63.

35　Although now known to be little more than a paper plot, this 'conspiracy' was sufficiently real – or *useful* – at the time to provoke a vicious backlash, which resulted in the regime being purged of its technocrats. Central to the rumours was the fact that, prior to the war, several of the key technocrats had worked for the commercial and banking house of Hypolite Worms. Worms was Jewish, which gave ready ammunition to the technocrats' opponents. Allegations of their involvement in an international Jewish financial conspiracy ensued, which were then grafted on to and reinforced by allegations of their involvement in a network of megalomaniacal freemasons, the Mouvement Synarchiste d'Empire. This was a potent mix, which flourished in the paranoid atmosphere of the Vichy hotels, and was no doubt fuelled by the imperious and cliquey behaviour of the technocrats themselves. The 'conspirators' were pursued tenaciously by the Chief of Pétain's Civil Cabinet, Henri du Moulin de Labarthète, which resulted in Darlan's fall in April 1942 and the return to power of the conservative Laval. Rather than giving Laval the satisfaction of dismissing them, several key members of Darlan's team quickly dispersed. The rest grew disenchanted and drifted away in their own time. (Kuisel, 1970, *passim*.)

36　Adrian Jones, 1986, *passim*; Griffiths, 1978, p. 738. The technocrats had also been forced to deal with the increasingly inordinate exaction of raw materials, finished products and labour by the Germans, and also with Germany's chipping away of what little remained of French sovereignty. Their efforts were crippled by the Allied blockade as well.

37 The information on Le Corbusier's Vichy career is taken from Fishman, 1977 (a), pp. 271–80.

38 Cited in ibid., p. 276.

39 Cited in Jencks, 1987, p. 131. (Originally cited in Jean Petit, *Le Corbusier lui-méme*, Geneva, 1970, p. 87.)

40 Kuisel, 1981, pp. 148–9. See *Home*, pp. 57–72 for Le Corbusier's arguments against the satellite city.

41 Bernard Ménétrel to Le Corbusier, 1 April 1942, cited in Fishman, 1977 (a), p. 276.

42 Details of the various politically motivated variations of Le Corbusier's plans for Algiers, with particular reference to their colonial arrogance, can be found in McLeod, 1980, pp. 55–85, *passim*. F. Sherry McKay provides a more in-depth account of how Le Corbusier's plans took part in a sophisticated kind of colonialism that distinguished it from that upheld by the Beaux-Arts urban proposals: 'There have been two "traditions" in *l'imaginaire d'Alger*, it was a place of conquest and the inferior "other", and a place of repair, the "salvational" and "ideal" France. Le Corbusier continually vacillated between these two representations citing the improvement brought by military intervention and the ideal of Arab urban form.' (1994, p. 355.)

43 The industrial centre piece of the North African colonies, Algiers held special significance for the syndicalists of *Prèlude* in that it was one of the four capitals of the projected Latin Federation of the European segment of the new world order. As Le Corbusier had observed: 'Algiers ceases to be a colonial city; Algiers becomes the head of the African continent, a capital city. This means that a great task awaits her, but a magnificent future too.' (Le Corbusier to Charles Brunel, Mayor of Algiers, December 1933, in *Radiant*, p. 228.) Despite such internationalist sentiment, however, these early plans continued to articulate the dominance of the interests of metropolitan France. (William B. Cohen, 1972, pp. 368–93, *passim*; McLeod, 1980, p. 67.)

44 Brunel to Le Corbusier, 26 December 1932, cited in ibid., p. 82, n. 16. See also *Radiant*, p. 248, for a transcript of the letter Le Corbusier had sent to Brunel on 10 December.

45 Le Corbusier, *Poésie sur Alger*, cited in McLeod, 1980, p. 74.

46 Le Corbusier, 'Note à l'intention de M. Dumoulin de la Barthète' [sic], 27 July 1941, cited in Fishman, 1977 (a), p. 275.

47 Le Corbusier to Maxime Weygand, 30 June 1941; Le Corbusier, 'Note relative au Plan directeur d'Alger', 12 June 1941, cited in ibid.

48 Kuisel, 1970, p. 395.

49 *Mairie de la Ville d'Alger, Extrait du Régistre des Délibérations du Conseil Municipal*, 12 June 1942, cited in McLeod, 1980, p. 79, see also p. 71; Jencks, 1987, pp.

113, 126–33. The 'Trojan Horse' phrase was part of an earlier attack made by Alexandre de Senger as a response to the League of Nations controversy. (See pp. 217-18, n. 30 above.)

50   Cited in Fishman, 1977 (a), p. 279. Le Corbusier later reflected upon this fiasco and the power of slander. (*New World of Space*, 1948, p. 109.)

51   *Routes*, p. 201.

52   Manfredo Tafuri, '"*Machine et memoire*": The City in the Work of Le Corbusier', trans. Stephen Sartarelli, in H. Allen Brooks (ed.), 1987, p. 204.

53   See *Radiant*, pp. 40–50 on 'Exact Respiration' and 'Air-Sound-Light'; and pp. 143–6 on 'The Biological Unit: the cell of 14 square meters per occupant'.

54   *Home*, p. 14; *Radiant*, p. 151.

The Science of Painting: Preface

1   Stephen A. Kurtz, 1972, p. 38; Serenyi, 1968, p. 198.

2   Le Corbusier, 'Unité', in *L'Architecture d'aujourd'hui*, April 1948, cited in Richard A. Moore, 'Alchemical and Mythical Themes in the Poem of the Right Angle 1947–1965', in Frampton (ed.), 1980, p. 135, n. 2.

4   Léger and the Purist Object

1   *New World*, pp. 13, 18–20, 127. For dates and exhibition venues, see the chronologies in Ivan Žaknić, 1997, pp. 133–40, and by Richard Francis and Helen Sloane in Raeburn and Wilson (eds), 1987, pp. 344–53.

2   Von Moos, 'Charles Edouard Jeanneret and the Visual Arts', in Viveca Bosson et al., 1995, p. 76; Green, 'The architect as artist at home: Porte-Molitor apartments, 24 rue Nungesser-et-Coli', in Raeburn and Wilson (eds), 1987, pp. 127–9.

3   Le Corbusier, '*Préface*', in *Le Corbusier, Oeuvre Plastique*, Paris, 1953, cited in Green, 'The architect as artist', p. 111.

4   This formalist interpretation is standard and longstanding. (Ibid., p. 118, n. 7.) Katherine Fraser Fischer believes all Le Corbusier's art to be a formal exploration of the 'boundaries' of objects and phenomena, while von Moos considers it to be a search for the formal '*mariage des contours*'. (Fischer, 'A Nature Morte, 1927', in Frampton [ed.], 1979, pp. 156–65; von Moos, 'Le Corbusier as Painter', pp. 89–107.) On Le Corbusier's private painting as a kind of laboratory for testing formal ideas before they were applied in the 'real' world of architecture, see Geoffrey H. Baker, 1996, pp. 243 ff.; von Moos, 'Charles Edouard Jeanneret and the Visual Arts', in Bosson et al., 1995, pp. 59–82; Bosson, 'Le Corbusier – the painter who became an architect', in ibid., pp. 16–58: 'When talking about the architecture of the paintings we mostly allude to the experimentation

with form which inspired Le Corbusier's future architecture' (p. 37). Christopher Pearson gives a fresh angle to the formalist standpoint by investigating Le Corbusier's concept of '*acoustique plastique*': forms that can 'radiate' out over their surroundings as a 'plastic speech'. (1997, pp. 168–83; see also Pearson, 1995, in which he argues that Le Corbusier sought to effect a 'synthesis' of art and architecture, again primarily by virtue of 'a shared formal language'.) Green, however, makes an important modification to the standard formalist interpretation and this has contributed much to my own approach, as we shall see later.

5   'Purism', pp. 58–73; quotations from pp. 60, 63.

6   *Towards*, pp. 16, 29, 153, 211. See also pp. 21–64 for the remarks concerning Mass, Surface and Plan.

7   *New World*, p. 14.

8   Le Corbusier, *Mise au Point* (1966), 1997, p. 89 (emphasis added). The following statement also gives quite a compelling sense that painting represented a formal 'workout': 'I have not stopped painting daily since [1918], extracting from whatever I could the secrets of form and developing a spirit of invention in the same manner that the acrobat trains his muscles every day and achieves control. I believe that if people are going to see something in my work as an architect, it is to this private labor that one should attribute its deepest quality.' (*Sketchbooks. Volume 1*, p. 12; see also *Sketchbooks. Volume 2*, p. 37, entry nos. 449–50.)

9   *New World*, pp. 16–18, 33. There is a temptation to read a Surrealist influence into this, but the only sustained attempt to do so, relying exclusively on alleged formal affinities with the work of Giorgio de Chirico and René Magritte, is unconvincing. (Alexander Gorlin, 1982, pp. 50–65.) Settling upon exactly the same artists as a possible source of influence, Green suggests that the debt, if any, was inconsequential, and that Le Corbusier's interest in Surrealism was superficial and erratic at best. Le Corbusier genuinely considered Surrealism a 'funereal institution', while Ozenfant himself rejected Surrealism as indulging in visions potentially too painful and disturbing to be comfortably viewed. (Green, 'The *objet à réaction poétique*, the figure and eroticism in painting', in Raeburn and Wilson [eds], 1987, pp. 124–6; 'The Architect as Artist', p. 116. S. L. Ball, 1987, pp. 152–4.) Another, rather silly response is to explain this new love of the organic in general as emerging out of Le Corbusier's lust for robust foreign women in particular. Apparently, he 'rediscovered' both during his trips to Algiers in the early 1930s. (Von Moos, 'Le Corbusier as Painter', pp. 89–91; Jencks, 1987, pp. 85, 99–110.) This is questionable: the young Jeanneret was enamoured of 'exotic' women, in particular the 'coquettish' Muslims, from as early as his Voyage d'Orient.

10   Ball, 1987, pp. 38–50.

11   Green, 'The *objet à réaction poétique*, the figure and eroticism in painting', pp. 125–6. Le Corbusier's later forays into lithography, sculpture, tapestry and enamel-work, and his preoccupation with certain cryptic themes, could be subsumed within a continuous project of searching for formal affect, albeit

now emerging from more private sources. And the transcription of these forms into his architecture was the next logical step: 'a private activity found compelling expression'. (Green, 'The Architect as Artist', pp. 117–18; see also Green, 'Other media and collaboration' and 'The *Taureaux*', in Raeburn and Wilson [eds], 1987, pp. 129–30, 306. For more on Le Corbusier's concern for private self-expression and his debt to Fernand Léger, see Serenyi, 1968, pp. 37–8, 191–8.)

12 '*Préface*', cited in Kurtz, 1972, pp. 41–73.

13 Le Corbusier, 'Préface', in *Le Corbusier, Oeuvre plastique, peintures et dessins, architecture*, Paris, 1938, cited in Green, 'The Architect as Artist', p. 116. For more on the personal content of these later works, see Green, 'The *objet à réaction poétique*, the figure and eroticism in painting', pp. 124–5.

14 'Purism', p. 62.

15 Ibid., p. 65 (emphasis added).

16 Ibid., pp. 70–73.

17 *New World*, p. 37.

18 Cited in Herbert Read, London, 1967, p. 88 (emphasis added).

19 Green, 'Léger and L'Esprit Nouveau: 1912–1928', in John Golding et al., 1970, pp. 29–31; see also Golding, 'Léger and the Heroism of Modern Life', in ibid., pp. 8–10, and Antliff, 1993, on the influence of Bergson on the early twentieth-century avant-garde. I am relying chiefly on Léger's *Functions of Painting* (1965), 1973. The consistency of themes in this volume ensures that the details under discussion may be found in it almost anywhere, but the following entries can be consulted as fairly representative (page references are used here only to indicate the direct quotations or especially salient passages): 'The Spectacle: Light, Color, Moving Image, Object-Spectacle' (1924); 'The Machine Aesthetic II: Geometric Order and Truth' (1925), p. 64: this state of everyday war, with its drama, clarity and heroism, is for Léger 'much more normal and more desirable than the state of peace'; 'New York' (1931), p. 88: he urges Pétain, under whose command he served at Verdun, to direct an artillery barrage at New York simply 'for the sport, for love of the profession!'

20 Léger, 1973: 'The Ballet-Spectacle, the Object-Spectacle' (1925); 'The New Realism' (1935), p. 111; 'The Human Body Considered as an Object' (1945); 'How I Conceive of the Figure' (1949), p. 155.

21 Léger, 1973: 'A New Space in Architecture' (1949), pp. 157–8; 'Color in Architecture' (1954), p. 184 (emphases added).

22 The following works are well known, so I shall not reproduce them needlessly. (See the exhibition catalogue of Carolyn Lanchner et al., 1998.)

23 Léger, 1973: 'The Ballet-Spectacle, the Object-Spectacle', p. 72; 'The Spectacle: Light, Color, Moving Image, Object-Spectacle', p. 38.

24 Léger, 1973: 'Spartakiades' (1960).

25 Léger, 1973: 'The New Realism'; 'The New Realism Goes On' (1937).

26 Siegfried Kracauer, 'The Mass Ornament' (1927), 1975, pp. 67–76.

27   But the 'individual' *does* persist for Léger in terms of the individuality of the artist leading the masses into a state of highly refined aesthetic awareness. (Edward F. Fry, 'Introduction', in Léger, 1973, pp. xix–xxviii; see also 'The New Realism Goes On'; 'Color in the World' [1938]; 'Art and the People' [1946].)

28   Léger considers the artistic 'subject' to be a regrettable throwback to the times before the emergence of widespread publishing and the mass media, when art was forced against its nature to communicate literary, religious and propagandist messages. The Renaissance is considered the low point of such misuse. (Léger, 1973: 'The Origins of Painting and Its Representational Value' [1913]; 'Contemporary Achievements in Painting' [1914]; 'The Machine Aesthetic I: The Manufactured Object, the Artisan, and the Artist' [1924]; 'The Wall, the Architect, the Painter' [1933]; 'The New Realism'; 'Mural Painting and Easel Painting' [1952].)

29   Léger, 1973: 'The Machine Aesthetic I: The Manufactured Object, the Artisan, and the Artist'.

30   Léger, 1973: 'The Spectacle: Light, Color, Moving Image, Object-Spectacle'; 'The Machine Aesthetic II: Geometric Order and Truth', p. 64; 'A New Space in Architecture', p. 158; 'New York'; 'Color in the World'; 'Modern Architecture and Color' (1946), p. 152; 'Color in Architecture', pp. 187–8.

31   Cited in Herbert Read, 1967, p. 88.

32   Curtis, 1986, p. 50. See also p. 49, where he mentions that Purist objects resemble 'engineering drawings'. Golding also observes that the Purists revealed 'the true structure of objects, so that their works often give the odd impression of being blueprints for objects that are already in existence'. Moreover, he continues, the Purists had reservations about Juan Gris's use of distortion in his painting, which gave the impression that 'the objects in it had no exact counterparts in the world'. (Golding, 'Léger and the Heroism of Modern Life', p. 19.) In Gris's own words, 'The forms I create are illusions, poetic metaphors, they are not materializable. Those objects would die if they were removed from their pictorial context. They only exist within their relationship one to the other.' (Cited in Peter de Francia, 1983, p. 72.) Green's account of Gris's 'synthetic process' in the immediate post-war years neatly clarifies this issue. Gris seemed to change his compositional approach from one that began with an analysis of concrete objects in the world to one that deployed abstract forms which would then be pared-down into synthetic 'objects'. Increasingly, he would attempt to fit vague object-ideas into *a priori* compositional structures, rather than more directly working from the observed and experienced object itself. (1982, pp. 87–111; esp. pp. 87, 95, 99–100, 102.) Despite the fact that Gris contributed to *L'Esprit nouveau* this approach to the object is inconsistent with Purism, and the Purists themselves opposed it. (Green, 'The Architect as Artist', p. 113.)

33   Interestingly, Léger's association with the Purists appears to have led to a brief reconsideration of his approach. In 1924, he stated that colour must 'create a

calm and anti-dynamic atmosphere . . . to facilitate a calm ensemble where the place for the sharp and unexpected is filled by the people who happen to be there. In this new environment a man can be seen, for the eye is not distracted by dispersed qualities. Everything is arranged. Against these big calm areas the human face assumes its proper status. A nose, eye, foot, hand or jacket button will become a precise reality.' (Léger, 'Polychromatic Architecture' [1924], in Golding et al., 1970, p. 96.) Léger is advocating here those qualities of the Corbusian cube that he was later to condemn: the clear definition and legibility of the room, against which objects and the individual stand out unequivocally. These were the years when Léger was closest to the Purists, and despite his rather non-committal statements as to their relationship and influence, it would seem that they briefly diverted him from his love of flux. His paintings from the mid- to late-1920s seem more willing to concentrate upon the object as a stable whole: 'the object achieves a status the equal of [his] austere pictorial architecture . . . the common object acquired true monumentality'. (Green, 'Léger and L'Esprit Nouveau: 1912–1928', pp. 57–63, 72–80, quotations from pp. 62, 80.) See also Green, 2000, p. 156, on 'What seems an uncomplicated shift from a Bergsonian stress on the dynamism of experience to a revived positivist accent on "objective" display within structured settings.' This change, however, was only temporary and perhaps misleading. Green maintains that Léger was attracted to Purism because he recognized the Bergsonian energy simmering under the positivist surface. (Ibid., pp. 156–8.) Golding observes that Léger never fully subscribed to the Purist concept of the object: he considered it a springboard for imaginative formal games, 'not an end but a means. He saw in orthodox Purism an element of "imitation" which he condemned.' ('Léger and the Heroism of Modern Life', p. 19.) Affron also discusses the fundamental constancy of Léger's position. (1994, pp. 1–21; 'Léger's Modernism: Subjects and Objects', in Lanchner et al., 1998, pp. 121–48.)

34 Cited in Green, 'The Architect as Artist', p. 116.

35 Green, 'The *objet à réaction poétique*, the figure and eroticism in painting', p. 125; 'Léger and L'Esprit Nouveau: 1912–1928', p. 50.

36 Green, 'The Architect as Artist', pp. 111–14. The statement by Le Corbusier is from *New World*, p. 115. For more on what Green maintains is Le Corbusier's dual commitment to uphold the concreteness of his objects, and to slip into looser, more expressive form, see 'Purist painting: principles and practises', in Raeburn and Wilson (eds), 1987, pp. 120–21.

5 Conventionalism

1 'ni artistes ni savants, mais ignorants véritables . . . Crise, parce que quelques ignorants, contre toute raison banissent comme surannée le 3e dimension, au

profit d'une nouvelle dimension, dénommée quatrième. Comme la quatrième dimension est purement hypothétique (le sens plastique de l'homme restant conditionné par ses sens, qui sont à trois dimensions) que font-ils? . . . Or, ils réduisent ainsi à deux dimensions oubliant qu'il saugrenu de prétendre, *à l'aide d'un moyen à deux dimensions, en materialiser une quatrième* . . . dans une oeuvre plastique la troisiéme dimension étant *nécessairement perspective*, on peut par corollaire affirmer qu'il n'y a pas oeuvre plastique *sans perspective* . . . Cela prouve que, dans l'intérêt du Cubisme, et de l'Art, il serait désirable que les plasticiens, architects de la matière ayant comme materiaux les propriétés de cette matière dans l'espace, connussent autant qu'il est possible ses loi organiques, afin de ne pas bavarder à fort et à travers sur ces lois mêmes.' Amédée Ozenfant, 'Notes sur Le Cubisme', in *L'Élan*, 10 December 1916, cited in Ball, 1987, pp. 191–4. My translation.

2   '[J]eux merveilleux de l'esprit, sans aucun contact matériel avec le monde réel, concevable mais non représéntable.' *Après le Cubisme*, pp. 16–17. My translation. See also Ball, 1987, pp. 23, 37.

3   Albert Gleizes and Jean Metzinger, 'Cubism', trans. T. Fisher Unwin, in Herbert (ed.), 1964, p. 8.

4   Ibid., pp. 6–7.

5   And if the artist 'ventures into metaphysics, cosmogony, or mathematics, let him be content with obtaining their savor, and abstain from demanding of them certitudes which they do not possess'. (Ibid., pp. 15, 18 [emphases added].)

6   Ibid., pp. 5, 6, 13–15 (emphasis added).

7   Gleizes and Metzinger were also indebted to Bergson's philosophy, although Antliff maintains that they misrepresented it somewhat. Bergson considered it necessary to break away from rational-scientific modes of thinking in search of the 'profound self', but this was meant to end in a renewed understanding both of self *and* of world. According to Antliff, however, Gleizes and Metzinger distorted this programme by overprivileging the exploration of their personal intuitions and experiences, which led them to disregard the need to communicate with others or to arrive at any understanding of the world. From the passages examined, however, it seems to me that they *did* maintain a commitment of this kind. (See Antliff, 1993, pp. 39–66; esp. pp. 61ff.)

8   Linda Dalrymple Henderson, 1983, *passim*.

9   Non-Euclidean geometry emerged in the first quarter of the nineteenth century. To give a rudimentary gloss of the kind of reasoning it involved, theorists observed that in orderly Euclidean space the internal angles of a triangle would always add up to 180°, but in concave or convex spaces, such as the inside or outside of a sphere, the internal angles of a triangle would add up to less *and* more than 180°. Theorists also explored the idea that space was not only curved but *irregularly* curved, which meant that the shapes and properties of geometrical figures would be deformed unpredictably as they moved over and through it.

10   These theories emerged later and less coherently than the non-Euclidean ones. Also, there was an insurmountable difficulty of visualizing a fourth dimension in spatial terms: one method was to suggest that just as a three-dimensional solid is bound by two-dimensional planes, so a four-dimensional 'hypersolid' must be bound by three-dimensional solids. Others dramatized the dilemma by pointing out the difficulty a hypothetical two-dimensional being, confined to life on a plane, would have in visualizing a *third* dimension. This difficulty led many to consider the fourth dimension as time.

11   Henderson, 1983, pp. 3–43, esp. pp. 3–10; quotations from pp. 6, 43. Tom Gibbons maintains that the occultist explanation of the fourth dimension as a transcendental reality was by far the most popular and influential in the early twentieth century. The individual could access this reality either through the 'normal' occultist channels of mediums, clairvoyancy or meditation, or through the more rational means of complex geometric exercises. (1981, pp. 130–47; see also Henderson, 'Mysticism, Romanticism and the Fourth Dimension', in Edward Weisberger [ed.], 1985, pp. 219 ff.)

12   Bernard Smith, 1998, pp. 81–2 for Pablo Picasso and Georges Braque's refusal to be associated with these ideas.

13   Apollinaire, *The Cubist Painters* (1913), trans. Lionel Abel, in Herschel B. Chipp, 1968, p. 243.

14   Ibid., pp. 221–8 for more references to the fourth dimension; quotations from p. 224. See also p. 227, in which Apollinaire notes that Cubism sought 'elements borrowed not from the reality of sight, but from the reality of insight'.

15   Gibbons, 1981, pp. 140–47: their interests and pronouncements on these new theories 'were a commonplace of contemporary semi-educated thought' (p. 142).

16   Henderson, 1983, pp. 44–116, 313–18.

17   Gibbons, 1981, p. 143.

18   Henderson, 'Mysticism, Romanticism and the Fourth Dimension', *passim*.

19   See Ball, 1987, p. 40.

20   Ozenfant, 1968, cited in Henderson, 1983, p. 301. See also *The Dictionary of Art*, vol. 23, p. 694.

21   Henri Poincaré, *Science et Methode*, Paris, 1920. This edition, which is held in Le Corbusier's personal library in the Fondation Le Corbusier (FLC), is inscribed as follows: 'Pour Jeanneret / 7 Dec 1920 / Ozenfant' (flyleaf: no pagination).

22   Gibbons, 1981, pp. 147, 142.

23   Poincaré, 'Sur les hypothèses fondamentales de la géométrie', in *Bulletin de la Société Mathématique de France*, xv, 1887, cited in Henderson, 1983, pp. 15–16; Poincaré, *Science and Hypothesis* (1903), 1952, pp. 48–50. For more details on this debate, see Henderson, 1983, pp. 10–17. In the works published around the time of his death in 1912, however, he argued for the reconciliation of perceptual and geometric space around a three-dimensional model not only for the sake of convenience or upholding convention, but rather in view of new 'proofs' that reality

was in fact three-dimensional. (Ibid., pp. 15–17, 36–8.) See also Smith, 1998, p. 78: the debate 'was eventually settled for all practical purposes by Henri Poincaré . . . who theorised that geometric axioms were neither a priori nor empirical: they were conventional'.

24 This summary is taken from Poincaré's most popular books dealing with the philosophy of science. See Poincaré, 1952, pp. xxi–vii, esp. pp. xxiii–iv on 'nominalism'; pp. 35–50 for the main non-Euclidean theorists, and a discussion of how conflicting geometries may all be *conceptually* elaborated and 'proved'; pp. 51–71 on how our physiological apparatus commits us to a three-dimensional experience of the world, how this is constructed around our 'sequential' encounters with solid objects, and also for Poincaré's hypothetical play with non-Euclidean and four-dimensional worlds and beings; pp. 72–88 on how experiment can be used to prove all spatial paradigms, which forces us to make a choice of 'convenience'. The later books revisit all these areas. See *The Value of Science* (1905), 1958, esp. pp. 112–42; pp. 37–74 for the arguments in favour of Euclidean, three-dimensional geometry; pp. 1–3 for the translator's discussion of 'conventionalism' as a kind of 'knowledge' that need only be *good enough*: 'with a sufficiency of conscious or unconscious omissions and doctorings and fudgings more or less wilful'; pp. 4–14 on how absolute truth is unattainable and the merely functional value of 'knowledge'. See also *Science and Method* (1908), no date. This is the volume in Le Corbusier's library, and it reiterates and elaborates all of the above points: pp. 15–24 on 'The Selection of Facts' are reprinted from pp. 4–9 of *The Value of Science*, thus Le Corbusier would have been aware of the centrally important points of Poincaré's philosophy; pp. 93–116 on how 'knowledge' is produced in the experiences filtered through human physiology as it negotiates the objects in its environment. Finally, see *Mathematics and Science: Last Essays* (1913), 1963, pp. 25–44 on 'Why Space Has Three Dimensions'.

25 Henderson, 1983, pp. 300–13, 318–21; see also appendix A, pp. 353–65, for a discussion of Albert Einstein's theories and the spread of their popularity and influence. As Henderson remarks, p. 320: 'Few of the other artists interested in the subject in the 1920s . . . would have agreed that a Euclidean, three-dimensional style was "better adapted" to the needs of a world that had been radically altered by Einstein.' Le Corbusier showed no 'interest in modern interpretations of the universe. For him the scientist is the revealer and the laws of gravity the unifier of the universe – both 18th century ideas, going back to the heyday of Newtonianism, but largely discarded by 20th century science and philosophy.' (Serenyi, 1968, p. 312.) This is correct and contradicts the seminal but superficial position of Siegfried Giedion, who attempted to explain *all* manifestations of twentieth-century art and architecture in terms of their reproducing the spatial awareness and possibilities of the new sciences. (1963. See especially pp. 431–2, 510–19.) As Christopher Pearson has observed, 'Giedion's totalizing

interpretations did not accord with Purist theory or practise, which emphasized the iconic presence of discrete and heterogenous objects in space rather than a "unified field" of space-time.' (1995, p. 82; see also p. 80.) Pearson later misrepresented the situation, however, when he said that Le Corbusier was interested in Poincaré's *Science et méthode* because it brought him 'up to date on the latest research' on 'relativity' and 'quantum theory'. (1997, p. 173.)

26   *Sketchbooks. Volume 3*, p. 46, entry no. 558. This is from a sketchbook dated 1955–6.

27   See again 'Purism', pp. 70–72.

28   In a phrase reminiscent of Golding's 'blueprints', Henderson observes that 'The Purist painter would depict these objects by means of a method resembling the descriptive geometry of the engineer.' (1983, p. 310.)

29   Poincaré, 1963, p. 44; see also 1952, pp. 51–71.

30   On the selective way these Cubists took up Poincaré's ideas, see Henderson, 1983, pp. 93–9.

31   Le Corbusier is unwilling to conceive form separately from its concrete manifestation in the world: see, for example, how he displays geometric solids in relation to how they appear in the actual buildings of Rome. (*Towards*, p. 159.) Daniel Joseph Naegele argues that Le Corbusier was fascinated by the mass media and the new spatial sciences, and used representational techniques like photography to 'de-materialize' his architecture: 'An architecture of illusion evolved which valued phenomenal sensation over the "thing" itself . . . [he] undermines the objectivity of architecture.' (1996, pp. viii, 23, 25; see also pp. 15–18 and 'Photographic illusionism and the "new world of space"', in Bosson et al., 1995, pp. 83–117.) Naegele maintains that Le Corbusier's city panoramas invoke 'invisible reality', 'construed' and 'continuous' space, despite the fact that Le Corbusier explicitly called them 'three-dimensional'. (*Radiant*, p. 204.) Like Colomina, Naegele overlooks those statements that contradict his argument. (See pp. 58–9 and p. 224, n. 23, above.) It is worth noting that Rosalind Krauss also refers to the strategies through which Purist painting sought to give objective knowledge of reality, although her terms differ from mine. ('Léger, Le Corbusier, and Purism', in *Artforum*, vol. x, no. 8, April 1972, pp. 51–3.)

32   Le Corbusier does not mention his active and eager collaboration with Vichy. Instead, he gives the impression that he complied only because he was coerced. (*The Modulor: A Harmonious Measure to the Human Scale Universally Applicable to Architecture and Mechanics* [1950], in *The Modulor 1 and 2*, 1986, pp. 36–43; quotation from p. 42.) Also, he contrasted his system with that of the Association Française de Normalisation, who had been officially charged by Vichy to determine an international proportional standard. In contradiction to the more idealistic Modulor, their system was a pragmatic 'cross-section' of methods and customs already in use by architects, engineers and manufacturers. (*The Modulor*, pp. 33, 36, 43, 78.)

33 Ibid., pp. 47, 57, 239: through the Modulor, international 'rivalries', 'oppositions', 'antagonism' and 'division' will be replaced by 'unification'.

34 Ibid., pp. 177–81; quotation from p. 180 (emphasis added).

35 Ibid., pp. 18–21, 47, 57, 114–5, 125; quotations from p. 115. See also *Modulor 2: 1955 (Let The User Speak Next)* (1955), in *Modulor 1 and 2*, 1986, pp. 49–51. See also pp. 16, 49–56, 189 for Le Corbusier's criticism of the more abstract proportional systems, and his praise for those – especially the Egyptian – that remain grounded in the measurements of the human body.

36 See ibid., pp. 89–91, 196–200.

37 François Rabelais, 1955, p. 710; see also pp. 642–6, 651–3, and 682–712.

38 *Modulor 2*, p. 200. Le Corbusier lampoons the attempts made to read mystical number symbolism into the Modulor, although he concedes that the misunderstanding may have arisen through its being released in a bookshop specializing in esoteric subjects. (*The Modulor*, p. 6; *Modulor 2*, pp. 22–3, 32–3, 79 ff., esp. p. 103: 'The "spokesmen" tend to speak in high-falutin' terms, implying deep knowledge and initiation. Sometimes they seem to be officiating at a cult.') Le Corbusier also expressed his scepticism through the image of a 'garden of delights' that he refused to enter. (See pp. 201–2, 298, and *The Modulor*, pp. 71, 238.)

39 Ibid., pp. 221–5; quotation from p. 225; see also *Modulor 2*, pp. 143–4.

40 *The Modulor*, pp. 50, 160; see also p. 65, n. 1.

41 Ibid., p. 184; see also pp. 78–80.

42 Ibid., p. 79.

43 Ibid., pp. 72–3: 'His eyes (of which he has two, and not ten or a hundred or a thousand) are placed in the front of his head, within *his own face*, looking forward; they cannot look sideways or backwards, and thus are incapable of appreciating the dazzling scene around them, with its combinations issuing from the philosopher's polyhedrons.'

44 Andreas Speiser, cited in *Modulor 2*, pp. 76–8; quotation from p. 76.; see also p. 205.

45 Ibid., p. 141. This passage is a paraphrase of Rudolf Wittkower at the Ninth Triennale in Milan in 1951, from a conference dedicated to 'Divine Proportion'.

46 Le Corbusier is convinced of his position at the head of this tradition: names that recur include Euclid, Vitruvius, Fibonacci, Alberti, da Vinci, Villard de Honnecourt, Dürer and so on. Also, a book exhibition at the Milan 1931 conference compared proportional conventions and culminated '*with a graphic demonstration of the MODULOR*'. (*The Modulor*, p. 5. See also *Modulor 2*, pp. 20, 141 ff.)

47 Wittkower commends the Modulor for answering a contemporary dilemma: 'the replacing of absolute measures of space and time by the new dynamic space-time relationship'. None the less, 'Le Corbusier's system of irrational magnitudes is still dependent on the conceptions which Pythagorean–Platonic thought opened up for western mankind.' Therefore it is 'a fascinating attempt to

co-ordinate tradition with our non-Euclidean world'. (Paraphrased in ibid., pp. 189–93, 141.)

48   *The Modulor*, p. 9.

49   Ibid., p. 25. Clearly Le Corbusier intends the Modulor to be seen as his personal project (pp. 36 ff. and 182).

50   Ibid., pp. 62–3.

51   Ibid., pp. 181–3. The Modulor's use of the Golden Section 'may represent a useful convention and, as often happens, the adoption of a convention – howsoever arbitrary it may be – can lead to substantial progress'. (Le Lionnais, cited in *Modulor 2*, pp. 18–20.) This 'conventional' knowledge may be arbitrary or incorrect, then, but it would appear to have some instrumental use. Consequently Le Corbusier is not committed to the Modulor, and occasionally reiterates his right to reject it when it fails to do its job. (*The Modulor*, pp. 56, 63, 163, 183, 234–5; *Modulor 2*, pp. 92–4.)

52   See Peter Collins, 'The Modulor', and Wittkower, 'Le Corbusier's Modulor': both expose the faulty mathematics and general arbitrariness of the system. (In Serenyi [ed.], 1975, pp. 79–83, 84–9.)

53   That Le Corbusier appears now to consider the new mathematical sciences is of no real significance, for if they *are* a factor in the Modulor, they are just the latest 'convention'. How else could he characterize his 'irrational magnitudes' as only '*somewhat closer* to reality' than the ASCORAL system? (*The Modulor*, p. 80 [emphasis added].) Henderson, 1983, p. 16, n. 32, notes that while Poincaré's general theory of 'conventionalism' has largely held, 'Euclidean geometry no longer seems the "most convenient" for physicists studying space.' The non-Euclidean becomes just another convention, which 'can be established empirically with the same certainty as other scientific "truths"'.

54   *The Modulor*, p. 84.

55   Ibid., p. 15; see also pp. 73–4.

56   Ibid., pp. 74–5.

57   Ibid., p. 84; see also p. 29: 'Music, like architecture, is *time and space*. Music and architecture alike are a matter of measure.'

58   *Modulor 2*, pp. 261–6.

59   *The Modulor*, p. 74.

60   Ibid., p. 111. One continually gets the impression of his chopping up the universe to his own measure. See, for example, *Modulor 2*, p. 284: 'everywhere and at all times, men have fitted their undertakings to the measure of their limbs, the amplitude of their gestures, creating a universe to the scale of their own movements'.

61   Ibid., pp. 144–5. While noting Le Corbusier's apology that his paraphrase of Hans Kayser has already suffered 'the double-dutch of translations which is part and parcel of polyglot international conferences', we can take the distinction drawn here to be broadly representative of Le Corbusier's own position.

62   The Modulor reasserts those earlier concerns with 'the "individual-collective" binomial'. (*Modulor 2*, p. 297; see also p. 154.)

63   The Modulor was not meant to remain a mere table of numbers, but was rather to be an iron grid set up on all building sites and a measuring strip used at the drawing board. (*The Modulor*, p. 37, pp. 60–61, p. 181.)

64   *Radiant*, p. 204.

65   See the photograph in *Decorative*, p. 191.

66   *Precisions*, pp. 198–200.

67   Ibid.

68   *Home*, pp. 89–99. See also the sketch in *Precisions*, p. 156; and the photographs in *City*, p. 200, and *Radiant*, p. 205.

69   I have been criticized for underestimating the aesthetic value that Le Corbusier can find in architectural design, and must concede that he was indeed keenly aware of such aesthetic value and considered himself a gifted connoisseur. But he did not expect the same receptiveness from the inhabitants of his ideal cities. For *them* to be enthralled by architecture would be a distraction. It is worth mentioning that Le Corbusier often advocated behaviour for others that he neglected to observe himself.

70   *Towards*, p. 246. After a brief moment when he appears to toy with the idea that mutual respect between individuals might be sufficient to maintain some kind of psychic boundary between them (p. 243), Le Corbusier returns to the demand for a more concrete demarcation of space. See also p. 260: 'What the student wants is a monk's cell . . . cut off by walls from his neighbours'; *Radiant*, pp. 143–7; *Precisions*, pp. 35–66, 85–103, 123–57.

71   *My Work*, p. 300; *Precisions*, p. 66. The first aim of the Marseilles Unité d'Habitation was 'to provide with silence and solitude before the sun, space and greenery a dwelling which will be the perfect receptacle for the family'. And beyond this, the internal detailing afforded privacy for the individual members of the family. (Benton, 'Unité d'Habitation, Marseilles', in Raeburn and Wilson [eds], 1987, pp. 220–23; citation from p. 220. See also *Le Corbusier Sketchbooks. Volume 4, 1957–1964*, 1982, p. 13, n. 137.) This preoccupation with the completely sealed dwelling unit surfaced time and again in Le Corbusier's thoughts. For example, in 1959 he envisaged creating a division within ASCORAL dedicated to solving the problem of noise pollution (p. 35, entry nos. 406–7). In 1962, an aerial view of Paris revealed to him the 'scandal' and 'sickness' of houses that 'see each other, hear each other hear each other' (p. 72, no. 866; see also p. 77, no. 912 on Le Corbusier's own hermetically sealed studio).

72   *Decorative*, pp. 73–5; see also p. 99: 'a triggering of our consciousness, a classification, and a normal perception of the objects in our life will emerge, which distinguishes the highly practical things of work from the intensely free, living, ideal things of the mind'.

73   *The Modulor*, p. 181.

74 Ibid., p. 224.

75 *Modulor 2*, p. 103.

76 I disagree with certain interpretations of the modernist grid, at least when it is thought representative of Le Corbusier's city grids, domestic layouts and Modulor. Generally, it is considered to be expressive of the spatial innovations of the new sciences, thus providing an homogenous, quantitative, infinitely extensible continuum. Jack H. Williamson reads this into the alleged 'dematerialization' of Le Corbusier's interiors and christens it the 'anti-object paradigm'. He considers this spatial development to be parallel to the loss of autonomous individuality under the new collectivist and determinist social and psychological sciences. Andrew McNamara similarly reads Le Corbusier's grid as evidence of a desire to collapse all boundaries – natural, spatial, social and aesthetic – into an undifferentiated field. Le Corbusier is apparently committed to imposing this field at all levels, 'to transform it into a broad social vision encompassing every aspect of life'. Although these readings may be applicable to other modernist grids, they are not applicable to Le Corbusier. (Williamson, 1986, pp. 15–30, esp. pp. 21–4, quotation from p. 23; McNamara, 1992, pp. 60–79, quotation from p. 65.)

77 *Sketchbooks. Volume 4*, p. 62, entry nos. 731, 733, 739, 741–3. For Le Corbusier's thoughts on an electronic lab-museum for Paris, see p. 54, nos. 668, 671; p. 57, no. 682. Le Corbusier proposed to include the 'Museum of Unlimited Growth' in several of his schemes, and succeeded in getting two built in India and one in Tokyo. (See Tim Benton, 'The Era of Great Projects', in Raeburn and Wilson [eds], 1987, pp. 165–6; Sunand Prasad, 'Cultural Centre, Ahmedabad', in ibid., pp. 300–02.)

6 Ozenfant's Impasse

1 A useful way to introduce Ozenfant's epistemological dilemma is to look at the different prefaces he wrote for his *Foundations of Modern Art*. Initially, in 1928, he emphasizes the need for the world, grown 'fugitive' and 'ephemeral', to be recalibrated according to those 'constants' that underlie all phenomena and give a promise of fundamental stability: 'how prodigiously stable mankind is . . . directed by the impalpable and rigid threads of the forces that govern the universe'. Anything that reveals and returns us to these constants is an 'ART', be it Purism, philosophy, science or religion: 'And why not? Art is not a matter of the particular technic used; that is merely the interpretative agent.' Purism is 'an attitude of mind and a procedure'. ([1928], 1952, pp. xiii–xiv.) By 1931, these 'certitudes' would appear to be few, and their capacity to reorient the world substantially diminished: '*the author feels himself drowned in the unseizable cosmos, and stretches his arms ardently towards the slightest blade of reality that floats*'. These

few certitudes, '*unhappily too rare*', might at least help us momentarily to '*forget the tragedy of our ignorance*' (p. x). By 1952, all constants are superseded by ever emerging 'new realities'. Atomic science has dissolved the materiality of the universe, 'all existence is motion and thus Time', and artists must forgo a past when 'their Muses needed mass and matter' (p. vii). See also p. 8, where Ozenfant discusses theories of Euclidean, non-Euclidean and *n*-dimensional space.

2 Ozenfant was aware that he was playing an intricate epistemological game: in order to help orient his reader in the 'mazes' of his argument, he provisionally 'colour-codes' its main threads like an electrician. (Ibid., pp. xv–xvi.) He also sets out a schema of what he considers to be all the methods of gaining knowledge, and seems to dabble in most of them (p. 178). It is worth noting Ball's point that Ozenfant shifted away from the increasingly unsustainable demands for epistemological order of *L'Esprit nouveau* into an appreciation of Bergsonian 'continuity and duration'. (1987, pp. 124–6.) Green maintains that a commitment to the Bergsonian 'experience' of modernity *always* underlay the more positivist aspirations of Purism. While this may apply to Ozenfant, I doubt it for Le Corbusier. (2000, pp. 156–8.)

3 Ozenfant, 1952, pp. xiv–xvi; quotation from p. xv. See also pp. 84–103 for Ozenfant's account of how a love of novelty and fashion has infected modern painting, particularly in terms of Picasso and his imitators, the so-called 'Picassoids'.

4 Ibid., p. xiii.

5 Ibid., pp. 339–43; quotation from p. 340. Incidentally, these 'preforms' and 'constants' are not *absolutely* constant: many are fundamental, but others are said to emerge in response to different circumstances and times (pp. 43–6, p. 342).

6 Ibid., p. xiii.

7 Ibid., pp. 130, 247–50. Ozenfant says that literature has a limited communicative power due to its use of culturally specific language conventions. It seems that we are physiologically predetermined to respond best to form and colour as they appeal to our 'Compulsive tropisms, energetic and universal enough to modify behaviour . . . Biophysics is here absolutely in accordance with aesthetics.' Ozenfant is therefore searching for a taxonomy of affect and provides a breakdown of the motifs and metaphors in modern French poetry, as well as of abstract shapes, in order to assess their effectiveness. These are intended to function as 'detectors' of our constants (pp. 31–7, 250–55, 308–11, 359 ff.).

8 Ibid., pp. 284–5. Poincaré is mentioned throughout this work: see, for example, pp. 4, 8, 173.

9 Ibid., p. 189.

10 Ibid., p. 196; see also p. 284: 'Is the world geometric? Is geometry the thread that man has seized which links all things? Or is it that the laws which guide the brain are geometric, and so it is only able to perceive what fits into its warp and woof?'

11   Ibid., p. 191.

12   Ibid., p. 312.

13   Ibid., pp. 311–13. Ozenfant believes that all conventions must ultimately 'harmonize', as they emerge from 'the laws of our intelligences' (p. 284). See also p. 175: science has come up against 'the armour plating of the unknowable. Armour plating? Every use of language is inappropriate, for we know nothing, and we but dupe ourselves with images.'

14   Ibid., pp. 181–3; quotation from p. 183 (emphasis added). It is not necessary to give more details concerning Pascal at the moment as we shall encounter him below.

15   Ibid., p. 173: 'Science is . . . incapable of discovering anything irrational in our universe.' Ozenfant finds an absurd irony in the attempts by modern science and religion to find fresh *rational* grounds and justification for faith: 'Reason can convince us of the impossibility of knowing, but it cannot give us reasons for faith' (p. 177). See also p. 181: 'In the annihilation of rational certitude we shall discover a justification for faith.'

16   Ibid., pp. 177–8. This is part of a table detailing and attacking the 'CATEGORIES OF BELIEVERS'.

17   Ibid., pp. 182–3, 190, 30.

18   Ibid., pp. 183–5; quotations from pp. 183, 130. See also p. 178, where art is described as 'A palliative and liberating hypnotic for the sceptic'; p. xv: 'Shut out from that splendid highway traced by Faith, which allowed us to traverse life without too much anguish, Art still remains on which to drift a while'; and p. 185: 'Religions were created to soften the fear of death, Art to enable us to forget it. The kind of buoy that rescues us is hardly relevant!' On a related theme, pp. 214–23, Ozenfant suggests that only art, with its promise of a quick fix, can successfully offset the frenzy and violence of the lives of modern people: 'They want their illusion compact, powerful' (p. 223). Further allusions to this can be found on pp. 230, 240.

19   Ibid., p. 289.

20   Ibid., p. 302.

21   Ibid., pp. 326, xv (emphasis added).

22   Ibid., pp. 4–5.

23   Again, he warns the reader that his theory will be inconsistent and full of contradictions. (Ozenfant, *Journey Through Life: Experiences, Doubts, Certainties, Conclusions*, 1939, p. 6.)

24   Ibid., p. 104; see also p. 20: 'To reason is to rationalise. That is all we do when we fancy that we understand. Even the superstitious, declaring that a will-'o'-the-wisp is the soul of a dead man, rationalise. To attribute to a phenomenon a definitely miraculous character is a sort of positivism. It comes from the refusal to remain in ignorance, the wish for a precise explanation. Many superstitious

folk are naïve rationalists who do not know themselves'; and p. 382: 'God is the
gilded name we give to our ignorance.'

25   Ibid., p. 129.

26   Ibid., p. 382.

27   Ibid., pp. 388–9, 383, 386.

28   Ibid., p. 382; more generally, see pp. 381–93.

29   Ibid., p. 291. For an account of Ozenfant's socialism, set against the backdrop
of the French Fascist upsurge of 1934, see pp. 290–340.

30   Ibid., p. 198: 'But the pursuit of purity for its own sake ends in sterility. I understood that as far back as 1925 and turned my mind towards research of a more
human kind.' See also pp. 197, 217–19.

31   Ibid., pp. 203, 252–3.

32   *Routes*, pp. 18, 100.

33   *Radiant*, p. 150.

34   Léger, 'Contemporary Achievements in Painting', p. 14. Léger's approach to the
modern city is typically modernist, full of overwhelming, unpredictable and
dangerous experiences. Ultimately, however, it is a liberating milieu to be
embraced optimistically, ripe with possibilities for the ceaseless change and
development of the individual. (Jodi Hauptman, 'Imagining Cities', in Lanchner
et al., 1998, pp. 72–119.)

35   Nina Lara Rosenblatt has argued that the Purists subscribed to a particular school
of thought that wanted to redress the social and psychological fragmentation
caused by the onslaught of modern life. But this did not involve shoring up the
individual psyche in defence, as individuality was considered socially undesirable.
Besides, all phenomena were believed to be aligned on a single interpenetrative
field of energy, and the human mind was no exception. The Purists' project
was to stabilize and control this field: a normative mass consciousness would
be synthesized through the effects of art, with all 'subjects' homogenized into
'unornamented surface'. While this may be a valid interpretation for Ozenfant,
it is not applicable to Le Corbusier. (1997, *passim*; quotation from p. 140.)

'Pascal's *Desideratum*': Preface

1   There are two outstanding collections that can be consulted: Henderson (ed.),
1987; Weisberger (ed.), 1985. Henderson offers useful definitions: 'Occultism'
indicates a large body of theory and practise involving 'supernatural agencies or
some secret knowledge of them', including such things as 'alchemy, the Cabala,
magic, astrology, Rosicrucianism, spiritualism, and Theosophy'. 'Mysticism' is a
more personal, meditative discipline involving 'the experience of mystical union
or direct communication with ultimate reality . . . it is based on an individual's
personal experience of transcendence'. (Henderson, [ed.], 1987, p. 5.) See

also Robert Galbreath et al., 'A Glossary of Spiritual and Related Terms', in Weisberger (ed.), 1985, pp. 368 ff.

2   Moore pioneered this approach and his thesis represents the outer limits of such interpretative complexity. (1977; quotation from the introduction, no pagination.) He will, for example, find significance in the way a particular door handle inclines towards a particular zodiacal constellation. Mogens Krustup, who concentrates rather more on the 'self-portraiture' elements within this iconography, substantially ratifies Moore's ideas. ('Persona', in Bosson et al., 1995, pp. 118–57.) See also Alice Gray Read's discussion of the 'Ubu' image as an expression of Le Corbusier's personality. (1998, pp. 215–26.) Peter Carl maintains that Le Corbusier's iconography reveals the 'three horizons of temporality' that 'mediate' between humanity and the divine, and which are manifest in the ornamental schemes of sculpture, painting and architecture throughout all time. (1991, pp. 48–65; 1992, pp. 49–64.) Frampton considers Le Corbusier's symbolism to be coherent to such a degree that even his alleged suicide in 1965 fits into the overall pattern: it was, he claims, 'consistent not only with his assumed Albigensian identity but also with his dualistic, alchemical preoccupations, coming close to the final sublimation of the body in the female ocean while swimming towards the male sun'. (2001, p. 202; see pp. 200–13 on 'Le Poème de l'Angle Droit'.) The most sustained recent attempt at this kind of approach is by Flora Samuel, who marshals Le Corbusier's iconography to present him as a maelstrom of Mariolatry, Orphism, Catholic yearning, and pioneering ecological feminism. (1999 [a], pp. 4–19; 1999 [b], pp. 111–25; 2000, pp. 181–99; 2001, pp. 325–38.) But the concern with Le Corbusier's iconography has also led to some more cautious and balanced studies. Mary Patricia May Sekler succeeds precisely because she is wary of becoming too immersed: 'We cannot know what Le Corbusier's vocabulary of forms meant to him. We can, at best, reconstruct contexts, analyse forms, and scrutinize verbal statements in the hope that by doing so we may at least begin to approach the artist's intention.' (1977; quotation from pp. 61–2.)

3   Samuel, 1999 (a), p. 14; Carl, 1991, p. 58. Jencks maintains that for Le Corbusier's 'Post-Modern' symbolism, 'multimeaning is an end in itself'. (2000; quotation from p. 275.) But Christopher Pearson makes the following point: '[Le Corbusier's] new iconographic language is at once apparently self-consistent and incomprehensible – in short, a system of hermetic symbols for which we have lost the key. Le Corbusier, it should be recognized, very probably constructed and encourages this iconographic obscurity quite deliberately . . . his desire was to pose a series of iconographic riddles that would ensure his lasting fame by piquing the interest of art historians.' (1997, p. 168; see also 1995, pp. 7–8.)

4   Green, 'Nature and the sacred: sign and symbol', in Raeburn and Wilson (eds), 1987, p. 246. A similar line is taken by Jaime Coll, who uses Roland Barthes's

theory of the 'Text' to argue that Le Corbusier's work involves the endless 'play' of pre-existing elements without origin, author or meaning: this 'prompts us to consider the work as a network of reciprocal and interchangeable relationships, where the substituted elements can be "loaded" with any symbolic content'. The continual round of 'transpositions', 'deformations', 'dislocations' and 'reconstructions' leads Coll to 'focus on the transformational strategies, rather than attempting an iconographic analysis'. (Coll, 1996, pp. 3–14, quotation from p. 7; see also Barthes, 'From Work to Text' [1971], in Barthes, 1977, pp. 155–64.) More generally, Smith also denies that avant-garde occultism and mysticism had any content. He alleges that it was merely a way for an artist to break the traditional constraints of making his art meaningful. Art was then freed for an exploration of pure *form*. Smith makes this claim to underwrite his thesis that modernism as a whole was preoccupied with form, which he christens the 'Formalesque'. (1998, esp. pp. 69–70, 73–4, 82; see also pp. 1–12.) But I agree with Robert P. Welsh's point that an interest in esoteric subjects was symptomatic of a desire to return to a stable pool of meaning as opposed to the senseless upheavals and inconsistencies of the times. ('Sacred Geometry: French Symbolism and Early Abstraction', in Weisberger [ed.], 1985, pp. 84–5.) It is also worth noting that Le Corbusier favourably cited a letter of 'around 1954' from an ex-member of his atelier on the subject of his 'pharaonic' poetry: 'To reproach you for formalism . . . becomes simply comic, were it not tragic!' (*Mise*, p. 96.)

5   Benton, 'The sacred and the search for myths', in Raeburn and Wilson (eds), 1987, pp. 238–45; quotations from pp. 240, 245.

6   *My Work*, p. 219. See also *Sketchbooks. Volume 4*, p. 43, entry no. 506.

7   Pascal: Preparing the Machine

1   As well as the references to Descartes that are sprinkled throughout Le Corbusier's writings, he also invites this comparison through his commitment to such things as stating the 'problem' clearly, working through its parts in a logical sequence, and so on. See, for example, *Radiant*, pp. 127–34 on 'Is Descartes American?', with its reference to 'The Cartesian skyscraper'; and *Cathedrals*, pp. 57, 112. Countless commentators have seized upon this. For example, Colquhoun remarks that 'the concrete frame [of Le Corbusier's Dom-ino] carries all the certainty of a Cartesian *a priori*'; while Lewis Mumford referred to 'his Cartesian clarity and his Cartesian elegance'. ('Rationalism: A Philosophical Concept in Architecture', in Colquhoun, 1989, p. 77; 'Architecture as a Home for Man' [1968], cited in Bacon, 2001, p. 180.) See also Chen, 1993, *passim*.

2   Le Corbusier kept a copy of this in his personal library, and I shall expand on how heterodoxy was an important source of his identity in due course. A full account of the history, motives and fortunes of the Jansenists, and also of Pascal's

final retraction in the face of papal censure, can be found in A. J. Krailsheimer's commentaries. (Pascal, *Pensées*, 1995, pp. x–xvii; *The Provincial Letters*, 1967, pp. 7–29.) But in brief, Jansenism emerged from the publication of the *Augustinus* of Cornelius Jansenius, Bishop of Ypres, in 1640 and was essentially a puritanical reaction to the extravagances and abuse of the Jesuit hierarchy. More specifically, the Jansenist–Jesuit conflict came down to the question of grace and free will. The Jansenists sought a return to the Protestant notion of man's wretchedness and helplessness, and consequent inability to influence his own salvation. They further said that the elect were few – only a small proportion would ever receive God's grace. Upheld in France primarily by Calvinism, this position had been overshadowed by Counter-Reformation notions of man as enjoying substantial free will, such that he might take actions in the world capable of directly influencing his own salvation. It was this that was taken up by the Jesuits, and attacked in turn by the Jansenists. And of course, in attacking this notion, the Jansenists were also attacking the highly profitable practice of papal indulgences. Pascal's own family were converted to Jansenism around the mid-1640s.

3   Le Corbusier appears not to have kept a copy of this book, but the fundamental affinities he holds with the theories elaborated here, the canonical status the text has held in French literature since its posthumous publication in 1670, as well as Ozenfant's frequent references to Pascal, allow us to speculate that he must have been acquainted with it. (On the morbid fascination with Pascal that runs throughout French intellectual life, see Anthony Vidler, 2001, pp. 17–24 on 'Horror Vacui: Constructing the Void from Pascal to Freud'.)

4   In slightly more detail: Descartes sought to find new grounds for certainty in knowledge, which he considered inaccurate for two reasons: first, because it emerged from a process of disinterested but vain academic revisionism; second, because it was gathered through empirical observation of phenomena, and the senses were untrustworthy. He attempted to redress this through the formulation of a new 'method' based upon philosophical logic and geometry/mathematics. Although, as human beings, we all come to different opinions and conclusions about things, this was not through any fundamental difference in us. Rather, it was attributable to the misapplication of reason, which is equally distributed within us all. We each possess a God-given 'rational soul' which is utterly fathomable and controllable. Through the application of Descartes's method, we are guaranteed to attain psychic uniformity and reach consensus on every issue. (Descartes, 1968, pp. 25–91; quotation from p. 57.)

5   Pascal, 1995, p. 61 (199). I shall be referencing this text both with its page and 'fragment' numbers. The vignettes on pp. 60–61 and 63 offer the best example of how physical phenomena recede infinitely beyond our perceptual grasp. (See also pp. 237–8 [782], and p. 18 [65]: 'A town or a landscape from afar off is a town and a landscape, but as one approaches it becomes houses, trees, tiles, leaves, grass, ants, ants' legs, and so on *ad infinitum*.')

6   Ibid., pp. 61–3; see also p. 130 (427): 'I see only infinity on every side, hemming me in like an atom or like the shadow of a fleeting instant.' We are strung up on a continuous 'chain' of creation, able to perceive dimly only a portion of 'the middle station allotted to us': 'I consider it as impossible to know the parts without knowing the whole as to know the whole without knowing the individual parts' (p. 64).

7   Ibid., and p. 16 (60). Pascal has borrowed the italicized sentence from Cicero. So-called natural or universal laws are therefore merely a matter of convention and 'habit': 'What are our natural principles but habitual principles? . . . Habit is a second nature that destroys the first. But what is nature? Why is habit not natural? I am very much afraid that nature itself is only a first habit, just as habit is a second nature' (p. 32 [125, 126]).

8   Ibid., p. 22 (83).

9   Ibid., p. 56 (188); see also pp. 19–20 (76), pp. 182–3 (512) and p. 127 (423, 424). Pascal considers it absurd that reason, unable to come to any certainty even in its own realm, should overstep its bounds and attempt to pronounce on other subjects: 'Tyranny is wanting to have by one means what can only be had by another.' (Ibid., p. 15 [58].) Descartes, with his 'geometrical demonstration' of God's existence, is the target here. (See p. 57 [190] and p. 151 [463]. Other attacks on Descartes can be found on p. 22 [84] and p. 330 [II].)

10 Ibid., pp. 28–9 (110); see also p. 4 (7).

11 The sensible will be obliged to concede to these paradoxes, 'finding no reason to reject them but [our] own inability to tell whether they are true or not'. (Ibid., pp. 49, 50 [149].) Entire series of fragments are dedicated to these issues: see XVIII–XIX (pp. 71–87) and XXIV (pp. 99–105). Also of interest is Section Three on 'Miracles' (pp. 255–81 [830–912]), in which Pascal explores the idea that, as God has allegedly shown his approval of Jansenism by allowing miracles to be performed at Port-Royal, the movement cannot be considered heterodox. (See p. xv for Krailsheimer's account of a miracle that was performed on Pascal's niece, Marguerite Périer.)

12 Ibid., p. 36 (131) (emphasis added).

13 See n. 2 above.

14 Ibid., p. 40 (136); see also p. 59 (198): 'Then these lost and wretched creatures look around and find some attractive objects to which they become addicted and attached. For my part, I have never been able to form such attachments.' For a definition of 'wretchedness' as the recollection of Original Sin, see pp. 29–30 (117), pp. 35–6 (131), p. 275 (889), and p. 19 (70): 'If our condition were truly happy we should not need to divert ourselves from thinking about it.' The childhood beginnings of our dependency on distractions are discussed on pp. 42–3 (139), and our dependency on the good opinion of others on p. 7 (31).

15 Ibid., p. 37 (132).

16   For Pascal's opinions on diversion and boredom generally, see ibid., pp. 37–41 (136), p. 26 (101); quotation from p. 8 (36).

17   Pascal reminds himself to 'write the letter about removing obstacles, that is the argument about the Machine, how to prepare it and how to use reason for the search'. (Ibid., p. 4 [11].) See also pp. 3–4 (5), p. 54 (172), and p. 29 (110): 'those to whom God has given religious faith by moving their hearts are very fortunate, and feel quite legitimately convinced, but to those who do not have it we can only give such faith through reasoning'.

18   Ibid., p. 123 (418).

19   Ibid., p. 125.

20   Ibid., p. 247 (821): see also p. 19 (72), and pp. 244–5 (808): 'we must open our mind to the proofs, confirm ourselves in it through habit, while offering our-selves through humiliations to inspiration, which alone can produce the real and salutary effect'. Further examples of how belief is a matter of being 'inclined' can be found on pp. 110–12 (380–82). Even religious observances come under this rubric: they are a matter of external routine only, preparing the individual but not giving any direct access to salvation. (p. 272 [874]).

21   Ibid., pp. 217–18 (688); see also p. 214 (673), where Pascal suggests that it is impos-sible to stay in love with someone as they inevitably change through time, and p. 117 (396), where he states that one becomes guilty of deceit by attempting to make oneself the object of another's affection. There is also a reference to Pascal's sister, Gilberte Périer, whom he censured 'for exchanging caresses with her chil-dren' (p. xi). See also p. 47 (149): 'do not expect either truth or consolation from men'; and p. 51 (151): 'we shall die alone. / We must act then as if we were alone.'

22   Ibid., p. 207 (618).

23   Ibid., pp. 37, 38 (136); see also p. 274 (879).

24   Ibid., p. 120 (414): rather than seeking diversion, this test 'would drive us to seek some more solid means of escape'. See also p. 208 (622) for a sense of the kind of psychic and spiritual hardships the individual is obliged to undergo. For the reference to Christ, see pp. 288–92 (919).

25   Ibid., p. 48 (149); see also p. 66 (202) and p. 47: 'Is it curing man's presump-tion to set him up as God's equal?'

26   Ibid., p. 194 (564), p. 110 (378). Further examples of this tension and paradox can be found on p. 119 (407) and p. 44 (143). On the topic of 'self-annihila-tion', see p. 66 (200).

27   Ibid., p. 126 (421).

28   Pascal, 1967, p. 10.

29   Pascal was committed to the setting up of a personal relationship with God, and rejected the ritual and mediation of Catholicism. But he was not insensitive to the condemnation of the papacy, and retracted his Jansenist faith shortly before his death. (Ibid., pp. 12–13; and Pascal, 1995, p. xvi, and p. xiii

on his experience of personal revelation and conversion, the so-called '*nuit de feu*'.)

30 See ibid., pp. xxvi–xxvii, for Krailsheimer's comments on how the individual, in following such 'mechanical actions', 'will on the purely human level be making himself a better citizen'.

31 *Routes*, pp. 18, 100.

32 *Mise*, p. 83.

33 *Radiant*, p. 9.

34 *Decorative*, pp. 30–31. Lubbock has identified this as one of the most representative statements of Le Corbusier's spirituality. (1995, pp. 308–12; see also James I. Dunnett, 1985, *passim*.)

35 *Towards*, pp. 120–21: 'the modern man is bored to tears in his home; so he goes to his club. The modern woman is bored outside her boudoir; she goes to tea-parties.'

36 Krailsheimer, in Pascal, 1995, p. xxiv.

37 *Routes*, p. 161; see also *Precisions*, pp. 86–7.

8 'Wisdom Builds Its Own House'

1 The Pavillon Suisse was built by Le Corbusier for the Cité universitaire, Paris, from 1930–33. (Benton, 'Pavillon Suisse, Paris', in Raeburn and Wilson [eds], 1987, pp. 179–80.) A diagrammatic sketch of the mural can be found in *The Modulor*, p. 207.

2 Although I am not going to trace Le Corbusier's iconography across the rest of his later works, it is helpful to be aware of some of the outstanding pieces. As well as *Taureau VIII* (fig. 5), see such paintings as *Les Lignes de la main* (1930) and *Icône III* (1956). See also the wood sculptures such as *Série Icône* (1953) and *Petite confidence* (1962), which were executed in collaboration with Joseph Savina. All of these seem to contain motifs that recur in the *Poème*. No single volume offers a comprehensive record of Le Corbusier's artistic work, but the following catalogues are quite good: Heidi Weber (ed.), 1988; Maria Cristina Poma (ed.), 1986. See also Christopher Green, 'Other media and collaboration', in Raeburn and Wilson (eds), 1987, pp. 129–30.

3 'Le Corbusier once noted with relish that the English had no translation for *indicible*.' (Benton, 'The sacred and the search for myths', p. 245, n. 52.) In Le Corbusier's words, 'the word *indicible* does not exist in English!!' (*Sketchbooks. Volume 2*, p. 17, entry no. 197. This sketchbook is dated 1950.)

4 Le Corbusier, *Le Poème de l'angle droit* (1955), 1989, D.3. The *iconostase* bears the dates 1947–53, but this 'seven year' aspect is probably another myth: other sources, such as the manuscript notes and the correspondence surrounding publishing arrangements, contain different dates. (See FLC, F2-20-301, -302, -303:

'Five years were consecrated to this work'. All translations of the material from these archives are my own. For the more important passages, I shall also provide the original French.)

5   Coll warns that the iconostasis should not be taken literally, but there is no justification for this. (1996, p. 4.) *The Penguin Dictionary of Architecture and Landscape Architecture* defines 'iconostasis' as follows: 'A screen in Byzantine churches separating the sanctuary from the nave and pierced by three doors ... Since the C14–15 it has become a wooden or stone wall covered with icons, hence the name.' (John Fleming et al., London, 1999, p. 277.) The four scenes of the Pavillon Suisse mural are reproduced in the *iconostase*: levels C.1, E.4, E.3 and C.5. (See *The Modulor*, p. 207.)

6   *Journey*, pp. 200, 203; other experiences in front of icon-screens are noted on pp. 62, 160. Although written in 1911–12, this work was not published until a few weeks before his death in 1965.

7   '4 est le nombre de la matière solide / 3 [est la nombre] de la puissance divine / 4 + 3 = 7 = accomplissement / . . . = accomplissement du dieu dans la matière'. FLC, F2-20-4; see also F2-30-32, -33, in which we find Le Corbusier experimenting with the different numerical schemes of a six- and seven-tier *iconostase*. Other interesting fragments are F2-20-1, -3, where there are sketches of Chinese ideograms, a Christian cross, Hindu swastika and suchlike.

8   FLC, F2-20-76, -77, -78, -79, -80, -81. An inscription dated 1942 in the flyleaf of his French edition of Shakespeare's sonnets (*Sonnets de Shakespeare*, translated by Gerard d'Uccle, no date or place of publication) again draws attention to sonnets 56 and 64. This book is held in Le Corbusier's personal library at the FLC, together with an English edition, in which sonnets 56 and 64 are again covered with Le Corbusier's translations. (*The Sonnets of William Shakespeare*, Edward Dowden [ed.], London, 1896.)

9   Shakespeare, 1991, pp. 1317–19.

10 FLC, F2-20-77. The English here is Le Corbusier's own. See also Le Corbusier, 'L'Espace indicible', 1946, pp. 9–17.

11 'Assis sur trop de causes médiates / assis à côté de nos vies / est les autres sont là / et partout sont les: "Non!" / Et toujours plus de contre / que de pour / N'accabler donc pas celui / qui vent prendre sa part des / risques de la vie. Laissez / fusionner les métaux / tolérez des alchimies qui / d'ailleurs vous laissent hors / de cause / C'est par la porte des / pupilles ouvertes que les regards / croisés ont pu conduire à / l'acte foudroyant de communion / . . . / Alors ne serons-nous pas / demeurés assis à côté de nos vies'. *Poème*, 'D.3'. Two English translations have been made of the *Poème*, one by Nancy Stephenson and Jean Canet which was included as an appendix to Moore, 1977, pp. 43–7; and another by Kenneth Hylton which provided an appendix to the facsimile reissue of the *Poème* in its original French (Paris, 1989). My transcriptions of the French are taken from the 1989 edition. The Stephenson and Canet translation is more

committed to preserving the literal meaning than making the English read elegantly. Hylton does the opposite, with the result that he occasionally misrepresents some of the content. I shall therefore primarily be citing the earlier translation, although I will also use certain passages from Hylton and some variations of my own.

12   It is interesting that Max Ernst's alchemical collage-'novel' *Une Semaine de bonté* of 1933–4 appears to pre-empt many of the motifs of Le Corbusier's *Poème*, as well as its structure: again, there are seven colour-coded 'days' or levels, each with its representative theme. See M. E. Warlick, 'Max Ernst's Alchemical Novel: *Une Semaine de bonté*', in Henderson (ed.), 1987, pp. 61–83; esp. pp. 61–2 on 'Alchemy in the Early Twentieth Century'.

13   Kurt Seligmann, *The History of Magic and the Occult* (1948), 1997. The French edition, *Le Miroir de la Magie: Histoire de la Magie dans le monde occidental*, trans. Jean-Mairie Daillet, Paris, 1956, is in Le Corbusier's personal library at the FLC.

14   Martica Sawin, 1986, pp. 76–81; 1995, *passim*. The details on Seligmann can be found throughout these works. Seligmann also contributed work to the International Surrealist Exhibition in Paris in 1947, which explored the mystical and occultist interests that had come to characterize much Surrealist activity (pp. 391 ff.). It is perhaps not a coincidence that Le Corbusier ostensibly began his *Poème* in the same year.

15   A further marker of Le Corbusier's general interest is that his library also contains a copy of *L'Art magique* by André Breton and Gerard Légrand (Paris, 1957). In broad terms, Breton believed 'the persistent vitality of an esoteric conception of the world . . . attests . . . to the perennial nature of certain major human aspirations'. These aspirations appear primarily to have involved humanity's desire to be connected with the creative genius and lawfulness of the universe, or with 'God' – 'an unknown superior principle'. This connection was to happen at the level of 'sensibility', and therefore represented a 'liberation' from an exclusively rational, utilitarian and scientific mind-set, and it would crystallize in the formation of a new 'myth' appropriate to modern times 'which it is our task to define and to coordinate'. Poetry and literature could liberate the reader into this new sensibility through the 'Alchemy of the Word': they contained 'too many gleams of the philosopher's stone for us not to repudiate the mean and miserable world that is inflicted on us'. Breton took the contemporary upsurge in occult and mystical activity as evidence of how urgently necessary this process had now become. (See 'Before the Curtain' [1947] and 'On Magic Art' [1957], in Breton, 1978, pp. 273–9, 292–6; quotations from pp. 276–7, 279, 294–5.) Breton's treatment of this subject is so rich and allusive that it would be possible to make links with Le Corbusier, but this would be misleading. Essentially they have little in common.

16   Le Corbusier recorded this fact in the flyleaf of his copy of *Gargantua and Pantagruel*. (Samuel, 2000, pp. 196–7.)

17 As well as relying upon Seligmann's discussion, 1997, esp. pp. 93–112, this summary is an amalgam of the few points common to the various treatments of the theme that we shall encounter below, especially that of C. G. Jung. Such a summary is possible only by suppressing all the inconsistencies and paradoxes that, although acknowledged as fundamental to this art, make it almost impossible to say anything definite about it. I have been extremely wary not to get ensnared in the complexities of its symbolism.

18 Ibid., p. 96. Seligmann offers a qualified confirmation of the position of E. A. Hitchcock (*Remarks upon Alchemy and the Alchemists*, New York, 1865): 'He denies the likelihood that any real chemical operations were performed by the adepts and affirms that all chemical processes were symbols of ennoblement not of the metals but of man himself. While we do not share such ideas, believing that both mystical contemplation and alchemical operations can coexist, yet the impulse which Hitchcock gave to psychological and psychoanalytic inquiry into the Hermetic art produced a rich harvest' (p. 93).

19 Ibid., pp. 96–7; also pp. 105–6.

20 Ibid., pp. 86–7. The philosophical gold was analogically linked with the sun, which 'mediated' between the realms of angels and men. Its attainment, therefore, was equivalent to taking a step up the ladder of creation towards God. See also p. 119: 'Alchemy's chief values were of a psychic nature; the Hermetic was the brother of the mystic.'

21 Ibid., pp. 88, 125 (emphasis added: the reference to 'protest' is crucial, and we shall return to it later).

22 The following summary of Gnosticism is taken from ibid., pp. 60–66, 79–82, 127–9, and from Chas S. Clifton, 1992, pp. 5–6, 49–54. Like the summary of alchemy, it is greatly simplified, providing only the major points of contact with our present concerns.

It was assumed that knowledge of alchemy had been imparted initially to women by fallen angels as a reward for sexual intercourse, 'with the intention that their companions make jewels, colourful garments and perfumes with which to adorn their beauty'. And complementing their debt to these 'betrayers of God's secrets', the alchemists also worshipped the Tree of Knowledge and the Serpent that first led man to it, which were 'to become the most cherished emblems of alchemy'. (Seligmann, 1997, pp. 79–82.) These ideas emerged from Gnosticism.

Gnosticism was a syncretic religious movement that flourished primarily, as did alchemy itself, in the cross-cultural milieu of Alexandria in the first to third centuries AD, combining such elements as 'Babylonian astrology, Zoroastrian Magism, Egyptian secret knowledge, Hellenic philosophy, Judaism and Christianity', in the belief that all the great world-systems held a grain of some greater truth. (Seligmann, 1997, p. 61.) This originated, it seems, from 'a type of world-weariness that particularly affected dissident intellectuals and people whose worldly status had shifted against their will from higher to lower. Feeling unappreciated and dishonored, these people were receptive to philosophies that rejected the world and the grinding processes of history.' (Clifton, 1992, p. 53.)

Already, then, we can recognize as fundamental a turning away from worldly values; but what were the specific terms of this? Gnosticism differed from orthodoxy in refusing to accept the notion of Original Sin: for many Gnostic sects, man was not some blameworthy being that had to seek reconciliation with an angered God. Rather, Original Sin had been brought about by the jealous and unjust restrictions that God placed upon mankind's rightful inquisitiveness, and the blame lay squarely with Him. The Serpent thus became a liberator, man's enlightener, giving him access to the knowledge through which he might save himself. Despite the fact that the Gnostic pantheon was fleshed out by many 'foreign' gods and goddesses, there were two overarching higher and lesser Gods. The lesser God, the malicious one responsible for Original Sin and ruler of the material world, was known as the 'Demiurge' and also as the Jehovah or Yahweh of the Old Testament. To turn away from the value- and meaning-systems of this world, then, was to turn away from this angry incompetent. The other, higher God was discovered through traces residing in the psychic depths of the individual, and consequently the acquisition of self-knowledge was fundamental: 'Gnostics generally accepted that the kingdom of God was an interior state, a transformed consciousness, rather than a future event.' Given such an individualist bias, the Gnostics were largely indifferent to organizing themselves into workable, long-lasting social groupings: rather, turning inward, 'Each Gnostic was his or her own ultimate authority' (p. 51). From the fourth century AD, *The Book of Thomas the Contender* contained the following sentiment: 'Whoever has not known himself has known nothing, but he who has known himself has at the same time already achieved knowledge about the depths of all things.' (Cited in ibid., p. 50.)

A further heterodox aspect was the importance accorded to women and sex. Sometimes this was taken literally, the sexual act seen by some as leading to an ecstasy that left the flesh behind. But this was also taken at a metaphorical level, such as the Gnostic 'bridal chamber' ritual in which the initiate would be spiritually united 'with his or her "image" or angelic counterpart'. In more 'concrete' psychological terms, 'this union may have been viewed as a marriage between the psyche or undying emotional self and the pneuma or undying spirit'. As the final blasphemy, 'Through this initiation . . . the Gnostic became "no longer a Christian, but a Christ".' (Ibid., p. 53. The final citation is from the *Gospel of Philip*.)

It was perhaps only by defining itself against these Gnostic heterodoxies that the notion of 'orthodoxy' was able to crystallize at all. These beliefs shaped alchemy at a fundamental level, and although not all later alchemists were directly aware of this strand of their heritage, the debt is very easy to see: it worked implicitly to maintain their art as ineradicably heterodox.

23   Alchemists later attempted to give their studies a conciliating gloss of orthodoxy. Indeed, medieval and Renaissance alchemists made the case that they were pious Christians, and sought parallels between their books and the Gospel as evidence. Theologians were unimpressed with such efforts, although outright persecution abated during these years. Indeed, alchemists were now often officially affiliated to the court, and when they *were* tortured and executed it was more usually because they had failed to deliver their much-vaunted gold. (Seligmann, 1997, pp. 82–3, 87–8, 126–7.)

24   See pp. 125–6, and p. 243, nn. 2–3.

25   'Le soleil maître de nos vies / indifférent loin / Il est le visiteur – un seigneur – / il entre chez nous'. *Poème*, 'A.1'.

26   'Ponctuelle machine tournante / depuis l'immémorial . . . / . . . / . . . Mais il la rompt / à deux fois brutalement le / matin et le soir. Le continu / lui appartient tandis qu'il / nous impose l'alternatif – / la nuit le jour – les deux temps / qui règlent notre destinée: / Un soleil se lève / un soleil se couche / un soleil se lève à nouveau'. *Poème*, 'A.1'. This deferential way of characterizing the sun, and the lithograph that accompanies the poem, are consistent with Le Corbusier's treatment of it elsewhere. (See *Cathedrals*, pp. xvii–xviii; *Mise*, pp. 92–3; *Radiant*, pp. 76–8.)

27   'Se couchant bonsoir dit-il / à ces moisissures (ô arbres) / à ces flaques qui sont partout / (ô mers) et à nos rides / altières (Alpes, Andes et / Himalayas). Et les lampes / sont allumées'. *Poème*, 'A.1'. The idea of considering the earth as mould and wrinkles seems to have come to Le Corbusier from his flights over South America. (*Precisions*, esp. pp. 5–8: '*you, trees*, all of you, seen from the sky, seem nothing but mould. And you Earth, Earth so desperately damp; you are nothing but mould!' [p. 7].)

28   'And from the Equator planetary / boiler the clouds take flight / then departed, grouped / regimented, drawn up / met and clashed . . . / the storm explodes'. 'Et de l'Equateur bouillotte / planétaire les nuées envolées / puis parties groupées / enrégimentées dressées / rencontrées se sont heurtées . . . / L'orage éclate'. *Poème*, 'A.2'.

29   'La face tournée vers le ciel / Considérons l'espace inconcevable / jusqu'isi insainsi. / Reposer s'étendre dormir / – mourir / Le dos au sol . . .' *Poème*, 'A.3'.

30   'Mais je me suis mis debout! / Puisque tu es droit / te voilà propre aux actes. / Droit sur le plateau terrestre / des choses saissables tu / contractes avec la nature un / pacte de solidarité: c'est l'angle droit / Debout devant la mer vertical / te voilà sur tes jambes'. *Poème*, 'A.3'.

31   'Il est la réponse et le guide / le fait / une réponse / un choix / Il est simple et nu / mais saisissable / Les savants discuteront / de la relativité de sa rigueur

/ Mais la conscience / en a fait un signe / Il est la réponse et la guide / le fait / ma réponse / mon choix'. *Poème*, 'G.3'.

32   *The Modulor*, pp. 181–3. See also *City*, pp. 18 ff., which I believe to be the first example of Le Corbusier's idea that the right angle is a tool with which humankind protects itself from a hostile universe.

33   'Entre pôles règne la tension / des fluides s'opèrent les / liquidations de comptes des / contraires se propose un / terme à la haine des / inconciliables mûrit l'union / fruit de l'affrontement / . . . / . . . si nécessairement / à concilier. / Seule possibilité de survie / offerte à la vie'. *Poème*, 'A.5'.

34   'Between bumps and in cracks / sliding on the hard and sinking / in the soft the crawling the / vermiculant the sinuant the / reptant have sketched the / first propulsion the worms / and serpents the worms hailing / from the potential of carrion. / The brooks the streams and / the rivers do the same'. 'Entre bosses et dans fissures / glissant sur les durs et s'enfonçant / dans les mous le rampant le / vermiculant le sinuant le / reptant ont ébauché la / propulsion première. Les vers / et les serpents les verns venus / du potentiel des charognes. / Les ruis-seaux les rivières et / les fleuves en font autant'. *Poème*, 'A.4'. This poem is also about Le Corbusier's famous 'law of the meander', which he formulated by looking at South American rivers from an aeroplane. He considered the forma-tion of these meanders, and the moment when the river broke through the tangle and flowed straight again, as symbolic of the entanglements and resolutions of human thought and affairs generally. (*Precisions*, pp. 141–3; *Radiant*, pp. 79–80.)

35   'A metter au bout des doigts / et encore dans la tête un / outil agile capable de grossir / la moisson de l'invention / débarrassant la rotue d'epines / et faisant le ménage donnera / liberté à votre liberté. / . . . Voilà la proportion! / la pro-portion qui met / de l'ordre dans nos / rapports avec / l'alentour'. *Poème*, 'B.2'.

36   *The Modulor*, p. 181.

37   *Poème*, 'B.3' and 'B.4'. The latter is especially interesting for its emphasis upon how the 'Unité' building-type puts humanity back into proper harmony with 'the dance' of the cosmos. In deference to the sun – the 'lord' and 'master' of 'A.1' – this building becomes a 'sundial'. (For an introduction to this building type, see Benton, 'Unité d'Habitation, Marseilles', in Raeburn and Wilson [eds], 1987, pp. 220–22.) *Poème*, 'B.4' refers to the 'sun-breaker' or 'brise-soleil', which became a common fixture for Le Corbusier's later buildings in hot climates. These were deep reinforced-concrete embrasures attached to the outer surfaces that served to cool the interior with shade and draughts. Beyond this utilitar-ian motive, however, is the more worshipful one of acknowledging the sun's primacy, as the lithograph corresponding to 'B.4' shows: the passage of the sol-stices of the sun is marked by a Corbusian Unité, the numbers on its end wall turning it into a monumental 'sundial'. It is important to note that, whilst in India from the early 1950s for his business with Chandigarh (see p. 257–8,

n. 55 below), Le Corbusier became fascinated with the eighteenth-century astronomical observatories of the Maharajah Sawai Jai Singh II, the 'instruments' of which were in fact sculptures and buildings at a considerable scale. Le Corbusier said in a sketchbook of 1951 that Jai Singh's astronomical instruments 'point the way. They bind men to the cosmos', and he echoed their forms in the sculptural outcrops on the roof of his Chandigarh Palace of Assembly. (*Sketchbooks. Volume 2*, p. 28, entry no. 329.) Moreover, the sculpture park that surrounds the government buildings in Chandigarh includes Le Corbusier's 'Temple of Shadows'. (See Curtis, 1986, pp. 188–201.)

38 See Coll, 1995, pp. 545–50; Green, 'The *Taureaux*', p. 306.

39 'Les éléments d'une vision se / rassemblent. La clef est une / souche de bois mort et un galet / ramassés tous les deux dans un / chemin creux des Pyrénées. Des / boeufs de labour passaient / tout la jour devant ma fenêtre. / A force d'être dessiné et redessiné / le boeuf – de galet et de racine / devint taureau'. *Poème*, 'C.1'.

40 'le voici chien éveillé. / Ainsi après huit années / se fixe le souvenir de "Pinceau" / le dénommé tel, mon chien. / Il était devenu méchant / sans le savoir et je dus le / tuer'. *Poème*, 'C.1'.

41 'Armé des dispositifs animé / des dispositions pour déceler / saisir défoncer lécher tous / sens éveillés voici la chasse. / Armé jusqu'aux dents / mufle et nauseaux oeil et / corne poil hérissé / s'en va-t-en guerre / Belzébuth. / Qui est donc en définitive / Belzébuth?' *Poème*, 'C.1'.

42 Seligmann, 1997, p. 150 (emphasis added). One feels silly attributing this allegorical importance to Le Corbusier's dog, but a curious fragment in the archives of the FLC offers some more justification. At the 1947 CIAM conference in Bridgwater, England, one of Le Corbusier's colleagues sketched out a number of Chinese ideograms for him on the back of one of their dinner menus. Their meanings: 'woman', 'scandal', 'mouth', 'words', 'heaven', 'wisdom/ancient', 'child', 'student', 'home', 'peace'. In pencil over the top of these, Le Corbusier wrote, 'solemn ideograms . . . the same ideograms as Pinceau'. This date corresponds to Le Corbusier's earliest serious thoughts about the *Poème*. (FLC, F2-20-1.)

43 'Un peut être deux et à deux / et ne pas conjuger les choses / qu'il serait fondamental de / mettre en présence chacun / hélas bien aveugle ne voyant / pas ce qu'il tient d'ineffable / à bout de bras'. *Poème*, 'C.2'.

44 'Les hommes se racontent / la femme dans leurs poèmes / et leurs musiques / Ils portent au flanc une / éternelle déchirure de haut / en bas. Ils ne sont que / moitié, n'alimentent la / vie que d'une moitié / Et la seconde part vient / à eux et se soude'. *Poème*, 'C.4'.

45 'Car le gîte profond is / dans le grande caverne du / sommeil cet autre côté de / la vie dans la nuit . . . / Passe la femme'. *Poème*, 'C.2'.

46   'En ces choses ici entendues / intervient un absolu sublime / accomplissement il est l'accord / des temps la pènètration des / forme la proportion – l'indicible / en fin de compte soustrait / au contrôle / de la / raison / porté hors / des / réalités / diurnes / admis / au couer / d'une illumination / Dieu / incarné / dans / l'illusion / la perception / de la vérité / . . . / mais il / faut / ête sur / terre et / présent / pour / assister / à ses propres / noces / être / chez soi / dans le sac de sa peau / faire ses affaires à soi / et dire merci au Créateur'. *Poème*, 'C.3'.

47   Elsewhere in his preparatory notes, under the heading 'Poème >+', Le Corbusier copies some lines from Stéphane Mallarmé that echo these ideas. They are presented as through they were a motto to his whole project: 'For I inaugurate through science / The hymn of all hearts spiritual.' (FLC, F2-20-10, -11. The English is taken from Henry Weinfeld's translation of Stéphane Mallarmé's 'PROSE *for des Esseintes*', in *Collected Poems*, Berkeley and Los Angeles, 1994, p. 46.)

48   'Je me suis miré dans ce caractère / et m'y suis trouvé / trouvé chez moi / trouvé'. *Poème*, 'E.3'.

49   This symbol preoccupied Le Corbusier for many years. Sekler has traced the importance Le Corbusier attributed to it, and its long and painful gestation – '*un travail intérieur ininterrompu*'. (Sekler, 1977, pp. 42–95; citation from p. 77.)

50   'Elle est ouverte puisque / tout est présent disponible / saisissable / Ouverte pour recevoir / Ouverte aussi que pour chacun / y vienne prendre / . . . / pleine main j'ai reçu / pleine main je donne.' *Poème*, 'F.3'.

51   *Tapisseries Le Corbusier*, Paris, 1975, cited in Nancy Stephenson, 'The Open Hand', in Moore, 1977, p. 36.

52   FLC, C1-15-61 ff. on 'Mains – Astrologie'. This collection stands in marked contrast to the more typical press-cuttings collected by Le Corbusier on technical and industrial subjects. (See, for example, F2–12-*passim*.)

53   'La forme de la main, son équilibre, sa proportion, la qualité et la couleur de sa peau, la valeur de ses monts révèlent le témperament et le caractère de l'individu aussi sûrement que le plus profond examen psychologique . . . mystérieuse, car rien ne peut expliquer encore comment toutes les grandes phases de notre vie se trouvent, à l'avance, marquées dans la main'. Marie-Louise Sondaz, 'les mains qui parlent' (no date), FLC, C1-15-69. This article is dominated by a woodcut illustrating the principle lines of the left hand after Jean-Baptiste Belot's *Œuvres* of 1649, which also appears in Seligmann, 1997, p. 269. Further evidence of Le Corbusier's fascination with the mystical properties of hands, in this case relating to their use in faith healing, can be found in the press clippings under C1-15-67 and C1-15-83. Elsewhere, Sondaz argues that time should be devoted to understanding the four elements and their equivalents in the 'tempéraments', or rather the 'humours', of man: 'Feu (bilieux), Terre (nerveux), Air (sanguin), Eau (lymphatique)'. This would form the basis for a

complete knowledge of all phenomena. This 'fundamental order', she says, 'has not been established in an empirical manner, but corresponds very closely to the order of human elevation and perfectioning . . . It constitutes the grand harmony of the worlds, the closed circle of universal activity, the type formula which permits of all classification, of all understanding, the basis of a synthetic science which, heading for the infinite, arrives at the individual and founds human psychology.' ('L'order fondamental . . . n'a pas été établi d'une manière empirique, mais correspond très étroitement à l'ordre d'élévation et de perfectionnement humain . . . C'est la grande harmonie des mondes, le cercle fermé sur l'activité universelle, la formule type qui permet de tout classer, de tout comprendre, la basse de la science synthétique qui, partant de l'infini, arrive a l'individu et fonde la psychologie humaine.') Interesting also are the sacred *and* alchemical connotations of this fourfold human psychology, for as well as more obviously taking the elements as representative of the human psyche, Sondaz makes reference to the central alchemical symbol of the '*uroboros*': 'It is the perfect circle, obtained through rotating a cross of equal branches, and represented by the serpent which bites its own tail.' ('C'est le *cercle* parfait, obtenu en faisant tourner une croix à branche égales, et représenté par le serpent qui se mord la queue.') Sondaz, 'Les Astres et le Destin: les quatre éléments' (no date), FLC, C1-15-68, C1-15-103.

54 Stephenson speculates that the fusion of the index, middle and ring fingers at their base in the Open Hand parallels a mild deformity in Le Corbusier's own hand, a condition known as the 'Mount of Libra'. Le Corbusier's own birth-sign was Libra, known in French as 'la Balance', and the symbol of the scales appeared quite frequently in his work. ('The Open Hand', pp. 36–7; see also her contribution to Moore, 'Alchemical and Mythical Themes in the Poem of the Right Angle 1947–1965', p. 138, n. 43.) Sekler considers the Open Hand to represent John Ruskin's ideal balance of individual and collective forces, and traces the origins of this to the young Jeanneret's exploration of tree motifs with his art teacher Charles L'Eplattenier. Under 'the principles ascertained in trees', Ruskin observes: '3. Liberty of each bough to seek its own livelihood and happiness according to its needs, by irregularities of action both in its play and its work . . . 4. Imperative requirement of each bough to stop within certain limits, expressive of its kindly friendship and fraternity with the boughs in its neighbourhood.' Sekler maintains that everything in Le Corbusier's ideal environments subliminally calls the dweller back to an awareness of this ideal binary: 'collective participation and freedom of the individual'. (1977; quotation from pp. 62–3; citation from p. 57 [John Ruskin, *The Elements of Drawing; in Three Letters to Beginners*, London, 1857].)

55 When, in 1950–51, the National Mint in Paris asked Le Corbusier to provide the designs for his own commemorative medal, he drew a self-portrait on one side and an Open Hand on the other, with the lines of the hand clearly marked.

(*Sketchbooks. Volume 2*, p. 5, entry no. 35, figs 34–7. See also the reproduction of the medal in Žaknić, 1997, p. 37.) Le Corbusier was invited to help develop the Punjabi city of Chandigarh in the early 1950s, and this occupied a good deal of his time up until his death. The best accounts of Chandigarh are Ravi Kalia, 1987; von Moos, 'The Politics of the Open Hand: Notes on Le Corbusier and Nehru at Chandigarh', in Walden (ed.), 1977, pp. 413–57; Sunand Prasad, 'Le Corbusier in India', in Raeburn and Wilson (eds), 1987, pp. 278 ff.; Madhu Sarin, 1982.

56 *Mise*, p. 85.

57 Cited in Benton, 'The sacred and the search for myths', p. 240. (Originally cited in Petit, 1970, p. 177.) Le Corbusier made this statement towards the very end of his life, as he did the following: 'One is a ball, a sphere . . . One is in one's own sphere and this shapes one's own destiny.' (*Mise*, p. 85.)

58 Ozenfant, 1952, p. xiv.

59 *Sketchbooks. Volume 4*, p. 89, entry no./fig. 1024. See also p. 76, no. 901, where the *Poème* is again identified with this single line. In a sketchbook from 1957, Le Corbusier stated the following: 'Every morning I awaken in the skin of an imbecile – in the evening, it gets better.' (*Sketchbooks. Volume 3*, p. 78, entry no. 966.) The symbol '>+' can be found in the lithograph 'G.3' of the *Poème*, and to judge by the frequency of its appearances in Le Corbusier's manuscript notes, it can be taken as a shorthand symbol for the poem as a whole. Occasionally Le Corbusier figured it '<+' instead, as he does here.

60 Cited in Warlick, 'Max Ernst's Alchemical Novel: *Une Semaine de bonté*', pp. 62 and 73, n. 68; see also Hopkins, 1998, pp. 55–9. The Chinese text was *The Secret of the Golden Flower*, and we shall be referring to Jung's 'commentary' on this below.

61 Moore claims that Le Corbusier was directly acquainted with Jung's work and that it was 'highly current' at 'the critical juncture of [his] career' in the 1940s. Benton concedes that Le Corbusier had made a study of Jungian texts during his wartime exile in Ozon. Jencks, sceptical of any such concrete connection, grants that it is likely Le Corbusier unconsciously absorbed and reworked such ideas from a variety of indirect sources. (Moore, 'Alchemical and Mythical Themes in the Poem of the Right Angle 1947–1965', p. 135, n. 3; Benton, 'The sacred and the search for myths', p. 243; Jencks, 1987, pp. 8–9.) These commentators emphasize similarities between the iconographies of Jung and Le Corbusier. I am more interested in the similarities between their philosophies of selfhood.

62 Seligmann, 1997, p. 93.

63 Le Corbusier's connection with these issues is, however, no less concrete than that of other members of the avant-garde more readily associated with them. John F. Moffitt, for example, concludes his study of the alchemical content of Duchamp's work by saying that it is based on 'largely circumstantial evidence'.

('Marcel Duchamp: Alchemist of the Avant-Garde', in Weisberger [ed.], 1985, p. 269.) Warlick admits that 'the significance of the alchemical tradition to Max Ernst remains unclear'. (Warlick, 'Max Ernst's Alchemical Novel: *Une Semaine de bonté*', p. 72.) And after subjecting both artists to a similar study, Hopkins also has to concede 'a lack of substantive biographical back-up'. (1998, p. 190.) In comparison with these, Le Corbusier's indebtedness to mystical and occult issues is perhaps rather *more* compelling. Although such issues seem to be present in the work and thought of a great many avant-garde figures, then, this can only be proved definitively for the small handful who were open with their affiliations, such as Wassily Kandinsky, Johannes Itten and Piet Mondrian.

64 Another account of these issues, particularly in terms of how they are figured in the imagery and allegories of alchemy, can be found in Nathan Schwartz-Salant (ed.), 1995, pp. 1–43.

65 Jung, *Psychology and Alchemy* (1953), 1993, p. 244.

66 Jung, *Memories, Dreams, Reflections* (1963), 1995 (a), p. 415. 'Individuation' is the centrally important concept for Jung. The psyche was a goal-oriented process that led ultimately to the fully 'individuated' human being, and this happened 'independently of external factors'. (1993, pp. 4–5.) Jung's 'analytical-psychology' sought not merely to treat sickness, then, but more importantly to 'perfect' those who were otherwise quite healthy. (*Modern Man in Search of a Soul* [1933], 1995 [b], pp. 32–62 on 'Problems of Modern Psychotherapy' [1931] and pp. 70, 75, 78.)

67 This projection betrayed the collective psyche at this point in history: Western man was too immature to deal with the process of his individuation internally. Organized religion was, for Jung, just a monumental projection of this psychic process: similar to alchemy, external practise and ritual were a safe substitute for the more personal confrontation with one's unconscious. (1993, pp. 299–301 and 242–83 on 'The Psychic Nature of the Alchemical Work'; 1995 [b], pp. 143–74 on 'Archaic Man' [1931].)

68 Jung, 'Psychology and Religion' (1938), in Jung, *Psychology and Religion: West and East* (1958), 1991, p. 56; Jung, 'The Visions of Zosimos' (1954), in Jung, *Alchemical Studies* (1967), 1981, p. 92.

69 See Jung, 'Commentary on "The Secret of the Golden Flower"' (1957), in Jung, 1981, pp. 44–8 on 'The Detachment of Consciousness from the Object': 'the interweaving of consciousness with the world has come to an end' (p. 44). See also 'The Visions of Zosimos', pp. 90–92.

70 *Decorative*, pp. 115–27 on 'Respect for Works of Art'; quotations from pp. 118, 126. Like Jung, Le Corbusier saw this psychic development as happening at an individual and a collective level: 'the passage from the age of subjection to the age of creation – the history of civilization, as also the history of the individual' (p. 118).

71 Another reason for Jung's admiration of alchemy is that it made possible the emergence of his 'analytical-psychology'. When the material side of alchemy was

sheared off into pure chemistry, alchemists became more directly concerned with the mystical and psychological side. Eventually, modern psychology emerged to deal with the leftover psychic material more adequately. (See Jung, 1993, pp. 227–8, 423–4; also 1995 [a], pp. 260–61, where Jung traces his ancestry to a Dr Carl Jung of Mainz, who appeared to move in alchemical circles.)

72   See 'Psychology and Religion', pp. 7–10 on the differentiation of the general *numinosum* into particular dogma and ritual, and esp. pp. 34–50 on 'Dogma and Natural Symbols' for the effectiveness of different kinds of dogma such as Roman Catholic versus Protestant. See also Jung, 'Psychoanalysis and the Cure of Souls' (1928), in Jung, 1991, pp. 348–54. For more on individuation, see Jung, 1993, pp. 24–5; 1995 (b), pp. 85–108, on 'A Psychological Theory of Types' (1931); 1995 (a), pp. 412–13 on 'archetype'. In brief, individuation involves two things: first, accommodating within the psyche the terrifying archetypical images emerging from the depths of the unconscious; second, striking a balance between the four antagonistic 'psychic functions' of 'thought', 'feeling', 'sensation' and 'intuition'.

73   Jung, 1993, pp. 35–7; see also 'Psychology and Religion', p. 97.

74   Jung, 1993, pp. 476–7 and n. 2, p. 306.

75   See Jung, 'Transformation Symbolism in the Mass' (1954), in Jung, 1991, pp. 280–81.

76   Jung, 1993, p. 314. For more on how alchemists dealt with or repressed their blasphemies, see pp. 306–19, 345–55; 'The Visions of Zosimos', esp. pp. 95–6, and 'Paracelsus as a Spiritual Phenomenon' (1942), in Jung, 1981, esp. pp. 120–21, 127–30; 'Psychology and Religion', pp. 50–63.

77   'Commentary on "The Secret of the Golden Flower"', p. 9.

78   Jung, *The Undiscovered Self* (1958), 1996, p. 16; see also pp. 9, 13 and more generally pp. 3–70: 'To-day, individuals and cultures are faced with a similar threat, namely of being swallowed up in the mass.' (Jung, 1995 [a], pp. 238–9.)

79   Jung, 1993, pp. 217–18, 7: the belief that all problems are susceptible to political or other communal solutions is attributed to 'the prevailing tendency of consciousness to seek the source of all ills in the outside world … The consciousness of modern man still clings so much to outward objects that he makes them exclusively responsible . . . The social and political circumstances of the time are certainly of considerable significance, but their importance for the weal and woe of the individual has been boundlessly overestimated.' (Jung, 1996, pp. 81, 85 and 112.) See also Jung, 1995 (a): 'We rush impetuously into novelty, driven by a mounting sense of insufficiency, dissatisfaction, and restlessness.'

80   Jung, 1993, p. 477.

81   Jung, 1996, p. 12; also pp. 9–10. Not unexpectedly, 'the Westerner who wishes to set out on this way . . . has all authority against him – intellectual, moral, and religious'. ('Commentary on "The Secret of the Golden Flower"', p. 18.)

82 'Psychology and Religion', p. 75 (emphasis added).

83 'Myth is the primordial language natural to these psychic processes, and no intel-
    lectual formulation comes anywhere near the richness and expressiveness of
    mythical imagery. Such processes are concerned with the primordial images, and
    these are best and most succinctly reproduced by figurative language.' This
    cannot be approached discursively, with 'words': '*It is futile, for everything valuable
    and important is ineffable*.' (Jung, 1993, pp. 25, 138.) And as he is constructed out
    of this language, the fully individuated man is also 'ineffable': 'When we now
    speak of man we mean the indefinable whole of him, an ineffable totality, which
    can only be formulated symbolically.' ('Psychology and Religion', p. 82; see also
    pp. 24 ff.)

84 Jung, 1995 (b), p. 181; see also pp. 175–99 on 'Psychology and Literature' (1929).
    Even though it may employ quite conventional figurative imagery, the disrup-
    tive effect of this 'language' remains immense: 'the principle of the unconscious
    is the autonomy of the psyche itself . . . with the result that the rationality
    of the cosmos is constantly being violated in the most distressing manner'. (Jung,
    1993, p. 146.)

85 Ibid., p. 49; see also esp. p. 89: 'it constitutes a secret which must be anxiously
    guarded, since the justification for its existence could not possibly be explained
    to any so-called reasonable person . . . The discharge of energy into the envi-
    ronment is therefore considerably impeded, the result being a surplus of energy
    on the side of the unconscious: hence the abnormal increase in the autonomy
    of the unconscious figures, culminating in aggression and real terror.'

86 Jung continues: 'The same procedure has also been used since olden times to
    set a place apart as holy and inviolable; in founding a city, for instance, they first
    drew the *sulcus primigenius* or original furrow.' (Ibid., p. 54; see also n. 6, in which
    the *temenos* is defined as 'A piece of land, often a grove, set apart and dedicated
    to a god.') For more on the cutting of the 'first furrow', its military uses and
    sacred connotations, see Leon Battista Alberti, 1997, pp. 100–03.

87 Jung, 1993, p. 167; see also p. 118: 'the dreamer reaches the shelter of the *temenos*
    as a protection against the splintering of personality'; 'Psychology and Religion',
    p. 95: '[the *temenos*] protects or isolates an inner content or process that should
    not get mixed up with things outside'; 'Commentary on "The Secret of
    the Golden Flower"', p. 24: 'It has the obvious purpose of drawing a *sulcus
    primigenius*, a magical furrow around the centre, the temple or *temenos* (sacred
    precinct), of the innermost personality, in order to prevent an "outflowing" or
    to guard . . . against distracting influences from outside'.

88 See Jung, 1995 (a), pp. 250–65 on 'The Tower'; quotation from p. 255.

89 Jung, 1995 (b), pp. 274–5.

90 Ibid., pp. 212–13; quotation from p. 213. Further references to how the psyche
    defies space–time conventions can be found in Jung, 1993, pp. 137–8, 182–3.

91 Jung, 1995 (a), pp. 323, 326.

92 Jung said from the *temenos* of his Tower that 'here is space for the spaceless kingdom of the world's and the psyche's hinterland'. (Ibid., p. 252.)

93 Ibid., pp. 198–9.

94 *Towards*, pp. 69 ff.; see also *Journey*, pp. 193–5, where Le Corbusier says that the task of architecture is to provide a home for the 'Mother of God'.

95 First, to balance the psyche, which will otherwise become too one-sided and end in breakdown. (Jung, 1995 (b), pp. 109–31 on 'The Stages of Life' [1931].) Second, to reverse the projection of unconscious material into the external world, which is dangerous: everything irrational and demonic is projected into our neighbours, which gives rise to endless conflict. (Jung, 'Commentary on the "Secret of the Golden Flower"', p. 36; 1995 [b], pp. 162–4; 1996, pp. 65–6, 82–3, 97.) Third, individuation heightens our instinct for 'adaptedness': it helps us negotiate all manner of changing circumstances. Fourth, the resulting self-awareness allows the individual to maintain a healthy antisocial distance without which it is impossible to criticize society effectively. (Ibid., pp. 4–5, 17–18, 39–41, 54–6, 58–9, 68–70.)

96 Ibid., p. 55. Also, pp. 50–52, and Jung, 1993, p. 479.

97 Jung, 1996, pp. 24–5, 81–2: 'A gentle and reasonable being can be transformed into a manic or savage beast.' ('Psychology and Religion', p. 15.)

98 See ibid., pp. 22–3.

99 Jung, 1996, p. 24; see also pp. 30, 102–6: 'the value of a community depends on the spiritual and moral stature of the individuals composing it'. But although a keen sense of individuality is necessary to counter the abuses of the state, too much individuality leads only to 'depotentiated social units' (p. 105).

100 See Jung, 1993, pp. 41, 204–5, and esp. pp. 18–19: 'the "self" – a term on the one hand definite enough to convey the essence of human wholeness and on the other indefinite enough to express the indescribable and indeterminable nature of this wholeness . . . Not only is the self indefinite but – paradoxically enough – it also includes the quality of definiteness and even of uniqueness.' Jung's account of his own individuation is also interesting: 'There were things in the images which concerned not only myself but many others also. It was then that I ceased to belong to myself alone . . . From then on, my life belonged to the generality.' (1995 [a], p. 217.) Ultimately, 'Individuation does not shut one out from the world, but gathers the world to one's self' (p. 415).

101 *Cathedrals*, pp. 131–2, 217.

102 *Radiant*, p. 97.

103 *Poème*, 'D.3'.

104 Clifton, 1992, pp. 5–12, 29–31. To be clear, 'Albigensianism' was a specific movement, while 'Catharism' is a generic term denoting any of a number of heterodox movements from the third to thirteenth centuries.

105 *My Work*, pp. 18–19. Jardot remarks upon Le Corbusier's studies of the 'Catharic Heresy' in his native region: 'Every facet of his mind, every instinct of his

temperament is there' (p. 10; see also Frampton, 1980, p. 149). In a sketchbook from 1955, Le Corbusier again mentions his ancestry, and calls the Jura region 'a land of exile and contrition'. (*Sketchbooks. Volume 3*, p. 26, entry nos. 315 ff.) Evidently Le Corbusier was always on the lookout for material that could give him more information on this issue. In April 1949 he sent a letter to Breton expressing interest in a book Breton had referenced in *La lampe dans l'horloge* (Paris, 1948) concerning the anarchist movement in the Jura mountains. Breton responded with the details and an offer to lend Le Corbusier his personal copy. (FLC, G2-10-253, E1-9-216.)

106   *L'Etendard de la Bible et Héraut du Royaume de Christ*, nos. 47–8, September–November 1964: FLC, C1-8-155. This was the revue of a nominally 'independent' lay missionary movement. Anti-papism would appear to have been a lifelong commitment for Le Corbusier, for in a letter to his parents dated 8 November 1909, he wrote, 'I am Luther's subject, not Pius X's.' (Cited in Benton, 'The sacred and the search for myths', p. 245, n. 4.) It is therefore something of a paradox that Le Corbusier should have accepted the commissions for the Ronchamp pilgrimage chapel and the La Tourette monastery from the Dominicans in the 1950s. But as he wrote to one of the monks at La Tourette, 'I do not bear grudges, despite everything which the Dominicans did to my ancestors.' (Benton, 'Notre-Dame du Haut, Ronchamp', in Raeburn and Wilson [eds], 1987, pp. 247–9; citation from p. 247; 'Monastery of Sainte-Marie de la Tourette, Eveux-sur-l'Arbresle', in ibid., pp. 250–52.)

107   *Routes*, pp. 109–10.

108   *My Work*, p. 19: 'CE QUE TU FAIS, FAIS-LE . . . La Royne [sic: 'le royaume' / 'la reine'?] de Quinte Essance [sic: 'quintessence'?], 5th book by Rabelais.'

109   Rabelais, 1955, pp. 645–6.

110   See Jung, 'Commentary on "The Secret of the Golden Flower"', p. 27; 1993, p. 183 on 'the entelechy of the self'.

111   In a sketchbook of 1950, Le Corbusier made proposals for the Colombian port town of Barranquilla that would transform it into 'an oasis, a summer city of the M'Zab'. (See also *Mise*, pp. 87–90.)

112   Clifton, 1992, p. 29.

9   Bataille and Camus: 'Vers la limite critique'

1   Georges Bataille, *La Part Maudite: Essai d'Economie Generale – Vol. I, La Consumation*, Paris, 1949; Albert Camus, *L'Homme Révolté*, Paris, 1951. These are the editions held in Le Corbusier's library in the FLC.

2   Bataille, *The Accursed Share: An Essay on General Economy – Vol. I: Consumption* (1949), 1988, pp. 72–4 on 'Ambiguity and Contradiction'; quotation from pp. 72–3.

3   Ibid., FLC edition, p. 96. More generally, see Bataille, 1988, pp. 63–77 on 'The Gift of Rivalry: "Potlatch" '.

4   Ibid., pp. 189–90 on 'Consciousness of the Ultimate End of Wealth and "Self-Consciousness" '; FLC edition, pp. 252 ff. It is also revealing that Le Corbusier heavily underscored Bataille's discussion of how the economics of growth, production and utility must give way to that of squander, if individuality and the sacred are to be uncovered. (Bataille, 1988, pp. 178–82 on 'From the "General" Interest According to François Perroux to the Perspective of "General Economy" '; FLC edition, esp. p. 240.)

5   Bataille, 1988, pp. 135–6; FLC edition, p. 179 and flyleaf. Note also Le Corbusier's interest in the following passage: 'Within the limits of strictly economic activity, the rigor has a precise object: the dedication of excess resources to the removal of life's difficulties and to the reduction of labor time. This is the only use of wealth that coincides with an adequation of man to *things* and it retains the negative character of action, whose goal for man remains the possibility of being entirely at his own disposal.' (Bataille, 1988, pp. 138–9; FLC edition, p. 183 and flyleaf.) 'Raising the living standard' is not the final answer, but merely the first step. (Bataille, 1988, pp. 40–41.)

6   Ibid., p. 129; FLC edition, p. 170.

7   Bataille, 1988, pp. 58–9.

8   Ibid.; FLC edition, pp. 75–6 and flyleaf.

9   *Poème*, 'D.3'.

10 Camus, *The Rebel* (1951), 1971, p. 265.

11 Ibid.; FLC edition, p. 372.

12 Camus, 1971, p. 158; FLC edition, pp. 235–6 and flyleaf.

13 Camus, 1971, pp. 73–5. It is unlikely that Camus would approve of the connotations of self-as-God that inform those 'heresies' discussed above: 'the only original rule of life today: to learn to live and to die, and in order to be a man, to refuse to be a god' (p. 269).

14 'Mon cher Camus, / Sans prétention aucune je me permets de vous remettre une étape de mon 'Poème de l'Angle Droit' (texte) pour que vous la mettiez dans un coin, et si par hasard vous avez quelques conseils à me donner concernant obscurités ou des inexactitudes qui peuvent s'y trouver, même des fautes de syntaxe ou autres, je les recevrai avec plaisir. / Amicalement à vous / LE CORBUSIER'. FLC, B3-7-489 (dated 10 October 1952); see also G2-13-222 for a signed copy of this letter. This and the following translations are my own. A sketchbook entry indicates that Le Corbusier also sent the finished work to Camus. (*Sketchbooks. Volume 3*, p. 42, entry no. 496.)

15 See FLC, G2-13-125, where Le Corbusier attempts to arrange a meeting to discuss the Marseilles script (dated 1 August 1952); and E3-2-343, in which André Wogenscky, Le Corbusier's right-hand man, makes Camus aware of several of the technical inaccuracies in his script (dated 9 December 1952). This film

was never made, but more details can be found in Naegele, 1996, p. 110, n. 59–60. See also McLeod, 1980, pp. 65–7, where the relationship between Le Corbusier and Camus is noted in terms of their love of Mediterranean culture. Le Corbusier also wanted to get involved in the construction of a theatre that Camus was planning for Paris. (Le Corbusier to Camus, 13 February 1957; FLC, G1-11-164.)

16   The relationship between the two men clearly goes back some way, as can be seen from the letter of sympathy Le Corbusier sent to Camus's widow upon his death in 1960: 'Camus was in our gang in 1931, 32, 33, in Algiers, when he sketched out for himself an heroic adventure! / Alas!' 'Camus était de notre bande en 1931, 32, 33, à Algers alors que s'esquissait une aventure peut-être héroïque! / Hélas!' FLC, E1-12-13; also reproduced under G1-17-27; dated 21 January 1960.

17   Bataille, 1988, pp. 19–26 on 'The Meaning of General Economy'; quotation from p. 21. This surplus energy *must* be wasted or else it will explode catastrophically beyond our control in violence and war, destroying us along with itself. The trick, then, is to select 'an exudation that might suit us', to indulge in 'unproductive works that will dissipate an energy that cannot be accumulated in any case' (pp. 24–5).

18   Ibid., p. 41.

19   Ibid., pp. 45–61 where Bataille explores this in relation to the 'Sacrifices and Wars of the Aztecs'; quotations from p. 58.

20   The utilitarian-minded individual may find this wastage difficult and even painful to accept. (Ibid., pp. 27–41 on 'Laws of General Economy'; quotation from p. 30.) See also pp. 81–110, where Bataille discusses this 'expenditure'-shift in terms of the rationally driven, aggressive and expansive methodology of Islam, as against the non-profitable, truly spiritual 'consumption' of Lamaism. He also maps this on to the USSR and the United States, urging the latter to curb its economic and industrial expansionism and follow the example of Lamaism (pp. 147–90).

21   This demarcation allows for our perception of the 'completion of *things* . . . a radical independence of *things* (of the economy) in relation to other (religious or, generally, affective) concerns'. It marks off the boundary for 'the return movement of man to himself (to the profundity, the intimacy of his being)'. But Bataille admits that, given our 'natual propensity to servitude', this 'counterbalancing' is 'an unattainable ideal in a sense'. It is open only to the 'strongest personalities'. (Ibid., pp. 129–42 on 'The Bourgeois World'; quotations from pp. 134–8.) See also Bataille, *The Accursed Share: An Essay on General Economy – Vol. II: The History of Eroticism; Vol. III: Sovereignty* (1976), 1991, pp. 198–200 on 'The Basic Elements: Consumption beyond Utility, the Divine, the Miraculous, the Sacred': 'the sovereign (or the sovereign life) begins when, with the necessities ensured, the possibility of life opens up without limit' (p. 198).

22   Bataille, 1988, p. 11 (emphasis added).

23 A moment of 'sudden illumination', this is 'The miraculous moment when anti-cipation dissolves into NOTHING, detaching us from the ground on which we were groveling, in the concatenation of useful activity.' (Bataille, 1991, pp. 201–4 on 'Considerations on Method'; quotations from pp. 202, 203. See also pp. 208, 225–9.) Prior to this moment, 'Not only was the individual integrated into the order of things but the order of things had entered into him and, within him, had arranged everything according to its principles. Like other things he had a past, present *and a future* – and an identity through that past, present and future.' (Ibid., pp. 213–17 on 'The Sacred, the Profane, the Natural Given and Death'; quotation from pp. 216. On the paradoxical nature and non-rational imagery of this sacred sense of self, see p. 215.)

24 'The consciousness of these inner aspects was diffuse; these aspects eluded those who could only perceive their external image, their crude embodiment . . . It seemed out of the question to look for this miracle within. (But we can no longer find it on the outside . . .)' (Ibid., pp. 229–35; quotation from p. 233.) But 'The past came close to this experience [the genuine sovereign experience], beyond the institutional forms, insofar as it granted that a solitary experience, given over to the freedom of the imagination, assumed a role that the one God played in objective sovereignty' (p. 235). Bataille presents this in an historical schema similar to that of Jung: Roman Catholic ritual and riches invested the exterior milieu with sacredness, but the Reformation challenged this. Increasingly, the world was 'desacralized' and considered only in terms of material utility and profit, which allowed the true religious experience to with-draw within. (Bataille, 1988, pp. 115–27 on 'The Origins of Capitalism and the Reformation'.) 'Religion in general answered the desire that man always had to find himself, to regain an intimacy that was always strangely lost. But the mistake of all religion is to always give man a contradictory answer: *an external form of intimacy.*' Even the Holy Grail is only a '*thing*', a 'cooking pot' (pp. 129–30).

25 The rebellion 'does not have to destroy as fire does; only the tie that connected the offering to the world of profitable activity is severed'. 'This principle opens the way to passionate release', but 'it liberates violence while marking off the domain in which violence reigns absolutely'. This limitation of violence is dif-ficult, however, as it is susceptible to 'contagion': 'it breaks forth without limits'. (Ibid., pp. 58, 59; see also p. 110 on Lamaist 'violence': 'Their triumph is its unleashing within. But it is no less violent for all that' [p. 110].)

26 Ibid., p. 189.

27 Ibid., p. 59. See also Bataille, 1991 p. 222: 'He has no more regard for the limits of identity than he does for limits of death, or rather these limits are the same; he is the transgressor of all such limits'; and p. 253: 'my being is never *myself alone*; it is always myself and *my fellow beings*'.

28 Even so, we must 'tear ourselves from the beaten track which connected us', and through this 'become conscious' of ourselves. 'This is where the opposition

between literature and politics comes in: one is rebellion with an open heart; the other is realistic.' But 'Still, we must ask whether a revolt that refuses tyranny can achieve anything other than ferment and discordant verbalism.' (Bataille, 'The Age of Revolt' [1951], in Bataille, 1994, pp. 159–61, 165–6; quotations from pp. 159, 165–6.) Again, this revolt reconnects the individual with others: 'the very movement of revolt signifies that the rebel shares this inviolable and sovereign element . . . with whoever rebels with him'. (Ibid., pp. 166–7; quotation from p. 161; see also Bataille, 1991, pp. 242–3.)

29 The drive 'to belong to oneself and no-one else' means that 'sovereignty resides in crime just as its divine and majestic humours do, being, like revolt, beyond all laws . . . the modern rebel exists in crime'. The 'initial meaning' of the sovereign moment of revolt 'lies in a refusal to accept man's common condition as a limit'; it is a 'refusal of human law'. (Bataille, 'The Age of Revolt', pp. 169–72.)

30 The rebel 'knows that this indomitable part of himself exists within *all* other people, even if they have denied it'. To overstep this boundary and attempt to enforce one's revolt by subjugating others, is to destroy the awareness of that 'complicity' with other human beings that forms the very basis and meaning of revolt, and 'At a stroke all the benefits of his revolt are nullified.' (Ibid., pp. 172–5; quotations from 173; see also Bataille, 1991, p. 221.)

31 Bataille, 'The Age of Revolt', p. 174; 1991, pp. 237 and 420: 'Traditionally, the work of art invites one to give some *real* form to the subjectivity that offers itself and yet is only a refusal of the *real* order.'

32 Camus, 1971, pp. 11–17.

33 Behind his borderline, the individual 'stubbornly insists that there are certain things in him which "are worthwhile" '. He also recognizes 'certain values which are still indeterminate but which he feels are common to himself and to all men'; thus, 'the affirmation implicit in each act of revolt is extended to something which transcends the individual in so far as it removes him from his supposed solitude and supplies him with reason to act . . . Therefore the individual is not, in himself, an embodiment of the values he wishes to defend. It needs at least all humanity to defend them.' (Ibid., pp. 19–28 on 'The Rebel'; quotations from pp. 19–22.)

34 Ibid., p. 28; see also pp. 23 and 27: 'Man's solidarity is founded upon rebellion, and rebellion can only be justified by this solidarity . . . In order to exist, man must rebel, but rebellion must respect the limits that it discovers in itself – limits where minds meet and, in meeting, begin to exist.'

35 Ibid., pp. 260–61.

36 Ibid., p. 25: 'Rebellion, though apparently negative since it creates nothing, is profoundly positive in that it reveals the part of man which must always be defended.'

37 See pp. 29–31 on 'Metaphysical Rebellion'.

38 Ibid., pp. 32–43 on 'The Sons of Cain: A Man of Letters'; quotations from pp. 35, 32. See also pp. 34, 38–9: 'The law of force never has the patience to await complete control of the world. It must fix the boundaries, without delay, of the territory where it holds full sway, even if it means surrounding it with barbed wire and observation towers. / For Sade, the law of force implies barred gates, castles with seventy-foot walls from which it is impossible to escape, and where a society founded on desire and crime function unimpeded, according to an implacable system.' These are 'his impassioned kingdom', his 'sordid fortress', 'strongholds of debauchery' and 'tortured communities', 'ideal societies'. Camus finds these sentiments flourishing again in Romanticism, with the fascination for Satan as a romantic hero, and in the nineteenth-century dandy who 'can only exist by defiance . . . and creates a unity for himself by the very violence of his refusal'. (pp. 43–9 on 'The Dandy's Rebellion'; quotation from p. 47.) On the countervailing tendency, the shift from the rebellious mind-set into the realm of organized political action, see pp. 50–56 on 'The Rejection of Salvation', pp. 72–5 on 'Nihilism and History', and the entire third section on 'Historical Rebellion', pp. 76–218.

39 Ibid., p. 11; see also pp. 36, 42–3.

40 Ibid., p. 76; see also pp. 250–51.

41 Ibid., pp. 212–18 on 'Rebellion and Revolution'; quotation from pp. 216–17 (emphasis added).

42 On the necessity and difficulties of taking rebellious action, see ibid., pp. 249–50, 253, 268.

43 Ibid., p. 72.

44 Ibid., see esp. pp. 246 ff. Camus makes some vague demands for 'a philosophy of limits, of calculated ignorance, and of risk . . . Authentic acts of rebellion will only consent to take up arms for institutions which limit violence, not for those which codify it . . . Moderation, born of rebellion, can only live by rebellion. It is a perpetual conflict, continually created and mastered by the intelligence.' (pp. 253, 256, 265; see also p. 258.)

45 Ibid., pp. 217–18.

46 Ibid., p. 219. See the entire fourth section on 'Rebellion and Art', pp. 219–42.

47 Ibid., p. 221; see also p. 229: 'Here we have an imaginary world . . . which is created from the rectification of the actual world . . . Man is finally able to give himself the alleviating form and limits which he pursues in vain in his own life.'

48 Ibid., pp. 234, 238; see esp. pp. 233–7 on 'Rebellion and Style'.

49 This art keeps open a 'dialogue' with others that must be clear and understandable. It is not completely withdrawn, incomprehensible, or even merely ambiguous, which Camus equates with 'death' and 'despair'. (Ibid., pp. 232, 236, 247–8.)

50 Ibid., p. 265.

51 'When we have only just conquered solitude, must we then re-establish it definitively by legitimizing the act which isolates everything? To force solitude

on a man who has just come to understand that he is not alone, is that not the definitive crime against man? . . . From the moment that he strikes, the rebel cuts the world in two. He rebelled in the name of the identity of man with man and he sacrifices this identity by consecrating the difference in blood.' (Ibid., p. 245; see also pp. 243–50.)

52 *Radiant*, p. 182. On this sense of splitting the individual, see *Decorative*, pp. 22, 73–4, 86 and 99: 'Life (and the cost of living) subjects us to labour . . . There is a time for work, when one uses oneself up, and also a time for meditation . . . There should be no confusion between them . . . Everything has its classification; work and meditation' (pp. 73, 86). The 'object' of architecture was '*to contain men*'. (*The Modulor*, p. 20.)

53 *New World*, pp. 20–21.

54 *Towards*, p. 289.

55 *Radiant*, p. 18.

Conclusion

1 See introduction, p. 4 and p. 204, n. 3.

2 Jane Jacobs, (1961) 1994. See esp. pp. 442–62 on 'The kind of problem a city is', where we get the most compelling sense of Jacobs's belief that the city is a fragile ecosystem. For the remarks on how it is only through community relationships that people can forge real identities, see pp. 66–9, 146–7. 'The uses of city neighbourhoods', pp. 122–51, discusses the creation of 'localized self-government' which mediates between neighbourhood interests and City Hall.

3 Sennett, (1970) 1996. The first part of his book deals with the psychological disadvantages of 'purified' identity, and the physical form and social mechanisms of the city that sustain this, while the second part deals with the advantages of the opposite.

4 The literature is extensive, but the following suffice for an introduction: Charles Knevitt and Nick Wates, 1987; Michael Leccese and Kathleen McCormick (eds), 2000.

5 *Sketchbooks, Volume 2*, p. 41, entry no. 487.

6 Serenyi provides another example of this kind of reaction. He speculates on Le Corbusier's indebtedness to the nineteenth-century social-Utopian ideas of Charles Fourier, who thought human beings had several naturally occurring anti-social 'passions'. The tendency was for people to drift apart or be hostile to one another, and Fourier's ideal society sought to manage this situation. It was to be divided up into small, habitable productive units of some 1,800 inhabitants each, which took the form of a large building known as the 'Phalanstère'. The affairs of each unit were to be managed by a professional executive, the 'Aeropagus'.

There were no participatory politics or socializing beyond this, for people were considered to be antisocial beings. The affinities with Le Corbusier are obvious and compelling, and I think Serenyi makes an important contribution to our understanding of him. It is therefore strange that Serenyi should go on to attack these individualist, antisocial trends in both Fourier and Le Corbusier as being symptomatic of pathological idiosyncrasies in their characters. He alleges that both were sick, socially dysfunctional loners: 'vagabond', 'rootless', 'uprooted', 'single', 'lonely'. (Serenyi, 1967, *passim*.) Vidler has argued similarly that Le Corbusier's proposals were the result of 'those phobias, pyschoses, and neuroses' induced by his fear of the city. (2001, pp. 51–64 on 'Framing Infinity: Le Corbusier, Ayn Rand, and the Idea of "Ineffable Space", quotation from p. 62.)

7   For example, the plan of a Western church can be generally identified as cruciform in shape, with a fairly consistent arrangement of elements like narthex, nave, chancel, transept, altar, chapels and so on.

8   Giulio Carlo Argan, 'On the Typology of Architecture' (1963), trans. Joseph Rykwert, in Nesbitt (ed.), 1996, pp. 242–6. Argan points out that the type is not an *archetype*, or ideal 'model'. To seek any such ideal would be to strip architecture of the possibility of developing and responding to new historical circumstances.

9   Aldo Rossi, (1966) 1997. These ideas are elaborated throughout in a highly allusive manner. Rossi also maintained that the fundamental 'myths' of humanity were inscribed into the city, and that these were revealed in the transformations of its built fabric throughout history. Human beings were bound up in this urban 'destiny', and must attend to the city as their shared destinies were slowly revealed. (1981, *passim*.)

10   Colquhoun, 1981. See esp. pp. 11–30 on 'Modern Architecture and Historicity', 'The Modern Movement in Architecture' (1962), and 'Symbolic and Literal Aspects of Technology' (1962), which discuss how the modernists tried and failed to get out of the loop of historical meaning, and also how their technological and industrial concerns amounted to just another symbol-system. See also 'Typology and Design Method' (1967), pp. 43–50, in which Colquhoun argues for the use and 'modification' of historical types to discover what they can contribute in changing cultural circumstances; and 'Rules, Realism, History' (1976), pp. 67–74, which discusses how architecture is shaped by its own internal historical-typological meanings and also by external social, economic and political meanings, and how it must 'dialectically' work within these circumstances. 'Form and Figure' (1978), pp. 190–202, runs over the same ground in terms of Colquhoun's preference for historical-typological 'figuration' over nominally self-referential modernist 'form'.

11   Colquhoun, 'Displacement of Concepts' (1972), in ibid., pp. 51–66. Von Moos reiterates Colquhoun's conclusions, remarking on the various 'traditional' precedents of Le Corbusier's architecture, and also that he 'continued to be

under [the] spell' of Beaux-Arts typology. Also, although he concedes that Le Corbusier's architecture does not always have an obvious correspondence with past typologies, he argues that it keeps them alive in subtler ways. Ronchamp, for example, completely disregards the inherited *formal* typology of the church, but respects it in terms of *atmosphere*, in 'the strong medieval overtones of the twilight interior'. (1979, pp. 69–142 on 'Typology and Design Method'; quotations from pp. 81, 103.) Other examples of this approach include Colin Rowe's intricate mathematical demonstration that Le Corbusier's Villa Stein at Garches reproduced the proportions of Palladio's Villa Foscari near Venice. ('The Mathematics of the Ideal Villa', in Rowe, 1976, pp. 1–28.) The most recent example is Adolf Max Vogt, who traces the typological origins of Le Corbusier's *pilotis*. Allegedly, they became of widespread interest in nineteenth-century Switzerland following the discovery of prehistoric settlements on the great lakes, which were lifted above the water on stilts. This archaeology had worked itself into the primary-school curriculum by the time of Le Corbusier's childhood, and he absorbed it so thoroughly that when he came to deploy *pilotis* in later years, he mistakenly thought he had invented them. Vogt maintains that this 'type' was reinforced in Le Corbusier's unconscious by his exposure in Istanbul to riverside pavilions and summer-houses similarly lifted up on stilts. (1998, *passim*.)

12   See *City*, pp. 287–8; *Precisions*, p. 199.

13   Le Corbusier, 'Réponse à moscou, avant propos', 1931, cited in Jean-Louis Cohen, 1992, pp. 146–50; see also p. 141 for the few artefacts Le Corbusier would have permitted to remain standing in central Moscow. As Entwistle observed, Le Corbusier promoted 'the abandonment of all preconceived forms that had become a language entirely without force or meaning both for the user and the viewer'. (*Home*, p. 8.) It is also interesting that Le Corbusier valued Berlin as 'the finest problem I have ever envisaged since it has to do with making the plan of a city completely destroyed and destined to be rebuilt all at one time!!' (*Sketchbooks. Volume 3*, p. 79.)

14   For an introduction to some pioneering phenomenologists and what they have to say about place, see the selections in Leach (ed.), 1997. Martin Heidegger, for example, says that 'dwelling' is the necessary pre-condition of 'being', and in order for us to be returned to this our homes must 'gather' the '*fourfold*' into '*a primal oneness* . . . earth and sky, divinities and mortals'. Elsewhere he equates this building with 'poetry': it is 'a high and special kind of measuring'. That is, it allows us to take our measure within this larger phenomenal reality. ('Building, Dwelling Thinking' [1954], '. . . Poetically Man Dwells . . .' [1954], trans. Albert Hofstadter, in ibid., pp. 100–19; quotations from pp. 102, 114.) For an introduction to the way this has been taken up by architectural theorists, see the selections in Nesbitt (ed.), 1996. Christian Norberg-Schulz, for example, reiterates that architecture has a duty to 'gather' around us the 'concrete phenomena' of our 'everyday life-world', from domestic furniture, through people and animals, to nature as a whole. This will give us an 'existential foothold', will 'orientate' us within our environment

and allow us to 'identify' with it. ('The Phenomenon of Place' [1976], in ibid., pp. 414–28; esp. pp. 414, 423.) Another example of how intimately the identities of human beings are thought to be interwoven with their built domain can be found in the work of Juhani Pallasmaa. He says that building must concern itself with the 'reality of experience', 'striving consciously to depict and articulate the sphere of our consciousness'. Our 'consciousness', then, is only possible in relation to all these phenomena, which it is the architect's duty to present to us: 'As architects we do not primarily design buildings as physical objects, but the images and feelings of the people who live in them.' ('The Geometry of Feeling: A Look at the Phenomenology of Architecture' [1986], in ibid., pp. 448–53; quotations from pp. 449–50.)

15   Baker, 1996, esp. pp. 274 ff., and the conclusion, pp. 284 ff.; quotations from pp. 293–4, 311; Henri Lefebvre, *The Production of Space* (1974), trans. David Nicholson-Smith, in Leach (ed.), 1997, pp. 139–46; quotations from pp. 144–5; Karsten Harries, 'The Ethical Function of Architecture' (1975), in Nesbitt, 1996, pp. 394–6.

16   Jencks, 'Semiology and Architecture', in George Baird and Jencks (eds), 1969, pp. 10–25: even 'In their denial of meaning, they create it' (p. 12); see also Geoffrey Broadbent, 1977, pp. 474–82.

17   Jencks, 1987, pp. 137–69 on 'Other Languages of Architecture 1946–65', esp. pp. 157–62 on 'The Repertoire of Invented Signs'; quotations from pp. 157, 160–61. See also p. 191, n. 19 for Jencks's 'incomplete list of the "words" or invented signs'. 'These forty points', Jencks maintains, 'could be classified according to their function and semantic weight, until one understood the coherent usage. Finally, one could read off the specific architectural messages in each building, and find what attitudes and values were being communicated' (p. 162). Jencks also identifies six distinct languages in Le Corbusier's career: 'naturalistic, geometric Art Nouveau', 'Regional Classicism', 'Purism', 'heavyweight Brutalism', 'metaphorical Post-Modernism' and 'lightweight, proto-High-Tech'. (pp. 158, 162 ff.; 2000, pp. 299–300.) See also Tafuri's intricate account of the complexities of Le Corbusier's architectural 'languages'. ('"*Machine et memoire*": The City in the Work of Le Corbusier', *passim*.)

18   The monofunctional zoning and vast spaces of Chandigarh have been heavily criticized for making almost impossible the dense interweaving of small-scale enterprises and vibrant street culture that is an important part of other Indian cities. It also serves to eradicate their visual interest. See Madhu Sarin, 'Chandigarh as a Place to Live in', in Walden (ed.), 1977, pp. 374–411; 1982, *passim*. But beyond the effect of the architecture Sarin also argues that many sources of employment and activity, which the urban working classes and poor depended upon both economically and for their sense of identity, are outlawed by the Chandigarh plan and its accompanying legislation. Rodrigo Perez de Arce provides a step-by-step diagrammatic account of how to 'fix' Chandigarh. Under de Arce's directions, the city would be made 'typologically' valid, given a sense

of historical continuity and made socially meaningful. ('Urban Transformations and the Architecture of Additions', in *Architectural Design*, vol. 48, no. 4, 1978, pp. 237–66, esp. pp. 260–64.)

19   But normally, says Eco, architecture is stuck within a 'limited repertoire' of meanings that serve to reify and project existing social values. It is not free, like language proper, to innovate new meanings. This gives architecture 'a real social utility . . . it permits certain social relations, confirms them, shows their acceptance on the part of those who are communicating with it, their social status, their decision to abide by certain rules, and so forth'. ('Function and Sign: The Semiotics of Architecture', pp. 187, 197.)

20   Plato, 1987, p. 297. See esp. pp. 177–259 on 'Guardians and Auxiliaries' and 'Justice in State and Individual', and pp. 181–2 on the dissemination of 'some magnificent myth' to replace history and make the people think their allotted stations in life had been ordained by 'god'. Of course Plato was not an urbanist, but he elaborated his philosophy with many metaphorical and literal references to city life and reconstruction.

21   Alberti, 1997, pp. 92–4 on how all the variations in human nature must be accommodated in the fabric of the city; pp. 100–07 on how war is made inevitable by human greed, and the fortifications necessary to defend against this; pp. 117–25 on the measures to be taken by the prince and tyrant to maintain their own safety at home and in the city; pp. 155–7 on the pacifying effect of good decoration; pp. 189–92 on zoning; pp. 294–6 on how one is obliged to be in the city due to business and civic obligations, and also the ideal of suburban retreat. Alberti is often portrayed as the great advocate of the glorious Renaissance city, but Caspar Pearson's has explored the anti-urban tensions in Alberti's thinking and has made a powerful argument to the contrary. (2003, *passim*.)

22   Cited in Anthony Grafton, 2001, pp. 42–3.

23   This can be traced as an underlying dynamic in Lubbock, 1995, although this book explores a different set of themes. The Elizabethan and Jacobean governments feared that the attractions of London were destroying rural society and the power structure and value systems that depended upon it. This led to the imposition of preventative policy measures. But by the eighteenth century, this outlook was complemented with a new fascination and justification for the city by city-dwellers themselves. The city came to be valued not only on the grounds of commerce, trade and the formulation of policy, but also for the international exchange of culture, news and ideas, the refinement of manners and taste, and the promise of exciting experiences. Increasingly it was believed that such things could *only* happen in the city, and that they were generated spontaneously by the clash of different elements. Writers like Bernard de Mandeville and David Hume were important figures in this shift. Of course many moralizers continued to condemn the city, such as William Cobbett in his *Rural Rides* of 1830.

24   Louis Aragon, (1926) 1971, pp. 28–9; see also pp. 38–47 for Aragon's condemnation of the plans to drive a boulevard through the 'passage'. Breton, (1928)

1960, pp. 11, 16, 59. See also Roger Cardinal, 1978, pp. 143–9; Dagmar Motycka Weston, 1996, pp. 149–78. Weston explores the idea that the traditional 'perspectival' approach to the city represented the desire for rational control and the maintenance of impersonal distance, while the Surrealists' 'non-perspectival' approach involved immersion and a richer experience of the city. I think this complements my observations on Le Corbusier's 'three-dimensional' city.

25   For the former position, see Gallagher and Shear (eds), 1999 pp. x–xi; for the latter, see Elliott, 2001, pp. 10–11. The essays in Porter (ed.), 1997, are *all* committed to debunking the first, so-called 'authorized version' of the self. See also Hays, 1992, esp. pp. 3–21 and 279–88, for an account of how this shift appears to have been reflected in twentieth-century architecture.

26   See introduction, pp. 5–6, and pp. 205–7, nn. 8–9.

27   Anthony Giddens, 1997; quotation from p. 215. See also Elliott, 2001, pp. 36–45. For a more general sense that individuality is maintained through constant negotiation with society, see Richard Jenkins, 1996.

28   Even so, Nikolas Rose does not believe that this does violence to some inner core of self, but in fact it is *only* this kind of external intervention – this providing of a psychological 'language' – that makes subjectivity possible at all. (1989, *passim*; 'Assembling the Modern Self', in Porter [ed.], 1997, pp. 224–48.)

29   Kenneth J. Gergen, 1991, *passim*.

30   Sennett maintains that the desire to be considered a unique individual is an unfortunate hangover from Romanticist ideas of interior depth, and the popularization of psychology. Everyone strives to emphasize their individualities, which only makes them mutually incomprehensible and prevents them from developing an effective 'public realm'. ([1977] 1993, *passim*.) Steven Lasch maintains that the calmness, efficiency, self-interest and self-control that seem to characterize the normal modern individual are in fact defence mechanisms against a world that has grown too unstable and traumatic to face more directly. This 'narcissistic' self shuts its boundaries to society and is incapable of taking responsible remedial action for these 'troubled times'. (1984, *passim*.)

31   Admittedly, certain psychoanalytic approaches locate the core of self in psychological processes and expectations that pre-date the influence of society. These are never elaborated in terms even remotely reminiscent of Le Corbusier, however. (See the selections under 'Psychoanalysis and psychosocial relations' in du Gay et al., 2000, pp. 119–276; esp. Jessica Evans's introduction, pp. 121–9.) Ian Craib, for example, believes in the existence of an inner 'psychic space' that is inaccessible to theoretical understanding, but this does not mean the individual should exclude external influences. Rather, it is only through expanding this space so that it begins to partake of the 'emotional intersubjectivity' of all human beings that its inner richness will emerge. (1998, *passim*.)

32   *Le Corbusier Sketchbooks. Volume 2*, p. 52, entry no. 624. Le Corbusier is implying perhaps that his philosophy of self may have been applicable to former 'epochs',

but even this seems unlikely. The essays in Porter (ed.), 1997, that explore self-hood in the Renaissance and Enlightenment periods offer nothing even vaguely comparable with Le Corbusier's ideal. Pascal barely receives a mention.

33 Aldo Van Eyck, in Alison Smithson (ed.), 1962, pp. 559–602; quotation from p. 559.

34 Maxwell Fry was one of Le Corbusier's collaborators at Chandigarh, and is speaking here of his dismay over how this city made highly socialized street life impossible. ('Le Corbusier at Chandigarh', in Walden [ed.], 1977, p. 361.)

35 The 'Urban Task Force' report, for example, which was commissioned by the British government, assumes without question that inner-city living is good and beneficial, and should be made as near as possible compulsory. (Richard Rogers et al., 1999.) See also Lubbock, 1999, pp. 15–17.

Bibliography

Occasionally the original publishing date and title differ from those of the edition consulted, but this will be noted only where it is pertinent. Many of the following works are anthologies, but for reasons of space the entries within them are referenced only in the notes. Especially important entries, however, are given an independent mention.

Ades, Dawn, et al., *Art and Power: Europe under the Dictators 1930–45*, London, 1995.

Adorno, Theodor, *The Stars Down to Earth and Other Essays on the Irrational in Culture*, Stephen Crook (ed.), London, 1994.

Affron, Matthew, 'Fernand Léger and the spectacle of objects', in *Word & Image*, vol. 10, no. 1, January–March 1994, pp. 1–21.

Affron, Matthew, and Antliff, Mark (eds), *Fascist Visions: Art and Ideology in France and Italy*, Princeton, 1997.

Alberti, Leon Battista, *On The Art of Building in Ten Books*, trans. Joseph Rykwert et al., Cambridge, Mass., and London, 1997.

Anderson, Stanford, 'Modern Architecture and Industry: Peter Behrens and the Cultural Policy of Historical Determinism', in *Oppositions*, no. 11, Winter 1977, pp. 52–71.

——, 'Modern Architecture and Industry: Peter Behrens, the AEG, and Industrial Design', in *Oppositions*, no. 21, Summer 1980, pp. 78–97.

Antliff, Mark, *Inventing Bergson: Cultural Politics and the Parisian Avant-Garde*, Princeton, 1993.

Aragon, Louis, *Paris Peasant* (1926), trans. Simon Watson Taylor, London, 1971.

Austin, Roger, 'Propaganda and Public Opinion in Vichy France: The Department of Hérault, 1940–44', in *European Studies Review*, vol. 13, no. 4, 1983, pp. 455–82.

Bacon, Mardges, *Le Corbusier in America: Travels in The Land of the Timid*, New Haven and London, 2001.

Baird, George, and Jencks, Charles (eds), *Meaning in Architecture*, London, 1969.

Baker, Geoffrey H., *Le Corbusier – The Creative Search. The Formative Years of Charles-Edouard Jeanneret*, London, 1996.

Ball, S. L., *Ozenfant and Purism: the Evolution of a Style, 1915–30*, Michigan, 1987.

Banham, Reyner, *Theory and Design in the First Machine Age*, London, 1960.

——, 'Corb's morning works: painting and sculpture by Le Corbusier. 1953', in *Architect's Journal*, vol. 185, no. 10, March 1987, pp. 56–9.

Barthes, Roland, *Image–Music–Text*, trans. Stephen Heath, Glasgow, 1977.

Bataille, Georges, *The Accursed Share: An Essay on General Economy – Vol. I: Consumption* (1949), trans. Robert Hurley, New York, 1988; *Vol. II: The History of Eroticism*; *Vol. III: Sovereignty* (1976), trans. Robert Hurley, New York, 1991.

——, *The Absence of Myth: Writings on Surrealism*, Michael Richardson (ed.), London and New York, 1994.

Berman, Marshall, *All That is Solid Melts Into Air: The Experience of Modernity*, London and New York, 1997.

Blatt, Joel, 'Relatives and Rivals: The Responses of the Action Française to Italian Fascism, 1919–26', in *European Studies Review*, vol. 11, no. 3, 1981, pp. 260–92.

Bosson, Viveca, et al., *Le Corbusier – Painter and Architect*, trans. Helene Anderson et al., Paris, 1995.

Brady, D., *Le Corbusier: An Annotated Bibliography*, New York, 1985.

Breton, André, *Nadja* (1928), trans. Richard Howard, New York, 1960.

——, *Manifestoes of Surrealism*, trans. Richard Seaver and Helen R. Lane, Michigan, 1972.

——, *What is Surrealism? Selected Writings*, Franklin Rosemont (ed.), New York, 1978.

Breton, André, and Légrand, Gerard, *L'Art magique* (1957), Paris, 1991.

Broadbent, Geoffrey, 'A Plain Man's Guide to the Theory of Signs in Architecture', in *Architectural Design*, vol. 47, nos 7–8, 1977, pp. 474–82.

Brogan, D. W., *The Development of Modern France: 1870–1939*, London, 1940.

Brooks, H. Allen (ed.), *Le Corbusier*, Princeton, 1987.

——, *Le Corbusier's Formative Years*, Chicago and London, 1997.

Brower, Sidney N., et al., 'Planners' People', in *Journal of the American Institute for Planning*, 32(4), 1966, pp. 228–33.

Buck, Robert T., et al., *Fernand Léger*, New York, 1982.

Camus, Albert, *The Rebel* (1951), trans. Anthony Bower, Harmondsworth, 1971.

Cardinal, Roger, 'Soluble City: The surrealist perception of Paris', in *Architectural Design*, vol. 48, nos. 2–3, 1978, pp. 143–9.

Carl, Peter, 'Architecture and Time: A Prolegomena', in *A. A. Files*, no. 22, 1991, pp. 48–65.

——, 'Ornament and Time: A Prolegomena', in *A. A. Files*, no. 23, 1992, pp. 49–64.

Chen, Hui-Min, *A Critique on Scientific Rationality in the Production of Architecture*, unpublished Ph.D. thesis, Georgia Institute of Technology, 1993.

Chipp, Herschell B., *Theories of Modern Art*, Berkeley, Los Angeles and London, 1968.

Claque, Monique, 'Vision and Myopia in the New Politics of André Tardieu', in *French Historical Studies*, vol. VIII, no. 1, Spring 1973, pp. 105–29.

Clifton, Chas S., *Encyclopedia of Heresies and Heretics*, Santa Barbara, 1992.

Cobham, Alfred, *A History of Modern France. Volume Three: France of the Republics 1871–1962*, Harmondsworth, 1965.

Cohen, Jean-Louis, *Le Corbusier and the Mystique of the U. S. S. R.: Theories and Projects for Moscow, 1928–1936*, trans. Kenneth Hylton, Princeton, 1992.

Cohen, William B., 'The Colonial Policy of the Popular Front', in *French Historical Studies*, vol. VII, no. 3, Spring 1972, pp. 368–93.

Coll, Jaime, 'Le Corbusier. *Taureaux*: an analysis of the thinking process in the last series of Le Corbusier's plastic work', in *Art History*, vol. 18, no. 4, December 1995, pp. 537–67.

——, 'Structure and Play in Le Corbusier's Art Works', in *A. A. Files*, vol. 31, 1996, pp. 3–14.

Collins, Peter, 'The Doctrine of Auguste Perret', in *Architectural Review*, August 1953, pp. 90–98.

——, *Changing Ideals in Modern Architecture: 1750–1950*, London, 1965.

Colomina, Beatriz, *Privacy and Publicity: Modern Architecture as Mass Media*, Cambridge, Mass., and London, 1994.

Colquhoun, Alan, *Essays in Architectural Criticism: Modern Architecture and Historical Change*, Cambridge, Mass., and London, 1981.

——, *Modernity and the Classical Tradition: Architectural Essays, 1980–1987*, Cambridge, Mass., and London, 1989.

Conrads, Ulrich (ed.), *Programmes and Manifestoes on Twentieth Century Architecture*, trans. Michael Bullock, Cambridge, Mass., and London, 1970.

Craib, Ian, *Experiencing Identity*, London, 1998.

Crinson, Mark, and Lubbock, Jules, *Architecture – Art or Profession?: Three Hundred Years of Architectural Education in Britain*, Manchester and New York, 1994.

Cuff, Dana, and Ellis, Russell (eds), *Architects' People*, New York, 1989.

Curtis, William, *Modern Architecture since 1900*, Oxford, 1982.

——, 'Modern Transformations of Classicism', in *Architectural Review*, vol. CLXXVI, no. 1050, August 1984, pp. 39–45.

——, *Le Corbusier: Ideas and Forms*, London, 1986.

Descartes, René, *Discourse on Method and the Meditations*, trans. F. E. Suttcliffe, Harmondsworth, 1968.

de Arce, Rodrigo Perez, 'Urban Transformations and the Architecture of Additions', in *Architectural Design*, vol. 48, no. 4, 1978, pp. 237–66.

de Francia, Peter, *Fernand Léger*, New Haven and London, 1983.

de Pierrefeu, François, and Le Corbusier, *The Home of Man*, (originally published as *La Maison des Hommes*, Paris, 1942), trans. Clive Entwistle and Gordon Holt, London, 1948.

du Gay, Peter, et al. (eds), *Identity: A Reader*, London, 2000.

Douglas, Allen, 'Violence and Fascism: The Case of the Faisceau', in *Journal of Contemporary History*, vol. 19, no. 4, October 1984, pp. 689–712.

Dunnett, James I., 'The Architecture of Silence', in *Architectural Review*, vol. CLXXVIII, no. 1064, 1985, pp. 69–75.

Elliott, Anthony, *Concepts of the Self*, Cambridge, 2001.

Etlin, Richard, 'Le Corbusier, Choisy, and French Hellenism: The Search for a New Architecture', in *Art Bulletin*, vol. LXIX, no. 2, June 1987, pp. 264–78.

Fishman, Robert, 'From the Radiant City to Vichy: Le Corbusier's Plans and Politics, 1928–1942', in Russell Walden (ed.), 1977 (a), pp. 244–83.

——, *Urban Utopias in the Twentieth Century: Ebenezer Howard, Frank Lloyd Wright, and Le Corbusier*, New York, 1977 (b).

Flaubert, Gustave, *Madame Bovary*, trans. Geoffrey Wall, Harmondsworth, 1992.

Frampton, Kenneth, 'The City of Dialectic', in *Architectural Review*, vol. XXXIX, no. 10, October 1969, pp. 541–6.

—— (ed.), *Oppositions*, special issue on 'Le Corbusier, 1905–1933', nos 15–16, Winter–Spring 1979.

—— (ed.), *Oppositions*, special issue on 'Le Corbusier, 1933–1960', nos 19–20, Winter–Spring 1980.

——, *Modern Architecture: A Critical History*, London, 1980.

——, *Le Corbusier*, London, 2001.

Fraser, Valerie, 'Cannibalizing Le Corbusier: The MES Gardens of Roberto Burle Marx', in *Journal of the Society of Architectural Historians*, vol. 59, no. 2, June 2000, pp. 180–93.

Freud, Sigmund, *The Origins of Religion*, Albert Dickson (ed.), Harmondsworth, 1990.

——, *Civilization, Society and Religion*, Albert Dickson (ed.), Harmondsworth, 1991.

Friedman, Gerald C., 'Revolutionary Unions and French Labor: The Rebels behind the Cause; or, Why Did Revolutionary Syndicalism Fail?', in *French Historical Studies*, vol. 20, no. 2, Spring 1997, pp. 155–81.

Gallagher, Shaun, and Shear, Jonathan (eds), *Models of the Self*, Thorverton, 1999.

George, Waldemar, 'Ozenfant: from Purism to Magic Realism', in *Formes*, no. 16, June 1931.

Gergen, Kenneth J., *The Saturated Self: Dilemmas of Identity in Contemporary Life*, New York, 1991.

Gibbons, Tom, 'Cubism and "The Fourth Dimension" in the context of the late nineteenth-century and early twentieth-century revival of Occult Idealism', in *Journal of the Warburg and Courtauld Institutes*, vol. 44, 1981, pp. 130–47.

Giddens, Anthony, *Modernity and Self-Identity: Self and Society in the Late Modern Age*, Cambridge, 1997.

Giedion, Siegfried, *Space, Time and Architecture: The Growth of a New Tradition*, Cambridge, Mass., and London, 1963.

Gildea, Robert, *The Past in French History*, New Haven and London, 1994.

Golding, John, et al., *Léger and Purist Paris*, London, 1970.

Gorlin, Alexander, 'The Ghost in the Machine: Surrealism in the Work of Le Corbusier', in *Perspecta*, no. 18, 1982, pp. 50–65.

Grafton, Anthony *Leon Battista Alberti: Master Builder of the Italian Renaissance*, London, 2001.

Gray, Christopher, *Cubist Aesthetic Theories*, Baltimore, 1953.

Green, Christopher, *Léger and the Avant-Garde*, London, 1976.

——, 'Synthesis and the "Synthetic Process" in the Painting of Juan Gris: 1915–19', in *Art History*, vol. 5, no. 1, March 1982, pp. 87–111.

——, *Art in France 1900–1940*, New Haven and London, 2000.

Griffiths, Richard, 'Anticapitalism and the French Extra-Parliamentary Right, 1870–1940', in *Journal of Contemporary History*, vol. 13, no. 4, 1978, pp. 721–40.

Hall, Peter, *Cities of Tomorrow*, Oxford, 1996.

——, *Cities in Civilization: Culture, Innovation, and Urban Order*, London, 1998.

Hays, K. Michael, *Modernism and the Posthumanist Subject: The Architecture of Hannes Meyer and Ludwig Hilberseimer*, Cambridge, Mass., and London, 1992.

Hegel, G. W. F., *Lectures on the Philosophy of World History*, trans. H. B. Nisbet, Cambridge, 1975.

Hellman, Geoffrey, 'From Within to Without', in *The New Yorker*, part one: 26 April 1947, pp. 29 ff.; part two: 3 May 1947, pp. 36–53.

Henderson, Linda Dalrymple, *The Fourth Dimension and Non-Euclidean Geometry in Modern Art*, Princeton, 1983.

—— (ed.), *Art Journal*, special issue on 'Mysticism and Occultism in Modern Art', vol. 46, no. 1, Spring 1987.

Herbert, Robert L. (ed.), *Modern Artists on Art: Ten Unabridged Essays*, Englewood Cliffs, 1964.

Hitchcock, Henry Russell, *Painting toward Architecture*, New York, 1948.

Hobsbawm, Eric, *The Age of Empire: 1875–1914*, London, 1987.

Hoffmann, Stanley, 'Paradoxes of the French Political Community', in Hoffman et al., *France: Change and Tradition*, London, 1963, pp. 1–117.

Hopkins, David, *Marcel Duchamp and Max Ernst: The Bride Shared*, Oxford, 1998.

Irvine, William D., 'French Conservatives and the "New Right" during the 1930s', in *French Historical Studies*, vol. VIII, no. 4, Fall 1974, pp. 534–62.

——, 'Fascism in France and the Strange Case of the Croix de Feu', in *Journal of Modern History*, vol. 63, no. 2, June 1991, pp. 271–95.

Jacobs, Jane, *The Death and Life of Great American Cities* (1961), Harmondsworth, 1994.

Jarry, Alfred, *The Ubu Plays*, trans. Cyril Connolly and Simon Watson Taylor, London, 1997.

Jeanneret, Charles-Edouard, 'La révélation 1908: Lettre à Charles L'Eplattenier', in *Aujourd'hui, art et architecture*, vol. LI, November 1965, pp. 10–11.

Jeanneret, Charles-Edouard, and Ozenfant, Amédée, *La Peinture Moderne*, Paris, 1925.

——, 'Purism' (originally published as 'Le Purisme', in *L'Esprit nouveau*, no. 4, January 1921), trans. Robert L. Herbert, in Herbert (ed.), 1964, pp. 59–73.

——, *Après le Cubisme*, (originally published Paris, 1918), Turin, 1975.

Jencks, Charles, *Modern Movements in Architecture*, Harmondsworth, 1977.

——, *Le Corbusier and the Tragic View of Architecture*, Harmondsworth, 1987.

——, *Le Corbusier and the Continual Revolution in Architecture*, New York, 2000.

Jencks, Charles, and Kropf, Karl (eds), *Theories and Manifestoes of Contemporary Architecture*, Chichester, 1997.

Jenkins, Richard, *Social Identity*, London and New York, 1996.

Jones, Adrian, 'Illusions of Sovereignty: Business and the Organization of Committees of Vichy France', in *Social History*, vol. 11, no. 1, January 1986, pp. 1–31.

Jones, Joseph, 'Vichy France and Postwar Economic Mobilization: The Case of the Shopkeepers', in *French Historical Studies*, vol. XII, no. 4, Fall 1982, pp. 541–63.

Judt, Tony, 'The French Socialists and the Cartel des Gauches of 1924', in *Journal of Contemporary History*, vol. 11, nos 2–3, July 1976, pp. 199–215.

Jung, C. G., *Alchemical Studies* (1967), trans. R. F. C. Hull, London, 1981.

——, *Psychology and Religion: West and East* (1958), trans. R. F. C. Hull, London, 1991.

——, *Psychology and Alchemy* (1953), trans. R. F. C. Hull, London, 1993.

——, *Memories, Dreams, Reflections* (1963), Aniela Jaffé (ed.), trans. Richard and Clara Winston, London, 1995 (a).

——, *Modern Man in Search of a Soul* (1933), trans. W. S. Dell and Cary F. Baynes, London, 1995 (b).

——, *The Undiscovered Self* (1958), trans. R. F. C. Hull, London, 1996.

Kalia, Ravi, *Chandigarh: In Search of an Identity*, Carbondale and Edwardsville, 1987.

Katz, Peter, *The New Urbanism: Toward an Architecture of Community*, New York, 1994.

Kitchen, Martin, *Europe Between the Wars: A Political History*, London and New York, 1988.

Knevitt, Charles, and Wates, Nick, *Community Architecture: How People are Creating their Own Environment*, London, 1987.

Kracauer, Siegfried, 'The Mass Ornament' (1927), trans. Barbara Correll and Jack Zipes, in *New German Critique*, vol. 5, 1975, pp. 67–76.

Krauss, Rosalind, 'Léger, Le Corbusier, and Purism', in *Artforum*, vol. x, no. 8, April 1972, pp. 50–53.

——, *The Originality of the Avant-Garde and Other Modernist Myths*, Cambridge, Mass., and London, 1985.

Kuisel, Richard F., 'The Legend of the Vichy Synarchy', in *French Historical Studies*, vol. vi, no. 3, Spring 1970, pp. 365–98.

——, 'Technocrats and Public Economic Policy', in *Journal of European Economic History*, vol. 2, no. 1, Spring 1973, pp. 53–99.

——, 'Auguste Detoeuf, Conscience of French Industry, 1926–47', in *International Review of Social History*, vol. xx, no. 2, 1975, pp. 149–74.

——, *Capitalism and the State in Modern France*, Cambridge, 1981.

Künstler, Gustav, and Münz, Ludwig, *Adolf Loos: Pioneer of Modern Architecture*, London, 1966.

Kurtz, Stephen A., 'Public Planning, Private Painting', in *ARTnews*, vol. 71, no. 2, April 1972, pp. 37 ff.

La Marche, Jean Hertel, *The Subject of Architecture*, unpublished D.Arch. thesis, University of Michigan, 1995.

Lanchner, Carolyn, et al., *Fernand Léger*, New York, 1998.

Lasch, Steven, *The Minimal Self: Psychic Survival in Troubled Times*, London and New York, 1984.

Leach, Neil (ed.), *Rethinking Architecture: a reader in cultural theory*, London and New York, 1997.

Leccese, Michael, and McCormick, Kathleen (eds), 'Congress for the New Urbanism', *Charter of the New Urbanism*, New York, 2000.

Le Corbusier, 'L'Espace indicible', in *L'Architecture d'aujourd'hui*, 1946, pp. 9–17.

——, *The Four Routes* (originally published as *Sur les 4 Routes*, Paris, 1941), trans. Dorothy Todd, London, 1947.

——, *When the Cathedrals were White: A Journey to the Country of Timid People*, (originally published as *Quand les cathédrales étaient blanches*, Paris, 1937), trans. Francis E. Hyslop Jr., London, 1947.

——, *New World of Space*, New York, 1948.

——, *My Work* (originally published as *L'Atelier de la recherche patiente*, Paris, 1960), trans. James Palmes, London, 1960.

——, *The Radiant City* (originally published as *La Ville radieuse*, Paris, 1935), trans. Pamela Knight et al., London, 1967.

——, *The Athens Charter* (originally published as *La Charte d'Athènes*, Paris, 1943), trans. Anthony Eardley, New York, 1973.

——, 'In Defense of Architecture' (originally published in *Stavba*, no. 2, 1929), trans. Nancy Bray et al., in *Oppositions*, no. 4, 1974, pp. 92–108.

——, *Le Corbusier Sketchbooks. Volume 1, 1914–1948*; *Volume 2, 1950–1954*, trans. Agnes Serenyi et al., New York and Cambridge, Mass., 1981. *Volume 3, 1954–1957*; *Volume 4, 1957–1964*, trans. Alfred Willis, New York and Cambridge, Mass., 1982.

——, *The Modulor 1 and 2* (originally published as *Le Modulor*, Paris, 1950, and *Modulor 2*, Paris, 1955), trans. Peter de Francia and Anna Bostock, Cambridge, Mass., 1986.

——, *Journey to the East* (originally published as *Le Voyage d'Orient*, Paris, 1966), trans. Ivan Žaknić, Cambridge, Mass., and London, 1987.

——, *The City of Tomorrow* (originally published as *Urbanisme*, Paris, 1924), trans. Frederick Etchells, London, 1987.

——, *The Decorative Art of Today* (originally published as *L'Art décoratif d'aujour-d'hui*, Paris, 1925), trans. James I. Dunnett, London, 1987.

——, *Le Poème de l'angle droit* (originally published Paris, 1955), Paris, 1989.

——, *Towards a New Architecture* (originally published as *Vers une architecture*, Paris, 1923), trans. Frederick Etchells, Oxford, 1989.

——, *Precisions on the Present State of Architecture and City Planning* (originally published as *Précisions sur un état présent de l'architecture et de l'urbanisme*, Paris, 1930), trans. Edith Schreiber Aujame, Cambridge, Mass., and London, 1991.

——, *Mise au point* (originally published Paris, 1966), trans. Ivan Žaknić, in Žaknić, 1997.

Léger, Fernand, *Functions of Painting* (originally published as *Fonctions de la peinture*, Paris, 1965), trans. Alexandra Anderson, New York, 1973.

Levey, Jules, 'Georges Valois and the Faisceau: The Making and Breaking of a Fascist', in *French Historical Studies*, vol. VIII, no. 2, Fall 1973, pp. 279–304.

Loos, Adolf, *Spoken into the Void: Collected Essays, 1897–1900*, trans. Jane O. Newman and John H. Smith, Cambridge, Mass., and London, 1982.

Lowman, Joyce, 'Corb as Structural Rationalist: The formative influence of engineer Max DuBois', in *Architectural Review*, vol. CLX, no. 956, October 1976, pp. 229–33.

Lubbock, Jules, 'Adolf Loos and the English Dandy', in *Architectural Review*, vol. CLXXXIV, no. 1038, August 1983, pp. 43–9.

——, *The Tyranny of Taste: The Politics of Architecture and Design in Britain, 1550–1960*, New Haven and London, 1995.

——, 'Letter from Notting Hill: London', in *RIBA Journal*, August 1999, pp. 15–17.

Maier, Charles S., 'Between Taylorism and Technocracy: European Ideologies and the vision of industrial productivity in the 1920s', in *Journal of Contemporary History*, vol. 5, no. 2, 1970, pp. 27–61.

Mallarmé, Stéphane, *Collected Poems*, trans. Henry Weinfeld, Berkeley and Los Angeles, 1994.

Martin, Pierre, 'Industrial Structure, Coalition Politics, and Economic Policy: The Rise and Decline of the French Popular Front', in *Comparative Politics*, vol. 24, no. 1, October 1991, pp. 45–75.

Marwick, Arthur, *War and Social Change in the Twentieth Century: A comparative study of Britain, France, Germany, Russia and the United States*, London, 1974.

McKay, F. Sherry, *Le Corbusier, Negotiating Modernity: Representing Algiers 1930–42*, unpublished Ph.D. thesis, University of British Columbia, 1994.

McLeod, Mary, 'Le Corbusier and Algiers', in Frampton (ed.), 1980, pp. 53–85.

——, '"Architecture or Revolution": Taylorism, Technocracy and Social Change', in *Art Journal*, vol. 43, no. 2, Summer 1983, pp. 132–47.

McNamara, Andrew, 'Between Flux and Certitude: The Grid in Avant-Garde Utopian Thought', in *Art History*, vol. 15, no. 1, March 1992, pp. 60–79.

Moore, Richard A., *Le Corbusier: Myth and Meta-Architecture. The Late Period (1947–65)*, New York, 1977.

Müller, Klaus-Jürgen, 'French Fascism and Modernization', in *Journal of Contemporary History*, vol. 11, no. 4, October 1976, pp. 75–107.

Mumford, Eric, *The CIAM Discourses on Urbanism, 1928–1960*, Cambridge, Mass., and London, 2000.

Naegele, Daniel Joseph, *Le Corbusier's Seeing Things: Ambiguity and Illusion in the Representation of Modern Architecture*, unpublished Ph.D. thesis, University of Pennsylvania, 1996.

Nesbitt, Kate (ed.), *Theorizing a New Agenda for Architecture: an anthology of architectural theory, 1965–1995*, New York, 1996.

Noll, Richard, *The Jung Cult: The Origins of a Charismatic Movement*, London, 1996.

Norberg-Schulz, Christian, *Intentions in Architecture*, Cambridge, Mass., and London, 1997.

Ozenfant, Amédée, *Journey Through Life: Experiences, Doubts, Certainties, Conclusions*, trans. Helen Beauclerk and Violet MacDonald, London, 1939.

——, *Foundations of Modern Art* (originally published as *Art: Bilan des arts modernes et structure d'un nouvel esprit*, Paris, 1928), trans. John Rodker, New York, 1952.

——, *Memoires, 1886–1962*, Paris, 1968.

——, 'Notes sur Le Cubisme', in *L'Élan*, 10 December 1916, in S. L. Ball, 1987, pp. 191–4.

Outram, Dorinda, *The Enlightenment*, Cambridge, 1997.

Panofsky, Erwin, *Meaning in the Visual Arts*, Harmondsworth, 1970.

Pascal, Blaise, *The Provincial Letters*, trans. A. J. Krailsheimer, Harmondsworth, 1967.

——, *Pensées*, trans. A. J. Krailsheimer, Harmondsworth, 1995.

Passanti, Francesco, 'The Vernacular, Modernism, and Le Corbusier', in *Journal of the Society of Architectural Historians*, vol. 56, no. 4, December 1997, pp. 438–51.

Pearson, Caspar, *Visions of the City in Leon Battista Alberti's* De re aedificatoria, unpublished Ph.D. thesis, University of Essex, 2003.

Pearson, Christopher, *Integrations of Art and Architecture in the Work of Le Corbusier: Theory and Practice from Ornamentalism to the 'Synthesis of the Major Arts'*, unpublished Ph.D. thesis, Stanford University, 1995.

——, 'Le Corbusier and the Acoustical Trope: An Investigation of Its Origins', in *Journal of the Society of Architectural Historians*, vol. 56, no. 2, June 1997, pp. 168–83.

Pevsner, Nikolaus, *Pioneers of Modern Design: From William Morris to Walter Gropius*, Harmondsworth, 1975.

Phillips, Peggy A., 'Neo-Corporatist Praxis in Paris', in *Journal of Urban History*, vol. 4, no. 4, August 1978, pp. 397–415.

Plato, *The Republic*, trans. Desmond Lee, London, 1987.

Poincaré, Henri, *Science and Hypothesis* (1903), trans. W. J. G., New York, 1952.

——, *The Value of Science* (1905), trans. George Bruce Halstead, New York, 1958.

——, *Mathematics and Science: Last Essays* (1913), trans. John W. Bolduc, New York, 1963.

——, *Science and Method* (1908), trans. Francis Maitland, New York, no date.

Poma, Maria Cristina (ed.), *Le Corbusier. Pittore e Scultore*, Milan, 1986.

Porter, Roy, *The Enlightenment*, London, 1991.

—— (ed.), *Rewriting the Self: Histories from the Renaissance to the Present*, London and New York, 1997.

Price, Roger, *A Concise History of Modern France*, Cambridge, 1993.

Rabelais, François, *Gargantua and Pantagruel*, trans. J. M. Cohen, Harmondsworth, 1955.

Raeburn, Michael, and Wilson, Victoria (eds), *Le Corbusier: Architect of the Century*, London, 1987.

Read, Alice Gray, 'Le Corbusier's "Ubu" sculpture: remaking an image', in *Word & Image*, vol. 14, no. 3, July–September, 1998, pp. 215–26.

Read, Herbert, *A Concise History of Modern Painting*, London, 1967.

Rogers, Richard, et al. ('Urban Task Force'), *Towards an Urban Renaissance*, London, 1999.

Rose, Nikolas, *Governing the Soul: The Shaping of the Private Self*, London and New York, 1989.

Rosenblatt, Nina Lara, *Photogenic Neurasthenia: Aesthetics, Modernism, and Mass Society in France: 1889–1929*, unpublished Ph.D. thesis, Columbia University, 1997.

Rossi, Aldo, *A Scientific Autobiography*, Cambridge, Mass., and London, 1981.

——, *The Architecture of the City* (1966), trans. Diane Ghirardo and Joan Ockman, Cambridge, Mass. and London, 1997.

Roth, Jack J., 'Georges Sorel: On Lenin and Mussolini', in *Contemporary French Civilization*, vol. 2, no. 2, Winter 1977, pp. 231–52.

Rowe, Colin, *The Mathematics of the Ideal Villa and Other Essays*, Cambridge, Mass., and London, 1976.

Safran, Yehuda (ed.), *The Architecture of Adolf Loos*, London, 1985.

Samuel, Flora, 'Le Corbusier, Women and Nature', in *Issues in Architecture, Art and Design*, vol. 5, no. 2, 1999 (a), pp. 4–19.

——, 'The Philosophical City of Rabelais and St. Teresa – Le Corbusier and Edouard Trouin's Scheme for St. Baume', in *Literature and Theology*, vol. 13, no. 2, June 1999 (b), pp. 111–25.

——, 'Le Corbusier, Teilhard de Chardin and *La Planétisation humaine*: spiritual ideas at the heart of modernism', in *French Cultural Studies*, vol. 11, no. 2, 2000, pp. 181–99.

——, 'Le Corbusier, Rabelais and the Oracle of the Holy Bottle', *Word & Image*, vol. 17, no. 4, October–December 2001, pp. 325–38.

Sarin, Madhu, *Urban Planning in the Third World: The Chandigarh Experience*, London, 1982.

Sawin, Martica, 'Magus, Magic, Magnet: The Archaizing Surrealism of Kurt Seligmann', in *Arts Magazine*, vol. 60, no. 6, February 1986, pp. 76–81.

——, *Surrealism in Exile and the Beginning of the New York School*, Cambridge, Mass., and London, 1995.

Schlesinger, Mildred, 'The Development of the Radical Party in the Third Republic: The New Radical Movement, 1926–32', in *Journal of Modern History*, vol. 46, no. 3, September 1974, pp. 476–501.

——, 'The Cartel des Gauches: Precursor of the Front Populaire', in *European Studies Review*, vol. 8, no. 2, 1978, pp. 211–34.

——, 'Legislative Governing Coalitions in Parliamentary Democracies: The Case of the French Third Republic', in *Comparative Political Studies*, vol. 22, no. 1, April 1989, pp. 33–65.

Schuré, Edouard, *The Great Initiates: A Study of the Secret History of Religions*, trans. Gloria Rasberry, San Francisco, 1961.

Schwartz-Salant, Nathan (ed.), *Jung on Alchemy*, London, 1995.

Sekler, Mary Patricia May, 'Ruskin, the Tree, and the Open Hand', in Walden (ed.), 1977, pp. 42–95.

Seligmann, Kurt, *The History of Magic and the Occult*, (originally published as *The Mirror of Magic: A History of Magic in the Western World*, New York, 1948), New York, 1997.

Sennett, Richard, *The Fall of Public Man* (1977), London, 1993.

——, *The Uses of Disorder: Personal Identity and City Life* (1970), London, 1996.

Serenyi, Peter, 'Le Corbusier, Fourier, and the Monastery of Ema', in *Art Bulletin*, vol. XLIX, no. 4, December 1967, pp. 277–92.

——, *Le Corbusier's Art and Thought: 1918–1935*, Michigan, 1968.

—— (ed.), *Le Corbusier in Perspective*, Englewood Cliffs, 1975.

Shakespeare, William, *The Complete Works*, Peter Alexander (ed.), London and Glasgow, 1991.

Shorrock, William I., 'France and the Rise of Fascism in Italy, 1919–23', in *Journal of Contemporary History*, vol. 10, no. 4, October 1975, pp. 591–610.

Silver, Kenneth, 'Purism: Straightening Up After the Great War', in *Artforum*, March 1977, pp. 56–63.

Simmel, Georg, *On Individuality and Social Forms: Selected Writings*, Donald L. Levine (ed.), Chicago and London, 1971.

Smithson, Alison (ed.), *Team 10 Primer*, in *Architectural Design*, December 1962, pp. 559–602.

Smith, Bernard, *Modernism's History: A Study in Twentieth-Century Art and Ideas*, New Haven and London, 1998.

Soucy, Robert J., 'The Nature of Fascism in France', in *Journal of Contemporary History*, vol. 1, 1966, pp. 27–55.

——, 'French Fascist Intellectuals in the 1930s: An Old New Left?', in *French Historical Studies*, vol. VIII, no. 3, Spring 1973, pp. 445–58.

——, 'French Fascism and the Croix de Feu: A Dissenting Interpretation', in *Journal of Contemporary History*, vol. 26, no. 1, January 1991, pp. 159–88.

Splawn, James M., *Under the Oak Tree: The Mythical Intentionality in Le Corbusier's 'Le Poème de l'angle droit'*, unpublished M.Arch. dissertation, McGill University, 1990.

Stevenson, David, 'French War Aims and the American Challenge, 1914–1918', in *Historical Journal*, vol. 22, no. 4, 1979, pp. 877–94.

Taylor, Brian Brace, *Le Corbusier at Pessac*, Cambridge, Mass., 1972.

Thorpe, Wayne, 'Anarchosyndicalism in Inter-War France: The Vision of Pierre Besnard', in *European History Quarterly*, vol. 26, no. 4, October 1996, pp. 559–90.

Tiryakian, Edward A., 'A Model of Societal Change and its Lead Indicators', in Samuel Z. Klausner (ed.), *The Study of Total Societies*, New York, 1967, pp. 69–97.

——, 'Structural Sociology', in John C. McKinney and Edward A. Tiryakian (eds), *Theoretical Sociology: Perspectives and Developments*, New York, 1970, pp. 111–35.

—— (ed.), *On the Margin of the Visible: Sociology, the Esoteric, and the Occult*, New York, 1974.

Trachtenberg, Marc, ' "A New Economic Order": Etienne Clémentel and French Economic Diplomacy during the First World War', in *French Historical Studies*, vol. x, no. 2, Fall 1977, pp. 315–41.

Troy, Nancy J., 'Le Corbusier, Nationalism, and the Decorative Arts in France, 1900–1918', in *Studies in the History of Art*, vol. 29, 1991, pp. 64–87.

Truzzi, Marcello, 'The Occult Revival as Popular Culture: Some Random Observations on the Old and the Nouveau Witch', in *Sociological Quarterly*, vol. 13, no. 1, 1972, pp. 16–36.

Turner, Paul Venable, 'The Beginnings of Le Corbusier's Education, 1902–07', in *Art Bulletin*, vol. LIII, no. 2, June 1971, pp. 214–24.

——, *The Education of Le Corbusier*, New York and London, 1977.

Udovicki-Selb, Danilo, 'Le Corbusier and the Paris Exhibition of 1937: The Temps Nouveau Pavilion', in *Journal of the Society of Architectural Historians*, vol. 56, no. 1, March 1997, pp. 42–63.

van der Laan, Lambert, and Piersma, Andries, 'The Image of Man: Paradigmatic Cornerstone in Human Geography', *Annals of the Association of American Geographers*, 72(3), 1982, pp. 411–26.

Vidler, Anthony, *Warped Space: Art, Architecture and Anxiety in Modern Culture*, Cambridge, Mass., and London, 2001.

Vogt, Adolf Max, *Le Corbusier, the Noble Savage: Toward an Archaeology of Modernism*, trans. Radka Donnell, Cambridge, Mass., and London, 1998.

von Moos, Stanislaus, *Le Corbusier, Elements of a Synthesis*, Cambridge, Mass., and London, 1979.

Walden, Russell (ed.), *The Open Hand: Essays on Le Corbusier*, Cambridge, Mass., and London, 1977.

Weber, Heidi (ed.), *Le Corbusier – The Artist. Works from the Heidi Weber collection*, Zurich and Montreal, 1988.

Weisberger, Edward (ed.), *The Spiritual in Art: Abstract Painting 1890–1985*, New York, 1985.

Weston, Dagmar Motycka, 'Surrealist Paris: The Non-Perspectival Space of the Lived City', in *Chora*, vol. 2, 1996, pp. 149–78.

Williamson, Jack H., 'The Grid: History, Use, and Meaning', in *Design Issues*, vol. III, no. 2, Fall 1986, pp. 15–30.

Wiskemann, Elizabeth, *Europe of the Dictators: 1919–1945*, London, 1985.

Žaknić, Ivan, *The Final Testament of Père Corbu*, New Haven and London, 1997.

Zdatny, Steven M., 'The Corporatist Word and the Modernist Deed: Artisans and Political Economy in Vichy France', in *European History Quarterly*, vol. 16, no. 2, April 1986, pp. 155–79.

Acknowledgements

I would like to thank the British Academy, the Arts and Humanities Research Board, and the Sir Andrew Carnwath Travel Bursary for funding this research. I would also like to thank the staff of the Fondation Le Corbusier in Paris for answering my enquiries with such polite forbearance, as well as Gillian Malpass, Sandy Chapman and Elizabeth McWilliams of Yale University Press for bringing the project to completion with such efficiency.

Dawn Ades and Chris Green offered many invaluable insights when they examined this work, and these have been incorporated to considerable benefit. Likewise, the staff and students of the Department of Art History and Theory at the University of Essex have been subjected to more than their fair share of my ideas, and I thank them for their generous contributions and criticisms.

At a time when so many academics seem to consider students an unfortunate professional hazard, it has been a great inspiration to enjoy the support of Jules Lubbock. As he proves, important research does not have to be conducted at the expense of quality teaching and student care, and I consider it a privilege to be able to continue working with him.

On a more personal note, Kumiko Tsuji and Lisa Wade helped keep me reasonably sane by taking my mind off these obscure reflections, and I deeply value their kindnesses. Finally, for their support and encouragement of many years, without which I clearly would not have been able to pursue these studies at all, I thank my mother and stepfather – Aldyth Megan Richards and Anthony Barber.

Index

Action Française 41–2, 212n.12
aerial attacks, defence against 219n.43
Alberti, Leon Battista 6, 198–9, 273n.21
Albigensianism 169, 175, 262n.104
alchemy 141–5, 250n.12, 251nn.18, 20,
     253n.23, 258–9n.63
     and Gnosticism 251–3n.22
     and *Le Poème de l'angle droit* 138–42,
        145–57, 168
     and psychology, *see* Jung, Carl Gustav;
        Seligmann, Kurt
     and religion 144–5, 160–62
Algiers, Le Corbusier's plans for 62–4,
     226nn.42–3
America, Le Corbusier's views 37–8,
     216n.6, 223n.13
anti-Semitism, *see* Action Française;
     Stavisky, Serge Alexandre; 'Vichy
     Synarchy' conspiracy
Antliff, Mark 217n.18, 232n.7
Apollinaire, Guillaume 26, 94
Après le Cubisme 25, 92
Aragon, Louis 199–200
Argan, Giulio Carlo 192, 270n.8
Art et Liberté 25, 212n.12
Association des Constructeurs pour une

Rénovation Architecturale (ASCORAL)
     100
Association Française de Normalisation
     235n.32

Bacon, Mardges 203–4n.1
Baker, Geoffrey 194, 227–8n.4
Barrés, Maurice 211n.3
Bataille, Georges
     The Accursed Share 127, 171–5, 176–80
     and Camus 180–81
     see also individual
Barthes, Roland 243–4n.4
Behrens, Peter 208–9n.12
Benton, Tim 126, 258n.61
Bergson, Henri 80–81, 232n.7
Blum, Léon 47–8, 219n.44
Braque, Georges 94
Breton, André 199–200, 250n.15,
     262–3n.105
Brunel, Charles 63
Burckhardt, Jacob 205n.8

Camelots du Roi 41
Camus, Albert
     and Le Corbusier 171–2, 175–6,

264–5nn.15–16
The Rebel 127, 171, 175, 180–85
    see also individual
Carl, Peter 243n.2
Cartel des Gauches 31
Catharism 169, 170, 262n.104
cells, *see* units
Chandigarh 156, 195–6, 254–5n.37,
    257–8n.55, 272–3n.18, 275n.34
cities
    general theories 6–7, 197–8
    plans by Le Corbusier, *see* Algiers;
        Chandigarh; Moscow; Nemours; Plan
        Voisin; Ville Contemporaine; Ville
        Radieuse
class system, and technocracy 29–30
Clemenceau, Georges 27, 213n.24
Clémentel, Etienne 27–8, 213nn.22, 24
collective
    Jung's views 165–6
    Le Corbusier's views 35–6, 40, 51, 107,
        166–7, 220n.57
    Léger's views 83–4
Coll, Jaime 243–4n.4
Colomina, Beatriz 224n.23
colonialism 57–8, 62–4, 223n.19, 224n.28,
    226nn.42–3
colour, effect of 82, 84, 230–31n.33,
    240n.7
Colquhoun, Alan 192–3, 203–4n.1,
    270n.10
Comité d'Études du Bâtiment 59–60
Comité d'Études de l'Habitation et de la
    Construction Immobilière 60
Communism 48, 51–2
'Community Architecture' 190
Confédération Générale du Travail (CGT)
    44, 217n.24
Congrès Internationaux d'Architecture
    Moderne (CIAM) 45, 48, 50–53, 202,
    217–18n.30, 220–21n.58
conventionalism 71, 90–91, 95–9, 191,
    237n.53
Craib, Ian 274n.31

Croix de Feu 42, 49, 53
crusaders 56–7
Cubism 91–5
Cuff, Dana 8, 207n.13

Daladier, Edouard 42, 48, 49, 53
Darlan, François 225nn.34–5
Daudet, Léon 212n.12
de Arce, Rodrigo Perez 272–3n.18
de Pierrefeu, François 58, 62, 221–2n.3
Délégation Générale à l'Equipement
    National 62
Depression 34, 37, 48
Derrida, Jacques 201, 207n.9
Descartes, René 128, 129, 134, 135,
    205n.8, 244n.1, 245n.4
distractions (socializing, street life, etc.),
    elimination of
    de Pierrefeu's views 58
    Fry's comments 202, 275n.34
    Gurlitt's comments 30
    Jung's views 162
    Pascal's views 131–3, 246n.14, 247n.21
    Le Corbusier's views 3–4, 34–6, 50–51,
        58, 135, 215n.66, 218–19n.40
    see also political participation; public
        buildings
Dominicans 169, 263n.106
Dom-ino housing project 25, 212n.11
dualism, matter and spirit 1–2, 11–12,
    135, 204n.2
Duchamp, Marcel 258–9n.63

Eco, Umberto 197, 204n.4, 273n.19
Einstein, Albert 98, 234n.25
L'Élan 25, 212n.13
Ellis, Russell 8, 207n.13
epistemology
    of Gleizes and Metzinger 92–5
    of Jung 159–60
    of Le Corbusier 100–07, 111, 121, 160,
        234–5n.25
    of Léger 70–71, 80–85
    of Ozenfant 71–2, 112–15, 118–19,

239–40nn.1–2
of Pascal   129–31, 134
of Purism   69–70, 85–9, 91–9
Ernst, Max   250n.12, 258–9n.63
L'Esprit nouveau   26, 31, 98, 211n.1
Euclidean and non-Euclidean geometry
3, 92, 93, 96–9, 106, 232n.9,
233–4nn.23–5

Faisceau des Combattants et des
Producteurs   42, 48, 53, 217n.18
Fascism   41–4, 48–50, 217n.18
Fischer, Katherine Fraser   227–8n.4
Fordism   32–3
Foucault, Michel   201, 206n.9
Fourier, Charles   45, 269–70n.6
fourth dimension   91, 93–5, 233nn.10–11
Frampton, Kenneth   243n.2
Front Populaire   47–8, 224n.28
Frugès, Henri   215n.61
Fry, Maxwell   202, 275n.34
functionalism   71, 105

Gergen, Kenneth   201
Gibbons, Tom   95, 233n.11
Giddens, Anthony   200–01
Giedion, Siegfried   234–5n.25
Gleizes, Albert   92–3, 94, 99, 232n.7
see also epistemology
Gnosticism   145, 251–3n.22
Goffman, Erving   200–01, 206n.9
Golding, John   230n.32
Grande route   44
Green, Christopher   77, 87–8, 126,
203–4n.1, 216n.13, 228nn.4, 9, 230n.32
Gris, Juan   94, 230n.32
Guarino of Verona   199
Gurlitt, Cornelius   30, 214n.39

hands, significance of   155–6, 256–8nn.53–5
Harries, Karsten   194
Hays, K. Michael   207n.13
Hegel, G.W.F.   17
Heidegger, Martin   271n.14

Hellman, Geoffrey   216n.12
Henderson, Linda Dalrymple   93, 94, 95,
234–5n.25
Herriott, Edouard   31
heterodoxy   145, 160–63, 168–70
see also Gnosticism
Hoffman, Stanley   215–16n.70
L'Homme réel   44
Hoover, Herbert   216n.1
house, as machine for living   59, 135–6,
224n.27
human body, proportions of   102–3
Hume, David   6, 206n.9

iconography, *see* alchemy; Le Corbusier
iconostasis, *Le Poème de l'angle droit*
138–40, 249n.5
individual
Bataille's views   177–80, 185
Camus's views   181–5
Jung's views   159–68, 185, 262n.99
Le Corbusier's views   4, 14–18, 40, 47,
51–2, 58–9, 85, 87, 88–9, 107–10,
122, 156–7, 166–7, 185,
220–21nn.57-8, 224n.26, 269n.52
Léger's views   70–71, 80–85, 88–9,
121–2, 230n.27, 242n.34
Loos's views   15–16
Ozenfant's views   116–18, 120–22, 157
Pascal's views   47, 59, 132–4, 185
individuation   159, 161–2, 165–8, 259n.66,
260n.72, 262n.95
International Exhibition (Paris, 1937)
219–20n.45

Jacobs, Jane   6, 189–90
Jai Singh II, Maharajah Sawai   254–5n.37
Jansenism   116, 134, 244–5n.2, 247–8n.29
Jardot, Maurice   210–11n.2, 262–3n.105
Jeanneret, Charles-Edouard, *see* Le
Corbusier
Jencks, Charles   194–5, 203–4n.1,
210–11n.2, 218–19n.40, 243n.3,
258n.61, 272n.17

Jeunesses Patriotes 42
Jung, Carl Gustav 127, 137, 158–68,
    258n.61, 259–60n.71
    see also collective; distractions;
        epistemology; individual; individuation;
        participation mystique; *temenos*
Jura 169, 262–3n.105

Kayser, Hans 107
Kracauer, Siegfried 83–4
Krailsheimer, A. J. 135
Krauss, Rosalind 235n.31
Krustup, Mogens 243n.2

Labarthète, Henri du Moulin de 62,
    225n.35
La Marche, Jean Hertel 207–8n.13
Lamour, Philippe 44
La Rocque, Colonel de 49–50
Lasch, Steven 274n.30
Laval, Pierre 225nn.34–5
League of Nations, competition scandal
    217–18n.30
Le Corbusier
    ancestry 169, 170, 262–3n.105
    and Camus 171–2, 175–6,
        264–5nn.15-16
    dualism 1–2, 11–12, 135, 204n.2
    formalism 74–80, 227–8n.4, 228n.8
    iconography 125–7, 243–4nn.2-4; *see
        also Le Poème de l'angle droit*
    nationalism 38–9, 56–7, 216nn.6, 13,
        222nn.10–11, 223n.13
    and Ozenfant 25–7, 70, 120–22, 157,
        191, 211n.1
    paintings/aesthetic theory 70–71, 73–5,
        85–9, 138, 186, 248n.2
    Le Poème de l'angle droit 138–42,
        145–57, 174, 175–6, 248–9n.4
    political and economic views 21–2,
        210–11nn.2-3, Part I *passim*. *See also*
        anti-Semitism; Communism;
        colonialism; Fascism; *planisme*;
        syndicalism; technocracy

pseudonym 23, 211n.1
public-private divide 1–2, 73–6, 78,
    203–4n.1
urban planning, *see* cities
see also collective; distractions;
    epistemology; individual; mass media;
    museums; ornamentation; Pascal;
    political participation; Purism
Lefebvre, Henri 194
Léger, Fernand
    and Cubism 94
    and Ozenfant 120
    paintings of 80–89, 230n.28
    affinities with Purism 70–71, 77,
        230–31n.33
    see also collective; epistemology;
        individual; mass media
Lehideux, François 62
Locke, John 205–6n.9
London, society 273n.23
Loos, Adolf 14–17, 208–9nn.12, 19–20
    see also individual; ornamentation
Loucheur, Louis 27, 28, 33, 213n.24
Lubbock, Jules 204n.5, 248n.34, 273n.23

machine ages 55–6
Mallarmé, Stéphane 256n.47
mass media
    de Pierrefeu's views 58
    Le Corbusier's views 58, 85, 189,
        223n.21
    Léger's views 80, 85
Maurras, Charles 41
McKay, F. Sherry 236n.42
McNamara, Andrew 239n.76
Mead, George Herbert 200–01, 206n.9
meander, law of 254n.34
Mercier, Ernest 31–2
Metzinger, Jean 92–3, 94, 99, 232n.7
    see also epistemology
Mill, John Stuart 205n.8
modernist grid 94, 239n.76
'Modulor' system 71, 90, 100–11, 120,
    149–50, 235n.32

monism   95, 118–19
Moore, Richard   243n.2, 258n.61
Moscow, Le Corbusier's plans for   51, 193, 271n.13
Mumford, Eric   50–51
Mumford, Lewis   52–3, 189, 190
museums, Le Corbusier's views   17, 111, 239n.77
Mussolini, Benito   48
mysticism   125, 242n.1
M'zab, Algeria   169

Naegele, Daniel Joseph   235n.31
Nemours, Le Corbusier's plans for   57
'New Urbanism'   190
Norberg-Schulz, Christian   271–2n.14
Le Nouveau siècle   42
numbers, symbolism of   140, 236n.38, 249n.7

occultism   94, 95, 126–7, 142–3, 233n.11, 242n.1
'Open Hand'   155–6, 257–8nn.54-5
ornamentation, eradication of   15–17
Ozenfant, Amédée
    and Cubism   91–2
    and Le Corbusier   25–7, 70, 120–22, 157, 191, 211n.1
    and Léger   120
    and Poincaré   96
    see also epistemology; individual; Pascal; Purism

Pallasmaa, Juhani   271–2n.14
participation mystique   159–60
Parti Social Français (PSF)   49
Pascal, Blaise
    desideratum   133–4, 197
    influence on Le Corbusier   9–10, 47, 59, 127, 128, 197
    Ozenfant's views   112, 116, 118, 120–21
    see also distractions; epistemology; individual; Jansenism
Pavillon Suisse   138, 248n.1

Pearson, Caspar   273n.21
Pearson, Christopher   228n.4, 234–5n.25, 243n.3, 273n.21
Perret, Auguste   208–9n.12, 212n.12
Pessac housing development   215n.61
Pétain, Philippe   54, 57, 61–2, 223n.20, 225n.34
Peyrouton, Marcel   224n.28
phenomenology   191, 193–4, 271–2n.14
Picasso, Pablo   94
pilotis   193, 270–71n.11
planisme   44, 47–8, 219n.44
Plans   44
Plan Voisin   30–31, 193, 214n.40, 223n.21
Plato   6, 198, 199, 273n.20
Le Poème de l'angle droit   138–42, 145–57, 174, 175–6, 248–9n.4
Poincaré, Henri   71, 96–9, 103, 233–4nn.23-4
Poincaré, Raymond   32, 53
political participation, elimination of   3–4, 30, 46, 189–91, 218–19n.40
    see also distractions; public buildings
Prélude   44, 217n.29
proportion, systems of   100–04
psyche   159–60, 164–5, 168, 198, 259nn.66-7
public buildings, lack of   30, 34–5
Purism
    and Cubism   91–2, 95–6, 99
    paintings/aesthetic theory   69–70, 76–80, 230–31nn.32-3
    social ideals   26–7
    see also epistemology

Rabelais, François   101, 170
Read, Alice Gray   243n.2
reconstruction
    interwar   28, 33
    Vichy period   59–60
Redressement Français   31–3
religion, see Albigensianism; alchemy; Catharism; crusaders; Dominicans;

Gnosticism; heterodoxy; Jansenism;
  Pascal
riots, Paris (1934) 42–3, 49
Romier, Lucien 31, 32
Ronchamp, chapel 270–71n.11
Rosenblatt, Nina Lara 242n.35
Rose, Nikolas 201, 274n.28
Rossi, Aldo 192, 270n.9
Rowe, Colin 270–71n.11
Ruskin, John 257n.54

Saint-Simon, Henri de 25
Samuel, Flora 243n.2
Sarin, Madhu 272n.18
scientific management, *see* Taylorism
Sekler, Mary Patricia May 243n.2, 257n.54
self, concepts of 2, 4–8, 133–4, 185–7,
  197–202, 204–5n.6, 205–7nn.8-9
  'self/other self' 5–6, 200, 205–7n.9
  'self-sufficient self' 5, 200, 205n.8
Seligmann, Kurt 127, 137, 142–5, 158,
  250n.14, 251n.18
semiology 191, 194–5
Sennett, Richard 189, 190, 274n.30
Serenyi, Peter 234–5n.25, 269–70n.6
Sert, José Luis 52
Shakespeare, William, sonnets 140, 249n.8
Silberer, Herbert 158
Simmel, Georg 6, 206n.9
Smith, Bernard 243–4n4
social interaction, *see* distractions; political
  participation; public buildings
Société d'Application du Béton Armé 25
Société d'Entreprises Industrielles et
  Etudes 25
solitude 4, 133–5, 238n.71
Sondaz, Marie-Louise 155–6, 256–7n.53
Sorel, Georges 217n.18
Speiser, Andreas 103
sport 35, 46
'stalemate society' 36, 50, 215–16n.70
Stavisky, Serge Alexandre 43–4

Stephenson, Nancy 257n.54
Surrealism 38, 142, 228n.9, 250n.14
Sutcliffe, Anthony 214n.44
syndicalism 44–8

Tafuri, Manfredo 64
Tardieu, André 34
Taylorism 24–5, 26, 29, 31, 212n.11
Team 10 202
technocracy 24–5, 29–34, 37, 61–2
  see also 'Vichy Synarchy' conspiracy
temenos 163–5, 261nn.86-7
trade unions 211–12n.6
typology 191–3, 270–71nn.10-11

Union Nationale 32
Unité building type 149, 191, 254n.37
units/cells, for living 35, 109–10, 238n.71
'Urban Task Force' 275n.35

Valois, Georges 41–2, 44, 48–9, 217n.18
Van de Velde, Henry 209n.19
Veblen, Thorstein 216n.1
Vichy regime 54–65, 235n.32
'Vichy Synarchy' conspiracy 62, 225n.35
Vidler, Anthony 270n.6
Ville Contemporaine 28–32, 34–6, 108–10
Ville Radieuse 45–7, 50–51, 193,
  218n.32, 219n.43
Ville Voisin, *see* Plan Voisin
Vogt, Adolf Max 270–71n.11
von Moos, Stanislaus 74, 192, 211n.3,
  227–8n.4, 270–71n.11

Welsh, Robert P. 243–4n.4
Weston, Dagmar Motycka 273–4n.24
Weygand, Maxime 63
Williamson, Jack H. 239n.76
Winter, Pierre 42
Wittkower, Rudolf 236–7n.47
Wogenscky, André 264–5n.15
Worms, Hypolite 225n.35